The Decalogue in the Sermon on the Mount

Studies in Biblical Literature

Hemchand Gossai
General Editor

Vol. 66

PETER LANG
New York • Washington, D.C./Baltimore • Bern
Frankfurt am Main • Berlin • Brussels • Vienna • Oxford

Dan Lioy

The Decalogue in the Sermon on the Mount

PETER LANG
New York • Washington, D.C./Baltimore • Bern
Frankfurt am Main • Berlin • Brussels • Vienna • Oxford

Library of Congress Cataloging-in-Publication Data

Lioy, Dan.
The decalogue in the Sermon on the Mount / Dan Lioy.
p. cm. — (Studies in biblical literature; v. 66)
Includes bibliographical references and indexes.
1. Sermon on the mount—Criticism, interpretation, etc.
2. Ten commandments—Criticism, interpretation, etc. 3. Bible. N.T.
Matthew—Relation to Exodus. 4. Bible. O.T. Exodus—
Relation to Matthew. I. Title. II. Series.
BT380.3.L56 241.5—dc22 2003019605
ISBN 0-8204-7082-1
ISSN 1089-0645

Bibliographic information published by **Die Deutsche Bibliothek**.
Die Deutsche Bibliothek lists this publication in the "Deutsche Nationalbibliografie"; detailed bibliographic data is available on the Internet at http://dnb.ddb.de/.

275 Seventh Avenue, 28th Floor, New York, NY 10001
www.peterlangusa.com

To my beloved wife, Marcia, for her affection and companionship;
and to my precious son, Joshua, for his love and playfulness.

Contents

Editor's Preface

More than ever the horizons in biblical literature are being expanded beyond that which is immediately imagined; important new methodological, theological, and hermeneutical directions are being explored, often resulting in significant contributions to the world of biblical scholarship. It is an exciting time for the academy as engagement in biblical studies continues to be heightened.

This series seeks to make available to scholars and institutions, scholarship of a high order, and which will make a significant contribution to the ongoing biblical discourse. This series includes established and innovative directions, covering general and particular areas in biblical study. For every volume considered for the series, we explore the question as to whether the study will push the horizons of biblical scholarship. The answer must be *yes* for inclusion.

In this volume, Dan Lioy examines the relationship between the Decalogue and the Sermon on the Mount. Noting the unsettledness in biblical scholarship regarding this relationship, the author explores the influence of the Decalogue as a way of understanding the role of the moral law in the contemporary Church. While the author orients this argument to an evangelical audience, it is equally clear that both the arguments and conclusions will have widespread relevance in all aspects of scholarship. Certainly the direction in which the author drives will have to be reckoned with.

The horizon has been expanded.

Hemchand Gossai
Series Editor

Acknowledgments

This book has its basis in a research project completed at Trinity Theological Seminary (in cooperation with the University of Liverpool) in 1997. In its revision for publication, I endeavored to take into account the literature written on the subject since the manuscript was first submitted. As a result, the current document, though reflecting much of the previous work, has undergone substantial revision.

I wish to express my appreciation to all those who have helped me in writing and preparing this book. I am especially indebted to Dr. R. J. Gore (Professor of Systematic Theology, Erskine Theological Seminary), who served as the chair of my dissertation committee at the time I pursued my studies at Trinity. He also expressed enthusiasm about the present version of the manuscript. Dr. Jeff Forrey (Department Chair of Biblical Counseling at Trinity Theological Seminary), Dr. Al Machiela (Senior Pastor of Sunnyslope Christian Reformed Church in Salem, Oregon), Doug Dawson, Esquire (a retired attorney), and J. Ed Komoszewski (former Director of Research at Josh McDowell Ministry) likewise deserve a note of thanks for their careful review of the book.

I especially want to express my love for and appreciation to my wife, Marcia. Without her encouragement, affection, and companionship, the long hours of writing would not have been possible. My son, Joshua, likewise remained patient and understanding during the manuscripting process. Finally, I am indebted to my other family members and friends for their prayers and support during this venture.

Chapter 1

The Enduring Relevance of the Moral Law

Scholars and theologians continue to debate the relevancy and applicability of the Old Testament to the New Testament and the church. They also continue to debate the meaning and importance of the Decalogue and the Sermon on the Mount[1] to biblical, theological, and ethical studies.[2] To set the stage for the study to follow, this chapter will explore the issue of continuity and discontinuity between the testaments, the relevancy and applicability of the moral law, the nature of the relationship between the Decalogue and the Sermon on the Mount, and the unsettled state of scholarship concerning these two portions of biblical literature.

The Continuity and Discontinuity between the Testaments

For centuries, biblical scholars have debated the exact relationship between the Old Testament (also known as the Hebrew Scriptures) and the New Testament (also known as the New Covenant).[3] One attempt at delineating the relationship between the testaments argues that the Hebrew corpus is essentially a non-Christian religious book. Rudolf Bultmann is one scholar who posited this view.[4] In his writings he analyzed the historical development of Israel as a people and nation. He concluded that Israel failed in doing what God desired. Bultmann also maintained that Israel's downfall gave birth to all that is familiar in the New Testament and Christianity. He stressed that the Old Testament was a miscarriage of history. In a sense, the Hebrew writings were merely a presupposition giving way to the New Testament. Bultmann's position devalues the Old Testament in terms of its historical relevance and theological importance. In this view, the discontinuity is substantial.

Walter Zimmerli took issue with Bultmann, arguing that the hopes and history of Israel had not simply been shattered.[5] More importantly, they found complete fulfillment in the pages of the New Testament. Zimmerli also maintained that the Christological concept of Messiah was not merely a myth or existential interpretation rising from the ashes of Israel's failure. The notion was also a historically grounded and theologically sound event that connected with and brought to pass that which God had pledged to His people in the Old Testament. Zimmerli noted that Bultmann saw no continuity between the testaments because he ignored or discounted the promises God had made to Israel, promises that were literally fulfilled in the Christ of history.

Friedrich Baumgärtel, like Bultmann, emphasized the discontinuity between the testaments.[6] Also, like Bultmann, Baumgärtel stressed the disaster of Israel's failure. Baumgärtel, however, did not maintain the idea of Israel's total failure. Instead, he argued that most of the Old Testament promises had no relevance for Christians. Nevertheless, Baumgärtel did say there was a basic promise in the Old Testament that had enduring relevance. This was the pledge that the divine was the Lord and God of His people. Baumgärtel rejected the notion that prophecy had to be fulfilled, arguing that such ideas are foreign to the modern historical-critical mind. He maintained that Israel and the Old Testament bear witness to a religion under the law, one that is non-Christian in character and import. For Baumgärtel the historicity of Christ is not to be found at all in the Old Testament; rather, it is based on the idea of the incarnation.

Franz Hesse, like Baumgärtel, reduced the many promises of the Old Testament to a single basic promise.[7] Hesse argued that the promises failed because God punished Israel and the nation stubbornly hardened its heart. Hesse saw a dialectical process taking place. There was the warning (thesis) and witness (antithesis) of God's proclamations and activities in Israel, which led to the cross event (the synthesis). Hesse saw many supposed factual inaccuracies and historical blunders evident throughout the Old Testament. For him the Old Testament only served the purpose of pointing the Christian to the salvation articulated in the New Testament. He claimed the prophecies of the Hebrew corpus were nothing more than an anti-Jewish apologetic having only limited relevance in the early history of the church.

Klaus Schwarzwäller argued that the Old Testament was related to the New Testament only insofar as it pointed forward to Christ.[8] Schwarzwäller also maintained that the incarnation of the Messiah pointed back to the history and promises made in the Old Testament and gave them relevance. Thus, the significance of the Hebrew corpus only existed in connection with the Christ event (namely, the Messiah's advent).

In contrast to the scholars previously mentioned, there are other experts who stressed the theological primacy and importance of the Old Testament.

Wilhelm Vischer advocated that the exegetical analysis of the Old Testament be influenced and dictated by the New Testament.[9] He moreover argued that the Old Testament was Scripture and that the New Testament merely elucidated the meaning and fulfillment of these writings through its proclamation of the gospel. Alfred van Ruler similarly maintained that the Old Testament was the true Bible and the New Testament was its handmaiden to explain how its many promises were fulfilled.[10] Van Ruler said the New Testament gave meaning to the Old Testament and vice-versa. According to this view, the kingdom of God (not redemption or reconciliation) is the primary link between the testaments.

Other scholars such as Walther Eichrodt and Gerhard von Rad made use of typology to determine the relationship and unity between the testaments. Eichrodt believes the types could be almost anything, including persons, institutions, and events of the Old Testament.[11] He regards as a legitimate type whatever is a spiritual metaphor or paradigm for New Testament salvation history. The exact historical details are not really of much concern to him. Rather, it is the shadowy prefigurations that can be discerned from them. Von Rad took a more cautious approach. He saw the Old Testament as being a history book written in anticipation of the New Testament.[12] In his view, the institutions and prophecies in the Hebrew sacred writings offered prototypes to the antitypes of the New Testament. For example, von Rad would see Joseph (in Genesis) as the type and Christ as the antitype.

Richard Lucas rejected the typological approach.[13] He saw this technique as a method that is based mostly on conjecture and supposition, not scholarly exegesis and research. Richard E. Murphy has delineated the relationship between the testaments in terms of promise and fulfillment.[14] He argued that the Old Testament promises find their realization in the New Testament. While there may be partial fulfillments in the Hebrew sacred writings, the New Testament is said to delineate the full and final fulfillment of what is anticipated in the Old Testament. The eschatological aspect is clear in the view espoused by Murphy. For instance, God's pledge of redemption, which was announced in the Old Testament, is brought to fruition by Christ in the New Testament. In critiquing this view, it is important to realize that the promise/fulfillment approach, like many others, cannot do full justice to the variegated nature of each testament and the multiplex dynamic between the testaments.

In this regard, Gerhard Hasel maintained that there is a fundamental connection between the testaments and that this relationship is historically and theologically real.[15] He argued that delineating the exact relationship cannot be done on the basis of simplistic assumptions or reductionistic approaches. For example, it would be incorrect to take the New Testament as the starting point and make it a straightjacket for what the Old Testament says and means. Hasel furthermore advocated an approach that recognizes the uniqueness and unity of the testaments, one that tries to show how the Old Testament leads forward to the New Testament without over emphasizing or deemphasizing either Testament. The approach of Hasel has merit, for his method takes into account the intricacies of the sacred writings. His procedure employs such models as salvation-history, promise-fulfillment, and typology to delineate the nature of the connection between the testaments. Hasel argued for discerning the many ways in which the testaments are related without adopting over generalized, conflicting, or limiting interpretations. He maintained that the theologian should be willing to accept both the continuities and discontinuities, and the similarities and dissimilarities evident between the testaments.

As one analyzes the relationship between the testaments, it seems wise to recognize and elucidate the original historical witness and to explain the theological and eschatological significance of that witness. In this scheme of thinking, the Old Testament is regarded as being more than a general history of religion. It is an inspired document that finds dynamic unity and fulfillment in the New Testament. Both testaments should be read together in order to obtain a full and complete understanding of the topic being investigated. Thus, biblical events and meanings are directly derived from a careful, objective, and scholarly exegesis of the biblical text, not an eisegesis of it. Both the original context of the sacred writings and its broader relation to the entire canonical corpus influence the final form of the interpretation adopted.

Hasel has identified several patterns of historical and theological relationships between the testaments,[16] seven of which are briefly discussed here. First, both testaments give witness to the continuous history of God's people and the redemptive work of God in the affairs of humankind. Second, the New Testament makes frequent reference to Scripture passages in the Old Testament, which signifies the theological interrelatedness between the testaments. Third, there is a common usage between the testaments of certain key theological terms. Fourth, there is an essential unity of major themes between the testaments. Fifth, there is a typological (as opposed to allegorical) relationship between the testaments that binds them together. Sixth, the presence of promises and prophecies in the Old Testament that find fulfillment in the New Testament underscores the interrelationship between the testaments. Seventh (and finally), there is a genuine salvation history binding the testaments together. God worked within the realm of human history, experiences, and events to bring about His redemptive plan, and both testaments give witness to this.

In connection with the preceding discussion, it is affirmed that the Hebrew Scriptures bear witness to Christ (John 5:39). Additionally, He is the fulfillment of all that the Old Testament has to say about the Messiah (Luke 24:27). Nevertheless, Jesus also taught that the law had not been abolished; rather, it was eternal in its relevance (Matt. 5:18) and every aspect of it has enduring significance (Luke 16:17). A person might fittingly assert that God is the One who enables His people to discern the proper relationship between the testaments (cf. Mark 4:9–12; 2 Cor. 4:3–4); yet each major theological system[17] has to wrestle with the issue of the continuity/discontinuity between the testaments. Since each theological system takes more or less differing views on the matter, the task of analysis is difficult, and one's position on a particular issue becomes evident at various junctures in the discussion.

With respect to the subject of continuity and discontinuity, one must wrestle with a litany of questions concerning each testament. For example, is there an overarching theme that unites the Old Testament or is it filled with unrelated themes?[18] Can a unified theological stance be taken that unites the Old Testament and provides the basis for continuity with the New Testament, or is there no unifying stance about which to speak? Finally, is the Old Testament to be used in formulating Christian theology, and if so, how?

Covenant theologians tend to argue that there are events, people, and covenants in the Old Testament that bear analogy to those of the New Testament.[19] Also, the Old Testament is said to form the historical and theological context for the New Testament and the New Testament is said to form the interpretive key for grasping the full meaning of the Old Testament. Moreover, the correspondence in the details between the testaments is said to help understand the witnessing intent of the Old Testament contexts.

While Reformed, or covenantal, theologies tend to stress intertestamental continuity, classical and revised dispensational theologies[20] tend to stress intertestamental discontinuity.[21] This is especially evident in the writings of such persons as Charles I. Scofield, Lewis S. Chafer, and James D. Pentecost.[22] These and others would distinguish God's program for the church from His program for Israel. In contrast to many Reformed thinkers, classical and revised dispensationalists maintain that the church did not exist in the Old Testament, but began on the Day of Pentecost. They also argue that the church is not presently fulfilling promises made to Israel in the Old Testament.[23]

The Relevancy and Applicability of the Moral Law

The preceding discussion helps set the stage for the study to be presented in this work. It is clear that the issue of continuity/discontinuity between the testaments remains a topic of debate among biblical scholars and theologians. It is also evident that scholars and theologians continue to debate the relevancy and applicability of the Old Testament to the New Testament and the church. Furthermore, many Old Testament scholars recognize the vast importance of the Decalogue, or Ten Commandments, to the study and understanding of the Hebrew Scriptures.[24] Similarly, many New Testament scholars recognize the vast importance of Jesus' Sermon on the Mount to the study and understanding of the New Testament.[25]

The importance of the Decalogue and the Sermon on the Mount is especially evident in the study of ethics from various non-Christian and Christian perspectives.[26] For instance, Gearey advocated that "a critical legal theory, an elaboration of a Law, above the law, can be discovered in the text of the Bible."[27] Also, Bloesch observed that the "commandments in the Bible, particularly the Decalogue and the Sermon on the Mount, should be regarded as road signs that set us on the straight and narrow way."[28] With respect to the Decalogue, many consider it to be the moral law, or the basic list of God's universal ethical norms for proper human conduct.[29] The Sermon on the Mount is also recognized as having unparalleled importance to the moral life of the Christian church.[30] Moreover, a cursory examination of the Sermon on the Mount indicates that Jesus made repeated reference to the Decalogue. For example, a comparison of Matthew 5:21 with Exodus 20:13, and of Matthew 5:27 with Exodus 20:14, suggest that there is some connection between these two great bodies of biblical literature. The exact connection and its precise relevance for biblical studies is a matter of debate.[31]

At one end of the spectrum, theonomists would say that the Decalogue, or moral law, as well as the civil law of the Old Testament, applies to the church today.[32] Of course, theonomists—along with many other theologians—would see the Sermon on the Mount, along with the rest of the New Testament, as being entirely applicable for the church today.[33] At the other end of the spectrum, classical and revised dispensationalists tend to limit the primary application of the Decalogue to Israel, whether it is the nation that existed in the Old Testament or the so-called restored and redeemed Israel of the future kingdom age.[34] These dispensationalists also are prone to limit the primary application of the Sermon on the Mount to a future kingdom age.[35] Supposedly the church is not in view; rather, people living during a so-called millennial kingdom only are in view.[36]

Interestingly, both classical and revised dispensationalists as well as theonomists acknowledge there is some connection between the Decalogue and the Sermon on the Mount; however, classical and revised dispensationalists argue that these portions of Scripture have either no relevance or only indirect relevance for the church, whereas theonomists say these two great bodies of literature have full and continuing relevance for the church.

The Relationship between the Decalogue and the Sermon on the Mount

The preceding discussion spotlights the importance of the Decalogue and the Sermon on the Mount to biblical, theological, and ethical studies. It has also been advocated that there is some connection between the Decalogue and the Sermon on the Mount.[37] But what is that connection, and how can an understanding of it be beneficial?

An examination of the pertinent literature[38] shows that there are numerous authoritative sources relating to the contemporary relevance of the Decalogue, the relation of the Decalogue to the New Testament, the issue of continuity/discontinuity between the testaments, Christ's use of the Torah, and the hermeneutics of the Decalogue and the Sermon on the Mount. There are also some monographs on the Mosaic law as a whole and on the theology of dispensationalism, the literary affinities of the Sermon on the Mount with the Deuteronomic legal code, and the interpretation of the Sermon on the

Mount in light of Jewish-Palestinian tradition. There are scholarly reference works dealing with the authority of God's law for today, the setting of the Sermon on the Mount, the Jewish sources of the Sermon on the Mount, the structural analysis of the Sermon on the Mount, critiques of dispensational theology and Christian reconstructionism, as well as a plethora of exegetical commentaries on the Decalogue and the Sermon on the Mount.

The preceding information indicates that there has been extensive research and dialogue in subject areas that will be of concern to our area of investigation. However, there is no comprehensive research specifically on the topic to be discussed herein. In short, this study will explore the relationship between the Decalogue and the Sermon on the Mount and how this relationship affects the extent to which the moral law has continuing relevance as a rule or guide of life for the Christian church today.

There are several reasons why it is important to investigate this issue. First, such a study clarifies Jesus' usage of the Decalogue in particular and the Mosaic law and Old Testament in general. Second, such a study illuminates the way in which Jesus' Sermon was organized. Third, such a study sheds light on the nature of continuity/discontinuity between the testaments. Fourth, such a study addresses and furthers the discussion about the relevancy or irrelevancy of the moral law and the Sermon on the Mount for the Christian church. Fifth, such a study augments the existing research concerning the use of the Decalogue in the rest of the New Testament.[39]

The Study to Be Conducted

To reiterate, this work analyzes and compares the Decalogue and the Sermon on the Mount. One goal is to determine the nature of the relationship between the two. A second aim is to consider how that relationship affects the extent to which the moral law has ongoing pertinence for the Christian church today. To accomplish this objective, five key questions are addressed:[40]

- In what ways are the Decalogue and the Sermon on the Mount biblically and theologically related?
- What influence did the structure of the Decalogue have on the way the material in the Sermon on the Mount was arranged?

- To what extent is the Christian church obligated to obey the Sermon on the Mount? Are believers duty bound to obey all of it, part of it, or none of it?
- Do the references and allusions in the Sermon on the Mount to the Decalogue imply that the moral law has full and continuing relevance, partial and continuing relevance, only indirect relevance, or absolutely no relevance for the Christian church?
- Based on the relationship between the Decalogue and the Sermon on the Mount, to what extent are Christians obligated to obey the moral law? Are they duty bound to obey all of it, part of it, or none of it?

The Unsettled State of Biblical Scholarship

An examination of the literature dealing with the Decalogue indicates that there is no general agreement concerning the authorship and time of writing of this work.[41] Some maintain that Moses—Israel's liberator and lawgiver—is the author.[42] It is said that he, under the guidance of the Spirit, used both oral and written records from early history to compile the various accounts that appear in the Torah. This view allows for the presence of minor editorial additions that scribes provided later to the text for clarification.[43] Others maintain that numerous editors contributed to the content of the Torah over a period of approximately six centuries (from the eleventh to fifth centuries B.C).[44] These scholars argue that editors creatively pieced together at least four earlier literary documents.[45] These experts additionally maintain that the redactors combined and reedited the documents into the form of the Torah we now have.[46]

There is also the unsettled question about the relationship between the versions of the Decalogue recorded in Exodus 20:1–17 and Deuteronomy 5:6–21.[47] Some think Moses authored both forms of the Ten Commandments. According to this view, the differences between the two passages could be due to Moses' restating the material to suit the needs of a new generation of Israelites.[48] Or the differences could be due to Moses' quoting the material from memory.[49] Others, however, think the differences between versions of the Decalogue recorded in Exodus and Deuteronomy are due to considerable expansion and revision of the Ten Commandments over and above their original literary form.[50] These experts think several teams of writers and editors (for example, royal scribes, prophets, priests, and elders) over numerous centuries cut apart, rearranged, and recombined different literary sources into one new whole.[51]

An examination of the literature dealing with the Sermon on the Mount likewise indicates that there is no general agreement concerning the authorship and time of writing of this work. Some think that Jesus' discourse reads as a seamless whole, that Christ gave His message at one time, and that Matthew authored the material.[52] Others, however, think the Sermon is an assembly or collation of different sayings of Jesus or those attributed to Him by His followers. These were later compiled and edited by redactors within the community of faith.[53] Still others argue that Christ gave portions of the Sermon at various times throughout His earthly ministry and that Matthew and others arranged these segments into a cohesive unit.[54]

There is also the unsettled question about the relation between the Sermon on the Mount recorded in Matthew and the Sermon on the Plain (Luke 6:17–49) recorded in Luke. Some think the Lukan version presents an abbreviation of the longer sermon recorded in Matthew.[55] Others, however, think the two passages represent different versions of a discourse Jesus gave on several occasions.[56] Still others think the gospel writers/redactors either took a single common sermon and expanded it with other relevant teachings of Christ, or took numerous teachings of Christ and weaved them into coherent, thematically related units.[57]

As it currently stands, there is little general agreement among scholars concerning the preceding issues. Also, it is beyond the scope of this present work to rehearse and resolve these matters. Furthermore, it should be noted that, while "many scholars look for redactional layers and source-critical units"[58] within the Ten Commandments and Jesus' discourse, they were not "read in such fashion throughout the history of the church, including the early church."[59] In a similar vein, this study will take the biblical text in its present literary form at face value. Contrary to the opinion of some,[60] this faith-affirming approach is sensible, for it seeks to operate in a rational and objective manner. Admittedly, the stance adopted in this work might seem like a break with established "scholarly tradition."[61] Nevertheless, sufficient precedent for my decision is reflected in the evangelical academic community.

For instance, Johnson observed that, regardless of how "any biblical text has been redacted, its final shaping is the text to be accepted and interpreted."[62] With respect to the Sermon on the Mount, Williams advocated that the text "must be read on its own terms within the Gospel of Matthew."[63] Similarly, Tuttle stated that the goal of his research into Jesus' discourse was not "an exercise in reconstructing a pre-literary stage but in understanding the Biblical data in its present shape."[64] Furthermore, Moo, in his discussion of Matthew 5:17–19, noted that, as "a working procedure, we will seek to determine the meaning of each verse within its present context, since it is certainly legitimate to suppose that the final redactor, at least, intended them to be understood in relation to one another."[65] Even a scholar such as Anderson is sympathetic to the "*a priori* presupposition" of examining "the Gospels as wholes, the Gospels as unified narratives."[66]

In light of what has been said, only those issues will be discussed that have a direct bearing on the in-depth analysis and comparison of the Decalogue and the Sermon on the Mount. This approach will prevent the present work from getting bogged down in lengthy deliberations about matters that do not focus on the main goal—to determine how the relationship between the Decalogue and Jesus' Sermon affects the extent to which the moral law has continuing relevance as a rule or guide of life for the Christian church today.

The preceding discussion indicates it would be erroneous to think that someone can approach the biblical text without any preliminary assumptions, for the aims and presuppositions of the interpreter will greatly impact his or her research. In this regard, Meier made the following cogent observation: "Too often writers of theses work with presuppositions that are never formally acknowledged. Such neglect can lead to unnecessary confusion in and disagreement with the body of the thesis."[67] Moreover, one's presuppositions will affect the way one handles the biblical text and the conclusions one obtains from one's investigation.[68] Thus, I acknowledge the presence of certain theological and hermeneutical presuppositions, and think it is important to state these at the outset. Because these presuppositions are commonly held by a number of orthodox Protestants, no attempt will be made in this work to establish the validity of them.

First, there are presuppositions concerning the nature of the Bible.[69] It is affirmed that: Scripture, in the words of the original manuscripts, is absolutely truthful and perfectly accurate in all that it asserts, whether that has to do with matters concerning God, humanity, ethics, or the various aspects of science; the Bible is the primary source of divinely revealed truth and the final arbiter of faith and practice; Scripture, as the expression of God's will for His creation, possesses the supreme and absolute right to define what one is to believe and how one is to behave; and all human traditions, institutions, creeds, and confessions are placed under the authority and scrutiny of the divine Word.

Second, there are presuppositions concerning the authorship of the Pentateuch, which includes the Decalogue.[70] It is affirmed that Moses was the human author of Genesis, Exodus, Leviticus, Numbers, and Deuteronomy.[71] Under the guidance of the Spirit, he used both oral and written records from early history to compile the various accounts that appear in the Torah. Sometime during Israel's forty years of wandering in the desert, Moses arranged his historical records and accounts. While the Pentateuch is a composite document in that it is made up of individual books, it nevertheless reads as a unified work.

Third, there are presuppositions concerning the authorship of the Gospel of Matthew, which includes the Sermon on the Mount.[72] It is affirmed that Matthew (surnamed Levi) was the human author of the first Synoptic Gospel. He was the son of Alphaeus (Mark 2:14) and a Jewish tax collector for the Roman government (Matt. 9:9). Under the guidance of the Spirit, Matthew used a variety of oral and written records to draft his account of the life, ministry, teachings, death, and resurrection of Christ. Matthew wrote the first Synoptic Gospel sometime before the destruction of Jerusalem in A.D. 70.

Fourth, there are presuppositions concerning the authorship of the Gospel of Luke, which includes the Sermon on the Plain.[73] It is affirmed that Luke was the human author of the third Synoptic Gospel. He was a highly literate Gentile physician (Col. 4:14) who accompanied the apostle Paul on his second and third missionary journeys and on his voyage to Rome (Acts 16:10–17; 20:5–15; 21:1–18; 27:1–28:16). Under the guidance of the Spirit, Luke used a variety of oral and written records to draft his account of the life, ministry, teachings, death, and resurrection of Christ. Luke wrote the third Synoptic Gospel sometime before the destruction of Jerusalem in A.D. 70.

Conclusion

In summary, this study will do an in-depth comparative analysis of the Decalogue and the Sermon on the Mount. We will begin in chapter 2, which deals with the concept of the law.

Chapter 2

The Biblical Concept of the Law

This chapter will conduct an overview of the concept of the law, beginning with a discussion of legal terms appearing the Old and New Testaments. This lexical information will provide a foundation of understanding for the analysis that follows. In turn, conclusions obtained from the latter investigation will influence the way in which the Decalogue and the Sermon on the Mount are interpreted and applied. Furthermore, such an endeavor will shape the conclusions reached in this work regarding the extent to which the moral law has continuing relevance as a rule or guide for the Christian church today.

Legal Terms in the Old Testament

There are several Hebrew words used to refer to God's law. The most frequently occurring one is the noun *tôrâ*,[1] which comes from the primitive root *yārâ*, a term that means "to throw" or "to shoot."[2] With respect to *tôrâ*, the possible idea might be that of "stretching out the finger, or the hand, to point out a route."[3] While the etymology of the noun is debated,[4] there seems to be general agreement that the word means "direction," "instruction," or "law,"[5] depending on the context in which it is used.[6] *Tôrâ* appears about 220 times in the Massoretic text.[7] In the Old Testament, it is the most comprehensive term used for law.[8] Furthermore, *tôrâ* represents a "balanced intermingling of story and law."[9] It includes "extensive narrative accounts, speeches, poems, and genealogies as well as 'laws'."[10] Moreover, the noun denotes ethical imperatives[11] that are more concerned with how people should live, rather than with abstract concepts about morality.[12]

A second legal term appearing in the Old Testament is the Hebrew noun *dāth*, which may be of Persian origin.[13] The meanings include "decree," "law," "edict," or "regulation."[14] A third legal term is the Hebrew noun *mishpāt*, which is derived from the verb *shāphat*, meaning "to judge," "to execute judgment," or "to govern."[15] Correspondingly, *mishpāt* means "judgment," "decision," "ordinance," or "sentence."[16] The term could be used to refer to all forms of government, whether legislative, executive, or judicial, though it was primarily used with respect to matters of litigation and the execution of judgment.[17]

A fourth legal term is the Hebrew noun *chōq*, which is derived from the verb *chāqâ,* meaning "to carve out," "to engrave," "to write," "to fix," or "to determine."[18] Accordingly, *chōq* means "something prescribed," "statute," or "due."[19] The term occurs 129 times in the Hebrew Bible.[20] Besides being used to refer to laws engraved on slabs of stone or metal, the word also was used to refer to orders, injunctions, regulations, requirements, and commandments.[21]

A fifth legal term is the Hebrew noun *dābār,* which is derived from the verb *dābar*, meaning "to talk" or "to speak."[22] Likewise, *dābār* means "word," "matter," "event," or "affair."[23] In some contexts it refers to commands or decrees given by some ruling entity (for example, the Lord in the Decalogue; cf. Exod. 34:28).[24] Just as the law as a whole can be viewed as *tôrâ,* so the revelation of God—especially the Mosaic covenant—can be regarded as *dābār*.[25] The ten words are part of God's revelation to His people. The syntactical form of their utterance denotes them as commandments.[26]

A sixth legal term is the Hebrew noun *'ēdût,* which some think is derived from the verb *'ûd*, meaning "to repeat" or "to do again."[27] The basis for the idea of "witness" or "testimony" in the root might be found in the sense of being present a second time or bringing something back, as in verbally repeating or rehearsing an event.[28] This etymology and its explanation, though, are debated. If the primary meaning of *'ûd* is "to warn," "to admonish," or "to call to witness,"[29] then it is clearer to see how the noun *'ēdût* can mean "witness" or "testimony."[30] Possible secondary meanings include "regulation," "commandment," and "contractual regulations."[31] The word is used consistently in reference to the testimony of God, especially as He makes His affirmations regarding His own person and purpose.[32] As a designation of God's law, *'ēdût* testifies to the principles of the Lord's dealings with His people.[33]

A seventh legal term is the Hebrew noun *mitswâ,* which is derived from the verb *tsāwâ,* meaning "to order," "to direct," "to command," or "to charge (someone to do something)."[34] Accordingly, *mitswâ* means "commandment";[35] it conveys the sense of "obligation" or "what is prescribed."[36] The word is used most commonly to refer to particular conditions of God's covenant with His people.[37] *Mitswâ* is used in contexts where it refers to a specific instruction from God that He intended His people to obey, rather than a general law that they were to observe. Thus, the emphasis is categorical, rather than casuistic, in nature.[38]

Legal Terms in the New Testament

There are several Greek words used to refer to God's law.[39] Perhaps the most common one is the noun *nómos*, whose principal meaning concerns "that which is conceived as standard or generally recognized rules of civilized conduct [especially] as sanctioned by tradition."[40] Such terms as "custom," "principle," and "norm" help capture this sense. *Nómos* can also denote "a formalized rule (or set of rules) prescribing what people must do."[41] Such terms as "ordinance," "rule," and "command" help to convey this notion.

Nómos occurs eight times in Matthew and nine times in Luke.[42] It usually refers to the Pentateuch;[43] however, it also can denote the Old Testament as a whole.[44] While *nómos* primarily refers to that which regulates behavior, it also can denote the promise of God (cf. Luke 24:44).[45] *Nómos* also refers to a word of instruction that is divine, not human, in origin and that indicates the path of righteousness and blessing.[46] *Nómos* is never used in the New Testament to refer to the oral Torah or the teaching tradition of Israel's religious leaders (cf. Mark 7:5, 8).[47]

A second legal term is the Greek noun *nomothesía* (cf. Rom. 9:4), which literally means "lawgiving"[48] and concerns the establishing of a law.[49] The focus is more on the result, rather than the act, of legislation.[50] A third legal term is the Greek verb *krínō*, which means "to judge," "to consider," "to assess," "to decide," or "to go to law."[51] Either God or people could be doing the judging, whether in an official or a personal sense.[52] A fourth legal term is the Greek adjective *énnomos*, which means "legal," "lawful," or "subject to (law)."[53] This term denotes one's adherence to the law.[54] That is why, when *énnomos* is used in reference to people, it means "righteous" or "upright."[55]

A fifth legal term is the Greek word *nomikós*, which means "relating to law" or "learned in the law."[56] In the Gospels of Matthew and Luke the word is used as a noun to refer to the religious leaders of Israel who were concerned with "the administration and understanding of the law"[57] (cf. Matt. 22:35; Luke 7:30; 14:3). A sixth legal term is the Greek verb *nomothetéō*, which means "to give a law" or "to establish a law."[58] Both the legislation and sanctioning of laws are denoted[59] as well as the notion of legally settling an issue.[60]

The Nature of the Law

The law is not an impersonal and foreign entity to God; rather, it reflects His holy character[61] and His purposes for human beings.[62] This means the law is more than a mere record of ordinances and decrees. It is a transcript of the will of God.[63] Thus, those who violate the law are transgressing God Himself, for He is the author of the law. Furthermore, the law is the precise expression of God's pure and perfect moral standard.[64] It is the measuring stick by which the Lord evaluates all human actions (cf. Rom. 3:20). The Mosaic law gave the Israelites guidelines for how they should relate to God and how they were to deal with Gentiles. The law also gave Israel insights concerning the Lord's holiness and purity. The law indicated the manner by which the people of God might continue to experience the temporal blessings associated with the divine promises once they arrived in Palestine.

The nature of the law was such that God's people could not pick which ones they wanted to obey and which ones they wanted to ignore. None of the commandments were open for review or revision by an advisory panel of Israelites, and God's people were not free to abandon ordinances and stipulations they found irksome or inconvenient.[65] The Lord required that His people fully heed the letter *and* the spirit of the law. This truth is reflected in *The Larger Catechism* of the Westminster Assembly.[66] Question 99 says that the law binds "the whole man...unto obedience forever"; "it is spiritual, and so reacheth the understanding, will, affections, and all other powers of the soul as well as the words, works, and gestures."[67] Valid implications of the law were also binding on God's people. "Where a duty is commanded, the contrary sin is forbidden; and, where a sin is forbidden, the contrary duty is commanded."[68]

The Larger Catechism was reflecting the scriptural teaching that both the desires as well as the actions of God's people must conform to the law. This emphasis is seen in Christ's teaching in the Sermon on the Mount concerning murder, adultery, divorce, and oaths (Matt. 5:21–37). The Savior condemned the hypocrisy of those who tried to conceal their inner corruption with an outward display of pious deeds (cf. 15:7–9; 23:25–28).

The Types of the Law

There were three distinct types of law evident within the Mosaic code.[69] Through the commandments, the Lord revealed His will for the Israelites with respect to *morality* and *ethics* (Exod. 20:1–26). Through a variety of ordinances, the Lord revealed His will for the Israelites with respect to *social* and *civil* concerns (21:1–23:33). Through concrete stipulations concerning worship and sacrifice, the Lord revealed His will for the Israelites with respect to *religious* and *ceremonial* concerns (24:12–31:18).[70] Thus, while there is an essential unity to the law,[71] it is not a juridical monolith.[72] Ethical, social, and religious distinctions are detectable within it.[73]

This information indicates there are various sorts of biblical law.[74] *Moral* laws specify the type of personal and community behavior that always is the duty of God's people, regardless of when and where they live. The *political* laws recorded in the Old Testament took the principles expressed in the moral law and applied them to Israel's national situation when it existed as a theocracy (a government in which God alone is the ruler). The laws in the Old Testament about *ceremonial* purity, diet, and sacrifice were temporary edicts that taught God's people important truths (for instance, about atoning for sin, properly worshiping the Lord, and regularly fellowshipping with Him). When Jesus fulfilled the symbolic meaning behind the ceremonial laws, they were cancelled; in other words, God's people no longer had to observe them (cf. Matt. 15:20; Mark 7:15–19; Acts 10:9–16; Col. 2:16–17; Heb. 10:1–14; 13:9–10).[75]

Those who hold to the tripartite division of the Mosaic law see it as being authoritative for the church, whereas those who reject this delineation view the law "merely as historical and illustrative source material"[76] for believers today. McQuilkin offers the typical rationale for the dissenting view:[77]

> Neither Moses nor the prophets made this distinction, and it is not always apparent what is moral and what is merely ceremonial. Furthermore, though Jesus seemed to distinguish the two by his behavior and what he stressed, neither did he make this distinction explicitly. But the gravest problem with this interpretation is that Paul himself did not seem to make this distinction. He seemed often to lump together everything in the Mosaic economy as "the law" and to teach that in Christ we have done away with it. In Paul there is no distinction between the Decalogue and the rest of the law. The law is one, the revealed will of God.

In evaluating the points made by McQuilkin,[78] one could observe that the widely held view of the doctrine of the Trinity, which teaches a distinction between the persons of the Godhead, is hard to find in the Old Testament and it is not always apparent in the New Testament. Nevertheless, it is a valid understanding of who God is, and a view that is affirmed when Scripture is examined carefully.[79] The same argument could be made concerning the division of the Old Testament law into three distinguishable parts. The tripartite division of the Mosaic law is a convenient and valid interpretation of the data present in the Old Testament. Even McQuilkin finds it advantageous to refer to distinctions within the Mosaic law when he wrote, "Ceremonial and national elements of the law, along with some moral laws, are clearly set aside."[80]

It is true that Jesus and Paul did not seem to make a distinction between different types of law (for example, Mark 7:10 citing Leviticus 20:9; or 1 Corinthians 9:9 quoting Deuteronomy 25:4). Yet this does not automatically mean the distinctions do not exist. One could argue that Jesus and Paul were reflecting the truth that God's law, despite its distinctions, is an essential unity.[81] Moreover, in both the Old and New Testaments, the law of God was not considered such a monolithic entity that it had no distinctions between ordinances that were considered to be either heavier or lighter. For example, Jesus taught that there were weightier matters to the law (cf. Matt. 23:23–24).[82]

God is the One who enacted the moral, judicial, and ritual aspects of the law in the Old Testament. In truth, He gave equal force to the entire Mosaic code. This is evident by the fact that all these laws were mingled together in the Pentateuch. Collectively the entire Mosaic law revealed that life under God is to be lived, not compartmentally, but as a variegated unity.[83] The unity of the Mosaic legislation, however, does not mean the laws were uniform in their type and purpose. There were different kinds of laws, and these served differing purposes. By the nature of Israel's theocratic state, the political and ceremonial laws had a limited application to that nation during the Old Testament era. In contrast, the moral law transcends the theocratic state of Israel. In fact, Jesus affirmed the unchanging universal force and relevancy of God's moral law for His people today (cf. Matt. 5:17–19; Luke 16:16–17).[84]

A related argument against the threefold division of the law is that such a convention is anachronistic, for ancient Israel made no such distinctions. But this line of reasoning misunderstands the intent behind the tripartite division of the law. The goal is not to give an historical account of the way the Israelites regarded and handled their own laws. Rather, the aim is to catalogue the constituent elements of the law, just as one might classify different types of literature according to their genre.[85]

In arguing against a division of the Old Testament law into three parts, Wenham made these points:[86] "First, the NT does not seem to distinguish between the different types of law. Second, it is difficult to draw the line between moral precepts and other law. Is the Sabbath a moral law or a ceremonial one? Third, much of the civil legislation is grounded on moral judgments, often expressed in the ten commandments."

The statement about the New Testament not distinguishing between different types of law has already been discussed. Wenham's second point—that it is difficult to discern between moral precepts and other forms of law—is well taken. But it does not necessarily invalidate the idea of a tripartite division of the law. Just because it is hard to distinguish the types of law does not make the distinctions invalid. For example, the hermeneutical principle of examining the grammatical and historical context of a passage is difficult at times to perform; nevertheless, it is an immensely valuable step in the interpretive process. Similarly, making the effort to distinguish between different types of law, though admittedly hard, is worth the effort.

McQuilkin also recognizes the difficulty of discerning between the moral, ceremonial, and civil aspects of the Mosaic legislation.[87] His suggestion, which seems to have merit, is to use the Ten Commandments to discern between ethical precepts and other forms of law. The basis for this is that the Decalogue represents the epitome of truth and a summary of what God expects of people. Others have advocated the idea of principalism.[88] In this case the Ten Commandments, the Sermon on the Mount, and the Pauline commands are some of the key materials used for discerning broad moral ideas of an enduring character. The merit of this view is that it seeks to make Scripture applicable for New Testament Christians.

Nevertheless, both of the previously mentioned approaches suffer from the same deficiency attributed to a tripartite division of the law, namely, that they can be overly subjective and arbitrary in nature. What interpretive standard does one use to determine which passages to principalize and which to disregard or ignore all together? Also, what hermeneutical guidelines should one follow to discern and apply the timeless ethical nuggets found in Scripture? Moreover, what safeguards exist within these approaches to ensure that the analysis and application of Scripture does not become "a matter of one's own interpretation" (2 Pet. 1:20)? The peril of having a ghettoized and compartmentalized approach to God's Word is a potential threat in these methods. Consequently, the Ten Commandments and the Sermon on the Mount remain useful and necessary starting points for discerning supracultural ethical truths. Furthermore, these serve as an objective, concrete expression of God's moral law that is straightforward to recognize and apply.[89]

Tiessen has furthered the discussion by articulating a "hermeneutic for discerning universal moral absolutes."[90] He begins with a disclaimer that it is wise not to "underestimate the complexity of discerning...the underlying moral intent that must be translated into active obedience in our own situation."[91] The reason is that Scripture is filled with a "multitude of specific commands of God addressed to diverse situations." Despite the culturally conditioned aspects of the Word, it is still valid to maintain that "universal moral absolutes do exist" and that the Lord has "revealed them to us"; moreover, "with the guidance of the Holy Spirit and the use of good hermeneutical and exegetical procedures we can discern them."[92]

Tiessen's interpretive principles are summarized as follows:[93]

1. Universal norms are identifiable by their basis in the moral nature of God.
2. Universal norms are identifiable by their basis in the creation order.
3. Universal norms are identifiable by transcendent factors in the situation of their promulgation and by the lack of situational limitation in their formulation.
4. Universal norms are identifiable by their consistency throughout the progressive revelation of the divine will.
5. Universal norms are identifiable by their consistency with the progress of God's redemptive program.

In the preceding discussion regarding Wenham, his third point concerning the moral underpinnings of the Old Testament civil legislation is valid; it is also a reminder of the essential unity of Hebrew law. The oneness and interpenetrating nature of the law means there are moral implications to commands that are civil or ceremonial.[94] But recognizing the essential unity of the law does not necessarily invalidate the notion of moral law as distinct from civil law and ceremonial law. In fact, Wenham made the following pertinent observation:[95] "Though the threefold division of the law is in my view arbitrary and artificial, it does provide a convenient framework for our discussion." My point is that the tripartite division of the Old Testament law is a legitimate and useful one for accurately interpreting and applying legislative material for the church today.

Some classical and revised dispensationalists argue that the Bible makes no distinction among the laws. For example, R. Lightner asserted the following:[96] "That the Law contains legislation related to Israel's moral, religious, and civil life is not disputed. However, when the parts are divided to support the contention that some of the Law is still operative as a rule of life today while other parts are not, then a totally new and unwarranted concept is introduced, a concept foreign to the Old Testament."

In response to Lightner's statement, it is interesting to note that he indirectly concedes the presence of various discernible aspects to Old Testament law, namely, legislation related to the moral, religious, and civil life of Israel. This supports the idea that distinctions among Israel's laws can be made and used as the basis for further theological discussion. It is also important to note that Lightner provided no scriptural support for his claim that "a totally new and unwarranted concept is introduced, a concept foreign to the Old Testament." The validity of the threefold division of the law already has been presented. The conclusions of that discussion make it clear that the tripartite division of the Mosaic law is not new, unwarranted, or foreign to the Hebrew Scriptures. Rather, it is a convenient and valid interpretation of the data present in the Old Testament.[97]

Some classical and revised dispensationalists furthermore maintain that the Christian is not obligated to obey any portion of the Mosaic law, including the moral law. Lightner made this assertion:[98] "The Bible teaches that the Law of Moses in its entirety has been set aside as a rule of life and therefore is not operative as a stewardship, or a way by which God manages His 'household affairs,' today."[99] But the contention that the law is not in force in the present age appears to contradict direct statements made in the New Testament. For example, Jesus said in John 14:15, "If you love me, you will keep my commandments."[100] In 1 Corinthians 9:21 and Galatians 6:2, Paul made mention of the law of Christ.[101] In 1 John 5:2–3, the apostle John wrote, "By this we know that we love the children of God, when we love

God and obey his commandments. For the love of God is this, that we obey his commandments. And his commandments are not burdensome."

Some classical and revised dispensationalists seem to draw an artificial distinction between the testaments, as if law was chiefly present in the Old Testament, while grace prevails in the New Testament. It is valid to say that Christ is "full of grace and truth" (John 1:14), suggesting that God's grace and truth achieve their fullest expression and highest potential in the coming of the Son. Nevertheless, God's grace was evident throughout the Old Testament period and undergirded the Lord's relationship with His people (cf. Gen. 6:8; Exod. 34:6; Jer. 31:3; Lam. 3:22–23).

Geisler maintained that the Ten Commandments have faded away, and he bases his argument on 2 Corinthians 3:7 and 11.[102] Charles Ryrie made a similar point when he wrote, "Paul...dares to label the moral part of the Law as a ministry of death and condemnation."[103] But an examination of verses 7–11 suggests that Paul was talking about the old covenant, not the Decalogue as such (cf. Heb. 8:13).[104] Geisler also made reference to Ephesians 2:15 as another indication that the Ten Commandments have faded away.[105] But an examination of that passage suggests that Paul was referring to the ceremonial aspects of the law.[106] Christ offered in His own body the final sacrifice to which the temple sacrifices pointed. The ceremonial laws, having been fulfilled in Christ, are no longer necessary for saved Jews and Gentiles to observe.[107]

In Geisler's thinking, "the whole law of Moses which was given to Israel was taken away by Christ."[108] Geisler based this conclusion on Galatians 3:24 and 25: "Therefore the law was our disciplinarian until Christ came, so that we might be justified by faith. But now that faith has come, we are no longer subject to a disciplinarian." Supposedly Paul included the moral law in his comment. But an examination of the passage and its context suggests that the apostle was talking about the pedagogical use of the law, not the abrogation of the moral law. Paul was saying that the law—especially its ceremonial aspects—pointed out sin and punished it. With the coming of Christ, however, it is no longer necessary to be under the tutelage of the law. This does not mean that Jesus has nullified the moral law, as Paul's subsequent statements in 5:13–14 and 6:2 corroborate.[109]

Geisler furthermore maintained that the law of Moses was given only to Israel.[110] Geisler based this argument on Hebrews 7:11–12, 18; 8:1–2, 9, and

13. He concluded: "The language could hardly be clearer: the whole covenant given to Israel by Moses, which included moral laws, has been done away with." A careful examination of Hebrews 7–8, however, does not support Geisler's sweeping conclusion. The writer of the epistle was specifically talking about the Levitical priesthood with its rituals, ceremonies, and sacrifices as well as the old covenant connected with it. The point is that with the coming of Christ, God has inaugurated a new covenant with a new Mediator. His high priestly service and sacrifice are infinitely superior to what existed under the old economy and has replaced it. Expressed differently, the writer of Hebrews was focusing on the ceremonial aspects of the Mosaic law. While the ceremonial law has been fulfilled in Christ and is no longer binding on believers, the moral law still remains in force.[111]

Geisler's final point is that one cannot take the blessings of the law without its curses. This argument is based on Galatians 3:10, 13, and 21. "According to Paul, with the law it is either all or nothing at all. So on the one hand, if any of the law is binding on Christians, then all of it is. On the other hand, if some of the Mosaic law does not apply to Christians, then none of it does."[112] An examination of these verses and the context of the passage, however, does not support Geisler's either-or conclusion. It is true that Paul considered the law, with all its precepts, as a unity. But in Galatians 3, the apostle was talking about the misuse of the law by his antagonists. They believed that by observing it, one could attain righteousness before God.[113] Paul's argument was that one minor infraction of the law made one irreversibly guilty before God and thus deserving of His punishment.[114]

Thus, the apostle was not saying or even implying what Geisler asserted. In fact, if Paul had been teaching that the moral law was no longer binding on Christians, why would he later make reference to it in Galatians 5:13 and 14: "For you were called to freedom brothers and sisters; only do not use your freedom as an opportunity for self-indulgence, but through love become slaves to one another. For the whole law is summed up in a single commandment, 'You shall love your neighbor as yourself.'"

Perhaps the greatest challenge to the threefold division of the Old Testament law has come from adherents in the theonomistic movement. Some Christian reconstructionists, as they are called, maintain that God and His holy nature are immutable. Therefore, His law, which is a reflection of His being, is immutable.[115] But the biblical record is that God has changed and abrogated certain portions of the law.[116] For example, He no longer requires Christians to practice circumcision, observe the Passover, and abstain from pork and shellfish (cf. Acts 10:9–16; 11:5–10; Col. 2:16, 20–21).

The theonomists try to work around the biblical record by making ambiguous distinctions in the term "law." As the argument goes, the law is the transcript of God's perfection. Nevertheless, it is not the precepts of the transcript of the law that are immutable, but the underlying principles. In this scheme of thinking, immutability pertains to the principles behind the laws, not the laws themselves.[117] Interestingly, theonomists acknowledge that entire classes of law are subject to alteration as situations require different applications.[118] But this line of reasoning undercuts the argument for the unchangeableness of the law. If whole categories of legislation are subject to change, depending on the situation, then certain portions of the law can be altered and/or abrogated. The central issue is not whether changes are made but rather how the changes are made and the criteria used for recognizing the changes.[119]

Even theonomists have tended to make distinctions in the Old Testament laws. For example, Bahnsen favors a two-level division between the moral law (namely, general precepts and illustrative applications) and the ceremonial law (namely, typological and separational precepts).[120] He maintained that the ceremonial precepts were conditional, being based on the historical situation in which they occurred, and thus are no longer obligatory. He also argued that the judicial precepts are part of the moral law, and thus are universally binding.[121]

Perhaps the most disputed contention made by some theonomists such as Bahnsen is that "*civil magistrates ought to mete out the punishment which God has prescribed in his word.*"[122] Though not all reconstructionists agree with everything Bahnsen has advocated, his views remain a dominant and influential force among theonomists, and thus merit analysis and critique. He argued that just as the ruling official in the Old Testament had divine injunctions that he was responsible to execute, so too ruling officials in the New Testament era were obligated to those commands recorded in Mosaic law that applied to "civil affairs and social penology."[123] Bahnsen also maintained that Christians in a democratic society should enact the Mosaic standing laws pertaining to civil government through the persuasive political process.[124]

There are several reasons to take issue with Bahnsen. First, unlike other nations, God entered into a unique relationship with Israel as a theocratic state. For example, Exodus 19:6 says the Israelites were "a priestly kingdom and a holy nation." Second, in the Old Testament, only the citizens of Israel were members of the community of the redeemed, for "all were baptized into Moses in the cloud and in the sea, all ate the same spiritual food, and all drank the same spiritual drink" (1 Cor. 10:2–4). Third, those who professed to be part of the covenant community submitted to circumcision, which was the sign of the covenant (Gen. 17:9–14; Rom. 2:28–29). In 2 Samuel 7:23 and 24, King David expressed his awareness of the unique status of Israel as a theocratic state among all the nations of the world:

> Who is like your people, Israel? Is there another nation on earth whose God went to redeem it as a people, and to make a name for himself, doing great and awesome things for them, by driving out before his people nations and their gods? And you established your people Israel for yourself to be your people forever; and you, O Lord, became their God.

While Bahnsen acknowledged Israel's privileged status as the people of God, he maintained that the nation was not entirely unique from other surrounding states, for Israel shared common civil functions with them.[125] In response to this view, one should note that, while it is true that Israel had civil laws which were parallel to those of other surrounding nations, Israel's political use of those laws was conditioned by its unique theocratic status. Unlike other states, the theocracy of Israel did not have to make sharp distinctions between the various uses of its law (that is, its civil, ceremonial, and moral codes). An examination of Deuteronomy 15, for example, reveals that the Mosaic law—though having different kinds of legislation—was an integrated unity. This indicates that every aspect of the life of this covenant community was subordinated to the will of God, who was Israel's Creator, Redeemer, and covenant Lord.[126]

Unlike other nations, the social framework that was operative in ancient Israel was unique to it as a theocratic state under Yahweh. For example, what other ancient Near Eastern nation had laws like Israel's sabbatical year or the year of Jubilee (cf. Lev. 25)? What other state required the judges to appeal to the priests when they could not arbitrate difficult cases (cf. Deut. 17:9)? What other nation had to abide by the rules of warfare that God placed upon His covenant people Israel (cf. Deut. 20)? In each of these examples, it is evident that the standing laws of Israel reflected the nation's unique status as a theocratic state under Yahweh. Moreover, contrary to some theonomists' sentiments, God entered into a theocratic covenant relationship only with the descendants of Abraham, Isaac, and Jacob. The Hebrew Scriptures were originally the body of laws for the community of the redeemed in ancient times. That is why no nation-state today can claim the civil and ceremonial aspects of the Old Testament law as their constitution.

God's people are to abide by the ethical principles reflected in the judicial laws recorded in the Old Testament (cf. 1 Cor. 9:8–10).[127] They are also to abide by the ordinances established by the governing authorities God has established (cf. Rom. 13:1–7; 1 Pet. 2:13–14).[128] A contemporary form of government might choose to frame its laws around those found in the Old Testament; but it is not required by God to do so. Likewise, believers are not divinely obligated to enact the Mosaic standing laws pertaining to civil government through the persuasive political process.[129]

The Divine Intent Behind the Law

Scripture is clear about the presence of God's moral law and what it contains. Such passages as the Decalogue, other statutes of Moses, messages declared by Israel's prophets, the teachings of Jesus (for example, the Sermon on the Mount), and the rest of the New Testament letters bear witness to the existence of God's moral law. Furthermore, that God has a moral law is evident from the lingering testimony of humanity's fallen conscience.[130] The inward moral law and the outward Mosaic law are in agreement. If Gentiles, who know nothing about the Mosaic law, would obey the dictates of conscience, they at least superficially would conform to many of the demands of the Mosaic law (Rom. 2:14). The fact that they do, by natural impulse, many of the things that the Mosaic law requires proves that God's law is written inwardly (vs. 15).

The conscience that God has endowed to people examines their deeds and reaches a verdict about them. Moreover, God will sit in judgment on all the ethical decisions that people make and condemn them when they ignore or stifle the voice of conscience. Every secret deed will come to light when Christ hails people before His bar of justice (vs. 16). Thus, God did not create human beings to be a law unto themselves. Rather, He made people to be subject to His law (cf. Gen. 2:15–17). In the Lord's eyes this was not to be a hardship, for He created people to experience true fulfillment and joy in life by obeying the law (cf. 1 John 5:2–3). One can see the presence of duty *and* delight in the life of Christ (John 4:34), and His experience in this regard is the divine ideal for all people (cf. Pss. 112:1; 119:14, 16, 47–48, 97, 113, 127–128, 163–167).

The human heart, which is fallen and prone to sin (cf. Jer. 17:9), despises God's law, for it originates with One who is holy and righteous and it censures the evil things the human heart delights in doing (cf. John 3:19–20). However, those who have trusted in Christ discover that they delight in and desire to keep the law (cf. vs. 21). Their aim is to please God and express their gratitude to Him through obedience (Rom. 7:18–22; 12:1–2). Through the enabling of the Holy Spirit, they can achieve a degree of obedience to the law that was never theirs before (Rom. 7:6; 8:4–6; Heb. 10:16).

In Matthew 22:37–40, Jesus summarized the moral law when He declared that people are to love God and one another wholeheartedly. In fact, Christ said that all the Old Testament moral instructions depended on these two commandments. The moral teaching given by Christ and His apostles does not represent a break with the moral law of the Old Testament. Instead, it represents a clarification of the old law and a reapplication of it to new circumstances. Furthermore, God still expects His people to live as citizens of His eternal kingdom, where Christ reigns. In this post-Pentecost era of the Spirit, God wants His people to be sanctified in their behavior as they exist in a hostile world (John 17:6–19).

The Purposes of the Law

The law serves several interrelated purposes.[131] First, it is like a mirror that reflects the perfect righteousness of God and a person's own sinfulness and shortcomings.[132] God uses the law to make people aware of their misdeeds (cf. Rom. 3:20; 4:15; 5:13; 7:7–11).[133] Through the work of the law in one's life, a person sees that all have sinned and fallen short of the supreme standard of righteousness (3:23).[134] One learns that he or she needs divine pardon and stands in danger of being eternally damned (Rom. 7:21–24; Rev. 20:11–15).[135] While the law does not cause people to sin, it frames their actions as sin by revealing God's evaluation of what they have done.[136]

A second purpose of the law is that it not only shows people their sin, but also it steers them away from transgression and toward the Savior.[137]

God placed people under the guardianship of the law to lead them to salvation in Christ (Gal. 3:19–24).[138] During the time of Paul, some children had an adult attendant (a pedagogue) who saw to it that the child got to school. One purpose of the law has been achieved when a person comes to faith in Christ, who is the goal, or fulfillment, of the law (Rom. 10:4).[139] In this regard, the law is like a rule or a map that shows people the landscape of a God-pleasing life.[140] An upright person gives the Lord the highest priority, honors his or her parents, values human life, tells the truth, and learns contentment with God.[141]

A third purpose of the law is that it serves a civic function by restraining evil.[142] The law tells people what transgression is by laying out boundaries for them. They know that the law cannot change the wicked bent of the human heart. Nevertheless, the law can, to a certain degree, inhibit anarchy by its threats of judgment, especially when those threats are reinforced by civil codes that administer punishment for confirmed transgressions (cf. Deut. 13:6–11; 19:16–21; Rom. 13:3–4). Clearly, then, God intended the law more for the lawless than for the lawabiding. Put another way, the Lord did not establish the law primarily to control the righteous, that is, those who pleased Him by their upright lives. Instead, God instituted the law mainly to regulate and condemn those who willfully sin against Him and all humanity (1 Tim. 1:9). When the law is rightly applied and used, it helps maintain civil order, and it also protects the righteous from the unjust.

A fourth purpose of the law is that it reveals the moral precepts by which God's people must live[143] and alerts them to the good works God has planned for them (Eph. 2:10). It is true that believers are no longer under the condemnation of the law (Rom. 6:14; 7:4, 6; 1 Cor. 9:20; Gal. 2:15–19; 3:25), for Christ has freed them from it (Rom. 6:15). Nevertheless, the law still plays a viable role in the lives of believers. Its moral demands are worthy to be studied and heeded. The law continues to reveal whether believers are living for God as much as they should.[144]

The righteous commandments intended by the law may be fully met in believers when they allow the Spirit, rather than the sinful nature, to control them (Rom. 8:4). Paul said that where the fruit of the Spirit was growing in abundance, there was no condemnation from the law (Gal. 5:22–23). This implies that believers who are genuinely led by the Spirit and manifest the love of Christ will fulfill the spirit and intent of the law (Rom. 13:9–10).

Furthermore, believers are under the law of Christ as a rule or guide of life (cf. 1 Cor. 9:21; Gal. 6:2). In a sense, the law is like a family code in that it tells the regenerate what behavior will please their heavenly Father. Christ reflected this truth when He said that His followers were to teach new converts to heed all He had commanded (Matt. 28:20). In fact, He declared that obedience to His commands will substantiate the reality of one's love for Him (John 14:15).

A fifth purpose of the law is that it can serve as a reminder of what believers were like before they trusted in Christ. As they reflect on God's perfect moral standard, as revealed in the law, they will see how sinful they were. They will also appreciate God's grace in rescuing them from eternal punishment.

A sixth purpose of the law is that it can help believers recognize when they have done something wrong. Although Christians are saved, this does not mean they never sin again. Also, while they want to live for God, there will be times when they will be unsure about how to do so. The timeless principles taught in the law can give them guidance in doing what is right. By knowing what the law says, they will have a foundation of wisdom on which to build.

In summary, Christ on the one hand has abolished the civil and ceremonial aspects of the law. On the other hand, He has affirmed the continuance and authority of the moral law as the expression of God's will. Those who are indwelt by the Spirit and energized by God's love are enabled to do what the moral law requires. They behave in a way that was rarely ever seen in the Old Testament.[145]

Jesus and the Law

Jesus lived under the jurisdiction of the law (Gal. 4:4) and as a Jew submitted to it (Luke 2:21–23; 4:16).[146] Also, throughout His earthly ministry, He affirmed the abiding validity and relevancy of the moral law (Matt. 5:17–18). Furthermore, He explained its meaning and elucidated its perfect, ultimate significance. For example, Christ taught that both murder and hatred were condemnable in the eyes of God (Matt. 5:21–26). He also said that both adultery and lust were reprehensible to the Lord (vss. 27–28). Moreover, in 22:36 Jesus pinpointed the foremost commandments in the law as being completely comprehensive when He cemented together Deuteronomy 6:5

and Leviticus 19:18. In these verses the law urged love for God and all people, providing full coverage of the commandments (Matt. 22:37–40).[147]

Christ consistently affirmed the divine authority of the Old Testament (Matt. 23:23). As He related the teaching of the Hebrew Scriptures, Jesus revealed the inner meaning and essence of the law.[148] At the same time, He censured the legalistic interpretations of the Mosaic code (cf. 5:20, 38). He also condemned the traditions legalists added to the law (cf. 15:1–9; 23:1–36).[149] Understandably, then, Jesus was often at odds with those who were experts in the law (23:35). This conflict occurred because for many the law was like a ship that had become encrusted with the barnacles of the "tradition of the elders" (Mark 7:5), which amounted to humanly derived precepts and regulations (vs. 7). These rules had rejected the true commandments of God (vs. 9). Jesus did not come to impose new regulations that would add more barnacles to those already there. Neither did He come to set aside God's commands, as some accused Him of doing.

Jesus' death on the cross fundamentally changed the way God's people relate to the law. Before the cross, the law had the power to condemn all people, for all had sinned and fallen short of God's glory (Rom. 3:23). Christ, however, has destroyed the power of the law to condemn believing sinners. They are acquitted and saved from divine punishment through their union with Christ (Rom. 8:1).

As a result, Christ ended the need for the ceremonial aspects of the Mosaic code.[150] In a sense, He enacted the reality foreshadowed in the symbolism of the ceremonial laws.[151] He brought them all to completion by becoming *the* sacrificial lamb to satisfy the demands of the law once for all (cf. John 1:29; Heb. 7:26–28; 9:1, 9–10, 23–27).[152] Christ's fulfillment and completion of the entire system of ceremonial laws is consistent with the pattern of His life and ministry.[153] When He affirmed the authority of the Mosaic code, He was specifically referring to the moral law.[154] In contrast, even before the cross event, Jesus said that practices which reflected the demands of the ceremonial law were about to become nonbinding. For example, in Mark 7:19, He declared all foods to be clean. This set aside all the dietary regulations the Jews used to observe. Although the ceremonial aspects are no longer obligatory for Christians, they continue to be instructive.[155]

The Relevancy of the Moral Law for Christians

I have maintained that the tripartite division of the Mosaic law has the most validity. Although the civil and ceremonial codes of the Mosaic law are no longer binding on believers today, the ethical underpinnings of these codes are binding.[156] Likewise, the moral aspects the Mosaic law are binding on the Christian church.[157] The reason for this is that God's moral law is absolute, perfect, unchanging, and eternal in nature.[158] The Lord and His holy character, as reflected in His universal moral law, is the abiding standard for how people of all ages should live (cf. Matt. 5:48; Rom. 8:29; 2 Cor. 3:18; Eph. 4:13; Col. 3:10; 1 Pet. 1:15–16).[159] These statements imply that the moral law is relevant for Christians, regardless of the age or society in which they live.[160]

Neither Jesus nor Paul set the believer free from obeying the moral law.[161] Rather, Christ, through His redemptive work, enables His people to heed the moral law in ways and to degrees that were impossible before their salvation.[162] Christ's affirmation of the moral law is confirmed by what Paul said in Romans 8:4: "so that the just requirement of the law might be fulfilled in us, who walk not according to the flesh but according to the Spirit."

Throughout the New Testament, aspects of the moral law are repeated and reinforced.[163] For example, in Mark 12:29–31, Jesus quoted from Deuteronomy 6:5 and Leviticus 19:18: "Jesus answered, 'The first is "Hear, O Israel: the Lord our God, the Lord is one; you shall love the Lord your God with all your heart, and with all your soul, and with all your mind, and with all your strength." The second is this, "You shall love your neighbor as yourself." There is no other command greater than these.'" With His citations from the Old Testament, Jesus revealed the essence of the moral law and gave it His own stamp of approval.

The Ten Commandments often form the basis for exhortations found in the New Testament.[164] For instance, John urged his readers to "keep yourselves from idols" (1 John 5:21), which recalls the second injunction in the Decalogue against making an idol (Exod. 20:4; Deut. 5:8). Numerous other examples could be noted, showing that the writers of the New Testament upheld the personal standard of conduct revealed in the moral law of the Old Testament.[165] One should not be surprised by this, for the God of the Old Testament is also the God of the New Testament. In fact the personal ethics of both testaments are harmonious. By way of example, just as in Leviticus

19:2 the Lord said to His people, "You shall be holy, for I the Lord your God am holy," so in Matthew 5:48 Jesus urged His followers, "Be perfect, therefore, as your heavenly Father is perfect."

It is helpful to note the similarity of the theological backdrop behind the ethical imperatives appearing in the Old Testament and those appearing in the New Testament. In either testament, law forms an integral part of the covenant relationship between God and His people.[166] Admittedly, unlike the Old Testament, covenantal terminology is hard to find in the New Testament. Nevertheless, covenantal ideas are present throughout the New Testament.[167] Just as God is always present among His people, so the underpinnings of His covenantal relationship are also present, creating a similar theological backdrop between the testaments.

For instance, in the Old Testament God declared that He had liberated His covenant people from Egyptian bondage. They were not free, however, to live as they wanted. The Lord called them to be a holy nation and to keep themselves pure from sin and moral impurity; otherwise, He would severely discipline them (cf. Deut. 4:1–40). Similarly, in the New Testament God teaches that His people have been liberated from bondage to sin. Christians are not free, however, to live immorally; rather, they are servants of God. As such, their lives are to be characterized by moral purity (cf. Rom. 6:15–23). Thus, if believers choose to disobey God, He will discipline them (cf. Heb. 12:10–11). Another example from the Old Testament is the incident where God directed His covenant people to obey Him: "Hear, O Israel, the statutes and ordinances that I am addressing to you today; you shall learn them and observe them diligently" (Deut. 5:1). Similarly, in the New Testament, the Lord directed His covenant people to heed His commands: "If you love me, you will keep my commandments" (John 14:15).

From this information it is evident that covenant and law go hand in hand. The covenant relationship between the Lord and Israel was reflected in the law He had given them through Moses. The law explained how they were to live as the people of God. Their willingness to obey the law represented their grateful response to their covenant relationship with the Lord. Similarly, the moral law explains how New Testament believers are to live for God. Though the law is not a means of salvation, obedience to it is the Christian's grateful response. Believers who obey the moral law are saying by their actions that they are thankful for the salvation they have in Christ.[168]

Another similarity in the theological backdrop between the testaments is the presence of grace in God's relationship with His covenantal people, whether Israelites in the Old Testament or believers in the New Testament. It was grace that prompted God to call Abraham out of Mesopotamia, to free Israel from Egypt, and to choose David as Israel's king. The Lord took the initiative to redeem His people and to establish a relationship with them. Likewise, it was grace that prompted God to call sinners to repentance and to save them from their transgressions. As Romans 5:8 says, "But God proves his love for us in that while we still were sinners Christ died for us."

In light of the fact that the moral law has enduring relevancy, it behooves God's people to heed what the Lord has declared in the Decalogue. Concerning this issue, Wallace noted that through the Ten Commandments, "we hear the voice of the living Lord, the Good Shepherd, addressing us in a thoroughly pointed and personal way about the concrete problems of our actual behaviour."[169] Moreover, the Decalogue ushers us "into a world dominated by a living Lord, who desires to enter personal communion with His people and to give personal guidance to them when they are in every situation involving moral decisions."[170]

Conclusion

In this chapter the concept of the law was discussed. This involved examining various terms for the law used in the Old and New Testaments, investigating the nature of the law, discussing the types of law, considering the divine intent behind the law, examining the purposes of the law, exploring Jesus' relationship to the law, and commenting on the relevancy of the moral law for Christians. From this inquiry it was determined that the law is an expression of God's person and will, reflecting His holy character and purposes for human beings. God uses the law to make people aware of their sin and reveal their need for redemption. He also uses the law to restrain evil by reminding transgressors that they will be punished for their crimes.

It was furthermore maintained that it is legitimate to divide the Mosaic code into three parts: the moral law, the civil law, and the ceremonial law. While the civil and ceremonial aspects of the law are no longer in force, the moral aspect of it is. It is also clear that the moral teaching given by Christ and His apostles does not represent a break with the moral law of the Old

Testament. Instead, it represents an elucidation of the Old Testament law and a reapplication of it to new circumstances.

These observations lend support to the view that the moral law is relevant and binding for Christians today. The redemptive work of the Savior enables His people to obey the moral law and comply with its stipulations. He frees them from slavery to sin so that they might serve Him exclusively. This information will prove to be relevant and useful as this study unfolds.

Chapter 3

An Overview of the Decalogue

In this chapter an overview of the Decalogue will be conducted. This will involve discussing the prominence and enumeration of the Ten Commandments in various religious traditions, the issue of the Sabbath in various religious traditions, and the Decalogue as a suzerainty royal treaty. Discussing these issues will clarify the way in which the Ten Commandments are arranged and identify their prominent themes. Also, considering the structure of the Decalogue will affect the way in which this passage of Scripture is to be interpreted and applied. Moreover, the information obtained from this investigation will prove useful in the analysis of the Sermon on the Mount. Furthermore, information obtained from an overview of the Decalogue will be advantageous when the relationship between the Decalogue and the Sermon on the Mount is examined.

The Prominence of the Decalogue in Various Religious Traditions

The Ten Commandments are regarded by many as the ethical directives[1] that God spoke to Moses and which God wrote on stone tablets at Mount Sinai (cf. Exod. 19).[2] Given the origin and role of the Decalogue "in the faith and life of Israel and of the Christian Church," it has been called "the *Magna Carta* of the Covenant" and "the title deeds of the history of Israel's liberation."[3] Others similarly maintain that "the Decalogue constitutes the very essence of religion."[4]

This distinctive status of the Ten Commandments is underscored in 34:28, where they are literally referred to as the "the words of the covenant, the ten words."[5] In Deuteronomy 4:13 and 10:4, they are also literally called "the ten words."[6] The "ten words" of the Mosaic covenant are known as the Decalogue.[7] This term is a transliteration of the Greek word δεκαλογος.[8] Δεκα means "ten," while λογος means "word."[9] The Decalogue first appears in Exodus 20 and is repeated with some variation of details in Deuteronomy 5. This passage of Scripture holds a premier status within the liturgical and catechetical traditions of both Judaism and Christianity.[10]

Moshe Weinfield observed that, according to the Mishnah (*Tamid* 5:1), the Jews around the time of Christ read the Decalogue and the Shema daily.[11] Also, according to Weinfield, "the Decalogue is to be spoken daily in accordance with the Palestinian practice as reflected in the Cairo Genizah, and to this day pious Jews read the Decalogue daily at the end of prayer."[12] Weinfield furthermore maintained that Qumran phylacteries and the Nash Papyrus provide evidence that the Jews used the Decalogue and Shema in their liturgies.[13] Later, in the early church, ministers and priests used the Decalogue, along with the Apostles' Creed and the Lord's Prayer, to communicate the fundamental precepts of the Christian faith. After the Reformation, Protestants and Catholics continued and expanded this practice.[14]

The Enumeration of the Decalogue in Various Religious Traditions

The Jewish, Roman Catholic, Orthodox, Lutheran, Anglican, and Reformed religious traditions all recognize the existence of ten commandments in the Decalogue. However, they disagree concerning which decrees comprise the first through tenth commandments.[15] The following chart shows how these various traditions diverge in their enumeration of the Decalogue:[16]

Exodus	Reformed Anglican Orthodox	Jewish	Roman Catholic (RC) Lutheran (Luth)
I am the Lord		1	
No other gods	1	2	1
No graven images	2	2	1
Name	3	3	2
Sabbath	4	4	3
Father and Mother	5	5	4
Murder	6	6	5
Adultery	7	7	6
Theft	8	8	7
False witness	9	9	8
Covet wife	10	10	RC 9/Luth 10
Covet property	10	10	RC 10/Luth 9

The chart indicates that Judaism, unlike the other religious traditions, takes the opening words of the first commandment, "I (am) Yahweh [the Lord] your God" (Exod. 20:2; Deut. 5:6) as the first injunction. Other religious traditions, however, do not consider the opening words of the Decalogue as a commandment. Instead, they regard it as a declarative statement concerning God and His relationship to His covenant people.[17] The chart also shows that the Reformed, Anglican, and Orthodox traditions take the injunction "you shall not have any other gods besides Me" (Exod. 20:3; Deut. 5:7) as the second commandment of the Decalogue. In contrast, the Jewish, Roman Catholic, and Lutheran traditions agree in taking this injunction and the next one, "You shall not make for yourself a sculpted image" (Exod. 20:4; Deut. 5:8), as one commandment.

Finally, the chart shows that there are some differences of opinion among the religious traditions concerning the last two commandments. The Jewish, Reformed, Anglican, and Orthodox traditions label the injunctions concerning coveting the wife and property of one's neighbor as one commandment (Exod. 20:17; Deut. 5:21). Roman Catholics view the prohibition against coveting the wife of one's neighbor as the ninth commandment and the prohibition against coveting the property of one's neighbor as the tenth commandment. In contrast, Lutherans view the prohibition against coveting the property of one's neighbor as the ninth commandment and the prohibition against coveting the wife of one's neighbor as the tenth commandment. In this study, the Reformed, Anglican, and Orthodox enumeration of the Decalogue will be followed.[18] This breakdown seems to present the best explanation of how the Ten Commandments are actually compiled, as the following discussion will suggest.[19]

Concerning the overall focus of the Decalogue, Philo[20] regarded it as summary principles governing the entire Mosaic legislation.[21] He furthermore divided the Decalogue into two groups of five. He said the first group was concerned with service toward God, while the second group was concerned with service toward humanity (specifically maintaining human justice).[22] Moreover, Philo asserted that only those who adhered to both sections of the Decalogue were completely virtuous. He said that they were lovers of God and lovers of humankind.[23] Early church leaders viewed the Decalogue similarly as they used it for instructing converts in the Christian way of life.[24]

The Reformed, Anglican, and Orthodox traditions usually divide the Decalogue into four commandments dealing with one's duty to God and six dealing with one's duty to humankind.[25] Roman Catholics and Lutherans unite the first and second and divide the tenth. This results in a division of three commandments dealing with one's duty to God and seven dealing with one's duty to humankind.[26] A twofold division of the Decalogue might be implied in the fact that God gave Moses two stone tablets.[27] Deuteronomy 9:9 calls them "the tablets of stone, tablets of the covenant that Yahweh [the Lord] cut with you." One tablet revealed humankind's duty towards God, while the other tablet revealed humankind's duty towards their neighbors.[28]

Philo and Josephus maintained that five commandments were on each stone tablet. Augustine, however, thought the first three commandments were on the first stone tablet, while the other seven commandments were on the second stone tablet. In contrast, Calvin advocated that four commandments were on the first stone tablet, while the other six were on the second stone tablet.[29] Another possibility is that the two tablets were duplicates of the Decalogue.[30] This would reflect parallel practices in the suzerainty treaties of other ancient cultures.[31] According to this view, one tablet was for God and the other was for His people.[32] This would be a symbolic recognition that two parties were involved in the covenant ratification ceremony—God (the great King) and His people.[33]

Mendenhall and Herion take issue with the notion that some of the commandments primarily deal with one's relationship to God and the rest primarily deal with one's relationship with people. They argued that "*all* of the stipulations represent those characteristics of human behavior that constitute the definition of the will of God: they describe the highest value, the 'ultimate concern' of the community formed by covenant, for they are the principles upon which the one God directs the historical fate of the community."[34]

The point being made by Mendenhall and Herion is well taken; nevertheless, of the various views presented by scholars, the traditional classification of the Ten Commandments into four laws having to do with obligations to God (Exod. 20:2–11), followed by six laws having to do with obligations to fellow human beings (Exod. 20:12–17) seems to do the best job of reflecting the emphasis and scope found in the Decalogue.[35] It is a useful thematic model by which to analyze the Ten Commandments. Park moves the discussion forward by noting that the first through fourth commandments deal with religious duties, while the fifth through the tenth deal with moral duties.[36] He then divides the moral duties as follows: the sixth through the eighth commandments are directed against mean *deeds*, the ninth is directed against mean *words*, and the tenth is directed against mean *thoughts*.

Farrar, in his discussion of the symmetry and thematic divisions within the Decalogue, noted how various Jewish scholars "endeavoured to connect each commandment on the first table with each on the second."[37] He then offered the following summary points:[38]

> Thus, the first proclaims the majesty of God, and the sixth the sacredness of a life made in His image. The second forbids idolatry, and the seventh, adultery with which idolatry was always compared. The third forbids perjury, and the eighth theft which leads to perjury. The fourth ordains the Sabbath, the violation of which resembles false witness against God as the Creator, and the ninth forbids false witness against men. The ten forbids the covetous desires which lead to filial irreverence.

Kaiser proposes a different way of thematically understanding the Decalogue.[39] He maintains that Exodus 20:2–7 concerns humanity's relationship to *God*, that verses 8–11 concern humanity's relationship to *worship*, and that verses 12–17 concern humanity's relationship to *society*. Kaiser's proposal underscores the pivotal nature of the command regarding the Sabbath—"Remember the Sabbath day, to keep it holy" (Exod. 20:8).[40] Deuteronomy 5:12 alternately says, "observe the Sabbath day." This injunction relates to God in that His people were to set apart the Sabbath day as a time of rest to worship Him and meditate on His Word. The injunction also has some applicability to people and the rest of creation in that God wanted them to benefit from observing the Sabbath (cf. Mark 2:27).[41]

Keeping in mind the pivotal nature of the Sabbath, it appears that the Reformed, Anglican, and Orthodox traditions would see the first three commandments concerning God exclusively and the last six dealing with humans exclusively. Roman Catholics and Lutherans, however, would see the first two commandments concerning God exclusively and the last seven dealing with humans exclusively.[42] In either case, Brown seems close to the mark regarding "the Decalogue's initial instructions."[43] He notes that "once they are honoured," there is "every likelihood that the rest will be obeyed." In short, the commandments concerning humankind's relationship with God stress that "men and women must acknowledge, exalt, reverence and remember their Creator."

In terms of the Decalogue's literary features, commandments one through five and ten are longer than the rest, perhaps because they represent injunctions plus commentary.[44] If this is so, it would help explain why the Sabbath command in Exodus 20:11 has a different ending from the one in Deuteronomy 5:14c–15. In other words, the writer drew out different explanations and applications from the basic injunction. In a similar vein, the minor variations in the tenth commandment (Exod. 20:17; Deut. 5:21) would be due to the fact that the basic injunction is followed by exposition.

Some scholars think the differences between the versions of the Decalogue recorded in Exodus and Deuteronomy are due to considerable expansion and revision of the Ten Commandments over and above their original literary form.[45] In response, one could note that these "differences are slight compared to other laws that are present in more than one tradition."[46] Furthermore, "the two presentations of the Decalogue in Exodus 20 and Deuteronomy 5 are essentially the same. They perdure unchanged."[47] Moreover, after almost forty years, it is probable that Moses would have restated some of his thoughts to suit a new set of circumstances.[48] The variations between Exodus 20:1–17 and Deuteronomy 5:6–21 could also be due to the possibility that Moses quoted the material from memory.[49] These explanations undercut the necessity for adopting the earlier-mentioned view regarding the Deuteronomic version of the Ten Commandments.[50]

One more set of observations is in order. All the commandments are spoken to the individual.[51] In fact, the "Decalogue epitomizes God's requirements of the Israelites as individuals and as a nation."[52] Moreover, commandments two and three are reinforced by warnings, and commandment five is reinforced by a promise. Except for commandments four and five,[53] the rest of the injunctions are stated negatively (in other words, "You shall not...").[54]

The Issue of the Sabbath in Various Religious Traditions

Throughout the history of Christianity, a variety of religious groups have tried to bind the Old Testament Sabbath regulation on the New Testament church. This view is called sabbatarianism.[55] For instance, some adherents hold what might be called a "Christian Sabbath" view. They maintain that Sunday is the Christian Sabbath and that it takes the place of the original Jewish Sabbath on Saturday.[56] They also argue that the observance of the Sabbath is a moral obligation, one based on the universal character of the fourth commandment of the Decalogue. Supposedly, the particular day of the week on which the Sabbath is to be kept was not the main intent of the law. Rather, it was the observance of one day in every seven. It is further insisted that during the forty days between Jesus' resurrection and ascension,

He transferred the day of the Sabbath's observance from Saturday to Sunday.[57]

In the Christian Sabbath view a great deal of emphasis is placed on Mark 2:27–28. In these verses Jesus pronounced, "The sabbath was made for humankind, and not humankind for the sabbath; so the Son of Man is lord even of the Sabbath." Based on this statement, it is argued that the Sabbath is an institution rooted in the very nature of humankind.[58] God supposedly instituted the Sabbath from the beginning of time not only for Israel but also for the entire human race.[59]

Contrary to the Christian Sabbath view, Jesus' intent in this passage was not to teach the Sabbath as a timeless, transcultural institution. Instead, Christ was stating that God never intended the Sabbath ordinance to be a burden on His people. In fact, He wanted it to be a welcomed release from hard labor.[60] God instituted the Sabbath for His people's spiritual, mental, and physical restoration. As the covenant community observed the Sabbath, they shared in God's rest and celebrated His work of creation and redemption. The implication is that the Christian Sabbath view has incorrectly supposed the New Testament teaches a change in the Sabbath's observance.[61] It is true that after Jesus' resurrection, the early church began to meet on the first day of the week (cf. Acts 20:7; Rev. 1:10). They did not do this, however, as a way to fulfill a Sabbath obligation; rather, they met to commemorate and celebrate the truth of the resurrection (cf. Eph. 1:20–22; 1 Pet. 3:21–22).[62]

In brief, the Christian Sabbath view has redefined what "Sabbath" means. For them, it is a morally obligatory time for spiritual and physical refreshment on Sunday.[63] The phrase Ὀψὲ δὲ σαββάτων, τῇ ἐπιφωσκούσῃ εἰς μίαν σαββάτων, which appears in Matthew 28:1, is sometimes cited in support of this view. Matthew allegedly was suggesting by his double use of σαββάτων that, as a result of Jesus' resurrection, the old Jewish Sabbath (which was observed on Saturday) was being replaced by a new Christian Sabbath (which was to be observed on Sunday). This interpretation, however, reads too much into the meaning of Matthew 28:1. The Greek noun σαββάτων can mean either "Sabbath" (that is, the seventh day in the Jewish calendar) or "week," depending on how the word is being used by the writer.[64] Matthew 28:1 is an example where both meanings for the word apply. The first mention of σαββάτων refers to Saturday, while the second mention of σαββάτων refers to Sunday, that is, the first day of the week.[65]

The preceding analysis suggests that the verse is not dealing with the establishment of a new Sabbath day for the people of God. Rather, the concern is with the resurrection of Christ and the time when this event approximately occurred. Simply put, the verse says that sometime after the Sabbath when it was beginning to dawn on Sunday morning, the two Marys returned to the tomb where Jesus' body had been buried. From what has been said, it is evident that the efforts of Christian sabbatarians to redefine the meaning of "Sabbath" will not stand the test of scrutiny.[66] The New Testament does not refer to Sunday as a Christian Sabbath, and the Christian sabbatarian view does not find support in any New Testament writings.[67] Given this fact, if one insists that the observance of the Sabbath is still universally in force, then it must fall on the seventh day of the week, not on the first day, in accordance with the stipulations of the fourth commandment of the Decalogue.

This is exactly the view advocated by Seventh-day sabbatarians, which includes both the Seventh-day Baptists (who originated in England in the seventeenth century) and the Seventh-day Adventists (who originated in the United States in the nineteenth century). The Seventh-day sabbatarians assert that Christians are obligated to observe the seventh day of the week as the Sabbath. The Seventh-day sabbatarians mainly look to the Old Testament for biblical support.[68] For example, they would argue that the fourth commandment of the Decalogue is clear in its declaration that the seventh day of the week is the Sabbath and that God only appointed this day to commemorate His work of creation.[69] Supposedly, the fourth commandment is part of the "law of God" (as opposed to the "law of Moses") and thus both wholly moral in character and universally binding on humankind.[70]

The Seventh-day sabbatarians also appeal to the New Testament to support their view concerning the observance of the seventh day as the Sabbath.[71] For example, they would argue that Jesus and the apostles attended the synagogue on the Sabbath (cf. Luke 4:16; Acts 13:14, 42; 16:13; 17:1–2; 18:4). The Seventh-day sabbatarians would note that in Matthew 24:20, Jesus prophesied the destruction of Jerusalem and urged His disciples to pray that their fleeing might not have to be on the Sabbath. The Seventh-day sabbatarians would maintain that the mention of "the Lord's Day" in Revelation 1:10 is a reference to the seventh-day Sabbath.[72] The Seventh-day sabbatarians furthermore assert that the New Testament shows no evidence of seventh day observance being changed to first day observance. They teach that the Roman Catholic Church instituted this change in practice. Supposedly during the early centuries of the church, an apostate ecclesiastical leadership along with half-pagan Roman emperors gradually replaced the ancient Sabbath with the pagan festival of Sunday.[73]

In critiquing the Seventh-day Sabbath view, it should be noted that there is no biblical support for the distinction that is made between the "law of God" and the "law of Moses."[74] This observation, of course, undercuts the assertion that the fourth commandment is absolutely moral in character and thus universally binding on all people. It is true that there is a moral dimension to the fourth commandment in that it advocates the worship of God. Yet, there are also ceremonial elements to the commandment that applied only to the Israelites.[75] In fact, the biblical record makes it clear that the Sabbath is the day God established specifically for the nation of Israel, not the New Testament church. He placed the Sabbath at the end of the week—beginning at sundown on Friday and ending at sundown on Saturday—so that the Jews might faithfully observe it as a sacred day.

The Seventh-day sabbatarians are correct in noting that Jesus and the apostles faithfully attended synagogue services on the Sabbath. This does not mean, however, that they mandated Gentile believers to observe this practice.[76] In fact, the New Testament witness suggests that Christians in the early church gathered on Sunday, the first day of the week, for corporate worship (cf. John 20:19; Acts 20:7; 1 Cor. 16:2). The Seventh-day sabbatarians moreover are correct in noting that, in Matthew 24:20, Jesus made reference to the observance of the Sabbath. The eschatological nature of this verse, however, suggests that Christ was specifically concerned with a turbulent period surrounding the end times, not the present age. The Savior evidently expected the strict Sabbath law to be in effect during a future time of great distress.[77] Thus, it would be incorrect to suppose from this verse that Jesus was advocating a seventh-day Sabbath observance.

The Seventh-day sabbatarians have asserted that the mention of "the Lord's Day" in Revelation 1:10 is a reference to the seventh-day Sabbath. Others think the phrase is a reference to the eschatological day of the Lord.[78] The more widely held view, however, is that John was referring to Sunday, the first day of the week.[79] This interpretation seems to have the strongest exegetical support.[80] Thus, it would be mistaken to suppose from this verse that the apostle was advocating a Seventh-day Sabbath observance.

The Seventh-day sabbatarians are correct in teaching that the Roman Catholics supported corporate Christian worship on Sunday. However, there is no conclusive historical evidence to substantiate the claim that the Roman Catholic Church changed the Sabbath observance from the seventh to the first day of the week.[81] The writings of the early church leaders indicate that believers routinely met for corporate worship on Sunday, rather than Saturday, from the very beginning of the Christian church.[82]

Many Protestant Reformers advocated the Christian observance of Sunday. This is evident in several historic writings.[83] Nevertheless, they did not base Sunday observance on the Sabbath injunction appearing in the fourth commandment of the Decalogue.[84] Furthermore, contrary to the Seventh-day Sabbath view, nowhere in the New Testament is the Jewish Sabbath ever restated as a religious practice or requirement to be observed and perpetuated. In fact, the opposite is the case.

Note, for instance, Paul's comments in Romans 14:5 and 6. Some Christians in the church at Rome thought one day was more special than the rest, while other believers did not hold to such distinctions among the days of the week. Instead, they viewed every day as being equally sacred. In their minds each day was to be dedicated in wholehearted service to God.[85] Paul said each group should act in accordance with their personal convictions. For example, the believers who were convinced that one day was more important than another did so to honor and serve the Lord. Likewise, Christians who were assured that it was proper to eat meat did so to glorify God, for they consumed the food with a heart of gratitude. Those who, out of personal conviction, refrained from eating meat also sought to honor God with a thankful attitude.

In Galatians 4:10 and 11, Paul revealed how distressed he was that his readers were deeply involved in observing ceremonies. They had become fanatical in keeping the Jewish religious holidays. The temptation was to think that, by honoring them, one had fulfilled one's duty to God. However, keeping such holy days could not take the place of faith. Paul's disappointment because of what the Galatians had done reached rock bottom when he was almost, but not quite, ready to say that his time with them had been wasted. But the Greek phrase φοβοῦμαι ὑμᾶς (literally, "I fear [for] you") is very important. It was Paul's way of saying that however close he may come to giving up on them, he had not done so. Thus with new resolve, Paul was ready to do everything in his power to see them brought back to their spiritual senses.

The preceding examination of the passages from Romans and Galatians provides no support for the Seventh-Day Sabbath view. Colossians 2:8–23 goes even further in stressing the believer's freedom in Christ from having to observe certain religious holy days. Paul urged his readers not to allow anyone to judge them concerning what they ate or drank, or whether they abstained from keeping Jewish religious festivals, New Moon celebrations, and Sabbath days. The apostle explained that these ceremonial aspects of the moral law were a shadow, or dim outline, of the good things to come in association with Christ.

In a similar vein, the writer of Hebrews declared that the new covenant, which Christ inaugurated, made the old covenant obsolete (Heb. 8:13). Because of this, the ceremonial aspects of the old covenant were ready to be phased out, for they were no longer valid or effective. The writer of Hebrews elsewhere declared that there was a spiritual and eternal form of rest for believers, a rest unlike the one God had offered the Israelites in Canaan (4:1). The ancient Hebrews had heard the good news of Canaan rest, but their persistent unbelief spurned the message of hope.[86] Believers in Christ were wise not to miss the opportunity of spiritual rest that the gospel of salvation provided (vs. 2). Jesus' death made it possible for God to issue His invitation for believers to enter into His salvation rest. This rest exceeds in blessings both the rest that followed creation and the rest the Israelites could have had in Canaan (vss. 3–5). Both the creation rest and the Canaan rest were past when the psalmist advised of an available rest (Ps. 95:7–11; Heb. 4:7– 8). At best these prior kinds of rest can only typify the salvation rest that remains for believers (vs. 9).

From what has been said it is evident that God intended the Sabbath ordinance for the covenant community of Israel in the Old Testament.[87] It represents the end of God's creative work. Conversely, the Lord's Day represents the first day of God's re-creative work. These statements do not mean the Sabbath ordinance has no bearing on New Testament believers. An examination of the fourth commandment indicates that it contains principles that are applicable to all people.[88] For example, all humankind is obligated to worship their Creator, for they exist because of Him. Also, all humankind should acknowledge the Lord as their Redeemer, for He alone provides them with deliverance from sin through faith in Christ.[89]

In anticipation of fully experiencing the Sabbath rest of Christ in the eternal kingdom of God,[90] believers should set aside stated times and places for worship, spiritual devotion, and instruction from God's Word.[91] Believers are spiritually blessed when they designate a special time in which they can regularly celebrate God's presence in a unique way.[92] By setting apart a particular day each week for spiritual worship and service (for example, Sunday) this can be effectively achieved.[93]

The Decalogue as a Suzerainty Royal Treaty

Throughout the Fertile Crescent during the second millennium B.C. a superior feudal lord would make a compact with his inferior subjects in which he demanded unwavering fidelity from them. A vassal would enter into an oath of loyalty and trust toward the overlord and his successors out of gratitude for royal favors that had already been received.[95] These compacts often included an historical prologue emphasizing benefits conferred, a demand for exclusive loyalty, stipulations to be followed, a provision for the treaty's deposit in a shrine, a list of gods as witnesses, and a list of blessings and curses.[96]

In 1954, G. E. Mendenhall proposed that the structure and language of Hittite suzerainty treaties were closely parallel to those of the Decalogue and other covenant passages.[97] In his ground-breaking work, *Treaty of the Great King*, M. G. Klein similarly argued that the Decalogue contained the basic elements of a suzerainty pact, especially Hittite state treaties.[98] Further research by others has affirmed Mendenhall and Kline's basic observations.[99] The Old Testament traditions of the Sinaitic covenant closely resemble the general form and specific content of these secular treaties.[100] This means that the Lord patterned His covenant relationship with Israel after the prevailing international political treaty form.[101]

Like many other ancient political treaties and royal covenants, the Decalogue began with a preamble in which the great King identified Himself (Exod. 20:1–2a; Deut. 5:6a). Yahweh declared that He was the Lord and God of Israel. The preamble of the Decalogue was followed by a brief historical prologue. In this section, Yahweh summarized the gracious acts He had displayed toward His covenant people. He noted that He had rescued them from Egypt, the land of slavery (Exod. 20:2b; Deut. 5:6b). The Lord was not just reviewing Israel's past to give a history lesson. Rather, He recounted the past to instill a sense of gratitude in His people. God also used the epic events of the past to form the foundation for the Israelites' obligation to remain obedient to the stipulations of His covenant with them.[102]

Yahweh next delineated the stipulations of the covenant He was making with His people. The Lord expected His subjects to obey these directives, which were ten in number (Exod. 20:3–17; Deut. 5:1–3, 7–21). Later prophets of Israel held God's people accountable for heeding the stipulations recorded in the Decalogue (cf. Jer. 7:9; 29:23; Ezek. 18:5–18; 22:6–12; Hos. 4:2). The prophets also held the priests accountable for not fulfilling their duty to make the moral demands of the Decalogue known among God's people (cf. Hos. 4:1–9; Mal. 2:1–9). Yet, unlike other ancient treaties, the Decalogue does not contain any mention of penalties for violating Yahweh's compact with His people.[103] One possible reason is that the Decalogue is not strictly a legal code, as other treaties would have been in ancient times. Instead, the Decalogue is a foundational covenant document. It served as a creed for the Israelites.[104]

Some scholars have argued that the lack of some late Bronze Age treaty elements in the Decalogue[105] is evidence that the Sinai covenant was not a suzerainty compact. These experts maintain that the Decalogue was a pious literary invention, having no connection with late Bronze Age treaty patterns and covenant traditions. However, Mendenhall and Herion think this line of reasoning is overly simplistic, for it attempts to draw an historical conclusion from an observation about mere literary forms.[106]

Yahweh took the covenant principles outlined in the Decalogue and expanded on them in the Covenant Code or Book of the Covenant (Exod. 20:22–23:19), which was a set of laws with penalties attached. The severity of the Ten Commandments is such that violation of most of them is elsewhere said to be punishable by death. God moreover inscribed the text of the Decalogue on two stone tablets (cf. Exod. 31:18; 32:16) and He instructed Moses to place them in the Ark of the Covenant (Exod. 25:16, 22; Deut. 10:1–5). Consistent with ancient Near Eastern suzerainty treaties, one copy of the Decalogue belonged to each treaty partner and the copies were stored in the respective shrines. Yahweh instructed Moses to place both copies in the ark because it was the focal point of Israel's sanctuary and the special dwelling place of God. Both the Mosaic covenant and its stipulations were to be adopted by the Israelites and used as the basis for their behavior.[107]

The fact that the Decalogue is similar in its literary form to other ancient political and royal treaties suggests that the opening declaration appearing in Exodus 20:2 (cf. Deut. 5:6) was not a separate commandment.[108] In other words, the stipulations of the Decalogue begin in Exodus 20:3 (cf. Deut. 5:7). Furthermore, the fact that the basic elements of the Decalogue are similar in literary form to other suzerainty treaties points to a crucial truth, namely, that God was the great King of the Israelites and that they were His subject people.[109] Both He and they were bound by the stipulations of the covenant that are recorded in Exodus 20:3–17 (cf. Deut. 5:7–21). As His subjects, God expected the Israelites to be absolutely submissive to Him and His will. They were to obey Him out of gratitude for His redemptive acts, worship Him because He was sovereign over creation, trust Him to provide for their needs, and depend on Him to protect them from harm.

Conclusion

In this chapter an overview of the Decalogue was presented. It was noted that the Decalogue retains a premier status within Judaism and Christianity. It was also concluded that the traditional classification of the Ten Commandments into four laws having to do with obligations to God (Exod. 20:2–11), followed by six laws having to do with obligations to fellow human beings (vss. 12–17) seems to reflect best the emphasis and scope found in the Decalogue. Moreover, this classification was determined to be a useful thematic model by which to analyze the Ten Commandments.

The discussion regarding the Sabbath emphasized the key place it occupies within the Decalogue. Connected with this issue is the attempt of some religious groups to bind the Old Testament Sabbath regulation to the New Testament church. It was concluded that the New Testament does not teach either a change in the Sabbath's observance or the establishment of a new Sabbath day for the people of God. It was also determined that Christians are not obligated to observe the seventh day of the week as the Sabbath. Furthermore, it was maintained that there are timeless principles connected with the fourth commandment of the Decalogue and that these are the way in which the Sabbath has continuing relevance for believers.

With respect to the structural analysis of the Decalogue, it was concluded that within the Ten Commandments were the basic elements of a suzerainty pact, especially Hittite state treaties. The Decalogue begins with a preamble in which the great King identifies Himself (Exod. 20:1–2a; Deut. 5:6a). The preamble of the Decalogue is followed by a brief historical prologue. In this section, Yahweh summarized the gracious acts He displayed toward His covenant people (Exod. 20:2b; Deut. 5:6b). Finally, the Lord delineated the stipulations of the covenant He was making with His people. God expected His subjects to obey these directives, which were ten in number (Exod. 20:3–17; Deut. 5:1–3, 7–21).

Chapter 4

A Content Analysis of the Decalogue

In this chapter a content analysis of the Decalogue will be conducted. The investigation will build upon the findings of the structural analysis presented in chapter three. For example, the outline used in this study of the Decalogue is based on the fact that the Ten Commandments contain the basic elements of an ancient Hittite state treaty. Also, the labeling of commandments one through four as obligations to God and commandments five through ten as obligations to fellow human beings is based on what was previously discussed.

Historical Prologue (Exodus 20:1-2; Deuteronomy 5:1-6)

Exodus 19 records the meeting of Yahweh with His people at Mount Sinai. Of significance is God's establishment of a covenant, or treaty, with the Israelites.[1] If the Hebrew people lived up to the stipulations of this agreement, they would remain the special, treasured possession of the Creator and Master of the entire universe (vs. 5). Thus, obedience was an essential element to this covenant. God used the meeting at Mount Sinai to instill a sense of reverential fear and awe in His people in their relationship with Him. Not only were they to respect, honor, and worship the Lord, but also they were to obey His ordinances and stipulations. God was serious about His commitment to His people, and they were to respond with a similar attitude (cf. Exod. 20:18–21; Deut. 5:1–5).

Like many other ancient political treaties and royal covenants,[2] the Ten Commandments that God communicated to Moses at Mount Sinai began with a preamble in which the great King identified Himself (Exod. 20:1–2a; Deut. 5:6a).[3] The Lord did not define Himself abstractly. Rather, He made Himself known by what He had done, particularly in the redemption of His people from Egypt.[4] Concerning the Hebrew of Exodus 20:1a, it might be literally rendered, "And God spoke all these words." The one declaring these injunctions was none other than אֱלֹהִים (*'ĕlōhîm*).[5] This masculine noun seems to be the plural of אֱלוֹהַּ (*'ĕlōah*), which means "god" or "God."[6] This word (also a masculine noun), in turn, is probably derived from אֵל (*'ēl*), a primary root that means either "god" or "God."[7] By and large, *'ēl*, *'ĕlōah*, and *'ĕlōhîm* are interchangeable.[8]

In the Old Testament, *'ĕlōhîm* is used for rulers and judges, gods and goddesses, and the one true God.[9] The term does not appear outside the Hebrew corpus and at times seems to be a "generic name for God."[10] Scholars have noted that, despite the plural form of the noun, it is consistently used in the Old Testament original as a singular term. Three hypotheses to explain this phenomenon are worth mentioning:[11] 1) the form is a "plural of majesty"; 2) the plural reflects either an "intensification or an absolutization" of the term; and 3) the form is "representative of the multiple Godhead," which would make it "an earlier reflection of the Trinity." Admittedly, these theories and even the basic etymology of *'ĕlōhîm* remain contested.[12]

When used as a proper name, *'ĕlōhîm* portrays the Lord as the one, true, and unique God.[13] The body of occurrences leaves one with the impression that *'ĕlōhîm* is the fountain and source of all things and the person who unifies all the forces of time and eternity.[14] An overview of the Old Testament corpus furthermore indicates that *'ĕlōhîm* is absolute in power, supreme in authority, and unique in His being or essence.[15]

In Exodus 20:2, God personally referred to Himself using the Hebrew word יַהְוֶה (*yāhweh*). It most likely is derived from the primary root הָוָה (*hāwâ*), which means "to be" or "to become."[16] The meaning of *yāhweh* in the Qal stem is "he is/becomes/will be(come)," while in the Hiphil stem it means "he causes to be/become."[17] A debate exists over how this special name for the covenant-keeping God of Israel[18] should be pronounced.[19] The reason is both simple and complex.[20]

Old Testament Hebrew was written using only consonants. There were no written vowels, and a reader was expected to add the appropriate vowel sounds. Thus, this distinctive title for the divine was written יהוה (*yhwh*). But by the time the name was translated into English, the original pronunciation had been lost. The reason, however, for the confusion is more complicated. Around 1100 A.D., a group of Jewish scholars produced what is known as the Massoretic text. In this document, the scholars added a series of vowels to the Hebrew manuscript, the vowels being represented by various placements of dots and dashes. The special name of God was so sacred that no observant Jew would pronounce it. Instead, when reading the Scripture, a person coming to that name would substitute an entirely different word.

This is a technical rule known as "kethive Kere." This phrase means "written one way, to be read another." It directed readers of the sacred Hebrew text that when they came to the four consonants YHWH, they were to attach vowel signs indicating that in its place they should read the Hebrew word אֲדֹנָי (*'ădônāi*), which means "lord." In this case, the scholars who produced the Massoretic text added the vowels "e," "o," and "a" to the consonants "Y," "H," "W," and "H" (in other words, "YeHoWaH").

The translators of the King James Version of the Bible followed this convention to translate YHWH as "Jehovah" (the sound of the consonant "Y" being represented by "J" and the sound of the consonant "W" by "V"). In other words, they used the vowels of the term to be pronounced (namely, *'ădônai*) rather than the vowels associated with *yhwh*, which represented the correct pronunciation of this most sacred name of the divine. This explains how the name "Jehovah" was introduced into the English language Bible. And it is for this reason that the form "Jehovah" most likely does not represent the correct way to pronounce the covenant name of God. The majority of Hebrew scholars think the consonants יהוה were originally pronounced "yahweh," though, a minority of others remain unsure.[21]

In making sense of the lexical data surrounding *yāhweh*, Gianotti concluded that the term, rather than conveying the abstract notion of God being static and motionless, instead emphasizes that the sovereign Lord is characterized by awesome power and dynamic effectiveness.[22] Gianotti furthermore maintained that *yāhweh* is the One who faithfully displays His visible presence through active involvement in human history.[23] Thus, despite the ongoing debate surrounding the etymology and meaning of *yāhweh*, the Old Testament remains clear that the One the Israelites served was the ever-present, ever-living God (cf. Exod. 3:13–14).[24] He eternally existed[25] without beginning or end,[26] and He was both the Source and Sustainer of life.[27] In contrast to pagan deities,[28] Yahweh abided with His people "to deliver them, to fulfill his promises to them, and to grant them his blessings."[29]

The preamble of the Decalogue recorded in Exodus 20:2[30] is followed by a brief historical prologue. In this section, Yahweh summarized the gracious acts He had displayed toward His covenant people.[31] He specifically noted that He had rescued them from Egypt, the land of slavery.[32] The freedom He had obtained for His people was the necessary foundation for the inauguration of His covenant with them.[33] The prologue indicates that the laws of God are a reflection of His personal relationship with His people. The laws were not to be substituted for or elevated above that relationship. Rather, the Lord intended these ordinances to help His people live in a way that reflected their personal relationship with Him.

Yahweh's mention of the redemption of His people is theologically significant. Before the Lord stated any explicit stipulations, He initially focused on His character and conduct in relationship to His people. He revealed Himself to be the almighty and gracious One, who had demonstrated His selfless and sacrificial devotion to His people through the exodus event. This historical incident became the basis for His issuance of His commandments.

The Decalogue concisely summarized the essential elements that should have characterized the Israelites' vertical relationship with God and their horizontal relationships with other people. The Ten Commandments were also an expression of the Lord's unmerited and undeserved favor toward His people. Thus, love and loyalty to the Lord and His people were the appropriate responses to what He had done for the Israelites.[34] They, in turn, were to visibly demonstrate their thankfulness for God's gracious deliverance "by living in obedience to the covenant requirements."[35]

Stipulations to Be Followed (Exodus 20:3-17; Deuteronomy 5:7-21)

Obligations to God (Exodus 20:3–11; Deuteronomy 5:7–15). The Decalogue should be classified as apodictic, or absolute, law.[36] This legal material is characterized by unconditional commands, prohibitions, and categorical directives.[37] Also, these laws feature direct forms of address such as "you shall/shall not."[38] They thus represent absolute decrees concerning right and wrong, with no exceptions being allowed.[39] Furthermore, the Ten Commandments should be seen as "'categorical imperatives of universal validity, above time and independent of circumstances."[40]

This legal material does not appear in isolation, but as a series or collection of laws, as is evident from the grouping of the Ten Commandments together to form the Decalogue.[41] Additionally, the Decalogue is not "just an abstract code of laws"; it is more about a "personal relationship" between God and His people.[42] Also, unlike "elsewhere in the Torah," there are no "specific punishments stated"[43] in the Decalogue. This implies that "the primary motivating factor for obedience is not fear of punishment but God's absolute authority and the people's desire to live in accordance with His will."[44]

The first commandment (Exodus 20:3; Deuteronomy 5:7) says, "You shall not have any other gods before My face" (Exod. 20:3; personal translation). The Hebrew phrase rendered "before My face" (עַל־פָּנָֽיַ) could also be translated "in My presence," "against Me," or "in hostility toward Me."[45] The idea is that the Lord had exclusively claimed Israel as His own;[46] thus He would permit no rivals—whether real or imagined—in His presence.[47] Such would create a hostile dynamic, one that would go against God and His relationship with His people.[48] That is why it would be incorrect to think of Yahweh as "the head of a pantheon"; likewise, He "does not have a consort," for "there are no gods in his presence."[49]

The first commandment should be understood as the "natural or logical consequence of the oneness of God."[50] As such, the opening stipulation of the Decalogue spotlights the monotheism of the Jewish and Christian faiths.[51] Whereas the Israelites worshiped, served, and obeyed the one true God (cf. Deut. 4:39), others believed in many gods (polytheism)[52] or in one supreme god and an assortment of lesser gods (henotheism).[53] On the surface it would seem that the first commandment is strictly limiting the worship of other gods while in the presence of the Lord. But since God is omnipresent in both time and space, there is no restriction on the application of this injunction.[54] Moreover, Patai noted that belief in the one God was a key element of Judaism.[55] He also observed that "a belief in the special relationship between God and Israel is not demanded explicitly in the Bible, but it is the underlying axiom of much that is said about Israel's duties toward God."[56]

Students of comparative religion have conjectured that the Israelite faith, like other religious traditions, evolved from primitive polytheistic forms to its more refined monotheistic form.[57] For example, they posit that the Israelites may have first been animistic, that is, believing "every natural object" was the dwelling place of "a supernatural spirit."[58] Then they supposedly figured out that "some spirits were more powerful than others and deserved to be called 'gods'."[59] Subsequently, over a long period of time, the Israelites decided that there was one spirit who was supremely powerful and who alone should be worshiped. Finally, they concluded that other gods were either inferior or nonexistent altogether.[60]

This evolutionary process of Israel's religion from animism to polytheism to henotheism to monotheism is contrived, being denied by the clear witness of Scripture.[61] The Old Testament opens with the declaration that the one true God already existed (Gen. 1:1). He created all things and deserved to be worshiped exclusively by His creatures. Subsequently, this theme is stressed throughout the Hebrew Scriptures (cf. Deut. 6:4; 1 Kings 18:39). The New Testament witness also speaks against the notion that Israel's religion underwent a process of evolutionary development. For example, Romans 1:21–23 reveals that humankind was originally monotheistic and gradually degenerated into henotheism, polytheism, and animism.[62]

There are other Old Testament passages that command God's people to worship Him alone. Exodus 34:14 declares that the Lord is jealous; in other words, He maintains a holy zeal for His people. Since He reserved the exclusive right to possess Israel and to claim the people's affection and allegiance, He could command them to worship no other god but Him alone.[63] Leibowitz aptly noted that the commandment against having other gods was transgressed "by worshipping values and objects which are transitory, and that only exist to be subordinate to the service of God."[64]

Deuteronomy 6:4 affirms the uniqueness and unity or singularity of God; thus, He alone was to be worshiped and served (vss. 13–14). Second Kings 17:35 repeats the divine injunction for the Israelites to venerate Him exclusively. As Psalm 81:9 makes clear, they were to have no foreign god in their midst, and they were not to bow down to any alien god. If the Israelites did follow after other gods to serve and worship them, they would provoke the Lord to anger (Jer. 25:6). In fact, the Lord exiled His people from the land of Canaan because they failed to heed His warnings against idolatry (35:15).

There are several New Testament passages which affirm that people should worship the Lord exclusively. In Jesus' encounter with Satan, He declared that only God was to be worshiped and served (Matt. 4:10). Christ underscored the importance of putting God and His kingdom rule first (6:33). The Savior recognized that His people's rejection of Him signified their rejection of the one true God (cf. 22:37–40). Many religionists of the first century failed to understand that by rejecting Christ, they were serving people rather than God (cf. Acts 5:29).

The second commandment (Exodus 20:4–6; Deuteronomy 5:8–10) says, "You shall not make for yourself a graven image, or any likeness which (is) in the heavens above, or which (is) in the earth beneath, or which (is) in the waters under the earth.[65] You shall not bow down to them, and you shall not serve them; for I am Yahweh your God, a jealous God, visiting the iniquity of fathers on children, on the third generation and on the fourth generation, to those that hate Me; and doing kindness to thousands, to those loving Me and to those keeping My commandments" (Exod. 20:4–6; personal translation). With respect to the connection between the first and second commandments, Bunch observed that while they are "closely related in that they both prohibit idolatry and false worship, there is, nevertheless, a distinct difference between them."[66] For instance, "the first deals with the question of who is the true God, and the second, of how He shall be worshiped." Expressed another way, while the "first commandment reveals the true object of worship," the second discloses "the true mode of worship."[67]

There are several Hebrew words in the second commandment worth investigating. The noun rendered "graven image" (פֶּסֶל, *pesel*) comes from the verb פָּסַל (*pāsal*), which most likely means "to carve out" or "to hew."[68] It refers to a variety of idols (that is, "solid or graphic representations" of a deity[69]) that one may cut or carve from wood, stone, metal, and pottery for use as an object of worship.[70] Many people in ancient times believed gods could reside in stone, wood, or metal.[71] Jewelers and other workers would make miniature idols, or amulets, and scarabs from steatite and semiprecious stones. Idols made from silver or gold might be cast hollow because of the value of the metal. Bronze or lead idols were often overlaid with silver or gold.[72]

The Hebrew noun rendered "likeness" (תְּמוּנָה, *tᵉmûnâ*) comes from an unused verb, the meaning of which is debated.[73] In addition to "likeness," תְּמוּנָה can mean "form," "semblance of," or "representation."[74] The idea is that God banned the Israelites from making idols that resembled "anything which [He had] created."[75] This statement is reinforced by the phrase, "which (is) in the heavens above, or which (is) in the earth beneath, or which (is) in the waters under the earth," and signifies anything in the sky (such as the sun, moon, stars, and birds), on the earth (such as animals), and in the waters below (such as fish, crocodiles, and other aquatic life).[76] All these entities were worshiped among ancient nations.[77] The Lord prohibited the Israelites from serving these things and from falling prostrate before them in worship.[78]

Those who worshiped the Creator in the form of an idol reduced Him to the substance of creation, for the idol was made from it, not Him.[79] Thus idol-worship fundamentally undermined the concept of God as being the transcendent Creator.[80] The idol gave the devotees the false idea that they were physically close to the deity and that they could somehow harness its power.[81] Although Israel's God was immanent, His presence among His people could not be expressed in physical or tangible form. The divine immanence remained the essence of faith and experience.[82] The Lord declared that to create a false image or impression of Him would be to misrepresent Him. He wanted no challengers to compete with Him for His people's love and loyalty. Their reverence and respect were to be placed in Him alone—just as in a relationship between a husband and wife.[83]

These truths are borne out by the Hebrew adjective translated "jealous" (קַנָּא, *qannā'*). It comes from the verb קָנָא (*qānā'*), which variously means "to act zealously" or "be zealous."[84] Emotional intensity forms the backdrop of both the verb and its adjectival derivative.[85] While envy is a concept associated with these terms,[86] such a notion is alien to God.[87] The Lord's "exclusive claim"[88] on His people is being stressed in Exodus 20:5.[89] The idea is that He maintained a burning zeal and passion[90] for them and would deal with all rivals firmly.[91]

Thus, any Israelites who violated the second commandment or encouraged its infraction among others would bring disastrous consequences upon themselves and their loved ones.[92] Also, because the Lord wanted to be the sole God of Israel, He would not share His claim for their worship and love with any other entity. His unbending demand for exclusive worship was unparalleled in the history of religion, for in ancient times, one sect usually was not antagonistic toward another. In fact, devotees of one group readily would worship the gods and goddesses of another group. Even the various temples were often considered as common ground for the deities of different cults.[93]

In the second commandment, the Hebrew verb rendered "visiting" (פֹּקֵד, *pāqad*) carries the sense of seeking something out to bring about affliction or punishment.[94] The basic meaning is for a superior "to exercise oversight over a subordinate."[95] The overlord might inspect the latter's behavior or take action that would bring about a sizeable "change in the circumstances,"[96] resulting in either good or evil for them. In Exodus 20:5 and Deuteronomy 5:9, the term conveys the idea of God, in His righteousness, visiting punishment upon the transgressors of the second commandment.[97]

The Hebrew noun rendered "iniquity" (עָוֹן, *'āwōn*) is derived from the verb עָוָה (*'āwâ*), which has a variety of meanings including "to be bent," "to twist (the law)," and "to do wrong."[98] The corresponding figurative image for *'āwōn* is of "a bent, twisted or crimped item laid alongside a standard straight edge."[99] In later Old Testament usage, *'āwōn* "became the central term for human sin, guilt, and fate,"[100] especially in the presence of God.[101] Accordingly, the ideas of ethical perversion and moral evil were closely associated with the noun,[102] which, in addition to "iniquity," can also be rendered "punishment of sin" and "transgression."[103]

The Hebrew verb for "hate" (שָׂנֵא, *śānē'*)[104] connotes such strong emotions as disdain, ill will, and abhorrence between two parties.[105] Put another way, *śānē'* conveys the ideas of opposing, detesting, or despising others.[106] The objects of this emotion are avoided at all costs. The term thus is the "opposite of love,"[107] for whereas love attracts and joins together, hatred repudiates and divides. Those who hate and those who are hated are regarded as mutual antagonists and view each other as "utterly unappealing."[108]

The preceding lexical data indicates that those who worshiped and served false deities instead of God were rejecting His ownership and rulership in their lives. Such individuals spurned the covenant that the Lord had made with the Israelites. The transgressors also disdained the moral fabric of Israelite society and culture.[109] The penalty for such idolatry was divine punishment throughout an intergenerational family. *The Net Bible* aptly notes, "Such people are doomed to carry on the sins of their ancestors, and bear the guilt with them."[110]

In the ancient Near East it was typical for intergenerational families to exist within the same household.[111] Parents, children, and grandchildren might live in personal, close proximity to one another.[112] In this arrangement, one individual might be the de facto leader for an entire unit or community. In reality that person served as the group's representative head, and what he did inevitably affected them, whether positively or negatively.[113] Moreover, what the leader did could easily influence the lives of others in the family group.[114] Thus, it is not difficult to understand how the negative consequences of one person's behavior could impact adversely the lives of other family members up to possibly three and four generations removed who are living with him (cf. Num. 16:31–34; Josh. 7:24).[115]

Exodus 20:6 spotlights a different outcome for God's people, to whom He shows "kindness." This renders the Hebrew noun חֶסֶד (*chesed*), which most likely is derived from the verb חָסַד (*chāsad*).[116] The latter possibly denotes the ideas of goodness, loveliness, or kindness.[117] The noun, building on these key notions,[118] includes such nuances as fidelity, loyalty, faithfulness, commitment, and mercy.[119] *Chesed*, as a term that "incarnates itself in action,"[120] is used both with respect to people showing kindness to each other and God showing kindness to people.[121] With respect to the חֶסֶד of God, it is undergirded by "his covenantal relationship with his people"[122] in which He provides for their needs, watches over them, and protects them. They, in turn, respond in service, fear, and devotion.[123]

The notion of mutual commitment is reinforced by the presence of the Hebrew verb rendered "loving" (אָהֵב, *'āhēb*).[124] This primary root is the main term for love used in the Old Testament.[125] It has a broad range of meaning paralleling that of the English word "to love."[126] In particular, *'āhēb* is used in reference to God's love for people and nations; likewise, the verb refers to people's love for inanimate things, for one another, and for God.[127] While it is true that affection and intimacy were to characterize the feelings the Israelites had for Yahweh, such was to be "expressed by obedience to God's commandments, serving God, showing reverence for God, and being loyal to God alone."[128] The Lord's covenant with His people, as seen in "his deeds of redemption and care,"[129] was the impetus for the Israelites responding to Him in gratitude and single-minded devotion.[130]

Such commitment is evident in the Hebrew verb rendered "keeping" (שָׁמַר, *shāmar*).[131] This primary root has a range of overlapping meanings,[132] including "to keep," "to watch over," "to take care of," "to preserve," and "to protect."[133] The verb conveys the fundamental notions of "to exercise great care over"[134] and "to pay careful attention to."[135] With respect to God's people, they were to give heed to the ordinances and decrees of His covenant with them. In fact, such obedience formed the foundation of their worship and service.

This ideation can be found in the Hebrew noun rendered "commandments" (מִצְוָה, *mitswâ*), which is derived from the verb צָוָה (*tsāwâ*).[136] The basic meaning of this root is "to command."[137] In the Old Testament, the verb is used in contexts in which a superior orders subordinates to do something (or forbids them to do something);[138] in turn, they are expected to obey.[139] Likewise, the noun *mitswâ* can refer to a "commission" (as in to carry out an assigned task), an "(individual) commandment," or a "(set of all the) commandments."[140] With respect to the Lord's decrees, they reflect "the particular conditions of the covenant."[141] Furthermore, because God issues the *mitswâ*, it represents, not an "arbitrary demand or constraint," but "the expression of God's will for his people" that carries His "moral authority."[142]

In a more general sense, Exodus 20:6 teaches that those who maintained their wholehearted loyalty and commitment to God experienced the same from Him for generations to follow. For instance, a person's example of complete allegiance, continuing trust, and consistent obedience could influence many physical descendants after him to live in the same manner. If these descendants devoted themselves to the Lord, they too would experience His loyalty and faithfulness in their lives. The "thousands" mentioned in verse 6 stand in sharp contrast to the third and fourth generations referred in verse 5. This antithesis is a reminder that "God's mercy transcends his wrath."[143] Divine justice, "which is the penalty for persisting in sin," is infinitely outstripped by "the beneficent consequences of a life of goodness."[144]

There are several Old Testament passages that, in harmony with the second commandment of the Decalogue, speak against idolatry.[145] Exodus 20:23 forbids the making of gods of silver and gold, while 32:8 notes the way the Israelites were quick to cast for themselves an image of a calf and then worship and sacrifice to it. Both 34:17 and Leviticus 19:4 prohibit making cast idols or images and worshiping them instead of the Lord. In Leviticus 26:1, God banned His people from making idols, erecting carved images or pillars, and placing engraved stones in their land to worship these detestable objects.

Deuteronomy 4:15–20 explains that when God spoke to His people from Mount Sinai, He remained invisible. The Israelites therefore were to be careful not to commit the sin of worshiping idols, regardless of whether they were shaped like people, mammals, birds, reptiles, or fish. God did not even allow the Israelites to bow down to the sun, moon, and stars, despite the fact that these were noteworthy objects in the nighttime sky. The Lord rescued His people so that they might exclusively worship and serve Him, not the created realm.

If the Israelites encountered the idols of pagans, they were to burn these images with fire (Deut. 7:25). God would be provoked to anger if His people began to worship idols (32:21). Psalm 115:4–7 relates that idols were powerless and lifeless. People made these objects from silver and gold. Although the images had mouths, ears, noses, hands, and feet, they could not speak, hear, smell, feel, or walk. Isaiah 44:12–20 relates similar information, adding that those who created these objects bowed down in worship before them and begged them for deliverance from calamity. This, of course, was impossible, for the images were lifeless objects.

The New Testament also has a complement of passages that speaks against the sin of idolatry. Matthew 6:24 and Luke 16:13 note that no one can serve two masters. People must choose either God or wealth. Acts 17:29 relates that God is not an image people have formed out of gold, silver, or stone. First Corinthians 8:4–6 teaches that there is only one God and that the idols people make are really lifeless entities. First John 5:21 exhorts believers to keep themselves from idols, for these are the opposite of the true God and eternal life.

The third commandment (Exodus 20:7; Deuteronomy 5:11) says, "You shall not take the name of Yahweh your God in vain; for Yahweh will not leave unpunished (him) who takes His name in vain" (Exod. 20:7; personal translation). In Old Testament times, a person's name was not simply a convenient form of identification but practically equivalent to bearer of the title.[146] For example, 1 Samuel 25:25 says, "My lord, do not take seriously this ill-natured fellow, Nabal; for as his name is, so is he; Nabal is his name, and folly is with him." This passage illustrates that a person's name often reflected his character, nature, and reputation.[147]

Likewise, there is an essential identity between God and His name.[148] This truth is seen in the Old Testament when the name and being of God are used in parallelism with each other. For instance, Psalm 18:49 says, "For this I will extol you, O Lord, among the nations, and sing praises to your name." Isaiah 25:1 similarly reads, "O Lord, you are my God; I will exalt you, I will praise your name." Furthermore, Malachi 3:16 says, "Then those who revered the Lord spoke with one another. The Lord took note and listened, and a book of remembrance was written before him of those who revered the Lord and thought on his name."

The Lord's name is characterized by sacredness and reflects the fact that He is infinitely exalted as well as set apart from His creation. In addition, He is morally pure and perfect in the most unsurpassed way. The holiness of God dictated that any reference the Israelites made to Him had to be done in a manner that expressed reverence and respect. After all, God's name was a gift of grace to Israel. The people had access to the Lord, not through an idol, but through His holy name.[149] The Lord also regarded a holy disposition as the essence of the covenant privilege and as the precondition for continuing to enjoy the blessings of the covenant. In this regard, Murray noted that the holiness of God demanded that His subjects be conformed to His virtuous character.[150] The Israelites displayed a holy disposition by obeying God's commandments. In contrast, they displayed an unholy disposition by violating His ordinances. From these observations it is evident that only those who heeded the Lord could have fellowship with Him.

Hence, in the third commandment, Yahweh was directing His people to honor and revere His name. To do anything less would be to misuse and disrespect the very person of God.[151] This truth is brought out by the appearance of the Hebrew noun rendered "in vain" (שָׁוְא, *shāw'*). The etymology of the term is unclear. It may be derived from the root *šw'* I, which means "to treat badly."[152] It is also possible *shāw'* is related to *šw'* II, which means "to be or make desolate or waste."[153] The noun variously can mean "worthless,"[154] "deceit,"[155] "emptiness," or "falsehood."[156] With respect to the latter possibility, Shepherd makes the intriguing conjecture that the third commandment specifically prohibits "against the use of the Lord's name in giving false testimony."[157]

A more likely possibility[158] concerns the common belief that ancient Near Eastern people had regarding the "power of the spoken word."[159] Allegedly what someone said could either positively or negatively affect the outcome of a situation.[160] Correspondingly, to utter the divine name meant invoking all that it represented with "God's identity and will."[161] The third commandment banned the practice of associating "the powers and purposes of Yahweh" with what someone declared and the objective inherent in that pronouncement. To do otherwise would be a "misrepresentation of God, a false claim to divine power and endorsement, and a miscommunication of truth."[162]

To sum up, Exodus 20:7 and Deuteronomy 5:11 forbid the use of God's name in false worship, for incantations or divination, as well as for attesting falsehood or speaking irreverently (Lev. 19:12; Deut. 28:58).[163] The Lord regarded the knowledge of His name to be a privilege, for it meant that the Israelites did not venerate an unknown, far away deity, but rather someone "whose personal name was known."[164] Since God's name represents the essence of His person (which is holy), to use it carelessly, thoughtlessly, or by rote was an offense to Him.[165] The Israelites thus were not to regard God's reputation as being empty, meaningless, or worthless.

Anyone who displayed such a reckless attitude toward the Lord would be held guilty of dishonoring Him and would one day be punished by Him.[166] This truth is stressed by the Hebrew verb rendered "leave unpunished" (נָקָה, *nāqâ*). The etymology of the term is debated, with some seeing it being derived from a single root or from two roots.[167] *Nāqâ* has a variety of meanings, including "to be desolate," "to be cut off,"[168] "to be free," "to be without blame,"[169] and "to be exempt from punishment."[170] The "derived juridicial meaning" of acquittal "is exclusive to the OT."[171] In Exodus 20:7, the idea is that the Lord would not acquit the violator of the third commandment. God would charge transgressors with guilt and discipline them accordingly.

In the ancient Near East, the most common example of taking the Lord's name in vain would have been to swear falsely by it in the taking of an oath or vow (cf. Lev. 19:12; Ps. 139:20). Another abuse would have been to use the divine name in magic incantations.[172] The idea was that by invoking the name of the deity, one could exploit God's power for evil and selfish intents.[173] In today's society, a common example of taking God's name in vain would be to use it in some obscene way.[174] Although this includes cursing, it is not limited to profane language. Any use of God's name that demeans His sovereignty over creation and His ability to redeem His people would represent a violation of the third commandment.[175]

There are several Old Testament passages that speak against misusing the Lord's name.[176] Exodus 22:28 prohibited reviling God and cursing the leader of one's people. Leviticus 18:21 banned the Israelites from giving any of their offspring in sacrifice to Molech (the god of the Ammonites), for this would profane the name of their God. In 19:21, the Lord forbade His people from swearing falsely by His name, for this would profane it. In Leviticus 22:2, the Lord urged Aaron and his sons to deal carefully with the sacred donations that the Israelites gave for the work of the tabernacle. Any mishandling of these donations would be a profaning of God's holy name. If either a citizen of Israel or an alien blasphemed the name of the Lord, the people were to stone the violator to death (24:16). God wanted to make known His holy name among the Israelites and the nations of the world. That is why He would not allow His people to profane it (Ezek. 39:7).

Several New Testament passages speak against misusing the name of the Lord. In Matthew 5:33–37, Christ prohibited swearing at all by heaven, by earth, or by Jerusalem. He urged His followers to make their oaths either a simple "yes" or "no," nothing more elaborate than that. As they prayed, they were to acknowledge the sacred nature of God's name. In 23:16–22, Jesus censured corrupt religious leaders for abusing oath-taking and for gravely misunderstanding the third commandment.

The fourth commandment (Exodus 20:8–11; Deuteronomy 5:12–15) says, "Remember the Sabbath day, to keep it holy. Six days you shall labor and do all your work. And the seventh day (is) a Sabbath to Yahweh your God; you shall not do any work, you,[177] and your son, and your daughter, your male slave, your female slave, and your cattle, and your stranger who (is) in your gates. For (in) six days Yahweh made the heavens and the earth, the sea, and all which (is) in them, and He rested on the seventh day; therefore Yahweh blessed the Sabbath day and sanctified it" (Exod. 20:8–11; personal translation).

The Hebrew verb translated "remember" (זָכַר, *zākar*) is a primary root that has the basic sense of "to call to mind" or "to give thought to."[178] More is implied, though, than the mere recollection of information or an event.[179] To meditate upon something or pay attention to some matter[180] was an "act of covenantal or legal obligation"[181] in which one recognized one's responsibilities and fulfilled them.[182] Thus, the goal of remembering was an increased active "appreciation and commitment"[183] toward the Lord and His covenant community. Exodus 20:8 makes it clear that *zākar* ultimately has "the law as its object."[184]

In Deuteronomy 5:12, זָכוֹר is not used; rather, שָׁמוֹר (the Qal infinitive absolute of שָׁמַר) appears.[185] This is the same term that is used in Exodus 20:6 and Deuteronomy 5:8. When Exodus 20:8 and Deuteronomy 5:12 are taken together, they stress the importance of both remembering the Sabbath and observing it as a holy day.[186] In terms of the Hebrew noun rendered "Sabbath" (שַׁבָּת, *shabbāt*), while the "etymological data is highly debated,"[187] it most likely is probably derived from the verb שָׁבַת (*shābat*).[188] This root generally means "to cease," "to stop," or "be at a standstill."[189] With respect to the notion of the Sabbath, *shābat* referred to the cessation of activity and the engagement in a time of "rest and celebration," which could involve people, animals, land, and God.[190]

Scholars have debated the origin of the Sabbath and its relationship to similar customs and institutions in other ancient Near Eastern cultures.[191] For example, one view is that the Sabbath represents a modification of a corresponding day in Mesopotamia.[192] The biblical record, however, makes it clear that the Sabbath institution has its origins in creation (cf. Gen. 2:1–2).[193] This being the case, the Sabbath is not derived from any pagan custom or institution.[194] In fact, over the years, general interest in this view has declined, for scholars have not been able to find any alleged parallel with other ancient accounts that can definitively explain the origin of the Sabbath.[195] Thus the Sabbath, as it is revealed in the Old Testament, is a distinctly Israelite institution and practice[196] in which the covenant community desisted from "the weeks' work."[197] Bosman accordingly notes that, while "seven-day periods were well known" in the Ancient Near East, "there is no clear instance of a similar seventh day of rest outside of Israel."[198]

An examination of the Decalogue reveals that the Sabbath regulation is treated more fully than any of the other commandments. Observance of the Sabbath is grounded in the fact that on the seventh day of creation, God rested or ceased from His activity.[199] God's original intention was to bring order, control, and stability to the creation.[200] In Genesis 2:2, Moses indicated that this was achieved.

Because the work and results of God's creating activity were final, complete, and absolutely perfect, they drew attention to the Lord's sovereignty "over all creation,"[201] especially over "the gods of the pagan nations."[202] Additionally, when God brought His endeavors to a close, He signaled that all He had willed and designed for His creation was now in place.[203] These truths are reinforced by the Hebrew verb translated "rested," which denotes the enjoyment of something accomplished and the celebration of that completed task.[204] This is an ascribing of human actions to God (in other words, an anthropomorphism). It is a literary technique employed by the writers of Scripture to make intelligible to the finite, human mind some truth about the infinite God.[205]

Genesis 2:3 declares that "God blessed the seventh day and hallowed it, because on it God rested from all the work that he had done in creation." Some have maintained that the Hebrew root translated "blessed" (בָּרַךְ, *bārak*)[206] is a denominative verb from the feminine noun בֶּרֶךְ;[207] however, many scholars have rejected this etymology.[208] When used in the sense of "bless," *bārak* means "to endue someone with special power."[209] Such "denotes the favorable relationship between object and subject."[210] In terms of Genesis 2:3 and Exodus 20:11, the idea is that God bestowed His goodwill and grace on the Sabbath and on those of His chosen people who would consecrate it as sacred.[211] God's blessing included both the temporal and spiritual graces He bestowed. Those who were so favored by Him enjoyed a rich and abundant life.[212]

These truths are emphasized by the presence of "hallowed" in Genesis 2:3 (קָדַשׁ) and "sanctified" in Exodus 20:11 (קָדַשׁ). קָדַשׁ (*qādash*) is the denominative verb from the masculine noun קֹדֶשׁ (*qōdesh*).[213] The latter means "apartness," "holiness," or "sacredness."[214] In turn, *qādash* denotes that which is "withheld from ordinary use" and "being treated with special care."[215] Such phrases as "to be treated as consecrated" and "to dedicate for God" help to further capture the essence of the meaning.[216] In the present context, the setting apart of the Sabbath[217] was intended to protect it from being profaned.[218] The holiness of God was at the heart of dedicating the seventh day to Him.[219]

According to Genesis 2:3, when God had finalized His creation activity, He placed His divine approval upon it all by pronouncing a blessing on the seventh day.[220] The bestowal of His approval was so commemorative that God set apart the seventh day for a distinctive purpose. It was dedicated to the cessation of activity, for at that time He ceased from all of His creative activity. The occasion furthermore provided humankind with a model for the cycle of labor and rest. Those who imitated this divine pattern confessed God's lordship in their lives and their consecration to Him. They also acknowledged that He was the source of their existence and the provider of their freedom. They furthermore recognized that God gave their life meaning and purpose.[221]

It is noteworthy that the first biblical record of obligatory Sabbath observance appears in Exodus 16, in the context of which is Israel's journey from Egypt to Sinai.[222] Nehemiah 9:13 and 14 suggest that the Lord made the observance of the Sabbath an official covenant obligation when He instituted the Mosaic law at Mount Sinai.[223] This implies (as was mentioned earlier) that the Sabbath was a uniquely Israelite institution.[224] Its observance was mandated in the Torah and the Israelites were to keep the Sabbath weekly. The focus of this observance was a sacred time, rather than a hallowed place. This enabled the Israelites to observe the Sabbath anywhere, even in captivity.[225]

Both Exodus 20:9 and 10 relate how the Israelites were to treat the Sabbath. Deuteronomy 5:13 and 14 also discuss this issue, but these verses contain some additional information. The different expansions of the fourth commandment in these two parts of Scripture should be seen as complementary, rather than contradictory. In each text God directed His people to observe, remember, and hallow the Sabbath as a testimony to His saving activity both in creation and in deliverance from captivity. When examined together, the verses in Exodus and Deuteronomy reveal that God directed the people to perform their labor during the first six days of the week. However, He forbade them from doing any labor on the Sabbath.[226] Neither they, their family members, their servants, the visitors within their city gates, nor their animals were to do any work. Every creature was to be given the opportunity to rest.[227]

Exodus 20:11 gives one reason why the Israelites were to observe the Sabbath. During the first six days of creation, the Lord brought all things into existence—the heavens with their stars, planets, and moons, and the earth with all its land, seas, fish, animals, birds, and plants. On the seventh day, however, He ceased from His creative activity. In this way He blessed the seventh day of the week and made it holy. Deuteronomy 5:15 gives another reason why the Israelites were to observe the Sabbath. The Lord explained that His people had once been slaves in Egypt, when He reached out His mighty arm and rescued them. Just as God gave them rest from their oppressive situation in Egypt, so they were to give themselves, their families, their servants, their resident aliens, and their animals an opportunity to rest from the wearying labors of the first six days of the week.

When taken together, Exodus 20:11 and Deuteronomy 5:15 reveal that the Sabbath ordinance is rooted in both the orders of creation and of redemption.[228] The implication is that the Sabbath looks backward to the good and perfect creation of God (cf. Gen. 2:2–3) and forward to the final redemptive Sabbath rest for the people of God (cf. Heb. 4:1–11). As Childs pointed out, in both cases Israel's memory of the Creation and the Exodus did not act as the motivation for observing the Sabbath; rather, it was the reverse—Israel observed the Sabbath to remember God's work of Creation and the Exodus.[229] Furthermore, as Cover noted, the Israelites' thereby affirmed their belief that "there is no other God than YHWH" as well as that He who "created the whole world and triumphantly rested" is "the only God who deserves worship and obedience."[230]

Just as circumcision was the sign of the Abrahamic covenant (cf. Gen. 17:1–14), so the observance of the Sabbath became a sign of the Mosaic covenant (cf. Exod. 31:13). The Sabbath reminded the Israelites of God's purposes for them in creation and of their deliverance from slavery in Egypt.[231] From a New Testament perspective, the Sabbath points to Christ, the Creator and Redeemer of His people, who brings them eternal rest (cf. Matt. 11:28; Col. 2:16–17).[232]

John Calvin noted three particular reasons why God instituted the Sabbath for Israel.[233] First, the Lord furnished His people with a "type of the spiritual rest by which believers were to cease from their own works, and allow God to work in them." Second, "he meant there should be a stated day on which they should assemble to hear the Law, and perform religious rites." Third, "he meant that servants, and those who lived under the authority of others, should be indulged with a day of rest, and thus have some intermission from labour."

There are numerous Old Testament passages that stress the importance of the Israelites observing the Sabbath.[234] The principle is set forth in the creation account (Gen. 2:3) and mentioned in the context of God's provision of manna and quail (Exod. 16:23–30). The Lord concluded His instructions for building the tabernacle and making the priestly garments by stressing to His people the importance and necessity of keeping the Sabbath (31:13–16). Furthermore, because of their relationship with the Lord, the Israelites were morally obligated to observe the Sabbath (Lev. 19:30). God promised to bless those among His people who refrained from desecrating the Sabbath (Isa. 56:2). Exodus 35:2 and 3 provide some specific Sabbath regulations. God forbade His people from lighting a fire in any of their dwellings on that holy day. Those who violated the Lord's injunction had to be put to death. Jeremiah 17:21 and 22 banned the Israelites from carrying any load on the Sabbath.

There are also numerous New Testament references to the Sabbath. For example, in Matthew 12:1–12, Christ declared that it was lawful to do good on the Sabbath. In essence, Jesus was claiming the right to redefine the status of the Sabbath.[235] Such authority could only belong to someone who was equal to God.[236] The Savior's remark contradicted the teaching of those who prohibited healing on the Sabbath (cf. Mark 3:1–6; Luke 6:1–11).[237] Later, during one of the pilgrim feasts held in Jerusalem, Jesus went to the holy city and healed an invalid on the Sabbath. Although this infuriated some of the religious authorities, Christ nevertheless stressed the validity of what He had done (John 5:1–18). He wanted people to know that meeting urgent human needs was more important than their way of observing the Sabbath.

Obligations to fellow human beings (Exodus 20:12–17; Deuteronomy 5:16–21). The *fifth commandment (Exodus 20:12; Deuteronomy 5:16)* of the Decalogue says, "Honor your father and your mother so that your days may be long on the land which Yahweh your God is giving to you" (Exod. 20:12; personal translation). Deuteronomy 5:16 adds that the Lord, Israel's God, commanded them to honor their parents. In addition to the promise that those who observe this commandment would enjoy long life, Moses noted that it would go well for them in the land which Yahweh was giving to His covenant people.

Inherent within the Decalogue is the understanding that "the worship of the one God implies respect for the integrity of others," and that "respect for the integrity of others implies the worship of the one God.[238] Hyatt furthers the discussion by noting that the "position of the fifth commandment" within the Decalogue "is significant."[239] It appears "immediately after commandments which inculcate proper worship and respect for Yahweh." The fifth commandment also comes before the directives "concerning neighbours." This central positioning thereby stresses the "importance of filial respect."

Furthermore, "the commandment forms a bridge between those concerning God and those concerning the neighbour."[240]

Within the fifth commandment one also finds an emphasis on the way in which the existence of God's covenant people could be ensured and sustained, an existence that is rooted in the faithfulness of the Lord. He pledged in the covenant to bless His people with land and offspring. The people, in turn, would enjoy the fulfillment of the promise only as parents taught their children and as children honored their parents and embraced their faith in the Lord. Thus, just as God and His people were to be committed jointly to the stipulations of the covenant, so too there needed to be joint commitments within the human family (namely, between parents and their children).[241]

During the Old Testament period, family relationships were concentric.[242] This means the husband and wife formed the innermost circle, their children formed the second circle, and grandparents and cousins formed a third circle.[243] At the time when God gave the fifth commandment, some cultures banished aged dependents from society, many of whom were eaten by wild animals or died alone in the desert. God, however, wanted parents to be honored—no matter how old they were.[244]

This emphasis is seen in the Hebrew verb rendered "honor" (כָּבֵד, *kābēd*),[245] which means "to be heavy," "to be weighty," or "to be oppressing."[246] "Weight" seems to be the core sense around which literal and figurative meanings with either positive and negative connotations arise.[247] For instance, the verb can be used to refer to something that is burdensome or awkward as well as someone who is powerful or influential.[248] Carrying the latter thought further, *kābēd* can be used to refer to respecting, esteeming, or revering someone.[249] In terms of parents, Exodus 20:12 is stating that they are worthy to be treated with respect and dignity by their children.[250]

Wrapped up in the concept of honor are the ideas of prizing someone highly (Prov. 4:8), providing care (Ps. 91:15), showing respect (Lev. 19:3), and obeying (Deut. 21:18–21). Through what the children thought, said, and did, they were to honor their parents for their excellence in station, character, and service (cf. Isa 29:13).[251] The Lord commanded His people to honor their parents because they were instrumental in rearing their children, providing for their needs, protecting them from danger, and training them to be responsible adults in society.[252] Honor toward parents provided a stabilizing force in society and bound children to parents in the community of faith.[253]

Another reason to show honor is that parents were the Lord's representatives to their children in the divine administrative order (namely, God-parent-child).[254] Parents were supposed to be God's representatives and partners in the rearing of their children.[255] Thus, children who failed to respect their parents were also being irreverent to God.[256]

As was mentioned earlier, if each Israelite heeded the fifth commandment, God promised them a long and prosperous life in Canaan. Patai offered this assessment of how the Jewish mind interpreted this aspect of Exodus 20:12 (cf. Deut. 5:16):[257]

> Talmudic teachers felt that this was an insufficient reward for so great a *mitzva* (commandment) and found a way of interpreting the relevant Biblical verses so as to derive from them a divine promise of rewards both in This World and in the World to Come. Moreover, they found it possible to extend the reward for honoring father and mother to the children of the person who fulfills this great commandment, and even to his remote descendants.

While the preceding interpretation is novel, it overstates what is in the biblical text. God's promise did not automatically imply that every cooperative child and their descendants would reap temporal and eternal blessings.[258] The fifth commandment also did not necessarily mean that every person who honored his or her parents would live a long life, just as the promise did not necessarily mean that a disobedient child would have his or her life cut short.[259] Rather, it conveyed the general principle that esteeming parents would contribute to a longer life.[260]

It stands to reason that if the entire nation consciously and consistently chose to act in this manner, Israel's longevity in Canaan would be extensive and productive. There are four reasons for these conclusions.[261] First, by honoring their parents, the Israelites would be honoring the Lord, who gave them their parents. Second, God's people would be showing respect for His command, which He had given to them. Third, by heeding this stipulation, the Israelites would reap the temporal and eternal blessings of the covenant, which the Lord had promised to bestow on His loyal people. Fourth, those who honored and obeyed their parents would benefit from the godly wisdom they imparted. Submissive children of devout parents would learn to avoid the evils of life and be encouraged to embrace and practice the time-honored truths of Scripture.

There are other passages of the Old Testament that stress the importance of honoring one's parents.[262] Exodus 21:17 declares that those who cursed their father or mother were to be executed by the covenant community. It is not clear how often—if ever—the Israelites implemented this harsh measure. Nevertheless, it is clear that ancient Hebrew society did not produce entire generations of children who brazenly violated the law and brought disgrace to their parents.[263] Leviticus 19:3 stresses that one's relationship to the Lord is the basis for respecting one's parents. Deuteronomy 6:2 says that parents were to teach their children to revere the Lord and obey His commands. The children, of course, had to follow their parental instruction in these areas. The teaching process did not merely take place in formal settings. Parents were to impart wisdom and instruction in informal settings as well.[264]

The Israelites were not to take lightly incidents where children rebelled against the authority of their parents. Deuteronomy 21:18–21 declares that parents were to take their stubborn and defiant children to the elders at the gate of their town. After the parents had noted the depraved way in which the child had behaved, the leaders were to stone him to death. In this way, God's people would purge their community of those who were evil. Moreover, those who dishonored their parents were supposed to be cursed in Israelite society (27:16). Perhaps this is why Solomon insisted that children keep their father's commands and never forsake their mother's teaching (Prov. 6:20). Such obedient children would avoid many moral pitfalls and enjoy the favor of the Lord.

There are several New Testament passages that stress the importance of obeying one's parents. In Matthew 15:4–6, Jesus affirmed the validity of the fifth commandment. He even stressed that the spirit as well as the letter of this injunction needed to be heeded (cf. Mark 7:9–13). In Matthew 19:19, honoring one's parents was part of the list of commandments Jesus cited to a wealthy young ruler (cf. Luke 18:20). Christ did not just verbally uphold the validity of the fifth commandment. He also obeyed it Himself. For example, Luke 2:51 says that Jesus was obedient to His parents throughout His adolescence. Furthermore, as Jesus hung on the cross, He told John to care for Mary, Jesus' mother (John 19:26–27). One possible reason Christ gave John this directive is that the Savior's brothers still did not believe in Him (cf. 7:5).

In Ephesians 6:1–3, Paul stressed to believing children the importance of obeying their parents. The apostle noted that God would bless such children for consistently honoring their parents. Colossians 3:20 similarly teaches that children should honor their parents in everything not sinful, for this pleases the Lord. In 1 Timothy 5:8, Paul targeted believers whose parents and grandparents were struggling to survive financially. He sternly rebuked the unwillingness of some in the Ephesian church to provide for the material needs of their loved ones. The apostle said these ingrates, by their selfish and uncaring actions, had practically denied the faith. They were behaving in a way that was worse than unbelievers.

The sixth commandment (Exodus 20:13; Deuteronomy 5:17) says, "You shall not murder" (Exod. 20:13; personal translation). The Hebrew verb rendered "murder" (רָצַח, *rātsāch*)[265] conveys the ideas of killing, striking down, or slaying.[266] The commandment itself is a comprehensive ban against the unlawful "taking of a person's life by an individual or by a mob, who target an individual, with all the attendant savagery."[267] Some have argued that the Mosaic legislation only concerns premeditated murder.[268] But Number 35:11 makes it clear the Lord was also concerned "about unpremeditated, accidental killings."[269] Thus, *rātsāch* "applies equally to both cases of premeditated murder and killings as a result of any other circumstances."[270] The latter is "what English Common Law has called, 'man slaughter'."[271]

The sixth commandment is based on the biblical concept of "the sanctity of human life."[272] In other words, all human life has intrinsic value and worth, for it is precious in the sight of God (cf. Gen. 1:26–28; 5:1; 9:6; Matt. 5:21–26; Jas. 3:9).[273] This implies that every human life belongs to the Lord, and He alone has the right to take it or command when it should be taken. The sanctity of life also means that each individual has divinely ordained, inviolable rights and responsibilities to maintain and preserve life. Thus only human governments, not free-wheeling vigilantes, have the divine sanction and authority to execute individuals for their crimes against the state (cf. Gen. 9:6–7; Rom. 13:1–7).[274]

There are several Old Testament passages that speak against murder.[275] Genesis 9:6 reveals that God made people in His image and that murdering someone is a direct offense against Him, the Creator of the victim whose blood has been wrongfully shed. Murderers, by their actions, display contempt for God, as well as their victims. Perhaps this is why, as Leviticus 24:17 and Numbers 35:33 reveal, the government was to execute murderers.

There are several New Testament passages that also speak against murder. In Matthew 5:21–24, Jesus declared that the presence of anger and hate against others reveals a murderous disposition and would be in violation of the spirit of the sixth commandment. In 26:52, Christ taught that those who customarily resort to murder would themselves be murdered by others. In 1 Peter 4:15, the apostle noted that not all the suffering which believers experienced in Bible times was due to their faith. Sometimes they broke the law, and in these instances the authorities were right to punish them. Peter said his readers should not be guilty of criminal activities such as murdering and stealing. They should not even meddle in other people's affairs. All these offenses were wrong and brought shame, not honor, to the cause of Christ.

The seventh commandment (Exodus 20:14; Deuteronomy 5:18) says, "You shall not commit adultery" (Exod. 20:14; personal translation). The Hebrew verb rendered "adultery" (נָאַף, *nā'ap*)[276] principally means to engage in illicit sexual intercourse "with the wife or the betrothed of another man."[277] Silbermann noted that *nā'ap* is applicable only in the case of a married woman.[278] Scholars moreover tend to distinguish *nā'ap* from fornication, which is unlawful sexual relations by an unmarried person.[279] In ancient Israel *nā'ap* primarily referred to the physical act of adultery.[280] Over time, however, the significance of the term and the connotations associated with it seemed to deepen and widen. For example, the term was also used to refer to idolatrous worship and unfaithfulness to God.[281]

The emphasis of the seventh commandment is on safeguarding "the integrity of the husband-wife relationship"[282] through sexual purity and fidelity. The injunction stands in sharp contrast with the promiscuity and infidelity of ancient and modern cultures alike.[283] From God's perspective, adultery is a grievous offense against Him, people, and society, for it represents a reprehensible breach of the marriage covenant (cf. Mal. 2:14–15).[284] Adultery also signifies a willful violation of the divine ideal (cf. Gen. 2:24).[285] His intent for marriage was that the man and the woman should be committed to each other for life and share in the creative work of making new people (Gen. 2:23). Marriage, of course, was for believers and nonbelievers; however, it was God's will that His people should marry only fellow believers (cf. 1 Cor. 7:39).[286] From a biblical perspective, the deepest dimensions of intimacy in a marriage relationship were impossible when the partners were not united in faith.[287]

While the fifth commandment upheld the sanctity of the home and the sixth commandment upheld the sanctity of life, the seventh commandment upheld the sanctity of marriage.[288] From the biblical perspective marriage was not simply a relationship of convenience, and its fundamental characteristics were not to be altered. That is why infidelity carried with it the most serious of consequences and penalties.[289] Moreover, adultery represented thievery of the lowest sort (Job 31:9–11), and it was always committed with forethought (cf. Jer. 5:8).[290] Furthermore, because "the extended family was the cornerstone of Israelite society, threats to its stability could not be tolerated."[291]

When someone engaged in this crime, he revealed his lack of judgment (cf. Hos. 4:11–14). The transgressor not only destroyed his own reputation, but also opened himself up to unexpected trials and hardships (cf. Prov. 6:32–35). Those having sexual relations with their neighbor's wife morally defiled themselves with the illicit partner (Lev. 18:20). So serious was this crime that in Old Testament times the community was to execute the transgressors (20:10), whether by stoning or by strangulation.[292] In this way the evil would be purged from Israel (Deut. 22:22).

In Matthew 5:27–30, Jesus taught that looking on someone else with lust constituted a violation of the spirit of the seventh commandment. Of course, Christ will forgive adulterers (cf. John 8:1–11). But those who refuse to repent of their evil ways cannot inherit the kingdom of God (1 Cor. 6:9). In fact, God will judge the adulterer and the sexually immoral; therefore, it is wise to honor the marriage relationship and keep the marriage bed pure (Heb. 13:4).

The eighth commandment (Exodus 20:15; Deuteronomy 5:19) says, "You shall not steal" (Exod. 20:15; personal translation). The Hebrew verb rendered "steal" (גָּנַב, *gānab*)[293] refers to "taking anything, human, animate, or inanimate, without legal right."[294] While the focus is "restricted to acts of theft done secretly,"[295] such a distinction should not be overemphasized; after all, thievery and robbery are equally reprehensible crimes before God (cf. Obad. 1:5; John 10:1, 8).[296]

The eighth commandment is a "general dictum against taking anything that belongs to someone else or the community at large."[297] All such crimes were considered transgressions "against the community and a threat to its very stability."[298] In one sense the eighth commandment is dealing with the preservation of private property.[299] In a more fundamental sense, however, it is concerned with the safeguarding of human liberty and freedom from such things as slavery and exile.[300] The commandment forbade a person from exploiting or manipulating the lives of others for personal gain.[301]

There are other Old Testament passages that speak against stealing.[302] Leviticus 19:11 repeats the basic injunction against stealing, and verse 13 adds the prohibition against defrauding and robbing one's neighbor. A convicted robber had to return what he had stolen. In cases in which the robbery was accompanied by violence, an additional twenty percent in punitive damages was added as a deterrent (cf. 6:2–7).

In the New Testament, one finds the eighth commandment repeated by Christ (cf. Matt. 19:18; Mark 10:19; Luke 18:20) and Paul (Rom. 13:9–10). The apostle also taught that thieves should no longer steal, but rather be honest and work hard, so they would have something to give to people in need (Eph. 4:28). James 5:4 reveals that God is aware of those who steal and will judge them for their crimes against those they have defrauded.

The ninth commandment (Exodus 20:16; Deuteronomy 5:20) says, "You shall not testify against your neighbor a witness of falsehood" (Exod. 20:16; personal translation). Uncertainties exist concerning the etymological underpinnings[303] of the Hebrew verb rendered "testify" (עָנָה, *'ānâ*).[304] Such deliberations notwithstanding, this study sees the basic root having a locus of interrelated meanings, such as "to reply," "to give an answer," "to give evidence," and "to respond to what was said."[305] The core sense of the verb is "to react," regardless of whether the situation involves dialogue or behavior in the absence of words.[306]

The ninth commandment is predominantly set against the backdrop of a forensic proceeding[307] (such as in a law court)[308] in which one party bears false witness to another party based on what has happened.[309] Nevertheless, as *The Net Bible* points out, "the law probably had a broader application to lying about other people in general" (cf. Lev. 5:1; Hos. 4:2). With respect to Exodus 20:16, the perjury is against one's "neighbor."[310] This renders the Hebrew noun רֵעַ (*rēa'*), which is derived from the verb רָעָה (*rā'â*). The latter can mean "to get oneself involved with," "to join oneself to," or "to befriend."[311] The noun, correspondingly, has a range of meanings, including "personal friend," "confidant," "companion," "colleague," and "fellow human being."[312] Such an associate can be either "close or occasional."[313]

Most of the terms that are rendered "neighbor" in the Old Testament refer to a fellow member of the covenant community belonging to the Lord. These would be people who shared in the rights and duties implied by membership in the covenant. The associations the members of the covenant had with each other were sanctioned by divine law.[314] The way in which someone treated his neighbor was an important indicator of the extent to which righteousness prevailed in Israel. When people in Israelite society refused to respect the right of their neighbors, it was a sign that the nation had morally disintegrated and would eventually experience punishment from God (cf. Isa. 3:5; Jer 9:4–9; Mic 7:5–6).[315] From a New Testament perspective, a neighbor is not just someone who lives in close proximity. It also includes one's fellow human beings (cf. Luke 10:25–37).[316] Jesus forcefully rejected the notion that limited the definition of "neighbor" to one's relatives and friends. He commanded His followers to love even their enemies, for God loved all humanity (cf. Matt. 5:43–48).[317]

The prohibition in Exodus 20:16 concerns testifying in a fraudulent way against one's neighbor. The Hebrew noun rendered "witness" (עֵד, *'ēd*) is derived from the verb עוּד (*'ûd*). While the etymology of the latter is debated, its basic meaning is "to warn," "to admonish," or "to call to witness."[318] The noun, in turn, refers to a person who "testifies or is in a position to testify to throw light on the facts of a case in a trial."[319] Such legal affairs could include "civil matters" and "criminal proceedings."[320]

The underlying concept of *'ûd* was that the person testifying had first-hand knowledge of a matter.[321] This is supported by Scripture. Leviticus 5:1 says a witness is anyone who can testify on the basis of something he has heard or personally seen. Likewise, Proverbs 29:24 stresses that such a person is morally obligated to declare what he knows. In order for objectivity to be preserved, a testimony from at least two people had to be provided before guilt could reasonably be established (Num. 35:30; Deut. 17:6; 19:15). When the method of punishment was stoning, the witnesses cast the first stones (17:7).

Honesty and veracity formed the backdrop of such proceedings, as seen by the presence of the Hebrew noun rendered "falsehood" (שֶׁקֶר, *sheqer*) in Exodus 20:16. It is derived from the verb שָׁקַר (*shāqar*). While the basic meaning of the root is "to deal falsely,"[322] it connotes more than just lying to and being deceitful toward others.[323] It also signifies the breaking of an agreement or the breach of a trust.[324] The act of treachery can involve either "a person or a covenant."[325] From a theological perspective, bearing false witness before a court was seen as a violation of the covenant God had made with His people.[326] In short, the presence of *sheqer* represented a "breach of faith"[327] just as much with God as with the offended party.[328] God did not condone such behavior, for He was characterized by truth, objectivity, and faithfulness. His people were also to be characterized by these virtues.

It's important to note that in Deuteronomy 5:20, the term rendered "falsehood" is not שֶׁקֶר, but a different word— שָׁוְא (*shāw'*).[329] This term was used in the third commandment and rendered "in vain." Moses evidently changed the wording of the ninth commandment to tighten, rather than alter, its meaning.[330] The main emphasis is on the deceit and fraud associated with testifying falsely against one's fellow human beings.[331]

Exodus 20:16 denounces those who testify falsely. Elsewhere in the Old Testament, the Lord declared that lying lips were an abomination to Him (Prov. 12:22; 26:28). Zechariah 5:4 talks about God's curse being sent out on those who swear falsely, and in 8:17 the Lord declared His hatred for those who loved a false oath. Proverbs 20:17 fittingly declares that bread gained by deceit might be initially sweet to a man, but afterward his mouth is filled with gravel. In other words, dishonest gains can never truly satisfy.

Deuteronomy 19:16–21 deals with the issue of a witness falsely accusing someone else of a crime. Moses declared that the two people had to stand before the priests and judges who were on duty. The judges were to thoroughly check the matter to determine whether the witness was telling the truth or lying. If he testified falsely, he had to be punished for his crime. Ironically, he was subjected to the same penalty he had hoped to inflict upon the person he had wrongly accused.[332] In this way the evil would be purged from the redeemed community, and the rest of the people who heard about it would be afraid to bear false witness.

Those who spread false reports helped the wicked by being a malicious witness (Exod. 23:1). Also, those who disseminated fraudulent charges were subjecting innocent and honest people to unjust treatment, a crime the Lord would surely punish (vs. 7). Only those who spoke the truth from their hearts could dwell in the sanctuary of the Lord (Ps. 15:2). In contrast, the Lord would silence the person who secretly slandered his neighbor (101:5). Proverbs 10:18 reveals that some people tell lies to hide their hatred, and the person who spreads lies is a fool. In Jeremiah 9:3–5, the Lord denounced those among His people who were like this. He deplored the lies that came from their mouths and their use of dishonesty to increase their power. Rather than treat others fairly, they cheated them. Zechariah 8:16 declares that God prefers a completely different kind of person, one who spoke the truth to others and rendered true and dependable judgment in the law courts.

The New Testament also upholds the ninth commandment. Christ declared that when someone makes a promise, he should be clear and direct in stating his intentions (Matt. 5:37). Because believers are all united to Christ's spiritual body, they are to put off falsehood and speak truthfully to one another (Eph. 5:25). Lying was no longer permissible for Christians, for they had taken off their old selves with its evil practices and put on their new selves, which was being renewed after the moral likeness of its Creator (Col. 3:9). Slander was also no longer permissible for those who claimed to be followers of Christ (Titus 3:2). One reason is that the denigration of others was tantamount to robbing them of their good name.

The tenth commandment (Exodus 20:17; Deuteronomy 5:21) says, "You shall not covet your neighbor's house; you shall not covet your neighbor's wife, or his male slave, or his female slave, or his ox, or his donkey, or anything which (belongs) to your neighbor" (Exod. 20:17; personal translation). In Deuteronomy 5:21, the neighbor's wife is mentioned first, then his house, his field, his male and female slaves, his ox, his donkey, and finally anything else that belongs to him.

The Hebrew verb rendered "covet" (חָמַד, *chāmad*)[333] can have either positive or negative connotations, depending on the context in which it is used.[334] The root can also be directed toward something concrete (for example, an object) or something abstract (for instance, status or influence).[335] Such notions as "to desire," "to crave," "to demand," "to request," "to acquire," and "to entice" help to express the shades of meaning associated with this verb.[336] It is not wrong to have aspirations and desires.[337] The tenth commandment, however, is speaking against an "inordinate, ungoverned, selfish desire."[338] It is a situation in which people set their "hearts and affections on things that then take the place of God."[339]

To clarify the injunction, the Lord gave several examples of things His people were not to covet: house, wife, servant, and utility animals. Then God summed up the examples by commanding His people not to covet anything that belonged to their neighbors.[340] This injunction is the most inward of the ten, for it is a precept of the heart.[341] The commandment goes to the foundation of all wicked actions, namely, those profane desires and impulses of a predatory nature.[342] They are the cause of nearly every sin against one's neighbor.[343] Those who craved and tried to obtain the property of others revealed their dissatisfaction with what God had given them.[344] They thus showed their lack of faith in Him and lack of confidence in His love for them. Coveting usually prompts a person sooner or later to hurt his neighbor to get his possessions. This wanton act of violence is inconsistent with the primary duty of love.

The Old Testament reveals the tragedy that results from coveting what does not belong to oneself.[345] Achan's sin at Jericho was that he inordinately desired some of the plunder that the Israelites had captured in battle (Josh. 7:21). David lusted after Bathsheba, and this brought untold heartache on him, his family, and his nation (2 Sam. 11–12). Greed for the most desirable treasures of Samaria lay behind the plunderous actions of the Aramean officers (1 Kings 20:6).

The Lord commanded His people not to covet the silver and gold that their pagan neighbors made into idols. Rather, the Israelites were to burn the images of the Canaanites' false gods (Deut. 7:25). Job recognized that it was sinful to put one's trust in gold and to look to wealth for security. He knew that it was wrong to take more delight in his riches than in the Lord. Job acknowledged that it was abominable to give homage to the sun in its radiance and the moon in its splendor, rather than God (Job 31:24–28).

David spoke against trusting in extortion, taking pride in stolen goods, and becoming inordinately enamored with one's vast riches (Ps. 62:10). Solomon warned the upright not to lust after the beauty of a prostitute, for doing so would only bring anguish and ruin (Prov. 6:25). Furthermore, God announced that disaster awaited those who coveted and seized the fields and houses of others. Moreover, He declared that calamity would greet those who defrauded their neighbors' of their homes and inheritances (Mich. 2:2–3).

The New Testament likewise speaks out against coveting. In the parable of the rich fool, Christ declared that it was senseless to store up things for oneself on earth, but to be poor in the things of God (Luke 12:13–21). Rather than worry about obtaining the things of this world, believers were to put their trust in the Lord and give their hearts in service to Him (vss. 22–34). In Romans 7:7, Paul upheld the validity of the Mosaic law by stressing that God used it to make people aware of their covetous tendencies. In Ephesians 5:3–5, the apostle urged his readers to abandon all forms of sexual immorality, impurity, and greed, for those characterized by these vices had no inheritance in the eternal kingdom of God.

In 1 Timothy 6:3–10, Paul said there were some at Ephesus who taught things that were contrary to the gospel. For example, they thought that being godly was a way of getting rich. (It is possible that the false teachers, out of greed, sought leadership positions in the church.) Paul told the Christians at Ephesus to have no associations with such individuals. Paul did not deny the benefit of being godly, that is, pursuing a life of holiness and abiding reverence for the Lord. When godliness was joined with contentment there was great reward. The benefit, however, was spiritual, not material, in nature. Those who served the Lord faithfully and remained satisfied with what He provided were eternally blessed. This was the best perspective to have on life, for all people come into the world empty-handed and leave the world the same way. Thus it was senseless to devote one's life to accumulating material wealth, for it had no eternal value or relevance (cf. Matt. 6:19–21).

Finally, in Hebrews 13:5 and 6, the writer exhorted God's people to keep their lives free from the love of money and to be content with what they had. They could do so, for they knew that the Lord would never abandon them and would watch over them. However, if believers gave in to their licentious desires, it would lead to quarrels and fights among themselves. Such disputes, in turn, would weaken and divide the body of Christ (Jas. 4:1–2).

With respect to the entire body of the Decalogue, Farrar summed up the various commandments as "expressing the threefold duty of holiness towards God; self-control as regards ourselves; [and] justice towards our neighbours."[346] In a similar vein, as Brown reflected on the enduring relevance of the Decalogue for believers today, he cited four key points.[347] First, the Ten Commandments "teach us that spiritual obedience must have priority over *self*." Second, we learn that "social compassion must transcend the personal lust for *power*." Third, we see that "moral values are more important than *sexual satisfaction*." Fourth, we come to understand that "eternal realities are more satisfying than *things*."

Conclusion

In this chapter, a content analysis of the Decalogue was conducted. The historical prologue was overviewed first and then the stipulations God wanted the Israelites to follow were examined. The first four of these commandments pertained to one's obligations toward God, while the last six concerned to one's obligations to fellow human beings. A brief discussion was also provided to show how the Ten Commandments are reflected elsewhere in the Old and New Testaments.

The information obtained from the content analysis of the Decalogue will be useful when the structural analysis and the content analysis of the Sermon on the Mount are conducted. The findings of the research in the present chapter will also have a bearing on the conclusions reached in this study regarding the extent to which the moral law has continuing relevance as a rule or guide of life for the Christian church today.

Chapter 5

An Overview of the Sermon on the Mount

In this chapter an overview of the Sermon on the Mount will be conducted. This will involve surveying the content of Jesus' discourse, examining its structure, and analyzing in detail the best way to interpret and apply the Sermon on the Mount. It is important for these matters to be discussed, for the conclusions obtained will have a direct bearing on the content analysis of the Sermon. The issues dealt with in this chapter will also be useful as the relationship between the Decalogue and Jesus' Sermon is examined. Furthermore, the analysis to be conducted will help determine how the relationship between these two great passages of Scripture affects the extent to which the moral law has continuing relevance for Christian living today.

Content Survey

For some, the Sermon on the Mount is a "political allegory of the Law" that "provokes the reader to compare the claims that are made about the Law to the world of history."[1] For others Jesus' discourse embodies His expectations for those who would follow Him as His disciples. It is said to be a "code of conduct" or "rules to govern the way of life of the community."[2] Some even maintain that the Sermon represents the most concentrated teaching Christ gave in clarifying the meaning of the law.[3] In fact, Jesus' discourse is said to occupy in the New Testament the same place that the Decalogue occupied in the Old Testament.[4] Expressed differently, the Sermon is for the New Covenant what the Decalogue was for the Old Covenant.

Furthermore, just as the Ten Commandments were the moral law of the Old Testament, so too the Sermon is said to be the moral law of the kingdom of God. Kang offers this explanation: "As Moses proclaimed the law for the new life in the promised land, so Jesus manifested his law for the life in the Kingdom of Heaven. As Moses had blessed the twelve tribes of Israel, before they entered the promised land, so Jesus announced the future blessings which would be awarded to his disciples in the coming theocracy."[5] Others similarly consider the Sermon on the Mount to be Jesus' classic statement of the ethics of the divine kingdom.[6] This position highlights the bearing that the Sermon on the Mount has on Christian morality.[7] Some even hold that the Sermon embodies "missionary ethics" and that its injunctions "show the disciples how they are to act in the world so that by their extraordinary living men are attracted to the saving message of Jesus."[8]

Such lofty views of the Sermon on the Mount are a tribute to its beauty and power. Phillips, reflecting this sentiment, observed that "even the greatest of the world's moral, religious, and philosophical statements blush and stammer in the presence of this sublime declaration."[9] This high regard for Jesus' discourse is likewise reflected in the wide variety of designations it has received. For instance, the Sermon has been called the Christian Magna Charta, the Christian Manifesto, the Design of Life, or the Compendium of Rules for Christian Living.

There are several ways of analyzing the Sermon on the Mount. A prevalent approach is to overview the content as a literary unit in order to discern the progress and flow of thought in Jesus' discourse.[10] That is the methodology adopted here. The rationale for this decision lies in the fact that some "approaches tend to atomize the Sermon on the Mount."[11] This extreme can be avoided by treating Jesus' Sermon both "as a block of material" and as "fundamentally a narrative text."[12]

We will begin our content survey with Jesus' ministry in Galilee, which provides the geographical context for His extended teaching.[13] Kupp observed that "almost every geographical move of Jesus to this point in the story has resulted from conflict with his opponents in Jerusalem."[14] By way of analogy, "Galilee, as a focus for Jesus' ministry, is the antithesis of Jerusalem, the focus of opposition to the Messiah."[15] Christ had been urging people to repent, for the "kingdom of heaven" (Matt. 4:17) had come near. This theme of God's reign is also "emphasized in the sermon itself (for instance, 5.10; 6.10)."[16] The phrase "kingdom of heaven," while found only in Matthew's Gospel, seems to be synonymous with the phrase "kingdom of God" used in the Gospels of Mark and Luke.[17] Because Matthew evidently wrote for a mostly Jewish audience, some think he followed a typical Jewish reluctance about mentioning God's name.[18]

Another possibility is that Matthew was giving special emphasis to the transcendence and sovereignty as well as active lordship and rule of God both in heaven and on earth.[19] This view is reinforced by the usage of the Greek noun rendered "kingdom." It is βασιλεία (*basileía*) and refers to "the royal reign of God."[20] It would be incorrect to think of the kingdom simply as "referring to a particular area in which God rules."[21] Instead of the main focus being "a particular place or special period of time," it is more on "the fact of ruling."[22] Moreover, the "cosmic, universal, eschatological character" of the divine kingdom "in the teaching of Jesus" indicates that the kingdom "comes from beyond and is created by God himself."[23]

In Jesus' day, the concept of the kingdom was rooted in the Old Testament.[24] For instance, God's rule was eternal (Ps. 145:13) and universal (103:19), but it was only partially recognized on earth. In fact, all nations would not serve the Lord until the last days (Zech. 14:9). Jewish people prayed daily for the coming of God's reign. Also, when they prayed for His kingdom, they did not doubt that God presently reigned over His creation; yet they longed for the day when God would rule unchallenged and all peoples would acknowledge Him. Jesus' teachings about the kingdom show it was both present with Him on earth (Matt. 4:17) and also something that would be completely fulfilled at the end of the ages (13:24–30; 16:28). Jesus revealed that entrance into His kingdom is something that God gives to those who believe (25:34), but (paradoxically) it can cost a person everything he or she has (19:16–24).

Other portions of the New Testament describe God's kingdom as being heavenly (2 Tim. 4:18) and unshakable (Heb. 12:28). It is also inseparably linked to righteousness, peace, and joy (Rom. 14:17). Moreover, the divine kingdom is associated with suffering and patient endurance (Rev. 1:9), supernatural power (1 Cor. 4:20), promise (Jas. 2:5), glory (1 Thess. 2:12), and "the renewal of all things" (Matt. 19:28). God's kingdom is not the product of human striving or invention (John 18:36). It is given as a gift (Luke 12:32) and humbly received (Mark 10:15). The Lord brings His people into His kingdom (Col. 1:13), makes them worthy of it (2 Thess. 1:5), and preserves them for it (2 Tim. 4:18).

Perhaps more than anything else in the Savior's mind, the divine kingdom was a dynamic, eschatological concept.[25] The Lord declared what the kingdom would be like and that He also sovereignly established it.[26] The justice and righteousness of His kingdom is evident by His concern for the weak and oppressed (Matt. 5:3). He would reach out to the poor, hungry, and distressed with His unfailing covenantal love.[27] Benson likewise noted the eschatological aspect of Jesus' pronouncements.[28] However, he relegated the enjoyment of the blessings entirely to a future messianic age:[29]

> It is clear from the context and from all related passages that the blessings promised in Matthew 5:1–12 are not a present condition as if the saints had already inherited the kingdom; it is the prospect of conditions which pertain to the kingdom of the Messiah and which will be realized when that kingdom is introduced in history. Spiritual qualifications are present realities in this passage, but the blessings that accrue are reserved for the period of the kingdom's manifestation.

Benson's assertion seems too extreme and narrow to be supported by the teaching of Scripture. While it is true that the blessings mentioned in verses 3 through 12 find their ultimate fulfillment in the kingdom age, many aspects of them are now being enjoyed by believers. For example, Christ said the poor in spirit will one day inherit the kingdom of heaven (Matt. 5:3), while Paul declared that believers are already citizens of heaven (Phil. 3:20). Christ said God would one day comfort those who mourn over sin and evil (Matt. 5:4), while Paul revealed that God presently comforts believers in their distress (2 Cor. 1:3–7). Christ said the merciful would one day obtain mercy (Matt. 5:7), while Peter announced that God has already showered His mercy on believers (1 Pet. 2:10). Christ said the pure in heart would one day see God, while He assured His disciples that in seeing Him they had already "seen the Father" (John 14:9). Christ said that peacemakers will one day be called children of God (Matt. 5:9), while Paul declared that the Spirit bears witness with our spirit that we are already God's children (Rom. 8:16; cf. John 1:12).

In terms of Jesus' emerging Galilean ministry, He summoned four fishermen to be His disciples (Matt. 4:17–22). He followed this activity up by traveling throughout the region.[30] As He did, He taught in the Jewish synagogues, proclaimed the good news of the kingdom (namely, that it was at hand),[31] and healed people of their sickness and diseases (vs. 23). People living north of Galilee in Syria began to hear about what Jesus was doing, and they brought Him their sick to heal (vs. 24). Consequently, large crowds of people began to follow Him from Galilee, the Decapolis, Jerusalem, Judea, and the region east of the Jordan, namely, Perea (vs. 25).

The Greek noun rendered "good news" (εὐαγγέλιον, *euangélion*, vs. 23) is derived from the Greek verb εὐαγγελίζω (*euangelízō*), which means "to tell good news" or "to proclaim the gospel."[32] The noun, in turn, refers to the message of salvation heralded first by Jesus and then by His followers.[33] It is clarifying to note that the concept of "gospel" has Roman and Jewish roots.[34] Among Romans the word was used to describe good news about events in the emperor's life, such as his enthronement. These events were thought to affect the whole world.[35] Thus Matthew's use of *euangélion* shows that Jesus' ministry marked the beginning of a new era for the world. Jewish roots of the term are found in the Old Testament prophecy books, especially Isaiah (e.g., 40:9).[36] There the announcement of the future time of salvation is called "good tidings" and is set against a backdrop of joy.[37] Consequently, Matthew's Jewish readers knew that the era Jesus ushered in was the prophesied time of salvation.[38]

Matthew 5:1 notes that one day, as some crowds were gathering, Jesus walked up the side of a mountain and sat down, preparing to speak. In Christ's day, sitting was the standard teaching position of rabbis (cf. Matt. 23:2; 24:3; Mark 4:1; 9:35; Luke 4:20; 5:3; John 8:2).[39] Draper observed that the "solemnity of the Sermon on the Mount is emphatic: Jesus sits, waits for his disciples to come to him and then formally 'opens his mouth and teaches them' (5.2)."[40] Furthermore, while Jesus' took "the role of the scribes," it is clear from Matthew 7:29 that Christ was "greater than the scribes"[41] and deserved to be approached with reverence.[42]

A straightforward reading of Matthew 4:1–5:2a gives the impression that Jesus taught the Sermon on the Mount early in His public ministry.[43] Lenski, however, maintains that the Sermon "could not have been preached at the opening of Christ's ministry in Galilee."[44] Lenski argues that the Sermon's "entire contents, as well as the account of the circumstances connected with its delivery, point to the height of Christ's ministry at the time of the delivery."

Ridderbos disagrees with this assessment.[45] According to him, the discourse is a "specimen of Jesus' early teaching activity." Ridderbos notes that the Sermon is not "yet dominated by the conviction that the people do not want to repent."[46] There is also the "absence of parables." Furthermore, "Jesus' revelation of *Himself*"[47] is "still veiled" in the content of His discourse. Whatever He does say regarding His person and work seems "almost unintentional and merely incidental" in nature. Ridderbos additionally maintains that "the very wealth of material" found in the Sermon "displays, so to speak, the full force and vigor of an initial takeoff." When all the evidence is weighed, I tend to agree with Ridderbos that the Sermon "can be regarded as the culmination of Jesus' early preaching."

In terms of the main discussion, a direct reading of 5:1–7:29 suggests that Jesus gave His discourse at one time in one location,[48] namely, on the side of a mountain northwest of Capernaum.[49] Be that as it may, the exact location where Jesus taught His Sermon remains uncertain. The Greek noun rendered "mountain" (ὄρος, *óros*; 5:1) can also refer to a hill, mountainside, or mountain range.[50] According to 4:12, the Savior had been ministering in Capernaum.[51] Because of this, some think the mountain could have been located at the northwest corner of the Sea of Galilee near Capernaum.[52] The Horns of Hattim seven miles west of Tiberias was the older suggested location for the mountain. The more popular site now is the slope up from the Sea of Galilee southwest of Capernaum.[53]

There are differing explanations for why the sermon in Matthew was delivered "up the mountain" (5:1) and the sermon in Luke was delivered "on a level place" (6:17). Some think both expressions denote the same spot approached from different directions.[54] Others, however, think the phrase "up the mountain" (Matt. 5:1) means "up in the hills," while the phrase "on a level place" (Luke 6:17) refers to some kind of plateau.[55] Regardless of which view is taken, it is clear that there are literary and thematic parallels between the Matthean and Lukan accounts. For example, both Sermons begin with the Beatitudes and end with the lesson of the builders.[56]

There are several possible reasons why Jesus may have chosen to proclaim His Sermon on a mountain. His voice would have carried well there, He would have gained the effect of withdrawal from everyday surroundings, and He could have offered a parallel to the giving of the law on Sinai.[57] Just as in the preamble to the Decalogue the Lord presented Himself to Israel as their Redeemer (Exod. 20:1–2), so in the prologue to Jesus' Sermon He presented Himself to Israel as their Messiah (Matt. 5:1–2a).[58] Also, as Moses received the old covenant on a mountain (cf. Exod. 24:12), so Jesus expounded on the nature of the new covenant from a mountainside.[59]

Dumbrell postulates that the setting could be "consistent with a covenant renewal situation."[60] In this case, the "disciples, collectively, function at this point analogously to the way in which Old Testament prophets did."[61] The idea of a "covenant recall of Israel" is supported by the fact that John the Baptist's "message had clear covenantal connections" and that "Jesus' message at the outset is identical with John's."[62] While the "points of parallelism with Sinai are not to be overpressed," they "clearly cannot be ignored."[63] Kline carries the discussion further when he maintains that this sort of typological imagery helps to spotlight Jesus as the One who mediates and ratifies the new covenant.[64] In fact, Christ "is presented not as a new Moses but as one who utterly transcends Moses," especially as the "Lord of the Covenant."[65]

This truth implies that Jesus is "the teacher par excellence," who far exceeded and transcended Israel's "great lawgiver" and deliverer.[66] Moreover, what He taught is Torah,[67] especially when it is recognized that *tôrâ* can mean "instruction."[68] Such an inference is reinforced by the fact that the introduction (5:1–2a) and conclusion (7:28–29) of Jesus' discourse "cast the sermon in a didactic framework" and construe it as "having a didactic function."[69] Kang makes the following pertinent observation:[70] "The hesitation of direct application of the role of Moses to Jesus seems due to Matthew's concern that any explicit Mosaic designation of Jesus is against his Christological view that Jesus is more than Moses." Kang similarly notes later that, for "Matthew, Jesus is greater than Moses. He is the Messiah and the Son of God."[71] Kang surmises that "in the prologue Matthew deliberately, but implicitly refers to Mount Sinai and Moses in order to allude to the divine authority of Jesus and the legitimacy of his words in the Sermon."[72]

The exact relation between the Sermon on the Mount recorded in Matthew and the Sermon on the Plain recorded in Luke 6:17–49 remains an unresolved issue.[73] Only a portion of the first appears in the second, and thirty-four of the verses in Matthew's Sermon occur in different contexts in Luke.[74] Apparently Jesus repeated some of His weightier sayings in different forms, with varied application, to meet the need of the situation.[75] Observations such as these have led a number of scholars to argue that the Sermon on the Mount is a compilation of various teachings that were given on different occasions in several places.[76] According to this view, Luke presented an abbreviated version of the longer sermon recorded in Matthew.[77] Matthew either took a single sermon and expanded it with other relevant teachings of Christ, or he took numerous teachings of Jesus and weaved them into a coherent, thematically related unit.[78]

Those who say the Sermon on the Mount and the Sermon on the Plain are the same argue that the differences between the two discourses can be accounted for or harmonized.[79] It is also maintained that the healing of the centurion's servant shortly after the giving of the Sermon (Matt. 8:5–13; Luke 7:1–10) makes it more probable that the two discourses are one and the same.[80] Furthermore, it is asserted that the similarity of the beginnings, endings, and subject matter strengthens the impression that the two passages represent the same discourse.[81]

Those who hold the view that the Sermon on the Mount is a compilation of various teachings note that Matthew did not always follow strict chronological order in the arrangement of his material, and that his sequence of events often differs from Luke's.[82] For example, in Matthew's Gospel the healing of the man with leprosy is placed right after the Sermon on the Mount (8:1–4). However, in Luke the incident is placed well before the Sermon on the Plain (5:12–14).[83] In Luke's Gospel the call of Matthew, or Levi, appears well before the Sermon on the Plain (5:27–32). But in Matthew's Gospel the same incident appears well after the Sermon on the Mount (9:9–13).[84] According to the compilation view,[85] the Sermon recorded in Matthew contains so much concentrated material that it could not have been delivered at one time. Also, the wide range of topics addressed is said to be inconsistent with the idea that Jesus delivered a single discourse. Furthermore, it is claimed that certain sections in the Sermon[86] appear too abruptly.[87]

As it currently stands, there is little general agreement among scholars concerning the relationship between the Sermon on the Mount and the Sermon on the Plain.[88] Despite the differences of opinion on these issues, there are some broad conclusions that can be affirmed.[89] For example, an examination of Matthew 5:1–7:29 indicates that it is not a mere patchwork of isolated and unrelated sayings.[90] Rather, it "operates as a kind of anthology of some of Jesus' most basic teaching"[91] and reads as a finished composition.[92] The discourse contains related themes and a well-designed, discernible structure.[93]

Because of these facts, one should study the Sermon on the Mount as a complete literary unit.[94] Nutz made the following pertinent observation: "One should not underestimate the importance of the Sermon's unity. In unity with the Old Testament, Christ in the Sermon presents a unified picture of salvation and righteousness."[95] One should also consider the Sermon on the Mount to be an accurate and reliable account of what Jesus actually taught.[96] This remains true regardless of whether this discourse was given at one time or represents material He repeated numerous times under a variety of circumstances.[97]

Furthermore, amidst all the scholarly debate, Morris seems close to the mark when he notes that it would be typical for an itinerant preacher such as Jesus to make "repeated use of his material, often with minor or even major changes."[98] Most likely in His Sermon, Christ adapted "what he has used elsewhere to the situation now confronting him." Moreover, that "we find similar statements in other parts of the Gospels does not mean that Jesus did not use them on this occasion." In light of what has been said, we are wise to "be on our guard against thinking that it is Matthew's sermon rather than that of Jesus."[99]

Earlier remarks indicated that Matthew 5:1–2a is the prologue to Jesus' Sermon.[100] A straightforward reading of these verses leaves one with the initial impression that Christ spoke solely to His disciples.[101] In fact, Campbell asserted that Jesus limited His comments to His Jewish followers.[102] But 7:28 indicates that when the Savior finished speaking, "the crowds were astonished at his teaching."[103] This suggests that, although Christ primarily addressed His disciples, a larger crowd of people was listening to Him.[104] Another possibility is that "disciples" (5:1) is used in a broader context to refer to more than just the closest followers of Christ.[105]

If the sermon in Matthew and the sermon in Luke concern the same incident, Luke 6:17 would support the view that a large crowd of people listened to Jesus speak as He addressed His disciples.[106] The crowd included those from "all Judea, Jerusalem, and the coast of Tyre and Sidon." Verse 18 relates that the multitude had come to hear what Jesus had to say, as well as to be healed of their diseases and be cured of their evil spirits.[107] In fact, according to verse 19, "all in the crowd were trying to touch him, for power came out from him and healed all of them." This information generally corresponds with the description of Jesus' healing ministry appearing in Matthew 4:23–25. Both accounts indicate that Jesus' ministry of teaching and healing had wide appeal.[108]

It was previously noted that at the beginning of Christ's discourse, He went up on a mountainside, sat down, and began to teach His disciples important truths about God, humankind, and the way true believers are supposed to behave (5:1–2a). The prologue is followed by preliminary remarks concerning the joy, fulfillment, and responsibilities of those who follow Christ (vss. 2b–16). Jesus first described the unique spiritual joy and fulfillment that belongs to His disciples (5:2b–12). This is followed by comments regarding the role His disciples are to play in their world. They are to be a positive influence against evil and a witness for good in a sin-cursed world (vss. 13–16). These verses are characterized by ethical admonition.

Matthew 5:17–7:12 comprises the central section of Jesus' Sermon.[109] Lund noted that this material is adapted to distinguish Christian righteousness from the righteousness of legalists (cf. 5:20) and the righteousness of the Gentiles (cf. vss. 46–47).[110] This suggests that the central section of Jesus' Sermon concerns God's moral law and the nature of its absolute requirements. The appearance of the phrase "the Law or the Prophets" in 5:17 and the phrase "the Law and the Prophets" in 7:12 substantiates this observation.[111] These similarly worded phrases bracket off this entire body of material from the rest of the Sermon.[112] This forms an inclusio[113] and shows that Jesus was relating His teaching and redemptive work to the Hebrew Scriptures, especially the Mosaic law.[114] Jesus focused both on specific injunctions and on issues "comprehending the total conduct of man in relation to God and to his fellow man."[115] Kang, in his research, additionally maintains that "the author of the Sermon not only followed the deuteronomic tradition, but also took Deuteronomy as the model for his Sermon."[116]

In terms of the material appearing in the nexus of Jesus' discourse, Matthew 5:21–6:4 and 7:1–6 primarily concern the disciples' relationship with other people, while 6:5–34 and 7:7–12 mainly deal with their relationship with God.[117] Ethical admonitions appear in 5:17–20 and 6:1–7:12, whereas contrasts between Jesus' teaching and the legalistic traditions of others appear in 5:21–48. In verses 17 through 20, Jesus declared that He had not come to abolish what was taught in the Hebrew Scriptures, but to fulfill these sacred writings. Here we find Christ affirming the abiding validity of the law, clarifying His relationship to the law,[118] and asserting His "unparalleled authority"[119] with respect to the law. Then, in verses 21 through 48, Jesus properly interpreted the law, especially "the commandments of the Decalogue."[120] The literary unity of this section is evident by the recurring antithesis formula "You have heard it said...But I tell you..." (vss. 21, 22, 27, 28, 31, 32, 33, 34, 38, 39, 43, 44).

Betz maintains that there is "nothing extraordinary about these frequent self-references, for they merely conform to Jesus' role as a teacher."[121] While it is true that these statements "express Jesus' self-consciousness as a teacher,"[122] Betz seems off the mark in asserting that "Jesus' authority for doing this" was not "based on a special commission as messiah."[123] An examination of what He said, both in the Sermon on the Mount as well as in the entire Gospel of Matthew,[124] indicates that Jesus' messianic commission, assertions, and self-identity were at the heart of His authority to express disagreement with "a prerabbinic Judaism, characteristic of which is the opposition of Sadducees and Pharisees."[125] Furthermore, the Gospel of Matthew as a whole attributes "an exalted station to Jesus and an authority that is specifically divine."[126]

With respect to 5:21–48, Christ focused on specific aspects of the law that some religious leaders had misunderstood and misinterpreted and that needed to be clarified. As the content analysis of the Sermon in chapter 6 shows, much of the material in this section has thematic links with the Decalogue. In particular, Jesus explained the true nature of: committing murder (vss. 21–26), committing adultery (vss. 27–30), marrying and divorcing (vss. 31–32), taking oaths (vss. 33–37), seeking revenge (vss. 38–42), and showing love (vss. 43–48).

The Savior's proper application of the law is dealt with in Matthew 6:1–7:12. The literary unity of this section is evident by the fact that it is filled with the following recurring phrases shows: "Be careful not to..." (6:1); "And when you pray, do not..." (vs. 5); "When you fast, do not..." (vs. 16); "Do not store up...but store up..." (vss. 19, 20); "do not worry about..." (vs. 25); "Do not judge..." (7:1); "Ask...seek...knock..." (vs. 7). Jesus was dealing with specific aspects of the law that some religious leaders had misapplied and that needed to be handled correctly. Christ explained the true nature of: giving to the needy (6:1–4), praying appropriately (vss. 5–15), fasting with the right attitude (vss. 16–18), shunning greed (vss. 19–24), forsaking worry (vss. 25–34), ceasing to judge others (7:1–6), and praying persistently (vss. 7–12).

In 7:13–27, Jesus explained the direction, lifestyle, and spiritual foundation of His disciples. They follow the path that leads into the kingdom of heaven (vss. 13–14). The genuineness of their conversion and commitment to Christ is revealed by what they think, say, and do (vss. 15–23).[127] Also, their lives are founded on the Savior, His teaching, and His redeeming work, not on themselves or others (vss. 24–27). Verses 13–23 are characterized by ethical admonitions, whereas verses 24–27 are presented in the form of a short parable.[128] Verses 28 and 29 form the epilogue of Jesus' Sermon. One learns that the crowds were amazed at the authority with which the Messiah taught. This should not be surprising, for Christ's Sermon is an exquisite example of His teaching, which He delivered in His authority as the Son of God.[129]

Structural Overview

Luz noted that in "its structure, the Sermon on the Mount itself is a literary work of art."[130] Yet, oddly enough, while scholars have suggested many differing ways to understand the structure of Jesus' discourse,[131] there is lack of agreement among these proposals.[132] If one were to survey the best scholarly treatments on the Sermon, it would be discovered that each one presents its own unique way of outlining this passage of Scripture.[133] It is not the intent of this study to examine every view in detail.[134] In accordance with the nature and extent of this work, only five schemes will be summarized here. This information is drawn primarily from Carter's overview.[135]

First, some think the Beatitudes of Matthew 5:3–10 provide the organizing structure for Jesus' discourse. While this is an interesting theory, a number of scholars have rejected it because it seems to ignore the more obvious subdivisions of the Sermon. This approach also seems to obliterate the unity of various literary sections evident within the text. Furthermore, this hypothesis obscures, rather than clarifies, the overall development of the themes in the Sermon. Moreover, this approach lacks specific verbal clues and repetitions in the text that would guide one to the supposed connections in the Beatitudes.

Second, some think the Lord's Prayer provides the basis for understanding the structure of the Sermon.[136] This proposal helps to emphasize the key role that the Lord's Prayer serves in Jesus' discourse. However, this theory suffers from some of the same weaknesses as the previous one.[137] For instance, it does not adequately explain the arrangement of material in the Sermon. It also does not sufficiently elucidate the thematic development of certain portions of the text.[138]

Third, some have proposed that the Sermon reflects a situation in which a Jewish Christian community had recently split from a synagogue and was now establishing its own identity. Supposedly, this incident shaped the overall structure of Jesus' discourse. The problem with this theory is that it is based entirely on conjecture. There is no way of knowing with any measure of certainty whether such an incident stood behind the Sermon, and the hypothesis is not supported by the biblical text. In fact, to adopt this view one would have to reject the clear testimony of Matthew 5:1 and 2a.

Fourth, some have tried to organize the Sermon around various theological ideas, such as the kingdom of heaven or righteousness.[139] The strength of such an approach is that it spotlights important doctrinal concepts evident in Jesus' discourse. The weakness with this view is that no two scholars seem to agree on the theological ideas around which to organize the Sermon. Another weakness is that this theory tends to be rather subjective. Certain concepts or phrases are given too much prominence, while other equally important concepts or phrases are deemphasized or ignored altogether.

Fifth, some maintain that the Sermon follows a distinctive chiastic arrangement.[140] In this literary schema, the second half of the text corresponds to its first half in reverse, or inverse, order.[141] Likewise, each corresponding section has parallel content.[142] Chiasm, also known as ring-composition or inclusio, is more than an intriguing literary device.[143] As Klein, Blomberg, and Hubbard maintain, writers used it "to convey something about the meaning of the lines concerned."[144] The structural center, which lacks any parallel with other sections of the literary unit, is the climax, or crucial portion, of the text.[145] The two halves of the passage hinge, or turn on, this structural center.[146] In essence, the main point, or central thrust, of the passage may be found in the chiastic structural center.[147] The outlying frames of the text (namely, A/A', B/B', and so on) form the secondary emphases of the text. These frames, of course, are at the relative beginning and end of the text. Recognizing the presence of chiasm in a text can be helpful in properly interpreting it.[148]

Of the various proposals for the structure of the Sermon on the Mount, the view that the discourse is arranged as a chiasm has the most merit for three reasons.[149] First, this approach remains sensitive to the various literary sections evident within the text. Second, it clarifies, rather than obscures, the overall development of themes in the Sermon. Third, it bases its analysis and conclusions on verbal clues and repetitions in the material.[150]

Admittedly, it is possible to overstate the presence of chiasm in the Sermon. For instance, one might be so determined to find a chiastic arrangement everywhere in Jesus' discourse that the text is artificially rearranged and forced to fit within a preconceived scheme. The result is a contrived and distorted picture of what the Sermon is really saying. This problem can be avoided by not getting atomistic in one's chiastic analysis of the text. As Webb has observed, "Ultimately, one can only analyze carefully the text and ascertain structures that are revealed by it, exercising caution to avoid the imposition of what is only preferred."[151]

The following is my proposed outline of the macro-chiastic structure of the Sermon on the Mount:

A Prologue (5:1–2a)
B The joy, fulfillment, and responsibilities of Christ's followers (5:2b–16)
- i. Blessedness as a follower of Christ (5:2b–12)
- ii. Being salt and light in the world (5:13–16)

C The moral law of God and the nature of its absolute requirements (5:17–7:12)
- i. The moral law fulfilled by Christ (5:17–20)
- ii. The moral law properly interpreted by Christ (5:21–48)
    - a. Committing murder (5:21–26)
    - b. Committing adultery (5:27–30)
    - c. Marrying and divorcing (5:31–32)
    - d. Taking oaths (5:33–37)
    - e. Seeking revenge (5:38–42)
    - f. Showing love (5:43–48)
- iii. The moral law properly applied by Christ (6:1–7:12)
    - a. Giving to the needy (6:1–4)
    - b. Praying appropriately (6:5–15)
    - c. Fasting with the proper attitude (6:16–18)
    - d. Shunning greed (6:19–24)
    - e. Forsaking worry (6:25–34)
    - f. Ceasing to judge others (7:1–6)
    - g. Praying persistently (7:7–12)

B' The direction, lifestyle, and spiritual foundation of Christ's followers (7:13–27)
- i. The two ways (7:13–14)
- ii. The two fruits (7:15–23)
- iii. The two foundations (7:24–27)

A' Epilogue (7:28–29)

In light of what was said earlier, this literary arrangement indicates that the moral law of God and the nature of its absolute requirements are of central importance to understanding the overall thrust of the Sermon on the Mount. The outlying frames of text, which are in "antithetical correspondence,"[152] suggest that when the followers of Christ are rightly related to the moral law, their lives will be filled with joy, purpose, and eternal hope. The antithesis of this is that those who are improperly related to the moral law will experience sorrow, futility, and despair in their lives.

The main aspects of the literary structure advocated by Turner closely mirror what I have proposed.[153] For instance, he sees Matthew 5:1–2 as the introductory narrative framework and 7:28–29 as the concluding narrative framework of Jesus' discourse. He labels the Beatitudes recorded in 5:3–16 as the introduction and the material found in 7:13–27 as the conclusion of the Sermon. Finally, he considers 5:17–7:12 as the body of Jesus' discourse. Similarly, the broad contours of the chiastic structure that Wyse has proposed for the Sermon have some affinities to mine.[154] In particular, he sees Matthew 5:3–16, 5:17–7:12, and 7:13–27 as the three main sections of Jesus' discourse.[155] He also considers 4:23–5:2 and 7:28–8:1 to be literary transitions with the previous and following narratives, respectively.[156]

Lund offered the following as an alternate chiastic arrangement for Matthew 4:25–8:1:[157]

A Introduction: multitudes, mountain, teaching (4:25–5:2)
  B General observations on the nature and function of the church (5:2–17)
    C. The higher quality of Christian righteousness (5:17–7:12)
  B' General observations on the nature and function of the church (7:13–27)
A' Conclusion: teaching, mountain, multitudes (7:28–8:1)

While the verse divisions in Lund's proposal are slightly different from the one offered earlier, there are some significant similarities. First, both arrangements recognize the presence of a central body of material in the Sermon having to do with divine or moral law. Second, both arrangements recognize the presence of outlying frames of text that are parallel in thought and complementary to the central body of material. Third, both arrangements recognize the presence of introductory and concluding material. Lund's analysis, however, seems to go too far when he proposes further chiastic arrangements within the major breakdowns of the Sermon.[158] While I may not agree with every detail of his outline, it is clear from his analysis that chiasm is present in Jesus' discourse. Also, the overall chiastic arrangement and conclusions I mentioned earlier are supported by Lund's research.

Breck also advocates a chiastic arrangement for Jesus' Sermon,[159] and favors the research of G. Bornkamm and J. D. Kingsbury, especially the latter.[160] In this approach, "the Lord's Prayer (6:9–13) constitutes the conceptual center of the Sermon."[161] The passage is delineated as follows:[162]

[5:1–2 and 7:28–8:1 frame the major sections]

A (5:3–16): Introduction: On Those who Practice the Greater Righteousness.
B (5:17–48): On Practicing the Greater Righteousness Toward the Neighbor.
C (6:1–18): On Practicing the Greater Righteousness Before God.
B' (6:19–7:12): On Practicing the Greater Righteousness in Other Areas of Life.
A' (7:13–27): Conclusion: Injunctions on Practicing the Greater Righteousness.

In analyzing Breck's approach, I would agree that "the disciple's practice of righteousness" being "greater than that manifested by those who profess to abide by the Mosaic Law"[163] is an important theme in Jesus' Sermon;[164] however, I do not consider it the overarching emphasis of the passage. Likewise, while I think the Lord's Prayer is a noteworthy part of the Sermon, I would not regard it as being "at the very heart"[165] of the passage. In this regard, Draper noted that the evidence for the position advocated by Breck "is slim."[166] Wyse similarly notes that the Lord's Prayer is "an *excursus*, a further teaching on prayer."[167] For this reason, "it is not the central idea in the Sermon."[168]

Furthermore, rather than seeing 6:1–18 being the locus of the Sermon[169] and 6:19–7:12 comprising B', I consider all of 5:17–7:12 to be the nexus of the passage. Additionally, as I mentioned earlier, I regard the moral law of God and the nature of its absolute requirements to be the core focus around which the Sermon is structurally and conceptually arranged.[170] Moreover, I do not favor the separation of 5:1–2 and 7:28–29 from the rest of the passage. While Breck acknowledges their role in framing the Sermon, their inclusio-effect seems weakened in the way he has split them off. Furthermore, I would not include 8:1 with the Sermon; instead, I regard this verse as the beginning of the next narrative section in Matthew's Gospel.

Hernandez has offered a different approach to the Sermon on the Mount's chiastic arrangement. He has proposed "that the beatitudes form the major points of the discourse, and that the remaining section of the Sermon is an expansion of those major ideas."[171] This is said to be done "in reverse order in the verses which remain."[172] Hernandez's working theory is that Jesus' Sermon "contains primarily a conceptual chiasm."[173] This stands in contrast to my proposal that the passage's chiastic structure is literary in nature. The comments I made earlier about the Beatitudes also apply to Hernandez's approach. In particular, the Beatitudes do an inadequate job as an organizational plan for Jesus' Sermon of conveying its principal theological message.[174] Moreover, as Breck has noted, "debate continues over the very number of Beatitudes."[175] An additional layer of ambiguity surrounds whether "the Beatitudes serve as a sort of table of contents, in either direct or inverse order."[176]

In Draper's chiastic arrangement of Jesus' Sermon, he regards the concentric structure as hinging on the theme of "righteousness."[177] Draper's delineation of the chiasm is as follows:[178]

A Jesus calls the four disciples, Simon and Andrew, James and John, and begins his ministry of teaching and healing (4.12–25). When the crowds from the whole of Syria and Palestine begin to follow him, he takes the four apart up a mountain and speaks to them surrounded by the listening crowds (5.1–2).

B 5.3–10 Eight blessings for doing righteousness

C 5.11–16 Disciples warned to do good works

D 5.17–48 Greater righteousness needed to enter the kingdom

E 6.1–21 Righteousness not to be done for human judgment

F 6.22–34 Seek righteousness and his kingdom first

E' 7.1–5 Do not judge others

D' 7.6–14 Rules of entry and exclusion

C' 7.15–23 False prophets known by not doing good works

B' 7.24–27 Blessings and curses for doing/not doing Jesus' words

A' The crowds are amazed at teaching not like the scribes (7:28–29). Validation of authoritative teaching by three healing miracles (of a leper, a Gentile and a woman).

This approach is innovative in its attempt to propose a macrostructure for the Sermon that is detailed and substantive (in fact, significantly more so than the other ones mentioned). Be that as it may, I would not consider 4:12–25 as part of the "A" section. Moreover, I would not include any of the narrative material from 8:1ff in the "A'" section. Furthermore, despite Draper's contention that righteousness is the Sermon's overarching theme, the mention of it is strangely absent from most of the labels in his literary arrangement of the passage. This omission seems to weaken his position on this point.

These statements do not mean that Draper's work is without merit. On the contrary, he has surfaced and articulated relevant strands of information. For instance, his schema makes "the statement of 6.33 central to the purpose of the whole Sermon."[179] Also, he understands the injunction to "strive first for the kingdom of God and his righteousness" as a summons to "faithfulness to the Torah." In this way of thinking, then, the Mosaic law would be "the centrepoint of [Jesus'] teaching." Such an emphasis complements what I consider to be the foremost theme upon which Jesus' Sermon hinges, namely, the law of God and the nature of its absolute requirements.

A comparison of the chiastic structures overviewed indicates that there are some areas of agreement and some significant areas of disagreement among them. In fact, "no consensus has been reached as to [the] precise shape"[180] of the Sermon's chiastic arrangement. This observation underscores the subjectivity connected with this type of an approach to structural analysis. One might regard these different views as working hypotheses that are open to scrutiny and verification.

As with the other chiastic arrangements discussed, the one I favor recognizes the influence that Greek drama, Roman narrative poetry, and Hebrew literature have had on the way in which Jesus' Sermon is structured.[181] In each of these genres, "the climax falls near the center of the action."[182] The original recipients would not have considered such an approach as being odd and artificial. Rather, they would have found such a chiastic arrangement of the material conventional, easy to grasp and remember, and perhaps most of all authoritative.[183]

Before ending this section, I want to discuss three more proposals concerning the literary structure of Jesus' Sermon that are highly suggestive. First, Guelich recognizes a threefold demarcation to the passage that has some affinities with the chiastic structure I favor,[184] although his verse divisions differ somewhat from what I have proposed. He wrote that "the basic division of the Sermon tradition into the Beatitudes (5:3–12, par. Luke 6:20–23), Admonitions (5:21–7:12, par. Luke 6:27–42; cf. 43–45), and Warnings (7:13–27, par. Luke 6:[43–45] 46–49) still obtains for Matthew's Sermon." Based on these and other observations, Guelich proposed the following outline for the Sermon:[185] the blessings of the kingdom (Matt. 5:3–16); the greater righteousness (5:17–7:12); and the alternatives (7:13–27).

Second, Betz proposes a fourfold breakdown of the Sermon:[186] Matthew 5:3–16, exordium: the premises; 5:17–7:12, main part: the way of life (cf. 7:14); 7:13–23, eschatological warnings; and 7:24–26, peroration: a double parable describing success and failure. The commonality of this structural arrangement with some of the others mentioned earlier is that it recognizes 5:17–7:12 as the central portion of Jesus' discourse,[187] and thus the foremost literary section of the entire text.

Third, Kang maintains that there is a “structural similarity” between the “covenant features in Deuteronomy and the Sermon.”[188] He demarcates these correspondences as follows:[189]

	Deuteronomy	The Sermon *Matthew*
Preamble	1:1–5	5:1–2
Historical Prologue	1:6–4:49	5:3–20
The basic stipulations	5:1–11:32	5:21–48
The specific stipulations	12:1–26:19	6:1–7:11
Blessings and curses	28:1–68; 33:1–29	(5:3–12; cf. Lk. 6:24–26), 7:13–27
Recapitulation	29:1–30:20	7:12–29

This arrangement of the Sermon’s literary structure is innovative and suggestive. For instance, Kang thinks that “the author of the Sermon” deliberately molded it to “the deuteronomic setting” so that “the readers may understand the meaning of the Sermon in terms of the renewal of the covenant relationship at dawn of the Kingdom of God.”[190] The general contours of this hypothesis mesh somewhat with the notion that the Sermon is concerned with the moral law of God,[191] the nature of its absolute requirements, and especially “obedience to the commandments.”[192]

Nevertheless, I remain averse to the idea that Matthew operated as a redactor who edited and revised his source material to create Jesus’ Sermon.[193] Also, while I think the disciples’ fidelity to the covenant is a key emphasis in the Sermon,[194] I am unconvinced that it “contains all the covenant features in Deuteronomy.”[195] In particular, I would not regard the Beatitudes as the Sermon’s historical prologue. I also am not persuaded that Matthew 5:21–48 should be labeled as basic stipulations of the covenant and 6:1–7:11 as specific stipulations. Such distinctions seem too conjectural to be supported by the biblical data.[196] Furthermore, 7:13–27 hardly fits the notion of blessings and curses found in Deuteronomy.[197] Moreover, even Kang admits the presence of considerable variation in the way the respective material in Deuteronomy and Jesus’ Sermon is organized. In fact, Kang seems to undercut his main thesis when he states that “the author of the Sermon does not rigidly follow the deuteronomic structure, but arranges his material to fit each context of the Sermon.”[198]

Interpretation and Application of the Sermon on the Mount

Trites remarked that the "interpretation of the Sermon has been the subject of intense interest and debate through the years."[199] Moreover, a "glance at the history of interpretation reveals a kaleidoscopic variety of positions."[200] For example, scholars are divided in their views on the relationship Jesus had to the Mosaic law;[201] and at the heart of this debate is Jesus' opposing statements in Matthew 5:21–48. Luz, in his deliberation of the "meaning of the antithesis formula," states that the "main question is whether the antithesis refers to the Jewish-Pharisaic interpretation of the Old Testament—i.e., to the halakah—or to the Old Testament."[202] Moo advances the discourse by noting six primary views held by scholars.[203] Although there are other ways to organize the positions on the subject,[204] the analysis presented by Moo will be used here to frame the discussion that follows:[205]

1. Jesus abrogated the law, thus making it no longer binding on Christians.
2. Jesus' teaching is a new law that supersedes and replaces the Mosaic law.
3. Jesus radicalized the law, intensifying the demands of the law beyond what they originally intended. Some of the commands are annulled by this radicalization process.
4. Jesus intensified the requirements of the law and brought new demands of His own, without necessarily abrogating any moral commands.
5. Jesus' teaching fulfills the law in the sense that the law pointed forward to His teaching. His demands move in a different sphere, one that is above and apart from the law. In fact, the law only has continuing validity in and through Him.
6. Jesus is the greatest expositor of the law of God. He upholds the moral law, showing obedience to its commands and demonstrating its original intent by His teaching.

The first position is to be rejected, for it flatly contradicts what Christ said in Matthew 5:17.[206] Christ did not come to abolish, annul, or make the law invalid. Rather, His intent was to fulfill the law. There are various ways that Christ did this.[207] For example, He obeyed the law perfectly, doing all that it required. Also, He established and validated the law by His life, teaching, and redemptive work. Furthermore, He brought the law to full expression by showing forth its true meaning.[208] Moreover, He filled the law to its fullest possible measure by bringing all that the law stood for to its final conclusion.[209]

These observations imply that the second view is also incorrect, for it creates a false dichotomy between Christ and the law. The Savior was not teaching a new law that superseded and replaced the old law. Furthermore,

He did not criticize, emend, or try to perfect the Mosaic law, which He allegedly regarded as being in some way inadequate and imperfect. Rather, Christ's main concern was to correct faulty notions about what constitutes the kind of righteousness that God accepts.[210] From what has been said, it is evident that Christ was not rejecting, modifying, rescinding, or replacing the old law with a new one.[211] Rather, He was questioning the wrongheaded interpretations of the law that some advanced.[212] Jesus labeled these views as works-based forms of righteousness.[213]

The six examples Jesus gave in verses 21–48 illustrate how some in His day had profoundly misunderstood the true intent of the law.[214] This implies that the contrasts He gave were not between Old Testament law and His teaching, but between His teaching and legalism.[215] He set aside incorrect interpretations of the law, replacing them with what the Torah had always said.[216] This truth is especially manifest in the provocative formula Jesus used to introduce the six antitheses: "You have heard it was said... But I say to you."[217] The latter part of the expression "marked Jesus as the lawful and true expositor of the Torah."[218] Jesus distinguished Himself from the religious experts with their "casuistic distortions" by going "back to the original meaning of the Torah, to the will of God."[219] In this way Jesus "brings the Torah's demands to bear once more."[220]

The preceding comments indicate that Jesus was not radicalizing the law (the third view previously mentioned). Put another way, He did not intensify the demands of the law beyond what they originally meant. Rather, He reiterated what the law had always taught, but which some had obscured by their incorrect interpretations.[221] The fourth view is also incorrect, for it depicts Christ going beyond the stipulations of the law by intensifying old requirements and bringing new demands of His own. In reality, He enunciated and explained what the law had previously revealed.[222] His intent was to contrast the righteousness that was to be characteristic of believers with the hypocritical goodness displayed by legalists.[223]

There seems to be both truth and error in the fifth view. It is correct to say that the law finds its goal in Christ.[224] It is also valid to maintain that He is the One through whom the law finds its continuity and significance.[225] But it would be incorrect to portray Jesus as operating in a different sphere from the law, namely, one that is above and apart from it. Christ and the law both operate in the same realm, teach the same truths, and advocate the same ethics. In light of what has been said, only the sixth view accords best with the truth of Scripture. As the greatest expositor of God's law, Christ upheld it in His life and ministry. He perfectly obeyed the law's commands and demonstrated its original intent in His teaching.[226]

In terms of what Christ declared in His Sermon, even a casual reading of the biblical text reveals that His call to moral and ethical living is quite high. To what extent should one literally interpret and apply Christ's teaching? Scholars are divided on this issue.[227] The reason for this disagreement is that there tends to be a large gap between what Jesus expects from His followers and what they can accomplish, even at their best.[228] Virtually all the approaches to interpreting and applying the Sermon are attempts to alleviate this tension.[229]

Beginning with the Anabaptist-Mennonite movement, this tradition favors a literal interpretation of the Sermon, and has attempted to apply its teachings verbatim to every area of the Christian life, whether political, social, business, or personal.[230] It is also maintained that the ethics of Jesus' discourse supersedes the ethics of the Old Testament.[231] Unlike many Calvinist theologians, who teach that Jesus abolished the ceremonial law and revealed the true intent of the moral law, Anabaptist-Mennonite scholars believe He elevated the moral law to a higher plane.[232] Also, whereas many Calvinist theologians would argue that God required the same standard of morals and ethics in both the Old and New Testament eras, Anabaptist-Mennonite scholars assert that His standard is higher in the New Testament than in the Old Testament.[233]

Anabaptists tend to think that the promises in which the Old Testament believers trusted were more carnal than spiritual in nature.[234] Supposedly, the legal codes enacted by Moses did not measure up to the standards of the kingdom, and that is why Jesus rejected these for a higher moral law.[235] Anabaptist-Mennonite scholars maintain that the New Testament law of love stands opposed to the use of force and the punishing of humans,[236] for these supposedly include an attitude of malice and revenge.[237] From this comes the prohibition against participating in war of any kind.[238]

In analyzing the Anabaptist-Mennonite position, the positive aspects of what is taught will be noted first. For example, it is admirable that those within this tradition take Jesus' discourse seriously. Also, it is commendable that they strive to apply the Sermon to every area of their lives. Furthermore, they are to be applauded for wanting to be thoroughly consistent in their beliefs and actions. Yet, despite the laudable aspects of the Anabaptist-Mennonite tradition, there are several problems that should be addressed. For example, it seems odd that God, who is unchanging in His character, would establish one set of moral commands in the Old Testament era and a different set of commands in the New Testament era. It is also peculiar that His new commands might contradict His old ones. One is left to wonder whether God's own concept of right and wrong was flawed and in need of improvement.

To get around this theological problem, some Anabaptist-Mennonite scholars have asserted that in Old Testament times God allowed His people to do what was against His will. For example, Hershberger maintained that when the Israelites willfully turned their backs against God, He directed their leaders to allow them to have their way, even though this was not His will.[239] This line of reasoning, however, does not solve the theological problem. In fact, it leaves one with the false impression that God is disingenuous, limited in power, or ambivalent. The better approach is to see no contradiction between the injunctions of the Old and New Testaments. They reflect the absolute and unchanging moral character of God (cf. Mal. 3:6; Heb. 13:8).

A superficial reading of the Sermon has lead Anabaptist-Mennonite scholars to conclude incorrectly that Jesus denounced the law and replaced it with a different, more lofty moral standard; but, as was noted earlier, Christ was censuring the misinterpretation and misapplication of the law by some religious leaders. Thus, the problem was not with Old Testament moral codes, but with those who twisted the meaning of them to their own advantage. In fact, Jesus upheld the abiding validity of the law when He declared, "Do not think that I have come to abolish the law or the prophets; I have come not to abolish but to fulfill" (Matt. 5:17). Here we see that Christ was not establishing a higher law of His own to discredit the injunctions contained in the Old Testament. Rather, He was declaring that the requirements of the Mosaic law were more demanding than what some experts taught. This interpretation fits the facts better than the explanation put forth by Anabaptist-Mennonite scholars.[240]

These academics are correct to note that God is characterized by love (cf. 1 John 4:7–8), but they are incorrect to overemphasize this aspect of His divine nature.[241] The same God who reaches out to the lost in compassion (cf. John 3:16) also punished the Israelites through war when they engaged in immorality and idolatry (cf. 2 Kings 17:7–23).[242] In fact, sin is a foremost cause of war. As Murray noted, if there were no sin, there would be no war.[243]

The same God who declared that vengeance belonged to Him (cf. Lev. 19:18; Deut. 32:35) also commanded the Israelites on occasion to go to war against His enemies (cf. Josh. 1:2–5; 2 Sam. 5:17–19). The transition between the Old and New Testaments has not changed this, for the Lord will one day wage war against His enemies in a final battle that precedes the Second Coming (cf. Rev. 19:11–16).[244] The witness of Scripture concerning the revealed character of God is that His love and justice cohere in the divine nature. When the love of God is so emphasized as to obscure the more stern dimensions of His justice and wrath, one is left with a merely sentimental and humanistic concept of love.[245]

Anabaptist-Mennonite scholars are correct when they say that believers should seek to promote peace and harmony, rather than physical violence (cf. Matt. 26:52–54; John 18:36). The Bible, however, neither condemns all war nor denies the reality of the presence of war. In fact, God has authorized human governments to maintain rule and order, including going to war, if necessary (cf. Rom. 13:4).[246]

In the New Testament, there is the combined affirmation of government's using force against wrongdoers and the lack of condemnation of those exercising such authority. This supports the overall biblical distinction between government and the private individual and how each can respond legitimately to evil. God holds governments responsible for restraining evil, protecting their citizens, and maintaining order. Governments not only are to protect their citizens from criminals, but also from criminal nations. The teachings of Christ regarding the virtues of nonresistance apply to individuals, not nations, police, or parents operating in their official capacities.[247]

Some early church leaders such as Augustine argued that war should be fought to ensure justice and reestablish peace.[248] This has been called the "just-war" theory, for it holds that under certain circumstances the Christian may participate in war for the sake of preserving justice. According to this view, some (but not all) wars are morally justifiable.[249] In this scheme of thinking, war should be placed under the direction of the nation's established and collective leadership.[250] Armies should not slaughter those not involved in the military conflict (for example, neutral civilians).[251] Likewise troops should neither mistreat innocent families nor loot and destroy their possessions.[252] Armies should respect the human worth and dignity of war prisoners. Moreover, the sick and the wounded should be medically treated.[253] Finally, all forms of cruelty should be minimized.[254]

The preceding analysis and critique of the Anabaptist-Mennonite position indicates that the Sermon on the Mount is antiretaliatory, not pacifistic. Put another way, though Jesus' discourse condemned militant activity, it did not laud a pacifistic attitude. That is why the Savior urged His followers to respond to evil with love, not revenge. But it would be incorrect to suppose that God's people do not have to protect their lives, the lives of their loved ones, and those of innocent people. To shirk such a responsibility would be a denial of the moral law Christ affirmed.[255]

In contrast with the Anabaptist-Mennonite position, there are others who fully apply the Sermon only to special classes of Christians (such as clergy).[256] For example, during the Middle Ages, the Roman Catholic church advocated that only those living within monasteries were held responsible for keeping the ethics of Jesus' Sermon. All others were bound only to observe the Ten Commandments. These clergy-laity distinctions, however, are artificial and contrived, without having any solid scriptural and theological support. Why would God hold some Christians to one moral standard (which is supposedly higher) and the rest to another standard (which is supposedly lower)? Also, why would He demand that certain groups of believers adhere to a stringent code of ethics, but permit the rest to follow a more lenient body of law?

With respect to the various literalist views concerning the Sermon on the Mount, it should be affirmed that they safeguard the moral seriousness of Jesus' discourse. Nevertheless, the shortcoming of an overly literalist approach is that by freezing the language of the Sermon, it deprives Christ of freedom of expression.[257] In a different vein, there are some groups who have viewed the Sermon as being either too legalistic, or as a provisional, temporary code, or as a heightening of the law of Moses with the intent of producing repentance.[258] Moreover, a few have dismissed the Sermon as being completely unrealistic in its demands on the believer.[259] The problem with these views is that they needlessly restrict the relevance of Jesus' Sermon or they distort the intent of what He said. While His discourse deals with matters pertaining to God's moral law, it is incorrect to label the Sermon as legalistic. Also, there is nothing in the discourse to suggest that it is a provisional, temporary code. Furthermore, the lofty and absolute nature of Christ's injunctions does not warrant it being capriciously ignored.

A humanistic interpretation would reject the relevancy and applicability of the Sermon for enlightened modern man.[260] Humanism would also discount completely the notion that a carpenter who lived two thousand years ago could give the final authoritative word on human relations.[261] The statements made in the first chapter regarding the inspiration and authority of Scripture can serve as a cogent response to the humanistic point of view.

In light of these remarks, the humanistic interpretation of the Sermon on the Mount should be rejected.[262] Scripture teaches that there is a supernatural realm which transcends the natural realm (cf. Deut. 4:39; Josh. 2:11; Dan. 2:28). The Bible is also clear about the sinful condition of the human race (cf. Rom. 3:10, 23). Furthermore, those who reject the notion of God are foolish for doing so (cf. 1:22–23). Thus, despite the assertions of atheistic humanism, Jesus is not someone to be bypassed, for no one else can save people from their sins (Acts 4:12). Also, those who truly love Him will heed His commandments (John 14:12). Furthermore, they will be like the wise builder who constructed his house on a solid foundation. In this case, it is the foundation of Christ, His saving work, and His teachings (Matt. 7:24–25). Consequently, despite the assertions of atheistic humanism, the Sermon on the Mount is entirely relevant and applicable for people today.

There are those who favor interpreting the demands of the Sermon in a symbolic, representative, or metaphorical sense. In the opinion of some, Jesus was not so much concerned with outward conduct as He was with one's inward disposition.[263] In the opinion of others, Christ intended the severity of the Sermon to compel His listeners to make a decision, either for or against God's demands in their lives.[264]

There seems to be a mixture of truth and error in both of these views. It is true that there are metaphorical elements in the Sermon.[265] For example, there are places in the discourse where Christ used hyperbole, or intentional exaggeration, to illustrate that the requirements of God's law are absolute (cf. 5:29–30).[266] There are also other figurative or poetic elements in Jesus' discourse that He used to communicate in a vivid and memorable way the truths He wanted to be taken seriously (cf. 5:13–16; 6:20; 7:6, 13–27).[267] The presence of these literary devices neither invalidates nor diminishes the force of what Jesus taught. The Savior proclaimed radical teachings that were meant to transform both the attitudes and actions of His people.[268] They thus have a clear-cut responsibility to implement Jesus' specific commands.[269] Consequently, it would be erroneous to conclude that Jesus was more concerned with a person's inward disposition than with his outward conduct.

Moreover, Jesus used a variety of literary devices to help His listeners understand their own inability to live as God desired. It is true that Christ wanted His audience to recognize their need for God, to repent, and to partake of His mercy and grace. It would be mistaken, however, to infer from this that the Sermon is only relevant for the unsaved.[270] Jesus' discourse serves as an abiding standard for all Christians.[271] For the unsaved of Christ's day (whether Jew or Gentile) and for all unsaved people today the Sermon is a detailed explanation of what it means to repent (cf. 3:2; 4:17).[272] The discourse also serves as an elaboration of the spirit of the law (5:17, 21, 22, 27, 28). For all believers, the Sermon is an in-depth revelation of the righteous standards of God that should be evident in their lives.[273]

Some interpreters who favor a non-literal interpretation and application of the Sermon argue that Jesus only intended His message to show how short of perfection people really are and, consequently, their need for God.[274] Others go further by saying that Christ fulfilled the demands of the Sermon for sinful people, for He knew that they could not live up to the ethical and moral demands He advocated.[275] Yet any view that needlessly tries to qualify or limit the application of Jesus' Sermon does the church a grave disservice.[276] It may be uncomfortable for people to consider Jesus' urgent and radical teachings, and they may want to dodge His moral responsibilities; however, they should not. Moreover, if Christ's injunctions seem humanly impossible to keep, that is because they are. Keener fittingly advocated that "modern interpreters must let Jesus' radical demands confront us with all the unnerving ferocity with which they would have struck their first hearers."[277] Clearly, to abide by what Jesus taught, one is forced to depend on the Spirit's presence, provisions, and power.[278] When viewed this way, the Sermon depicts what God desires to make of His people, if they will offer themselves to Him as living sacrifices.[279]

Luther put forward the idea that human activity may be divided into two spheres, the temporal and the spiritual.[280] Supposedly the Christian is obligated to keep the commands of the Sermon only in the spiritual realm. He is permitted to follow a different standard of interpretation in the temporal realm.[281] Luther's approach seems to make artificial distinctions between the temporal and spiritual dimensions of life, and these distinctions do not seem to be supported exegetically by the data in the Sermon on the Mount. Those advocating the view espoused by Luther effectively undercut the radical nature of Jesus' teaching and the necessity for the believer to heed what He said in every area of life, whether temporal or spiritual.

Some groups have projected the application and fulfillment of the Sermon to a future kingdom. For example, Albert Schweitzer[282] maintained that the ethical demands of Jesus' Sermon were too radical for all times.[283] Supposedly His teachings were an interim ethic (literally, *Interimsethik*) for the early Christians, who thought the end of the world would soon come.[284] Schweitzer primarily saw Jesus as an eschatological figure. Schweitzer thus coined the term "interim ethics" to emphasize that the rigorous requirements of Christ's discourse could only apply to the distressing times immediately preceding God's introduction of His kingdom. Since this event has not yet occurred, the Sermon presumably does not apply to our modern day.[285]

In terms of the weaknesses of this view, there is little merit to the notion that the ethical demands which Christ espoused are too extreme for any time other than the early church period.[286] In fact, the interim ethic position is based on an overly reductionistic, skewed, and biased view of the Sermon.[287] Furthermore, the exegetical and theological data obtained from an analysis of Jesus' discourse does not support Schweitzer's assertions. It is better to view the stringent requirements of Christ's sermon as having applicability to all periods of church history, whether early or modern.[288] What Jesus taught is valid not only in the disposition He intended to convey by His commandments, but also in the very precepts and injunctions themselves. On the one hand, Christ's declarations will awaken repentance in sinners. On the other hand, His teachings serve as a moral guide for the redeemed.[289]

A number of classical and revised dispensationalists have argued that the context of Jesus' discourse is His proclamation of the arrival of the kingdom (4:17, 23).[290] In this scheme of thinking the Sermon is not a statement of principles for the Christian church, for it was yet unrevealed.[292] Also, the

Sermon was not an evangelistic message for the unsaved.[292] Instead, Jesus' discourse was supposedly a delineation of the principles that would characterize the remnant of redeemed Jews living in a so-called earthly millennial kingdom announced by Christ.[293] Some people try to soften the harshness of this view by saying there are secondary, indirect applications of the Sermon for the New Testament believer.[294]

A major weakness of the preceding theory is that it creates an artificial separation between the people of God in various ages of human history. Such a view is at odds with the historic doctrinal position of the Christian church. Throughout the history of the church since the days of the apostles, it has been generally held that the redeemed of the Old Testament are part of the same household of faith as the redeemed of the New Testament (cf. Heb. 12:22–24). The classical and revised dispensational view also creates an artificial distinction between the moral codes the Lord expected His people to follow in various time periods. This differentiation is evident in the following statement made by Campbell:[295] "The Bible provides three complete and independent rules of life—one for the past age known as the Mosaic Law and crystallized in the Decalogue, one for the present age and found largely in the epistles, and one for the future age appearing in the Sermon on the Mount."

It is hard to find this threefold division supported by Scripture, and it leaves one with the impression that the classical and revised dispensational view is based on conjecture, not facts. Its proponents seem to have ignored the fact that the Book of Matthew was written for the benefit of all New Testament believers, not just God's people who will be living in a future kingdom age (regardless of the nature of that kingdom).[296] Furthermore, though Jesus directed His message to His original disciples, He also had in mind the evangelistic efforts of missionaries who would urge others to become His followers (cf. 10:5–15; 16:17–19; 28:18–20).[297] Thus, the observation that the New Testament church had not been revealed—while it may be true—does not support the claim that the body of Christ was not in view when Jesus gave His discourse.

In light of what has been said, an objection should be raised against the idea that the Sermon has only a secondary application to the church. Such a notion can leave the believer with the impression that he is not really responsible to heed Jesus' specific injunctions. Also, the importance and urgency of Jesus' statements are removed by such a view.[298] It thus seems best to understand the Sermon as applying to all believers, whether the followers of Christ's day or those of the whole church today.[299] Jesus' discourse is His instructions to His followers, telling them how to be godly in a fallen world.[300]

The classical and revised dispensationalist contention that the Sermon is not an evangelistic message for the unsaved is partly correct and partly erroneous. It is true that the major thrust of Jesus' discourse was directed toward His followers, namely, those who had trusted in Him and decided to follow Him (cf. Matt. 4:18–22; 5:1). It is also true that Christ primarily delineated the righteous standards of God by which the community of faith needed to live.[301] Nevertheless, as was noted earlier in the chapter, a portion of Jesus' original audience included crowds of unsaved people (cf. 7:28).[302] Some of His comments were undoubtedly made with them in mind (for example, 5:20, 22, 29, 30).[303] As Christ delivered His message, the Twelve evidently formed a circle immediately around Him. A large group of other disciples formed a second circle of listeners.[304] Beyond these were a large number of interested and inquisitive listeners.[305] Thus, some dispensationalists go too far when they assert that there are virtually no evangelistic threads present in Christ's Sermon.

Classical and revised dispensationalists are correct to point out that the kingdom of heaven is a prominent theme in the Sermon (cf. 5:3, 10, 19, 20; 6:10, 33; 7:21).[306] They distort the truth, however, when they claim that Jesus' discourse only concerns a so-called earthly messianic kingdom, for there are conditions referred to in the Sermon (by way of example, persecution, adultery, and divorce) that seem to be incompatible or out of harmony with conditions that will exist in a future kingdom age.[307]

To get around this last point, Campbell asserted the following:[308] "This discourse will be pertinent when during the Tribulation period the gospel of the kingdom, heralding the coming King, will again be preached." The problem with this line of reasoning is that it is based on conjecture, not solid exegetical analysis. There is nothing within the text of the Sermon to suggest that those passages dealing with such things as persecution, adultery, and divorce represent conditions specifically during a so-called seven year period of great tribulation immediately preceding the Second Coming. Thus, it is better to view the Sermon as providing guidance for regenerate persons (namely, Christians) living in an unregenerate world throughout church history.

Classical and revised dispensationalists overstate the case when they declare that the Sermon is solely concerned with law and that grace is absent from it. While it is true that the law is a prominent theme in Jesus' discourse (e.g. Matt. 5:17, 18, 25; 7:12), so is the grace and mercy of God (e.g. the promises Jesus made in the Beatitudes, 5:3–12). Furthermore, while believers are saved by grace, this does not mean they are free of all responsibility for the law. In fact, the New Testament contains references *both* to God's grace and the believer's obligation to obey His directives (e.g. Eph. 2:8–10; Titus 2:11–12).[309]

What will be advocated in this study is a moderating and balancing position in which the core truths of the previous views are retained and their excesses avoided. For example, it is acknowledged that Christ used hyperbole, that His discourse is primarily concerned with the inner disposition of one's heart, and that His commands set forth the pure will of God. Nevertheless, the interpreter should avoid emphasizing one aspect of the Sermon to the virtual exclusion of other equally important aspects. A proper interpretation of the Sermon will examine objectively all the relevant views and retain the best insights they have to offer.[310]

It therefore seems best to take the injunctions in the Sermon of the Mount at face value. Such literary conventions as poetry, ethical admonitions, and hyperbole should be recognized and handled accordingly.[311] They should neither be over-interpreted nor under-interpreted.[312] Rather, the ethical values being stressed through these literary conventions should be detected and fully embraced.[313] Because such moral virtues as self-control, integrity, honesty, kindness, and compassion transcend all time and cultures, it is best to see the Sermon as having direct applicability to God's people in all ages. Its ethical precepts are enduring in their relevance. Also, its truths are worthy of consideration and practice by God's people regardless of where or when they live.

Conclusion

In this chapter, an overview of the Sermon on the Mount has been presented. This entailed outlining the content of the Sermon in order to discern its progress and flow of thought. It was determined that Matthew 5:1 and 2a are the prologue of Jesus' Sermon, and that the prologue is followed by preliminary remarks concerning the joy, fulfillment, and responsibilities of those who follow Christ (vss. 2b–16). It was observed that: Matthew 5:17–7:12 comprises the central section of Jesus' Sermon; that 7:13–27 explains the direction, lifestyle, and spiritual foundation of Christ's followers; and that 7:28 and 29 are the epilogue for the discourse.

Of crucial importance was the decision that the Sermon follows a literary chiastic arrangement with the central section—Matthew 5:17–7:12—forming the pivotal portion of the text. This schema indicates that the law of God and the nature of its absolute requirements are of foremost importance to understanding the overall thrust of the Sermon on the Mount. The outlying frames of text indicate that when the followers of Christ are properly related to the law, their lives will be filled with joy, purpose, and eternal hope. The antithesis of this is that those who are improperly related to the law will experience sorrow, futility, and despair in their lives.

It was surmised that Jesus' teaching in the Sermon did not connote a rejection of the binding character of the Mosaic law. Also, He neither challenged nor replaced what was written in the Hebrew Scriptures. Rather, Jesus questioned the excessive legalism and distorted interpretations of the law advocated by some influential people. Moreover, it was concluded that it is best to understand the Sermon as applying to all believers, whether the followers of Jesus' day or those of the whole church today. The Sermon's moral precepts are timeless in their relevance, and its truths are worthy of consideration and practice by God's people in any time period. All these conclusions have a direct bearing on the content analysis of the Sermon on the Mount, as evidenced by the information appearing in the next chapter.

Chapter 6

A Content Analysis of the Sermon on the Mount

In this chapter a content analysis of the Sermon on the Mount will be conducted. The goal is to examine how the moral law of God and the nature of its absolute requirements are of central importance to understanding the overall thrust of the Sermon on the Mount. The information obtained from this chapter, along with the data found in chapters 2 through 5, will make it possible to answer the five key questions raised in the first chapter of this study. This, in turn, will enable us to come to a conclusion regarding the nature of the relationship between the Decalogue and the Sermon on the Mount and the bearing it has on the extent to which the moral law has continuing relevance for Christian living today.

Prologue (Matthew 5:1-2a)

The information in Matthew 4:17–25 suggests that Christ delivered the Sermon on the Mount late enough in His ministry for His fame to have spread.[1] However, it was too soon for some leaders within the religious community to have united in opposition against Him. During the first few months of Jesus' Galilean ministry, He preached in the synagogues (cf. Mark 1:21–28; Luke 4:16–30). But before long, rapidly growing crowds forced Him to move outdoors.[2]

At first Christ announced that the kingdom of heaven was at hand (Mark 4:17). But by the time He delivered His Sermon, He focused His attention more on the nature of the kingdom. He also taught His disciples (and undoubtedly all who would listen) how a citizen of God's kingdom was supposed to act.[3] This ethical and moral discourse is the first of five great blocks of Jesus' teaching in the Book of Matthew (the others being 9:35–10:42; 13:1–52; 17:24–18:35; and 23:1–25:46).[4] Based on the chiastic structure of Jesus' discourse adopted in the previous chapter, Matthew 5:1–2a is understood to be parallel in thought to 7:28–29. These two passages respectively form the prologue (or preface)[5] and epilogue (or conclusion) to the Sermon on the Mount.

The Joy, Fulfillment, and Responsibilities of Christ's Followers (Matthew 5:2b-16)

As was noted in the preceding chapter, Matthew 5:2b–16 is parallel in thought to 7:13–27. This means these outlying frames of the text form the secondary emphases of the Sermon. These passages suggest that when the followers of Christ submit to the moral law, their lives will be filled with joy, purpose, and eternal hope. The antithesis of this is that those who do not submit to the moral law will experience sorrow, futility, and despair in their lives. Moreover, with respect to 5:2b–12, Jesus described the unique spiritual joy and fulfillment that belongs to His disciples. Then, in verses 13–16, He clarified the role His disciples are to play in their world. In brief, they are to be a positive influence against evil and a witness for good in a sin-cursed world. An examination of verses 3–12 shows that there are repeated references and allusions to the commandments of the Decalogue.

Blessedness as a follower of Christ (Matthew 5:2b–12; Luke 6:20–23). After Jesus' followers and a larger crowd of people had assembled around Him, He began to teach them important moral and ethical truths (Matt. 5:2b). In His discourse, Christ revealed the holy standards of God's kingdom.[6] The conventional wisdom of Jesus' day taught that the wealthy and influential enjoyed more of God's blessings than anyone else. The Savior's radical teachings stressed that material things are only temporary and certainly not as important as being a godly person. Jesus also confronted the commonly accepted legalisms of the day,[7] for He spoke to the spirit of the law.[8] Moreover, Christ focused on people's motives and attitudes, not just their outward actions.[9]

Jesus began His Sermon in a poetic way by discussing what sorts of people receive what sorts of blessings from God.[10] The values that Jesus upheld belong to "life under God's Law and effectively set the parameters for its interpretation."[11] Some classical and revised dispensationalists have asserted that these blessings are obtained through merit.[12] Allegedly these blessings stand in sharp contrast to the spiritual benefits believers enjoy as a result of their exalted position in Christ.[13] This view, however, will not stand up under careful exegetical scrutiny. Jesus primarily directed His comments to His disciples (Matt. 5:1), that is, those who had made or would make a faith commitment to Him (cf. Matt. 6:15–19; John 6:68–69; 11:25–27).

Moreover, an analysis of Matthew 5:3–12 shows there is nothing explicit in these verses to suggest that God's people had to merit the blessings recorded in this passage. For example, passive forms of Greek verbs appear in several of the verses (cf. vs. 4—παρακληθήσονται: third person plural future passive indicative of παρακαλέω; vs. 6—χορτασθήσονται: third person plural future passive indicative of χορτάζω; vs. 7—ἐλεηθήσονται: third person plural future passive indicative of ελλεεω).[14] This observation suggests that believers would receive, not earn, these blessings from God. Furthermore, His bestowal of them is based solely on grace, not merit.[15] Consequently, the idea of merit has to be read into the text.

Strecker maintained an equally mistaken notion of the Beatitudes, namely, that they are conditions which must be fulfilled in order to gain entrance into the kingdom of God.[16] Also, according to Strecker, the ethical demands of the Matthean Jesus cannot be harmonized with the Pauline notion of justification by faith. There are two primary reasons why Strecker's view is to be rejected. First, he sets up a false dichotomy between the teachings of Jesus and the doctrines appearing in other portions of the New Testament. The Christ of Matthew 5:3–12 is the same One who is presented in the rest of the Sermon on the Mount, the Book of Matthew, and the entire New Testament. Second, Christ Himself declared that the new birth, not flawless moral rectitude, was the entrance requirement into the kingdom of God (John 3:3). This agrees with the Pauline doctrine that the Messiah vicariously fulfills God's righteousness requirement for humankind (Rom. 3:21–31).[17]

Thus, in Matthew 5:3–12, Jesus was not simply giving His followers imperatives He expected them to heed perfectly if they ever hoped to obtain admittance into the eschatological kingdom. More importantly, Christ was declaring the ethics of the kingdom and urging His followers[18] to let their inward motives and outward conduct reflect these moral principles.[19] Christ offered nine pronouncements of blessedness,[20] the last one being in a somewhat different form than the others. These nine declarations functioned in two ways. First, they established the ideology of the teaching that was to follow. Second, they poetically and formally introduced the entire Sermon.[21] In connection with the second point, Jesus' declarations of blessedness follow a consistent literary pattern.[22] There are two clauses, the first pronouncing blessedness upon a certain kind of person and the second giving the basis for such blessedness.[23] The details of the blessing or its promise are discernible from the pronouncement or the surrounding context.[24]

Christ's various declarations of blessedness are commonly called the "beatitudes." This term comes from the Latin word *beatus*,[25] which was used by the Vulgate in Romans 4:6 and 9.[26] The word originally referred to a state of utmost felicity or bliss. In church usage, however, "beatitude" became associated with Jesus' various declarations of blessedness (cf. Matt. 11:6; 13:16; 16:17; 24:46; Luke 7:23; 10:23; 11:28; 12:37, 38, 43; John 13:17; 20:29), especially those at the beginning of the Sermon on the Mount.[27]

With respect to Matthew 5:3–11, Jesus repeatedly used the Greek adjective μακάριοι (*makárioi*), which is the masculine plural form of μακάριος (*makários*). Some think the basic meaning is "honor" or "honorable."[28] While it is true that Jesus "revalues what has been disvalued" and "honors what has been shamed,"[29] it seems more likely that μακάριος means to be "free from daily cares and worries."[30] Such terms as "blessed," "fortunate," "happy," and "privileged" help to capture the sense of the term.[31] Though the consolation of the afflicted seems to form the backdrop for Jesus' remarks in His Sermon,[32] the ultimate focus is "the distinctive religious joy which accrues to man from his share in the salvation of the kingdom of God."[33]

Happiness—as the world conceives it—is a feeling often dependent on outward circumstances. The believers' state of blessedness, however, is not based on feelings, for it is a condition that God has ascribed to them based on their spiritual union with Christ.[34] Spicq, with this understanding in mind, notes that *makários* refers to "much more than contentment."[35] It is "an interior joy that becomes external." The reason for this is that "God will be the source of this beatitude." Furthermore, such "happiness is no longer attached to wealth, to having enough, to a good reputation, power, possession of the goods of the world." Instead, this joy is connected to "poverty alone." The people in this state are "essentially religious souls, in submission to God's law, obedient to his will." They consider Him "their only recourse and their only hope, and they are entirely ready to accept his gifts."[36]

Jesus applied *makários* to those who were devout citizens of "the kingdom of heaven" (Matt. 5:3). Those who are members of God's kingdom presently enjoy the blessings of His reign in their lives.[37] They experience a distinctive spiritual joy that the unsaved do not comprehend. Likewise, the saved display attitudes and actions that run counter to those advocated by the world.[38] For example, the unsaved tend to be selfish, insensitive, and bent on advancing their personal goals. The saved, however, are supposed to be sacrificial, sensitive, and concerned with the needs of others.[39]

There has been considerable scholarly debate over the exact number of Beatitudes appearing in the Sermon on the Mount, with the number ranging from seven to ten.[40] The discussion that follows will operate under the premise that there are nine Beatitudes,[41] which reflects the observation that *makárioi* appears at the beginning of each pronouncement in Matthew 5:3–11.[42] Some might object to labeling verse 11 as a separate Beatitude. After all, it does not follow the form and flow apparent in the first eight Beatitudes. Likewise, it merely seems to amplify what appears in verse 10. Nevertheless, like the other Beatitudes, the one appearing in verse 11 begins with the distinctive term *makárioi*.[43] Additionally, the equivalent of this saying is found as one of the four Beatitudes in Luke 6:22. For these reasons, Matthew 5:11 will be treated as a separate and ninth Beatitude. Verse 12, on the other hand, will not be regarded as a separate Beatitude, for *makárioi* is not used in it at all. Also, the verse is Christ's further explanation of matters introduced in 5:11 concerning persecution. Moreover, there is no break in the logic between verses 10 and 11.[44] Thus, it seems best to regard verse 12 as being part of the Beatitude introduced in verse 11.

In analyzing the Beatitudes, it would be incorrect to suppose that they describe nine different classes of believers. Rather, these pronouncements of blessedness denote nine distinct elements of virtue that should be simultaneously present in every Christian.[45] For example, the poor in spirit will also be meek, and the merciful are likely to be peacemakers. Those who hunger and thirst for righteousness will also be pure in heart, while those who are persecuted for the sake of righteousness are likely to experience the consolation of God when they mourn.[46]

There are various views regarding the structure of the Beatitudes.[47] Some think the first four pronouncements of blessedness are negative and passive, while the second four are positive and active. Others think the first four Beatitudes signify what is present in a person who desires salvation, while the second four epitomize what is present in the person who genuinely has salvation. Still others think the pronouncements of blessedness show the distinct stages of development in the spiritual growth of a Christian.

The problem with these views is that they tend to see nine different classes of believers being represented by the Beatitudes. However, as was noted earlier, it is best not to see these pronouncements as setting forth separate types of Christian character. Instead, the Beatitudes enumerate qualities and experiences that are combined in the ideal believer, and which were exemplified in Christ's own life and ministry. Worthy of brief mention is the view of Farrer, who maintained that the Beatitudes are modeled on the Decalogue of Exodus 20:1–17.[48] Despite possible weaknesses with this approach,[49] it does underscore the literary and thematic link the Beatitudes have with the Ten Commandments. The discussion to follow will also bear this out.

The *first beatitude* that Christ mentioned talks about being poor in spirit, a concept that has its thematic roots in Isaiah 61:1–3,[50] especially verse 1 with its emphasis on humility.[51] The Greek noun πνεῦμα (*pneúma*)[52] refers to the human spirit, not the divine Spirit.[53] With respect to being poor, Christ was not so much talking about the presence or absence of goods and possessions in one's life.[54] Rather, He was confronting the high self-estimation so prevalent in people like the legalists of His day. Some have supposed that the poor in spirit refers *only* to those who live in physical poverty, especially those who have chosen to be impoverished.[55] However, an objective examination of the biblical text[56] makes it clear that Jesus was referring primarily to spiritual poverty, not just to physical poverty or a vow of poverty.[57]

Most likely, then, Jesus was contrasting the righteousness of the legalists of His day with true righteousness. Legalistic righteousness made one excessively proud and duped him into thinking he had something good in himself to offer God. In contrast, the truly righteous is someone who has nothing to offer God, but turns to Him in faith for eternal deliverance (cf. Pss. 34:18; 51:7).[58] Such a person is humble and lowly,[59] as opposed to the legalists who were self-absorbed with their religious accomplishments.[60]

Christ's declaration about being poor in spirit implies that the citizens of the divine kingdom are not to be haughty and detached from other people.[61] According to James 4:7–10, genuine humility can be developed when believers obey and draw near to God, resist the devil, maintain moral purity and integrity, turn away from sin, and have an unassuming attitude before God. Furthermore, the poor in spirit describes believers who are genuinely unpretentious and recognize their need for God.[62] They understand the importance of the first commandment of the Decalogue, which teaches that their relationship with God is of foremost significance. It is only when people embrace their spiritual poverty that they can come to stand in a right relationship with the holy Lord.[63]

The humble followers of Christ are spiritually prosperous, for to them belongs God's kingdom (Matt. 5:3; cf. Isa. 57:15; Luke 6:20).[64] They do not receive the kingdom *because* they are poor in spirit. Rather, their inheritance of the kingdom is the *result* of their spiritual poverty.[65] God is not so much recompensing His people as He is allowing the consequence of their faith to bear its eternal fruit.[66] The person who is genuinely poor in spirit realizes his moral bankruptcy before God.[67] He has an overwhelming sense that he is destitute of any claim to righteousness.[68] He confesses that he has no merit of his own, but must rely on God's grace for salvation (cf. Isa. 66:2).[69] He also does not see his own goodness or wealth as a passport to heaven. Rather, he solely relies on the Lord, not himself, for redemption.[70] He can do this, for he knows that God shows mercy to those who genuinely love Him (cf. the parallel thought recorded in the second commandment of the Decalogue; Exod. 20:6; Deut. 5:10).

The *second beatitude* that Christ mentioned is mourning over one's own ethical depravity,[71] a notion that finds its conceptual roots in Isaiah 61:2.[72] This person is grieving over his sin and confessing his guilt to God.[73] He is aware of his disobedience and evil, the enormity of his rebellion against God, and the malignancy of his motives.[74] He recognizes that he has violated every commandment of the Decalogue, whether it is the prohibition against being idolatrous, or telling lies, or coveting what others have. Furthermore, those who mourn do so in the power of the Spirit. They are seeking God's forgiveness and blessing, and they desire to bring Him glory. They mourn not only because of their sin, but also because of its consequences. They do not look to the world for satisfaction, joy, or comfort. Rather, they find these things in God alone.[75]

The mourning referred to by Christ in Matthew 5:4 stands in sharp contrast to the thinking of the unsaved, who try to get and remain happy at any cost. The unregenerate do not realize how shallow and eternally empty life is apart from the Lord (cf. Eccles. 7:2–6).[76] In contrast to the unsaved people of the world, the citizens of God's kingdom find their spiritual satisfaction and joy in worshiping and serving the Lord. They have taken to heart the first commandment of the Decalogue, which forbids worshiping any other entity but God (Exod. 20:3). As the Lord's true children live for Him, they often experience sorrow from the presence of sin in their life and from being persecuted. Nevertheless, they find joy in their relationship with the Lord.

Such believers are the privileged recipients of God's favor, for He will comfort them (Matt. 5:4; cf. Isa. 61:1–2; Luke 6:21; 2 Cor. 1:4). They experience God's consolation when they confess their sins (cf. Ps. 51) and when they draw near to the Lord in their time of need (Heb. 4:14–16). The comfort promised by Jesus is the ultimate consolation and encouragement that only God can bring to those who grieve over their sin and helplessness. By trusting in Christ, they not only have the promise but also the assurance of God's comfort.[77]

The *third beatitude* that Christ mentioned is meekness or gentleness[78] and has its conceptual roots in Psalm 37:11.[79] The meek are individuals who stand empty-handed before God and are totally dependent upon Him for redemption.[80] With the Lord as their base of support and strength, they are able to bear patiently the insults and injuries others inflict on them.[81] They readily accept the instruction and admonition of others, for they think more highly of others than they do of themselves. Despite the provocations of others, they remain humble and calm, for they have given their destiny over to God.[82]

The world says that being aggressive and ruthless will win an individual authority and dominance over people and possessions. God, however, says that believers who remain calm and patient despite their circumstances are the heirs of the earth (Matt. 5:5; cf. Ps. 37:11). According to Psalm 35:5–11, these are people who completely trust in the Lord and place the punishment of the wicked in His hands.

The world often thinks of those who are meek as being deficient in zeal and courage.[83] This does not match the biblical conception, however.[84] From the Lord's perspective, meekness is an indication of strength, courage, and self-control.[85] The presence of meekness is also an indication that one has understood and embraced the fifth through tenth commandments of the Decalogue. After all, the person who is meek will strive to honor others, not dishonor them. He will seek to uphold the sanctity of marriage and to affirm the right of others to have and enjoy their own possessions. He will never testify falsely against others and he will not allow greed and selfishness to gain a foothold in his life.

There is scholarly debate over what Jesus was referring to when He talked about inheriting the earth (Matt. 5:5). Some of the options include the entire planet, the land of Israel, the kingdom of God, and the new earth associated with the eternal state.[86] When these views are considered, it seems best to conclude that Christ had an eschatological focus in mind.[87] In other words, He was talking about the ultimate fulfillment of God's promise to Abraham (cf. Gen. 12:1–3). In fact, Paul said the patriarch would "inherit the world" (Rom. 4:13). From this it is evident that the hope and promises to which the people of God look forward in faith are heavenly, not merely physical (cf. Heb. 11:16). Their inheritance will one day include the new heaven and new earth of Revelation 21:1 (cf. Isa. 65:17; 66:22; 2 Pet. 3:13).

Christ is the best example of what it means to be meek (cf. Matt. 11:28–30). As the most powerful person in the universe said, He was gentle, humble, caring, and sensitive. If Jesus was, so should be His people. Like the Savior, His followers neither press their own claims nor battle for their own interests.[88] Rather, they lean on God to work out His good and perfect will in their lives (cf. Rom. 12:1–2; Phil. 2:3–8).

With Christ's mention of the *fourth beatitude* it is possible to discern a "real progression" and close interconnection in these various states of blessedness.[89] For instance, the "one who is conscious of need is led to mourn this condition, come before God in a meek, teachable fashion, and then earnestly seek to have the spiritual vacuum filled by God himself."[90] In Matthew 5:6, Jesus referred to this deep yearning as hungering and thirsting for "righteousness." The Greek noun is δικαιοσύνην (*dikaiosýnē*), which may be defined as the "quality or characteristic of upright behavior."[91] In this verse, a general sense of uprightness is in mind, whereas in 5:20 and 6:1, righteousness manifested in specific actions is in view.[92] In both instances, conformity to "God's plan or what God has decided"[93] is the core idea being expressed. This notion is especially evident in 5:10, where *dikaiosýnē* refers to "the act of doing what God requires."[94]

The noun is also used to refer to "uprightness as determined by divine/legal standards."[95] For instance, the phrase "the righteousness of God" might be paraphrased "uprightness that meets God's ethical and moral standard."[96] Such rectitude stands in contrast to external legalism, which is merely a form of self-righteousness (cf. 5:20).[97] People of faith see themselves as being in covenant relationship with God and wanting to live in conformity to His will—as expressed in the Mosaic law and the teachings of Jesus.[98] This God-approved form of righteousness is the outflow of a "life that is centered on submitting to, worshiping, and seeking after God and confessing Jesus as the Messiah"[99] (cf. 5:17–42).

These remarks underscore how important the concept of righteousness is in Matthew's Gospel;[100] in fact, it "is central to his message."[101] Moreover, for Jesus in the Sermon on the Mount, *dikaiosýnē* seems to have a dual emphasis. On the one hand, it is "an expression of the salvation of God, for which people" long (5:6).[102] On the other hand, *dikaiosýnē* "remains—in good OT and Jewish perspective—God's demand to mankind, a condition for their realization of salvation (5:20)."[103] This creates a dynamic tension "between the indicative of the divine promise of salvation and the imperative of the ethical demand for the disciples of Jesus."[104]

In terms of the fourth Beatitude recorded in Matthew 5:6, Jones thinks it concerns desiring God above all things, a sentiment that harkens back to the first commandment of the Decalogue.[105] Guelich, however, maintains that Jesus was referring to the person's dire need to be in a right relationship with God and others, a sentiment that harkens back to the fourth through tenth commandments of the Decalogue.[106] Perhaps Christ had both views in mind when He lauded the genuine longing of His disciples for integrity, obedience, and justice.[107]

In a world filled with sinful people, the righteousness of God is despised as being weak, cowardly, and pointless. In the kingdom of God, however, His righteousness is honored for its strength of character, courage, and eternal significance. This is an example of how the standards of God's kingdom stand opposed to the standards of the world.[108] The believers' longing for righteousness also stands in sharp contrast with the desires of the people of the world. They pursue their own goals and do anything to achieve them. Greed, injustice, and violence are common among the unsaved. The citizens of God's kingdom, however, yearn for justice and goodness to be established. They reflect the moral law of God by honoring others and taking a stand against such vices as murder, adultery, stealing, perjury, and greed.

Guthrie noted that some religious experts in Jesus' day believed a person could earn righteousness by doing good deeds.[109] Believers, of course, understand that personal righteousness can only be found in union with Christ (Phil. 3:7–11) and maintained by the power of the indwelling Spirit (cf. Gal.

5:16–18).[110] Perhaps Jesus had this truth in mind when He declared that His followers have distinctive spiritual joy, for they know that God will one day satisfy their longing for justice to prevail (Matt. 5:6; cf. Isa. 11:5; 42:1–4; Luke 6:21). They want God's righteousness to be established not only in society at large, but also in their own lives.[111] For example, they seek to be upright, fair, and objective in their treatment of others, virtues affirmed by the fifth through tenth commandments of the Decalogue.[112]

Morris, in his discussion of Jesus' Sermon, observed that the "first four beatitudes express in one way or another our dependence on God; the next three the outworking of that dependence,"[113] especially with respect to humankind.[114] For example, the *fifth beatitude* that Christ mentioned extols being merciful to others. In contrast, some in society think that people need to be savage and brutal if they are going to get what they want. An illustration of this from the ancient world would be a Roman triumphal procession, which was merciless in the way it shamelessly exposed its prisoners in chains.[115] God's Word, however, declares that benevolence and compassion are to characterize the citizens of the divine kingdom.

Some people think that being merciful is the same as being good-natured or ignoring what is morally questionable. The idea is that people should be completely open-minded and permit others to do whatever they want.[116] In contrast to the world's way of thinking, the Bible depicts mercifulness as a gracious disposition toward one's fellow creatures and fellow Christians. The merciful person is kind, charitable, and ready to empathize with the sufferings of the afflicted.[117] He longs for justice, but is not harsh and cruel. He lauds forgiveness, but does not downplay the heinousness of sin. He seeks to be generous to all, showing the love of God without partiality or preconditions.[118] Such a lifestyle reflects all that is noblest and best in the commandments of the Decalogue (cf. Matt. 22:37–40).

The legalists of Christ's day mistakenly thought that any hardship endured by others was a sign of God's punishment. These influential people thus presumed they had no responsibility to help those who were poor, sick, infirm, or destitute. Jesus, however, taught that showing mercy was the way the people of God lovingly responded to those in need.[119] Believers who live in this way are the privileged recipients of God's favor, for they are the beneficiaries of His mercy.[120] They in turn show their gratitude by demonstrating His mercy to others in tangible ways.[121] They understand that, just as they have received God's love through Christ, so too they are to display His love concretely to other people (cf. 1 John 3:18).

Jesus reminded His followers that just as God's forgiveness enabled them to be forgiving, so His mercy enabled them who were once stony-hearted avengers to exercise mercy. Also, just as God had shown mercy to countless people—a theme underscored in the Decalogue (cf. Exod. 20:6; Deut. 5:10)—so too His people were to be compassionate and forgiving to others. Thus, rather than exact courtroom equity, the children of God unconditionally loved others, for they had received His love. They became agents of His mercy by forgetting their own rights and not seeking to punish those who had wronged them. The recipients of God's mercy did not condescendingly reach down from a superior level to their supposed moral inferiors, for the Cross prohibited this. Rather, their display of mercy was supported by an awareness that they were the undeserving recipients of God's grace.[122]

The *sixth beatitude* that Christ spoke about is maintaining a pure heart. In Scripture, the heart represents the core of one's inmost being, including the mind, will, and emotions (cf. Ps. 4:7).[123] Moreover, in western culture, people tend to divide human existence into independent, isolated functions.[124] Contrastingly, in ancient Near Eastern culture, people tended to maintain the unity of human existence. The heart represented the psychological core of the entire person, including the spiritual dimension of one's being.[125]

Another contrast worth mentioning is that the world lauds deception and betrayal. God's people, however, as citizens of His kingdom, are to be genuine and honest in all their dealings.[126] Living in this way fulfills the intent and spirit of the fifth through tenth commandments of the Decalogue. Believers realize, of course, that they do not have the ability to honor others consistently, remain morally pure, avoid coveting and pilfering the possessions others, and refrain from lying. They must look to God in faith to create an ethically clean heart in them (cf. Ps. 51:10).[127]

Only the pure in heart will dwell in the Lord's presence (Matt. 5:8; cf. Ps. 24:3–4). In a sense, then, declaring someone to be pure in heart is equivalent to saying he or she is a believer, for only those who have trusted in Christ for salvation will enjoy communion with God (cf. 1 John 1:3).[128] They experience that eternal Sabbath rest that Christ has made available to them (cf. Exod. 20:8–11; Heb. 4:1–11). In light of what has been said, there is considerable incentive for remaining pure in heart. The children of God have the unshakable confidence of knowing that one day they will personally dwell with Christ and be made like Him (1 John 3:1–2). Also, just as Jesus is morally pure, so too His people—who have this future hope of seeing Him—remain morally pure by turning away from sin (vs. 3).[129] Moreover, the eschatological hope of being with the Lord in heaven—a theme harkening back to the spiritual implications of the fourth commandment of the Decalogue—undergirds the believer's desire to remain morally pure.

The *seventh beatitude* that Christ mentioned is being a peacemaker. In the world there is violence and chaos. People pursue personal peace and happiness at any cost, and they never really seem to obtain the things they crave. The citizens of God's kingdom, however, strive for peace and stability in the lives of themselves and other people.[130] As true peacemakers, they uphold the fifth through tenth commandments. They affirm the value of life and deplore those who murder. They take a stand against marital infidelity and encourage husbands and wives to reconcile their differences. They deplore all forms of dishonesty, whether it is in the form of stealing or lying, and laud those who are upright. Humility, not greed and selfishness, is the trademark of those who strive for peace.

From God's perspective, those who are genuine peacemakers do not have a hidden agenda. They are not exclusively trying to accomplish their own goals or advance their own fortunes. Rather, such people are most interested in promoting God's values and achieving His will.[131] They are people of genuine integrity and their peacemaking has eternal value.[132] This peacemaking activity should be evident in every area of life, whether it is religious, social, or political.[133] Believers who strive for such peace experience lasting spiritual joy, for they are truly children of God (Matt. 5:9). This means they take delight in an intimate and personal relationship with the Lord.[134] In addition, their lives demonstrate that they have taken to heart the fundamental implications of the first commandment of the Decalogue.

In Jesus' day, the rabbis used the expression "sons of God" (υἱοὶ θεοῦ) to refer exclusively to the children of Israel. Christ took a much broader perspective by declaring that peacemakers—regardless of their race or social status—would be called "children of God" (Matt. 5:9). Jesus' Beatitude must have astonished the national zealots of His day, whose driving passion was to be free from the rule of Rome.[135] Here we see that being a true peacemaker is radically different from promoting the common values of the world. The child of God strives for peace against all odds, despite the prospect of being ridiculed and rejected. The peacemaker also operates under the steadfast conviction that in the end God's kingdom will prevail. For this reason, the Lord will eternally reward such people.[136]

In commending the activity of peacemakers, Jesus was opposing any system that needlessly erected barriers between people and consequently promoted strife. The ethic of Christ saw all nationalities as being equal in God's sight, rather than one being exalted above another. Accordingly, Jesus wanted His followers to proclaim His message of peace and hope to all people, for all needed to be saved.[137] Of course, God is ultimately the true source of peace for governments (cf. Isa. 60:17) and people (cf. Rom. 5:1).[138] The Lord's peace surpasses all understanding, for it remains with believers in the most distressing of situations (cf. Phil. 4:6–7).

Believers can be peacemakers by showing care and compassion in real ways to other people (cf. Rom. 12:9–21).[139] Christians can also explain to others how to have peace with God. In this way believers can function as catalysts of forgiveness and agents of reconciliation (cf. Heb. 12:14; Jas. 3:17).[140] They seek to bring a message of peace to the lost so that they might be brought into harmony with God, from whom they have been alienated.[141]

The *eighth beatitude* that Jesus mentioned concerns being persecuted for the sake of righteousness. Christ's pronouncement of blessedness takes a special place because of its form and content.[142] One reason is that it appears at the end of a series of Beatitudes that Jesus stated in the third person plural. Another reason is that Matthew 5:10b repeats the second line of verse 3a, "for theirs is the kingdom of heaven." The repetition creates an inclusio, or bracketing effect.[143] According to Betz, the first set of four Beatitudes emphasized the theme of pursuing righteousness (cf. vs. 6), while the second set of four Beatitudes underscored the theme of remaining steadfast for the sake of righteousness (cf. vs. 10).[144] This emphasis on the importance of upright thinking, speaking, and acting in the lives of believers is dominant throughout the Beatitudes and is a theme fundamental to the entire Sermon on the Mount.[145]

In his study, Grounds noted that the real followers of Christ were radical non-conformists by society's standards.[146] They recognized their own moral insufficiency and their failure to be righteous. They had an ardent desire to pursue God's righteousness and actively practice it, even though they might suffer at the hands of an unrighteous world. Believers should not be surprised that the world would want to harass and harm them.[147] After all, unsaved humanity hates the truth that Christians stand for (John 3:19–20). In fact, the world detests believers because they first detested the Messiah (15:18–20). Additionally, believers are a standing reproach to the wicked.[148] This is why anyone who is united to the Savior by faith and wants to live in a godly manner as His follower will be persecuted by opponents of the gospel (2 Tim. 3:12). Thus, believers should come to expect trouble from others as they witness for Christ (1 Pet. 5:9). Persecution might arise in the form of coldness, ridicule, contempt, or more radical forms of ill-treatment.[149]

The followers of the Lord who suffered persecution had come to terms with the injunctions of the Decalogue. In accordance with the first commandment, they gave their relationship with God highest priority. Likewise, in agreement with the second commandment, they showed their appreciation for God's mercy to them by being merciful to others. Moreover, rather than commune with the wicked of the world, the upright chose to find eternal rest with God through Christ. This desire reflected their affirmation of the spiritual dimensions of the fourth commandment. Furthermore, they would rather live in conformity to the fifth through tenth commandments of the Decalogue (despite the prospect of being persecuted), than dishonor others, commit murder, be guilty of adultery, steal from others, commit perjury, or allow greed to control their desires and actions.

This attitude and lifestyle contrasts sharply with the weak commitments maintained by most people. They do not want to be inconvenienced by demands that others often place upon them. The citizens of God's kingdom, however, are not concerned about the personal cost of remaining unwavering in their commitment to the Lord and His people. When believers are persecuted for being faithful followers of the Lord, they can be encouraged by the fact that the divine kingdom belongs to them (Matt. 5:10). They can also rejoice in the truth that they are the recipients of the Father's favor and the Spirit's presence (1 Pet. 4:14).

The *ninth beatitude* that Christ mentioned is actually a restatement and expansion of the eighth one, for it deals with being persecuted.[150] Furthermore, the ninth Beatitude not only is "the transition which links 5:3–10 and 5:3–16," but it also "sets the stage for the examples of 5:13–16 that illuminate the disciples' role in the world."[151] Jesus declared that enemies of the faith would verbally slander, physically abuse, and spread maliciously false rumors about His disciples (Matt. 5:11). Antagonists would also shun Christians and brand them as evildoers because they belonged to the Savior (Luke 6:22). Despite these awful possibilities, Jesus' followers were the privileged recipients of His eternal blessings. They could accept their circumstances with an attitude of joy and exultation, for their spiritual reward in the divine kingdom was fabulous. They could also find comfort in knowing that the sufferings of the present moment did not compare with the eternal riches in Christ that awaited them in heaven (cf. Rom. 8:18; Eph. 1:3; 1 Pet. 1:3–5).

Jesus knew that human beings naturally crave acceptance, approval, security, and status. He also realized that His followers might think their upright behavior would be warmly received—if not tolerated—by the world. Jesus was frank in His statements because He wanted to shatter any illusions that His disciples might entertain concerning the success awaiting them. Their godly lives would contradict and challenge the world's cherished ideals. The unsaved would not shower Christ's followers with bouquets and acclamation; rather, the world would heap lies, hatred, and abuse on them, and they needed to be prepared for this possibility.[152]

Jesus ended this last Beatitude with the sobering reminder that His persecuted followers were not experiencing anything unusual, for God's enemies had oppressed His representatives in Old Testament times (Matt. 5:12; cf. 2 Chron. 24:21; Jer. 20:2). By mentioning the example of the prophets, Christ intended to show His disciples that the struggle between them and the wicked was not new, but had existed in previous centuries (cf. Acts 7:51–52).[153]

Being salt and light in the world (Matthew 5:13–16). After giving His pronouncements of blessing, Christ declared that His followers were the "salt of the earth" (Matt. 5:13). The Greek noun rendered "salt" (ἅλας, *hálas*) literally referred to a white, crystalline compound known chemically as sodium chloride.[154] The inhabitants of Palestine obtained their salt primarily from the shores of the Dead Sea and the Hill of Salt (Jebel Usdum), which was a 15-square-mile elevation at the southwest corner of the Dead Sea.[155] Unlike the purified sodium chloride available for use today, the substance obtained from the Dead Sea region was generally contaminated with other minerals.[156] Thus, the salt could be dissolved out of this mixture, leaving a tasteless substance behind.[157]

The people could also obtain salt from mineral deposits they found in the soil, and the saltiness of this compound could be lost in several ways.[158] If a vein of salt was exposed to the sun and other elements, it soon deteriorated to grainy sands. Also, the salinity of the chemical could be leached out by dampness or deteriorate from the heat of an oven. Despite these possibilities, people in Bible times used the crystalline form of salt to season and preserve their food,[159] especially because the chemical was effective in bringing out the flavor of what was eaten.[160] Another reason people used salt had to do with the hot, dry, and windy climate of the Near East where body electrolytes were quickly lost through perspiration. Ingesting salt helped to maintain these electrolytes and prevent dehydration from occurring. People moreover used salt as a fertilizer, as a weedkiller, and as a retardant to slow the fermentation of dung.[161] In addition, people would rub salt into meat to slow its decay.[162]

Commentators have noted that pure salt cannot lose its basic chemical properties, for sodium chloride is a stable compound.[163] But, as Betz observed, Jesus was not referring to the chemical properties of sodium chloride in the technical sense.[164] Rather, He was saying that when salt becomes contaminated with foreign substances, it can lose its distinctive flavor and preservative qualities.[165] Matthew 5:13 indicates that when this happened, the inhabitants of Palestine would discard such a worthless chemical.[166] This information indicates that Jesus was not just concerned with the ways in which salt could become contaminated. More importantly, He figuratively used ἅλας to refer to the spiritual qualities that should be present in His disciples.[167] Christ was saying that His followers needed to have a wholesomeness about them[168] which enabled them to be a blessing and a moral preservative in the world.[169]

The Decalogue formed the ethical backdrop for Jesus' discussion. His followers could be a positive moral influence when they worshiped and served God exclusively and when they honored His name in whatever they thought, said, and did. They would bring the world a distinctive spiritual flavor when they found their eternal Sabbath rest in Christ, treated all people with respect, avoided such vices as murder, adultery, and stealing, told the truth, and shunned all forms of covetousness and greed. When the citizens of

God's kingdom live for Him, He in turn uses them to help preserve and maintain the moral qualities found in His Word.[170] Conversely, when God's people are slack in their spiritual devotion, they loose their distinctiveness. Likewise, when they grow inactive in their commitment to Christ, they loose their morally preserving quality. As McNeile noted, human life would be both insipid and corrupt were it not for the abiding influence of godly believers.[171]

Jesus next declared that His followers were "the light of the world" (Matt. 5:14). The Greek noun rendered "light" (φῶς, *phōs*) is used as a symbol of life, truth, uprightness, virtue, joy, goodness, and blessing.[172] In this verse, Christ was urging His disciples to become spiritual illuminators of the salvation He had shone in their lives.[173] They were to do this by radiating the knowledge and presence of God to people living in spiritual darkness or ignorance.[174] The Savior moreover explained that a city located at the top of a hill cannot escape detection. In Jesus' day, cities on hills often were built out of white limestone. These towns gleamed in the sun and could not easily be hidden. Additionally, at night the oil lamps used by the inhabitants could be seen glowing over the surrounding area.[175] Similarly, believers who are fully devoted to Jesus cannot remain hidden, for the spiritual light of their lives will be visible to everyone.[176]

Christ next stated that people in His day did not light a lamp and place it under a wooden basket or clay bowl, which was used to measure ground meal or flour.[177] Rather, they placed the lamp on a stand so that it might radiate its light to every person in the house (vs. 15). The Greek noun translated "lamp" (λύχνος, *lýchnos*) refers to a small clay bowl that burned olive oil drawn from a flax or linen wick.[178] Jesus' comment presupposes a one-room home that could easily be lit up by a lamp.[179] The inhabitants might place it on a shelf extending from a nearby pillar, on a single stone emerging from the wall, or on a piece of metal driven into the wall.[180] The lamp symbolized the believers' works of righteousness, the light of which shined far into the darkness of the world and gave glory to God.[181]

The Savior knew that people estimate the worth of Christianity by the lives of its adherents, whom they saw and knew, not by the Beatitudes or even by the entire Sermon on the Mount.[182] That is why Jesus said God's people were to shine the truth of His Word in their lives to people all around them.[183] To do otherwise would be to fail "to observe or teach the Torah."[184]

Understandably, then, it was Christ's desire that the unsaved would see the spiritual principles of the moral law at work in those who claimed to follow Him. This occurred when Jesus' disciples were characterized by doing beneficial and profitable deeds. When the unsaved saw the good that believers performed, they might give praise to the Father in heaven (vs. 16).

The Moral Law of God and the Nature of Its Absolute Requirements (Matthew 5:17-7:12)

Matthew 5:17–7:12 comprises the central section of Jesus' Sermon.[185] This is evident by the appearance of the phrase "the Law or the Prophets" in 5:17 and the phrase "the Law and the Prophets" in 7:12. These similarly worded phrases bracket off this entire body of material from the rest of the Sermon.[186] This is an important observation, for it indicates that this central section of Jesus' discourse specifically concerns God's moral law and the nature of its absolute requirements. For Jesus the content of the Torah was normative and gave clear expression to "the will and intention of God."[187]

Legalistic traditions that were prevalent in Jesus' day form the backdrop of His ethical remarks.[188] While much of what the religious leaders had taught was true, some of them had misunderstood and misapplied what was contained in the law of Moses. Jesus' concern was that these experts had failed to comprehend the true intent of the moral law and the nature of its absolute righteous requirements. That is why Christ addressed both inward motives and outward conduct. He also contrasted what the moral law said with what some had erroneously taught. Jesus' intent was to uproot the falsehoods they promulgated and at the same time affirm the truth of God. In this way Christ delineated what the standard for righteous conduct should be for His followers.

As was noted in the previous chapter, the Sermon on the Mount has a literary chiastic structure. This is helpful information, for it underscores how centrally important the moral law of God was to Jesus' discourse. The inherent structure of the Sermon indicates that the moral law is not something passé. Rather, it is of prime importance to the lives of those who are followers of the Savior. Thus, as the discussion to follow will indicate, the moral law should neither be taken lightly nor ignored by them as they seek to live for the Lord.

The Moral Law Fulfilled by Christ (Matthew 5:17–20). In Jesus' day, scholars often referred to the Hebrew Scriptures as the Law, the Prophets, and the Writings.[189] This is evident in Luke 24:44, where Christ called the Old Testament "the law of Moses, the prophets, and the psalms."[190] The Psalms, of course, comprised the first book of the third division of Israel's sacred writings.[191] In Matthew 5:17, when Jesus referred to "the prophets," He would have understood this to include the Latter Prophets or Major Prophets (Isaiah, Jeremiah, and Ezekiel), the twelve Minor Prophets or the Book of the Twelve (Hosea, Joel, Amos, Obadiah, Jonah, Micah, Nahum, Habakkuk, Zephaniah, Haggai, Zechariah, and Malachi), and the Former Prophets (Joshua, Judges, Samuel, and Kings).[192] When taken together, "the law" and "the prophets" (Matt. 5:17) referred to the entire Old Testament,[193] including the Writings.[194] This conclusion is reinforced by Matthew 13:35, where the author introduced the quotation from Psalm 78:2, which was part of the Writings, as being "spoken through the prophet."[195]

From the outset of Christ's earthly ministry, some erroneously presumed that He tried to set aside and completely abandon the teachings of the Hebrew Scriptures.[196] Moreover, Jesus' opponents regarded Him as a revolutionary and a fanatical nonconformist who sought to destroy every tie with the past (John 5:18).[197] Their disapproving attitude toward Christ never waned, but rather grew progressively stronger (Matt. 26:59–61).[198] Although Jesus challenged the misguided authorities of His day, this did not mean He had come to do away with the Torah (5:17). Rather, His attitude toward the Mosaic law was one of profound respect.[199]

In making sense of verse 17, the Greek verb rendered "abolish" (καταλύω, *katalýō*)[200] is important to discuss.[201] Here it means "to put an end to the effect or validity of something."[202] Such notions as annulling, repealing, doing away with, or making invalid the law help to capture of the gist of what Jesus was saying.[203] With respect to the Greek noun νόμος (*nómos*),[204] Christ was referring to "the Pentateuch, the work of Moses the lawgiver."[205] The idea is that Jesus, during His first advent, did not seek to tear down the legal, moral, and ethical structure represented by the law. Rather, He came to dismantle the traditional misinterpretations of others concerning the law and thus open the way for the fulfillment of it in the lives of God's people.[206]

Jesus' comments regarding the law were made against the backdrop of what some influential people had declared. They not only taught the law and required others to conform strictly to it, but also rested their salvation on their law-keeping.[207] In the Sermon on the Mount, the Messiah challenged and rejected the way these individuals had perverted the law.[208] While He confronted them verbally, His own life and ministry—especially as seen in His atoning sacrifice on the cross—would be the ultimate expression of His restoring what God originally intended with respect to the law.

This truth is borne out in verse 17 by Jesus' use of the Greek verb πληρόω (*plēróō*).[209] The term has been understood in a wide variety of ways,[210] only three of which will be mentioned here.[211] *Plēróō* can be taken to mean: 1) "to fulfill" as in "to do" or "to carry out"; 2) "to bring to full expression" as in "to show it forth in its true meaning"; or 3) "to fill up" as in "to complete."[212] In the midst of all the discussion and debate regarding these various nuances, I would like to propose that Jesus could have had all three meanings in mind when He made His declaration.[213]

With respect to Jesus fulfilling the law, He did so in love[214] by perfectly obeying it (cf. Luke 23:41; 2 Cor. 5:21)[215] and by bringing to pass its types and prophecies, especially the messianic pronouncements recorded in the Mosaic code.[216] The Hebrew Scriptures foretold the birth, life, ministry, and death of Christ, and He fulfilled all these prophecies.[217] In fact, Christ was the One to whom the entire Hebrew corpus pointed.[218] Consequently, as the eschatological goal of the Old Testament,[219] Christ is its sole authoritative interpreter[220] and the only One through whom the Hebrew corpus finds its significance and continuity.[221]

Another way that Jesus fulfilled the law was by paying the complete penalty for sin that the law required from transgressors. Christ did this by sacrificing Himself on the cross in the sinners' place and as their atoning substitute.[222] Thus, Jesus did not just simply affirm the law and the prophets. He also brought the will of God to full realization from the standpoint of what the Lord had promised and demanded in His law.[223] Moreover, through the Savior's work on the cross, He underscored that believers can fulfill the law only through faith in Him, not by works of righteousness they do apart from Him.[224] Accordingly, Jesus is the ideal example of how Christians are to behave.[225] Here we see that Christ was not "an antinomian. He expected his followers to understand and apply the moral principles already revealed in Scripture."[226]

Furthermore, when Jesus fulfilled the law, He did so to its fullest possible measure.[227] Expressed differently, He brought all that the law stood for to its final conclusion. Both as to the law's purest *intent* and its perfect *extent*, Jesus carried out all that was "proper...to fulfill all righteousness" (Matt. 3:15).[228] Additionally, Jesus helped people to move from an external, legalistic understanding of the law to one that is in keeping with what the Spirit originally intended.[229] Christ directed the people's attention from mere outward observance to genuine inward compliance (cf. 5:21, 22, 27, 28), and in this way, affirmed the heart and soul of the law.[230]

The preceding observations regarding the way Jesus fulfilled the law implies that His teaching not only stands in continuity with the Hebrew Bible and the scripturally-based form of Judaism arising from it,[231] but also in discontinuity with legalistic traditions that were prevalent in His day.[232] Christ questioned the teachings of some by reiterating what His Father had originally said in the Torah.[233] Although Jesus clarified the divine revelation that some had obscured, He never retracted, denied, or tried to distance Himself from what God had unveiled to Moses long ago.[234] Furthermore, while Jesus affirmed the teaching of Moses recorded in the law, the Savior rejected the unscriptural notions being promulgated by some who were living at the time.[235]

The implication is that, in Matthew 5:17–7:12, Jesus was taking issue with the distorted ideas that some had about the law.[236] He did so by elucidating the true nature and application of the Torah.[237] That this portion of the Sermon on the Mount is concerned primarily with God's law is evident by the appearance of the phrase "the Law or the Prophets" in 5:17 and the phrase "the Law and the Prophets" in 7:12. Also, the chiastic structure of the Sermon on the Mount indicates that the moral law of God and the nature of its absolute requirements are the main point, or central thrust, of the passage. Furthermore, by properly interpreting (cf. 5:21–48) and applying the Torah (cf. 6:1–7:12), Jesus rejected erroneous interpretations of the law, which some had considered part of the law itself.

As was noted in chapter two, there are three distinct classifications of law evident within the Mosaic code:[238] the moral law, as summed up in the Decalogue; the ceremonial law, as represented in the ritual prescriptions found throughout the Old Testament; and the civil or political law, which concerned the national and political life of the Israelites.[239] The abiding validity and authority of the moral law is evident from what Christ declared in Matthew 5:18.[240] He solemnly assured His listeners that as long as heaven and earth endured, so would the law of God[240] and "the will of God which it embodies."[242] Not the smallest letter or stroke in a Hebrew letter would vanish from the law until God had achieved all that He had foreordained.[243]

Jesus emphasized these truths by His use of the Greek verb γίνομαι (*gínomai*).[244] In verse 18, the term means "to occur as process or result."[245] Such words as "happen," "turn out," and "take place" help to convey the sense of the verb.[246] More particularly, the verb conveys the notion of attaining to or arriving at something,[247] which the NRSV expresses as "accomplished." In this verse, *gínomai* partly refers to the imperatives of the law; in other words, all the demands of the Torah are satisfied in Christ. The verb also refers to the prophetic announcements of the Old Testament; in other words, these find their ultimate fulfillment in Christ.[248]

Jesus would have regarded His work on the cross as contributing to the fulfillment of the Mosaic covenant and law as well as God's redemptive purposes expressed in them.[249] Christ would also have considered the full manifestation of God's kingdom (cf. Matthew 24–25), for which His believers were to pray (cf. 6:10), as bringing to pass all that was announced in the Hebrew Scriptures. Furthermore, Jesus would have regarded the consummation of the age as bringing closure to what God intended to accomplish in human history.[250]

Carson thinks Jesus' statement in Matthew 5:18 undercuts the notion that He was referring only to the moral law.[251] Supposedly, "the interpretation is invalidated by the all-inclusive 'not the smallest letter, not the least stroke of a pen'." However, an examination of the rest of the New Testament does not support this conclusion.[252] Christ began to annul the ceremonial aspect of the law when He declared all foods to be clean (cf. Mark 7:19). The Lord affirmed this particular truth to Peter in Acts 10:15, and Paul likewise affirmed it in 1 Timothy 4:4. Furthermore, the writer of Hebrews said that the old Levitical priesthood with its ceremonies and sacrifices was no longer valid or effective (Heb. 8:13). Thus, it is reasonable to assert that Christ, in Matthew 5:18, regarded the civil and ceremonial functions of the law to be fulfilled, and that only the moral law remains in force.

The Savior's comment in verse 19 was primarily made with the legalists of His day in mind,[253] although it is true that anyone can violate God's moral law. Jesus was condemning the way some people had misinterpreted and misapplied the law.[254] He questioned why they used the law as a means of winning acceptance with God. Christ further opposed the notion that a person's relationship with God was determined simply by his outward conformity to what the law stipulated.[255] In view of that, Jesus commended those who strictly observed the law; but He taught that those who had an arrogant and smug attitude made a sham of their outward conformity. They focused so intently on external requirements that they avoided the real intent of the law, and thus obscured its foremost demands.[256] Likewise, they were so preoccupied with its details, that they ignored its broader principles. Moreover, the legalists were so transfixed on their actions, that they ignored their motives.[257]

Some leaders in Jesus' day were notorious for accommodating and compromising the law to fit their circumstances. By doing this, they did not allow God to use the law as a mirror to reflect His perfect righteousness and their own sinfulness and shortcomings.[258] Consequently, they never became aware of their need for His grace and for depending on Him for salvation. This is surprising in light of the fact that, by the first century A.D., scholars had written voluminous commentaries about the law. They tirelessly sought to explain what would be required to obey its stipulations. Some of these experts incorrectly supposed that by spelling out every conceivable implication in the Torah, those who obeyed their commentaries would measure up to the law's requirements.

There are two reasons why this sort of thinking was incorrect. First, no commentary—regardless of how massive the volume might be—can ever clarify all that is revealed in God's Word. Second, scholarly preoccupation with exhaustive commentaries tends to distract the attention of researchers away from the inspired text to the commentaries themselves. This was the predicament of some in Jesus' day. The religious experts had focused so much on human traditions and opinions that they had neglected the commandments of God.[259] Christ noted that some of these people did not hesitate to break, or set aside, the least of the ordinances of Scripture, and to teach others to do the same.

In Jesus' day, scholars had enumerated 613 commandments in the law.[260] There was also the tendency within some groups to distinguish between the "heavier" and "lighter" commandments of the Torah.[261] The lighter commandments were statutes that made only minor demands, whereas the heavy commandments were ordinances that made significant demands.[262] This distinction was subjective and open to dispute among legal experts.[263] To strict followers of the law, even the light commandments had to be meticulously obeyed.[264]

In the midst of this confusion, Jesus declared in Matthew 5:19 that whoever was guilty of rejecting the least important command in the law would be considered least important in God's kingdom. The punishment matched the crime.[265] The transgressors had depreciated God's law, and so the Lord would depreciate them. The corollary was also true. Whoever practiced and taught even the smallest injunction of Scripture would be considered great in the divine kingdom. Correspondingly, the reward matched the virtuous deed.[266] The upright had affirmed God's law, and so the Lord would affirm them.

Based on the teaching of this verse, as well as all of Matthew 5:17–20, Bahnsen maintained that the political standards and agenda of society should be set by Christians, not by the unregenerate.[267] But there are at least two key reasons why God's civil law is not binding either on believers or unbelievers. First, the Hebrew Scriptures originally were the body of laws for the community of the redeemed in ancient times.[268] Second, God only entered into a theocratic covenant relationship with the descendants of Abraham, Isaac, and Jacob.[269] These two truths explain why no nation or state today can claim the civil and ceremonial aspects of the Old Testament law as their constitution. A contemporary form of government might choose to frame its laws around those found in the Old Testament; but it is not required by God to do so. Likewise, believers are not divinely obligated to enact the Mosaic standing laws pertaining to civil government through the persuasive political process.

Despite the non-binding nature of the civil and ceremonial aspects of the Mosaic covenant, God's moral law remains absolute, perfect, unchanging, and eternal in nature. As was noted in chapter 2, this means the Decalogue is relevant for Christians, regardless of the age or society in which they live. It might also be stated that unbelievers are accountable to the ethical demands of God, as expressed in His moral law (cf. Rom. 3:19). In fact, the Lord's condemnation of unbelievers is based on their transgression of the demands made by the moral law (cf. 2:5–16; 6:23).

Chafer argued that the intensely legalistic and stern character of Matthew 5:19 implies that it relates either to the Mosaic system of the Old Testament or to a coming earthly, millennial kingdom.[270] It supposedly does not relate to the Christian in the age of grace.[271] Chafer likewise maintained that the scrupulously strict injunctions of the rest of the Sermon do not apply to the New Testament believer, who is saved by grace.[272] This is because the emphasis of the Sermon allegedly is on doing things meritoriously, and the extreme legal penalty for wrongdoing is eternal punishment in hell.[273]

The analysis of Chafer and other likeminded dispensationalists (such as Benson, Campbell, and Pentecost) does not bear up under scrutiny. It would be mistaken to limit the application of the Sermon to those living in a so-called earthly, millennial kingdom. Because Christ addressed the Sermon to all His disciples (cf. Matt. 5:1–2), it has continuing validity for believers today. Moreover, there is no compelling reason to suppose that Jesus' Sermon reflects the misguided notion that one has to obey God to merit His favor. For instance, an examination of the Beatitudes suggests that God is graciously blessing His people for their faithfulness, not because they have earned His favor.

Although Christ might have appealed to reward, He never said salvation was based on the believer's merit. In fact, He made it clear that whatever rewards believers received were a result of God's grace. Even the opportunities for service were a divine gift. In this light, eternal rewards for faithfulness are seen as the free, unmerited offering of God to His people.[274] Furthermore, classical and revised dispensationalists are mistaken to assume that Christ had eternal damnation in mind when He talked about being called least in the kingdom of heaven. Verse 19 suggests that God's discipline of His people, not His eternal condemnation of the unsaved, is in view. The Lord will permit believers who depreciate His commandments to enter His kingdom; however, they will be considered the least, not the greatest, in it.

It is likely that Christ's statements sounded drastic or extreme to some of His listeners, as they do to some today. The Savior, nonetheless, brought a needed balance to the abuse of God's Word that existed in His time. Jesus made it clear that whatever eternal blessings the citizen of the kingdom receives is by God's grace; absolutely nothing is earned. Yet the believer's rank, or position, in that kingdom will correspond to his respect of God's law.[275]

Certain prominent leaders in Christ's day would have been considered sterling examples of upright behavior, especially in their practice of religion.[276] If anyone was righteous enough to merit God's approval and entrance into the kingdom, it would be these individuals.[277] Jesus shattered this myth by saying that the quality of a person's righteousness had to go infinitely beyond that set by any group.[278] Unless an individual showed himself to be a far better person from a moral standpoint than the most pious leaders in society, he would never enter the divine kingdom (vs. 20).[279] In this verse, "the scribes and Pharisees are transparent figures representing the Jewish opponents, whose religion may be characterized as legalism and hypocrisy."[280]

Christ was not addressing the issue of imputed righteousness here.[281] Rather, He was focusing on the propensity of some to adhere meticulously to the technicalities of the law. They thought that, by their rigid moral conduct, they would qualify for entrance into the kingdom of heaven.[282] Jesus, however, declared that the demands of the kingdom were far greater than anything that ever entered the minds of people.[283] Even those who were considered experts had failed to come to terms with the actual standard for holiness revealed in God's Word.[284] Despite the assertions of Chafer,[285] Jesus was not advocating a work's righteousness theology in the Sermon.[286] His intent was to show how holy the moral law of God truly is and how incapable all people are of living up to its perfect ethical standards (cf. Rom. 3:9–20, 23; 7:12; Jas. 2:9). This fact serves as a reminder of one's need for salvation in Christ.

Jesus did not intend the comment He made in Matthew 5:20 to drive people to despair over their inability to keep the law. Rather, He wanted His listeners to understand that a literalistic or atomistic interpretation of the law is unacceptable. In order to enter God's kingdom, one needs a righteousness that goes to the core of one's being.[287] For that reason the law is like a mirror that reflects the perfect righteousness of God and a person's own sinfulness and shortcomings. Through the work of the law in one's life, a person sees that all have sinned and fall short of God's supreme standard of righteousness (Rom. 3:23).[288]

Consequently, if anyone wants to enter the kingdom of heaven, he has to rely on God, not himself, for admission. The Father has provided His Son as an atoning sacrifice for the sins of the world (1 John 2:2). When people trust in Christ for salvation, they receive His righteousness and the privilege to enter God's kingdom (John 3:3). This righteousness of Christ, which believers possess by faith, surpasses the righteousness that anyone could ever obtain on their own. In addition, believers enjoy the blessing of Christ's priestly intercession and mediation on their behalf before the throne of God in heaven (cf. 1 Tim. 2:5; Heb. 4:14–16). Furthermore, He writes the moral law of God on their hearts and enables them to do His will (cf. Rom. 8:4; Gal. 5:16–18).[289]

The Moral Law Properly Interpreted by Christ (Matthew 5:21–48). In verses 17 through 20, Jesus underscored the importance of practicing and teaching God's Word. Christ also declared that His people were to heed the least important command found in the law, and they were to teach others to do the same. Some living at the time of Christ kept the law externally, but they transgressed many of its details. Also, in their efforts to gain merit before God by superficially complying with His directives, they violated the spirit of the law. They believed that mere ritualistic practices were more important than a person's heart attitude. Likewise, they were convinced that a person's heritage and standing in society could earn him God's righteousness.[290]

This situation forms the backdrop of Matthew 5:21–48, which records Jesus' proper interpretation of the law.[291] The Savior's intent in the comments He made was to contrast His ethical teachings with those who held a legalistic view of the law.[292] Christ maintained that it was a sham to keep the law externally, yet violate it internally. He also rejected the view that a right standing before God could be obtained by doing good works. Jesus' desire was to contrast widespread misunderstandings of the law with the true intent behind it.[293] In this way, Christ further stressed the nature of the moral law's absolute requirements.

In the following verses, Jesus provided six examples of how some had perverted the law. As the discussion to follow will indicate, much of the material in this section has thematic links with the Decalogue. In fact, Kang maintains that "the author of the Sermon consciously follows the order of the Decalogue in the antithetical statements."[294] Christ's assertions demonstrate that God's ideals are too high and unattainable to be achieved through humanly devised methods. The seeker learns that only through faith in Christ and His work can a person be acquitted by God. Likewise, only through the power of God's Spirit can His standards be realized in the believer's life.[295]

As it was previously noted, the legalistic traditions of Jesus' day form the backdrop of His ethical remarks.[296] While much of what the religious leaders had taught was true, some of them had also misunderstood and misapplied what was contained in the law of Moses.[297] The Savior's teaching in the Sermon was not a rejection of the binding character of the Mosaic law, and He did not claim that His own teaching challenged or replaced what was written in the Hebrew Scriptures.[298] Rather, Jesus was questioning the excessive legalism and distorted interpretations of the law advocated by some influential people.[299]

Thus, Jesus' concern was that some scholars had failed to comprehend the true intent of the law and the nature of its absolute righteous requirements.[300] That is why Christ addressed both inward motives and outward conduct. He also contrasted what the law said with what some religious leaders had taught. Jesus' intent was to uproot the falsehoods they had promulgated and at the same time affirm the truth of God.[301] In this way Christ not only "brought the will of God to expression,"[302] but also delineated what the standard for righteous conduct should be for His followers.[303] Jesus also revealed that He is "the decisive arbiter" of the law's "meaning, not one scholar among many."[304] Furthermore, without "saying he is the Messiah," Jesus nevertheless spoke "as one empowered to utter the will of God with the highest possible authority."[305]

Committing murder (Matthew 5:21–26; Luke 12:58–59) was the first subject area Jesus dealt with. He cited the teachings of some experts concerning Exodus 20:13 (Deut. 5:17), in which they said that it was illegal to murder.[306] Christ also mentioned a common teaching that all murderers must be brought to judgment (Matt. 5:21).[307] A superficial examination of these teachings might suggest that their adherents had properly understood the sixth commandment of the Decalogue.[308] Jesus revealed, however, that these interpretations were woefully inadequate,[309] for they failed to give a full summary of the law concerning murder, and thus left people with a distorted understanding of the truth.[310]

In their writings and oral teachings, some experts had focused on the external application of the law's injunctions. While they may have faithfully read the letter of the law, they frequently missed or obscured the spirit of it.[311] Because the mass of people in Galilee during the time of Christ could not read, they learned the Scriptures by hearing what these scholars read and explained in the synagogues.[312] The people thus adopted interpretations of the law that were distorted.

Christ went to the heart of the moral law when He declared that any person who harbored malice against his brother[313] was subject to the punishment imposed by the court.[314] Unlike the legalists, who had voided the law by their misinterpretations, Jesus affirmed the Decalogue by explaining its true meaning and significance.[315] Jesus then mentioned a Jewish decree that prohibited insulting someone using the contemptuous word "raca" (ῥακά, *rhaká*). This term was reserved for those who were presumed to be "totally lacking in understanding."[316] Such words as "numskull" or "fool" might be modern-day equivalents.[317] Whoever was guilty of this sort of insult was liable to pay the penalty imposed by the Sanhedrin, the Jewish supreme court.[318]

That injunction notwithstanding, Christ revealed the essence of God's will[319] by declaring that any verbal abuse made one liable to eternal damnation (vs. 22). The Greek noun rendered "hell" (γέεννα, *géenna*) originally referred to the Valley of (the Sons of) Hinnom, a deep ravine south of Jerusalem.[320] During the reigns of Ahaz and Manasseh, the Valley of Hinnom became notorious as the place where people made human sacrifices by fire to Molech, the idol worshiped by the Ammonites (cf. 2 Chron. 28:3; 33:6).[321] Jeremiah called this spot the "Valley of Slaughter" (Jer. 7:32), making the location a symbol of God's judgment on the wicked.[322] The nearby residents used the Valley of Hinnom as a trash dump, and the fires in it burned constantly.[323] The spot served as a horrifying reminder of the eternal destiny that awaits all who perish without trusting in Christ.[324]

The Savior's remarks indicate that He wanted His followers to be thoroughly upright in their attitudes and actions. Accordingly, He provided two examples in Matthew 5:23–26 of dealing with anger by means of reconciliation. While verses 23 and 24 deal with the reconciliation of an offended brother, verses 25 and 26 concern the issue of resolving legal conflict. The point in both illustrations is that believers are to work for reconciliation in all areas of life, whether private or public.

Jesus first had His listeners imagine that a worshiper brought some type of offering to the temple to be sacrificed on the altar. This would be intended as an expression of reverence and devotion to and a desire to "become reconciled with God."[325] However, if this same person remembered that his brother had a grievance against him, the Lord considered his religious devotion to be empty of meaning (vs. 23). Jesus said it would be better for the devotee to leave his offering at the altar, exit from the temple, and become reconciled to his offended brother. Once his relationship with his brother was restored, the worshiper could then present his offering with a clean conscience (Matt. 5:24; cf. Ps. 66:18).

Jesus next had His listeners imagine a lawsuit that existed between two individuals. Since the person was summoned into court by his opponent, the case most likely concerned the owing of debts.[326] The Savior recommended that the person being sued quickly come to peaceful terms with his accuser while they were on their way to the law court. This was especially pertinent advice if the person being sued was guilty of the crime. Christ then noted that if the two did not quickly settle their dispute, the authorities would hand the accused over to the judge, who in turn would place him in the custody of the prison ward so that the accused could be incarcerated (Matt. 5:25). Jesus solemnly assured His listeners that the authorities would not release the accused from prison until he had paid the last fraction of a penny (vs. 26).[327] The Savior made it clear that there was no room for malicious anger. Even the presence of enmity against someone else was a violation of the sixth commandment.[328] In fact, animosity was so evil that God would certainly judge it.[329]

Committing adultery (Matthew 5:27–30) was the second subject area Christ discussed. Undoubtedly, many would have approved of His citation of Exodus 20:14 (Deut. 5:18). The Savior, however, went far beyond the common understanding of this commandment.[330] His assertions indicate that it was the prevailing legalistic explanation of the law, not the law itself, that was at fault.[331] For instance, some scholars in Jesus' day had applied the seventh commandment only to the mere physical act of adultery.[332] They thought that as long as they were not guilty of this specific conduct, they had not violated God's moral law.[333]

Jesus, however, declared that if a man gazed at a woman with lustful intentions, he had already committed adultery with her in his heart (Matt. 5:27–28). Here the heart represents the center of one's feelings and desires.[334] The Savior was not talking about a brief glance, but a prolonged and deliberate stare in which the looker harbored lustful desires for the woman.[335] Doing this aroused sexual yearnings, and the illicit desires would lead to sinful acts.[336] Christ's teaching reflected the original biblical prohibition against premarital and extramarital relations.[337]

Next, Jesus graphically illustrated the importance of eliminating all sources of sin in a person's life. While the illustration was an exaggerated statement, it did not invalidate the specific injunction being stressed by the Messiah.[338] He declared that if a person's right eye caused him to disobey God, he should remove the eye and throw it away. Christ reasoned that it would be better for one member to be eliminated than for the entire body (in other words, the entire person) to suffer eternal punishment in hell (vs. 29). It would be absurd to think that Jesus was advocating self-mutilation, for even someone who was blind could still harbor lust.[339] Christ was saying that His followers should not take sin lightly.[340] They needed to adopt whatever drastic measures were necessary to overcome their wrongful desires.[341]

Jesus furthermore declared that if a person's right hand caused him to rebel against God, the hand should be severed from the body and cast away. In ancient times, people highly valued the right hand, for they saw it as being primarily responsible for the advancement of humanity throughout civilization.[342] Christ reasoned that it was better for a person to loose his hand than to have his entire body (in other words, his entire person) suffer unending anguish in hell (vs. 30). The severity of this demand illustrated the radical nature of the ethics of the Decalogue, and the need for believers to deal with sin in their lives. Christ knew that His followers sometimes tolerated sin and that these vices could spiritually undo them. Jesus taught that it was better for them to remove the source of sin—regardless of how painful that process was—than to allow the continued practice of sin to bring God's judgment.

Marrying and divorcing (Matthew 5:31–32) were the third subject areas Christ discussed. A "potentially polygamous society"[343] formed the backdrop of Jesus' remarks concerning the sin of divorce. This transgression not only undermined the marriage relationship but also was a violation of the spirit of the seventh commandment.[344] Jesus prefaced His remarks by mentioning Deuteronomy 24:1–4, which authorized a husband to issue a certificate of divorce to his wife (Matt. 5:31). Undoubtedly many in Christ's day would have affirmed the teaching of Deuteronomy 24:1–4.[345] Nevertheless, various experts debated the issue of divorce and remarriage,[346] because in first-century Palestine divorce was rampant and was permitted for the slightest matter.[347] Furthermore, once a divorce had occurred, the estranged wife would usually remarry, for being in a husband-wife relationship was her only means of support.[348]

There were some religious experts who had failed to consider fully the divine perspective regarding marriage and divorce.[349] Rather than deal with the spirit of the Decalogue (the ethical expectations of which were immutable),[350] they tried to avoid and circumvent it with a host of clever interpretations and traditions, which they added to the law. As a result, the true intent of the Mosaic legislation was concealed and nullified.[351] Jesus, in His remarks, "did not abrogate, nor did he disapprove of, the legislation of Moses."[352] Instead, He brought corrective and needed balance to the topic[353] by stating that divorce for any reason other than sexual immorality—namely, any form of marital unfaithfulness or unchastity[354]—caused the rejected spouse to commit adultery. Likewise, marriage to an improperly divorced person was an act of adultery (Matt. 5:32).

Jesus' statements, rather than transcending "the Torah's divorce halakhah," brought it "into focus"[355] and demonstrated that "the *Torāh* taught a stricter way of righteousness than anyone could have desired."[356] Moreover, rather "than pitting His own teaching as new and therefore going beyond what the Torah taught," Jesus sought to "implement the true heart of the Torah" by "displacing the traditions which had usurped the Torah's effectiveness and spiritual dynamic."[357] Furthermore, Jesus' comments signified both a revocation of "the halakhah of polygamy" and a denial of "a man's right to have more than one wife."[358] The antithesis, then, is not "between the 'old Law' and the 'new,' but between a body of halakah which had been constructed for the sake of the few, and the abiding and enduring word of God which was fair to all."[359]

Because the occurrence of divorce is a tragedy, the Christian community should model God's compassionate and gracious character towards those experiencing it.[360] Believers should also welcome and accept those suffering through this experience (rather than sternly condemn and reject them for their deficiencies). Furthermore, Christians should help the divorced emotionally readjust and stabilize, especially as they experience feelings of guilt and loneliness. Moreover, believers should extend material care when necessary.

The taking of oaths (Matthew 5:33–37) was the fourth subject area Christ discussed. This raised an issue of concern that was dealt with in the third commandment of the Decalogue.[361] Christ mentioned the ancient teaching that it was important to heed, rather than violate, one's sworn pledge to the Lord (Matt. 5:33). This truth reflected the Old Testament's sanctioning of oaths, except for those that profaned the name of God (cf. Lev. 19:12; Num. 30:2; Deut. 23:21). Tragically, some in Jesus' day had brought hypocrisy and abuse to oath taking.[362] For example, legalists required a specific oath to make spoken words binding (cf. Matt. 23:16–22).[363] Likewise, supposedly any oath that did not include the name of God was not binding.[364] The implication for honesty was that one did not have to be truthful except under oath.

To eliminate these kinds of abuses,[365] Jesus declared that no oath should be made whatsoever. His preference was to abolish oaths, especially if these became occasions for lying and deceiving, rather than encouraging truthfulness.[366] The letter and the spirit of the Decalogue was that one should be truthful in every area of life. Thus, if one did not swear at all, one would not swear falsely.[367] Christ declared that heaven, the throne room of God, that earth, the footstool of His feet (cf. Isa. 66:1), and that Jerusalem, the city of the great King (cf. Ps. 48:2), were not to be cited as witnesses to any type of pledge, especially false ones. When a person appealed to any of these entities while making an oath, these became as binding as if the individual had invoked the name of the Lord.[368] Even oaths made against a person's head were to be avoided, for no person but God could control the lightness or the darkness of one's hair (Matt. 5:35–36).[369]

Christ declared that it was far better to make simple "yes" or "no" declarations of what one intended to do (cf. Jas. 5:12).[370] Anything said beyond this was not only evil in character but also had its origins in Satan, the evil one (Matt. 5:37; cf. John 8:44).[371] The Savior's point was that unambiguous language must suffice for human communication.[372] Telling the truth and shunning all forms of deceitfulness were of prime concern to Christ. This was also at the heart of the ninth commandment. When Jesus issued His prohibition of oaths, He was stressing the importance of maintaining integrity of speech.

Some religious groups[373] have taken Christ's prohibition as being absolute and universal.[374] Jesus supposedly banned all oaths from ever being made, favoring instead simple declarative statements of truth. On the surface this view seems convincing, but an examination of Scripture disproves such an interpretation.[375] For example, Christ Himself submitted to an oath (Matt. 26:63), and Paul invoked God as his witness concerning his claim that he constantly prayed for the believers living in Rome (cf. Rom. 1:9).[376] Furthermore, the Lord used an oath to confirm the unchanging nature of His purpose to bless the world through the descendants of Abraham (cf. Heb. 6:17).[377]

In point of fact, the Savior's prohibition against oaths in Matthew 5:33–37 was conditioned by the hypocritical practices of some in His day.[378] These legalists ingeniously tried to classify oaths in order to discount those that did not mention God specifically. For example, if they wanted to be relieved from certain oaths they had made, they could argue that these vows were nonbinding, for God Himself was not involved. Christ, however, revealed that such reasoning—though deceptively subtle—was false, for God still was implicated by the oath. Because Christ was addressing specific abuses occurring in His day, His ban on all oaths is not absolute and universal. Rather, it is time-bound in its application to a specific group of people, namely, those living under the law in first-century Palestine. Thus, it would be incorrect to assert that God prohibits believers today from making oaths.[379]

Seeking revenge (Matthew 5:38–42) was the fifth subject area Christ discussed. He mentioned the ancient teaching that the punishment given by the authorities had to be equitable and match the crime, not exceed it (vs. 38). The original intent of Exodus 21:24 (cf. Lev. 24:20; Deut. 19:21) was to limit the occurrence of vengeance,[380] to help the court mete out correction that was neither too strict nor too lenient, and to prevent having different penalties for different social classes.[381] Scholars have labeled this ordinance the law of retaliation (*lex talionis* in Latin).[382] The premise was to offer protection for the guilty party from disproportionate retaliation on behalf of the victim.[383] The law also ensured that the victim had the right to equal recompense.[384] In the absence of such an equitable enforcement of justice, lawlessness and turmoil would result.[385]

God originally intended the law of retaliation to be carried out by the appointed judges, who were responsible for maintaining law and order.[386] However, at the time of Christ some used the law to excuse their vendettas against others.[387] They turned a negative injunction into a positive authorization for them to take justice into their own hands.[388] Jesus opposed this view of the legalists[389] when He declared that God wanted His people to be characterized by humility and patience.[390] This meant that, except for the case of self-defense, a believer was not to resist someone who was violent against him. The believer was also not to exact revenge for any wrongs done against him. This teaching is in harmony with the spirit of the fifth commandment of the Decalogue, for being kind and conciliatory, even toward one's enemies, is at the heart of showing respect to others.

A court of law probably would have been the context of Jesus' teaching.[391] The implication is that He was not condemning the government's right to prosecute and punish those who were guilty of robbery and violence. Rather, Christ was denouncing a spirit of revenge.[392] To illustrate His point, Jesus said that if a person slapped one of His disciples on the right cheek, the believer was to turn the other cheek so that the person might slap it, if he so desired. The slap on the right cheek would have been a backhanded one, and would have been both an insult as well as an injury.[393] In the ancient Near East, people would have regarded the right side of the face as being more important than the left side. Thus, striking the right side would have been most humiliating.[394]

Within the context of Matthew 5:39, Jesus was indicating that His followers were not to seek restitution (cf. Isa. 50:6). Thus, for example, if a person chose to sue a follower of Christ with the intention of confiscating his coat,[395] the believer was also to give him his cloak.[396] Likewise, if a citizen of God's kingdom was forced by a Roman soldier to walk one mile,[397] he was also to be willing to walk two miles (Matt. 5:39–41). During the time of Christ, the armies of Rome occupied Palestine. A Roman soldier had the right to force a person to carry his possessions, in order to facilitate the transport of goods from one place to another.[398] Yet Roman law also protected conquered citizens from injustice by stipulating that a soldier could compel someone to carry his load for only one mile.[399]

If a person asked one of Jesus' followers for something, the believer was to give it to him. Likewise, if a person wanted to borrow something from a disciple of the Savior, the believer was not to deny the request (vs. 42). It would be incorrect to take Jesus' comments as legal prescriptions. For instance, He was not commanding His disciples to give endless amounts of money to everyone who sought it (cf. Prov. 11:15; 17:18; 22:26).[400] Rather, He was emphasizing the importance of showing kindness and benevolence to the poor (cf. Deut. 15:7–11; Ps. 112:5, 9).[401] The only limit to the believer's response is what compassion and the Scriptures imposed.[402]

In short, Jesus was urging believers to be more concerned about eternal matters than temporal issues and about "showing a forgiving, loving and generous attitude."[403] For example, the creaturely comfort and respect a believer had was less crucial than the goal of bringing glory to God. Likewise, ensuring that one never was insulted or taken advantage of was less vital than heeding God's Word. This meant that preserving one's material wealth was not as critical as helping other people in need. If Jesus' followers wanted people to treat them with kindness, generosity, and respect, they were also to treat others in the same way (Luke 6:31).

At issue here was being just and merciful. Instead of demanding their rights, Christ's disciples were to give them up freely.[404] Such a concept undoubtedly would have been radical and offensive to some nationalists living at the time of Christ. After all, they were accustomed to hating and retaliating against their enemies.[405] Likewise, they probably balked at the notion of a Messiah who would turn the other cheek against their enemies. It was inconceivable to them how such a person could lead their fellow citizens in a revolt against Rome.[406]

Showing love (Matthew 5:43–48) was the sixth subject area Christ discussed. The experts taught others to love their neighbors and hate their enemies (Matt. 5:43; cf. Lev. 19:18; Pss. 139:19–22; 140:9–11).[407] The idea of hating one's enemy, however, was an extra-biblical injunction maintained by some.[408] It was based on the narrow understanding that a neighbor included only one's fellow citizens.[409] Jesus carried on His ministry in the midst of this intensely prejudiced, exclusivist, and intolerant environment.[410] One of His goals was to tear down the walls that existed between sinners and God. Doing this would enable God's love to flow freely and not be hindered by such potential barriers as nationality, race, party, age, and gender.[411]

Thus, Jesus commanded His people not only to love their enemies but also to bless those who cursed them, do good to those who hated them, and pray for those who abused and persecuted them. Such compassionate behavior would demonstrate that Christ's disciples were true children of their heavenly Father (Matt. 5:44–45). Jesus was stressing that goodwill must not allow itself to be limited by ill will. In fact, those who were genuine children of the Father demonstrated their parentage by their moral resemblance to

Him who is love.[412] For example, the person who regarded showing forgiveness as a sign of weakness was hypocritical in asking God to forgive him. Likewise, the person who felt enmity toward others could hardly be an effective peacemaker for the Lord.[413]

God demonstrated His love for sinners by allowing His Son to die for them, even though they were His enemies (Rom. 5:8). The mercy, generosity, and fairness of God are also evident when one realizes that He provides sunshine for all people, regardless of whether they are evil or good. He likewise supplies rain for the righteous and the unrighteousness (Matt. 5:45). These truths underscore the universal goodness of the Creator, which is to be the model for the believer's conduct.[414] Theologians have used the phrase "common grace" to refer to the merciful favor that God bestows without discrimination on all people.[415] Despite what has been said, it would be incorrect to conclude from verse 45 that God's love is amoral. It would also be mistaken to deduce that He shows love without any distinction toward people and that therefore all people must be saved. Jesus taught otherwise (cf. 25:31–46), and the rest of the New Testament reveals that some aspects of God's love are linked to His moral character and the prerequisite of obedience (cf. John 15:9–11; Jude 1:21).

Since God was so gracious to His enemies, believers were also to be compassionate toward those who hated them. Christ reasoned that if God's people only loved those who loved them in return, there was nothing commendable or distinctive about that.[416] Society might regard the display of mutual love to be normal, customary, and sufficient to fulfill moral expectations. Christ, however, stated that it was ethically inadequate. Merely responding in love to those who have first shown love is indistinguishable from an exchange of favors. Jesus called His followers to show the love of God without preconditions or self-imposed limitations.[417]

Jesus' followers should not expect to receive any heavenly reward for displays of love that were narrowly focused and conditional in nature, for the most despised people of society—namely, those who made a sizeable profit by collecting taxes from their fellow citizens on behalf of the Roman government[418]—showed love to the same extent.[419] Jesus also said there was nothing uniquely Christlike in greeting only one's brother,[420] for even unsaved people did that. It was unusual to display kindness not only to one's brother but also to one's enemy (Matt. 5:46–47). Moreover, if a believer lent his money or goods only to people from whom he expected to receive an interest payment, there was nothing commendable about that, for sinners did the same thing (Luke 6:34). It was distinctively more godly not only to lend one's possessions to other people but also to expect to receive nothing in return for one's kindness.

When Christ's followers operated in the manner previously described, their spiritual reward in the kingdom of God would be great. They would demonstrate that they were His true children, for He extended His kindness even to people who were ungrateful and wicked. Therefore, just as God was merciful, likewise His people should be merciful (vss. 35–36). The implication is that, in every area of life, God's people were to adhere to the perfect moral standard revealed in the Decalogue. They were to obey all the directives of Scripture, not just those they felt were most convenient. For instance, they were to love other people—including their enemies—with the sacrificial love of Christ. In fact, there was to be no limit to the compassion and kindness that God's people displayed, for He placed no limits on these virtues.

The consequence is that the high ideals of the Torah were to be the goal that believers strove to achieve. Jesus went so far as to say that His followers were to be as perfect as His heavenly Father (Matt. 5:48; cf. Lev. 19:2).[421] The Greek adjective rendered "perfect" in Matthew 5:48 is τέλειος (*téleios*). In the context of Jesus making a comparison with God, the word means "to be fully developed in a moral sense."[422] *Téleios* could also refer to "maturity of behavior."[423] In both cases, Jesus' emphasis was on "wholeness of consecration to God,"[424] as seen in being unreservedly compassionate.[425] Just as God was "unrestricted in His goodness,"[426] in the same way the disciples were to be unmitigated in their love.[427]

This attitude stands in contrast to the Dead Sea Scroll writings (found at Qumran)[428] of the Essenes. They were concerned with "correct, flawless fulfillment of the entire Torah," whereas Jesus was talking about a "deepening of the law that culminates in the renunciation of vengeance on the one hand, and love of one's enemies on the other."[429] With respect to the legalists of Jesus' day, they were satisfied with partial obedience to the moral law of love. Christ, however, wanted something profoundly different for His disciples.[430] They were to allow their lives to be reshaped and transformed[431] by the perfect example of their heavenly Father.[432] If they acted in this way, they would fulfill every aspect of the moral law revealed in the Decalogue (cf. Rom. 12:8–10).

In summary, Christ was focusing on ethical purity and spiritual maturity, which were demonstrated by the believers' willingness to heed God's commands.[433] This aspect of God's perfection is evident in His gracious provision of food and clothing to both the righteous and the unrighteous. He is not generous because He expects the wicked to respond with gratitude and reverence. In fact, He knows that apart from His saving grace the unrighteous will never appreciate His benefits.[434] Furthermore, God's generosity to His enemies is neither a sign of weakness nor an indication of moral indifference to the good and evil practiced by humans. Scripture teaches that the Lord will one day judge the righteous and the unrighteous (cf. Dan. 12:2; John 3:18). In the meantime, God's gracious provisions are given freely and unconditionally, thus removing any justification the wicked might claim in wanting to hate Him.[435]

The Moral Law Properly Applied by Christ (Matthew 6:1–7:12). Jesus ended the central section of His Sermon by properly applying the moral law. For instance, in 6:1–7:12 Christ focused on specific aspects of the law that some had misapplied and that needed to be handled correctly.[436] Jesus instructed His listeners not to perform righteous acts so as to gain attention from people. He explained how these good deeds were to be performed and what eternal rewards would flow from doing them. An examination of these verses shows that there are repeated references and allusions to the commandments of the Decalogue.

Giving to the needy (Matthew 6:1–4) was the first issue that Jesus discussed. It is clarifying to note that in verses 1–18, the acts of piety which Christ mentioned follow a consistent logical structure.[437] First, there is a warning not to do a pious activity in order to win the praise of others. Second, there is a guarantee that those who ignore this warning will get what they sought, but nothing more. Third, there is instruction on how to perform a virtuous activity in private. Fourth, there is the promise that the Father, who sees all that His people do in private, will reward them in public.[438]

Jesus made His remarks against the backdrop of prominent individuals who engaged in pious activities for a variety of reasons, most of them being self-serving. For instance, they performed public acts of righteousness[439] to be noticed by others.[440] Jesus, however, stated that good deeds should be done with no thought of being noticed or praised by anyone. Also, when engaging in religious activities, one's motives must remain pure and free from any self-serving tendencies. Otherwise one could expect to receive no eternal reward from the Father in heaven (vs. 1). The acclaim one received from other people was the only reward he could expect to get. Moreover, when pious activities are performed for self-serving reasons, the person doing the act is getting the admiration that alone belongs to God. This represents a fundamental violation of the first commandment of the Decalogue, for the egocentric person has made himself, rather than the Lord, his god. His self-serving ways also represent a violation of the second commandment, for he wants others to adore him, rather than the Lord.

In Jesus' day, public and private contributions were collected on a regular basis and used to care for the poor and needy. The people of Judea made additional contributions during special feast days and synagogue services. Some donations were made in private, while others were collected in public places.[441] Jesus said that whenever God's people gave to the poor, they were not to draw attention to themselves. The practices of some in first-century Palestine formed the backdrop for this injunction. When a charitable deed was performed, someone would blow a trumpet in the synagogues and streets to announce the deed to the public. In this way the benefactor would receive praise and admiration from others.

There has been a considerable amount of discussion concerning whether the Greek phrase rendered "sound a trumpet"[442] should be taken literally or metaphorically.[443] The reason for the debate is that no statement can be found in any ancient Jewish writings that refer to the custom of sounding a trumpet before giving charitable gifts on the Sabbath.[444] Some try to resolve the problem by suggesting that Christ was referring to "the practice of sounding trumpets on the occasions of public fasting in times of drought."[445] Others think Jesus was talking about "the modern custom of beggars in the East, who blow the trumpet before him from whom they ask alms."[446] These are possible options, but there is no way of verifying that Christ specifically had them in mind when He criticized the practices of some benefactors.

Still others think Jesus was referring to the clanking of money as it was thrown in the thirteen trumpet-shaped money chests used in the temple to prevent pilfering.[447] The problem with this view is that it does not adequately explain the practices of some benefactors when they were outside the temple.[448] Perhaps Christ was speaking metaphorically; in this case, He would have been deliberating exaggerating and caricaturing the abuses of some.[449] Expressed differently, Jesus was pointing to real practices as He made them a spectacle of ridicule.[450] Christ thus used satire to underscore that the motives of some benefactors for giving to the poor were self-seeking and hypocritical.[451]

The Greek noun rendered "hypocrites" (ὑποκριτής, *hypokritēs*) originally referred to play-actors or role-players in ancient tragedies or comedies.[452] Eventually, the noun took on the metaphorical nuance of "pretender" or "dissembler."[453] Those who fit the label were hypocrites in the truest sense of the word (namely, feigning to be other than they really were).[454] Just as the stage was a sham world and its actors imposters, so too some pious-looking individuals were frauds who deceived the people.[455] These fakes were supposed to be telling the truth and shunning all forms of deceitfulness. Instead, they made a career out of lying and dishonesty. Their hypocrisy represented a violation of the spirit of the ninth commandment of the Decalogue.[456]

Jesus' argument was clear—the imposters did not do charitable acts out of compassion for others, but for the sake of appearance. The world would say that their deeds were good, but God would say that their motives were deceitful. Christ declared that the recognition these frauds received from the public was the only reward they could expect to get (vs. 2). The Savior's comments indicate that the main intent of some benefactors was not to give to the poor, but to buy the accolades of the public.[457] This is what they paid for and this is all they received.[458] It is ironic that their good deeds merited the applause of people, but reaped the condemnation of God.[459]

Christ taught that it was far better to engage in a charitable activity without any desire to be noticed by others. One should not seek to be admired and praised by the public for giving to needy people. One's intent should be to honor God and give Him recognition. When this is a person's true motivation, he is honoring the sentiments of the first and second commandments of the Decalogue. This humble attitude is reflected in Jesus' comment about not letting the left hand know what the right hand is doing (vs. 3). Christ's statement should not be taken literally; rather, He meant that one's participation in a charitable activity should be so secret that the giver readily forgets what he gave.

One does not need to announce to the public his acts of kindness and compassion. If one's motivation is only to glorify God, he should do his charitable giving in secret or private. In this way the Father in heaven, who is well aware of such actions, will reward the giver (vs. 4). God might do so by enabling the person to grow and mature spiritually. He might also bless the believer with eternal riches of some kind. It would be mistaken to conclude from Jesus' remarks that charitable giving is improper. He was attacking the manner in which some benefactors gave alms, not the pious activity itself. Christ was teaching that instead of such ostentation, secrecy should characterize the performance of the believer's works of righteousness.[460]

Praying appropriately (Matthew 6:5–15; Luke 11:2–4) was the second issue that Jesus discussed. Regrettably, some people in Christ's day used this pious activity to obtain recognition. They loved to stand in prominent spots in the synagogues and on the corners of busy streets so the public could see what they were doing.[461] In Jesus' day, one normally prayed while in a standing position.[462] One might lead the congregation in prayer during the synagogue service or while standing before the ark where the Torah scrolls were stored. Also, one might be standing on a street corner or in a public place during one of the prescribed times for prayer.[463] No doubt many onlookers admired what appeared to be a display of pious devotion; however, God knew these practices were a charade. Jesus said that the recognition these attention-seekers received from the public was the only reward they could expect (Matt. 6:5).

It is ironic that an activity which was intended to bring honor and praise to God would be used to bolster the reputation of the worshiper. This violated the first commandment of the Decalogue, for the person had made himself, rather than the Lord, his god. He also violated the second commandment, for he was so preoccupied with serving himself that he had no real desire to serve God. Christ taught that to foster a humble attitude, it would be better for His followers to pray in a private, secluded spot.[464] By taking this approach, they would ensure that they were not drawing attention to themselves. Jesus promised His listeners that God, who is unseen, was well aware of their prayers and would reward them accordingly (vs. 6). Despite what has been said, it would be a mistake to assume that the Savior condemned praying in public, for even He prayed in public settings (cf. John

11:41–42).[465] His point was that the true citizens of God's kingdom were to pray with pure motives, rather than self-serving ones.[466]

Another problem involving prayer was that some of the unsaved engaged in meaningless repetition.[467] The pagans believed that their gods thrived on incantation and repetition.[468] They thought that by saying the same words over and over in prayer, they would influence the deity to hear their requests (cf. Matt. 6:7).[469] Jesus stated that such beliefs about prayer were based on superstition, not on trust in God. That is why the Messiah's followers were not to repeat themselves endlessly in prayer, for the Father already knew what they needed even before they asked (vs. 8). Therefore, meaningless repetition was unnecessary and insulting to God.[470] The more believers engaged in this practice, the more they violated the spirit of the third commandment of the Decalogue, for they were treating the person and character of God in an empty or meaningless way.

Jesus' remarks notwithstanding, it would be incorrect to infer that He was condemning everyone who prayed long prayers or repeated their requests, for even He prayed all night (cf. Luke 6:12) and repeated His petitions (cf. Matt. 26:44).[471] Rather, Christ was censuring the notion that prayers are like incantations that can compel God to do what He otherwise is unwilling to do.[472] Jesus was also denouncing the idea that through prayer people can overcome God's unwillingness by tiring Him with their words.

After commenting on the detestable practices of the hypocrites,[473] Jesus then instructed His disciples to pray in a certain manner. What He said is not a rigid magical formula that He wanted them to mechanically repeat over and over, for this would contradict what He had said earlier in this passage.[474] Rather, Christ intended the prayer to be a model after which to pattern other petitions.[475] The prayer, which is "Jewish in language and thought,"[476] briefly sums up the great themes of Jesus' teaching and expresses the desire of His disciples for God to establish His kingdom.[477] Through this petition, they acknowledge their dependence upon the Father to supply their daily needs. They also confess that He has reconciled them to Himself and that it is only through His power that they can resist temptation.[478]

Some dispensationalists have argued that Jesus did not intend the Lord's Prayer to be applied to believers in the church age. Supposedly, the context and the character of the prayer—as well as the entire Sermon—have an earthly millennial kingdom in view.[479] Another eschatological interpretation maintains that the Pater Noster refers to "the period of the last days, involving the return of Christ, the destruction of the forces of evil, and the definite establishment of God's rule."[480] An examination of the biblical text, however, indicates that these notions are mistaken concerning the applicability of the Sermon for believers today.[481] Neither Christ nor His apostles prohibited believers from using the prayer. Moreover, the Bible does not insinuate that the prayer was designed solely for use in the eschaton. The fact that the prayer appears in both the Gospels of Matthew and Luke indicates that it was intended for Jewish and Gentile Christians alike.[482] In light of these observations, an entirely eschatological interpretation seems too narrow and restrictive to accept as legitimate.

With respect to Matthew 6:9–13 and Luke 11:2–4, scholars have debated how they are related.[483] The Matthean version is longer than the Lukan rendition, and it is also more rhythmical and liturgical in its composition.[484] In addition, all of the Lukan version is contained in the Matthean rendition.[485] Some think that Matthew's version of the Lord's Prayer was the original, and that Luke borrowed and condensed it. Others say that Luke's version of the model prayer is the original and that Matthew expanded on it to reflect his theological and linguistic perspective. Still others maintain that the Matthean and Lukan versions originated from different, independent sources. Each of the theories has a considerable degree of subjectivity to it, which makes it difficult to determine which one is the most accurate. Of fundamental importance to the debate is the fact that the historical contexts are quite different for the Matthean and Lukan versions of the Lord's Prayer. This suggests that Jesus taught this form of prayer on more than one occasion during His earthly ministry.[486]

Jesus' model prayer contains various elements that should be included in all types of prayer to God. Some aspects of what Jesus said concern the believers' relationship with God, while others deal with their relationship with people. Thus, the thematic emphases of the Lord's Prayer parallel those of the Decalogue.[487]

In His model prayer, Christ first mentioned praise or adoration. The idea is that, before one ever mentions his needs and concerns, he should first acknowledge the holiness of his heavenly Father (Matt. 6:9). The Greek noun rendered "Father" (πατερ, *patēr*) is a term of intimacy that denotes a "close, familial relationship."[488] Moreover, the verb rendered "hallowed" (ἁγιάζω, *hagiázō*)[489] means "to treat as holy"[490] and implies the ideas of reverence,[491] honor, and obedience.[492] Also, in Bible times a person's name often denoted his nature or character.[493] Accordingly, God's name is a self-revelation of His nature, especially in terms of His saving acts in history.[494] Thus, to say that God's name is holy is to confess that He alone is morally pure and absolutely transcendent from His creation.[495]

This truth helps to explain the rationale behind the second commandment of the Decalogue—namely, that since God is infinitely distinct and set apart from His all He has made, it is an offense to make an idol to represent Him.[496] For that reason, to acknowledge the holiness of God is a corrective against any self-seeking motives in prayer. This assists us in understanding why Christ wanted His followers to focus their attention first on God, not themselves or others.[497] Jesus' directive reflects the concern of the first commandment of the Decalogue that as we pray, we should worship only God.

When believers commune with God in prayer, they not only are asking that His creatures would keep His name holy, but also that He Himself would sanctify His name by being the holy Judge and Savior.[498] These truths serve as a reminder that the Father is in heaven, that He cares for His people on earth, and that He can be approached on a personal basis.[499] They learn that in Him they can find eternal spiritual rest, a truth made evident by the fourth commandment of the Decalogue.[500]

As one prays to God, he should focus on the Lord's continuing rule in his life and the successful accomplishment of His will. The believer should long for God to manifest His kingdom and His will completely on earth, even as He fully implements His rule in heaven (vs. 10). Believers understand that in one sense God's kingdom already exists in the hearts and lives of those who obey the Lord and yield to His will. They also know that the kingdom will not come until God's will is perfectly done throughout the world, and it is for this that they pray.[501]

The implication of these truths is that believers should regularly ask God to help them and their fellow Christians remain submissive to His guidance and directives. When Jesus' followers obey God, they demonstrate that they are subject to His rule and that they want His will to be accomplished in their lives.[502] Verses 9 and 10 moreover indicate that when believers pray, they should first focus their attention on God and His glory. Then, as verse 11 makes clear, they should concentrate on their personal needs. From this we see that it is perfectly acceptable for believers to petition God concerning their ongoing needs, for He is the One who provides them with their daily sustenance.

With respect to the Greek adjective rendered "daily" (ἐπιούσιος, *epioúsios*), it is a rare term whose "attestation in Greek literature is doubtful and its derivation uncertain."[503] A variety of meanings have been suggested, including "necessary for existence," "for the current day," and "for the following day."[504] When all the options are considered,[505] Jesus probably meant either "bread for tomorrow" or "the bread that is necessary."[506] The differing views regarding the derivation and meaning of *epioúsios* have led to a variety of interpretations concerning what Jesus meant in verse 11. Three of these explanations are worth mentioning.

The sacramental interpretation is that Jesus was referring to the bread received in the Lord's Supper.[507] The eschatological interpretation is that Christ's reference to bread symbolizes life in the coming kingdom.[508] This would make the petition equivalent to the appeal in verse 10, "Your kingdom come." The problem with these two explanations is that they present the interpreter with an unusual figure of speech that is incongruous with the simple phraseology of Jesus' prayer. The third interpretation understands verse 11 as a straightforward petition for God to supply the daily needs of His people.[509] This explanation is best,[510] for it is a theme that is developed in other portions of Jesus' Sermon (cf. vss. 19–24).

It would be incorrect to infer from Christ's statement that God will give believers everything they desire. Jesus not only wanted His disciples to depend on God, but also to moderate their longings.[511] Furthermore, when believers pray to God to supply their daily needs, they are indicating their desire to be content with what He gives them.[512] Additionally, by depending on God to meet their needs, they are less likely to worry about their continued well-being. This, in turn, will minimize their inclination to violate the eighth and ninth commandments of the Decalogue, which concern stealing and coveting respectively.

Verse 12 stresses the importance of believers confessing their sins, or moral and spiritual debts, to God (cf. Luke 11:4).[513] Jesus evidently was speaking in Matthew 6:12 about daily forgiveness, for the moment a person is saved, God forgives his sins (cf. Eph. 1:7).[514] Daily forgiveness is necessary to restore the believer's broken fellowship with the Lord (cf. 1 John 1:3, 9).[515] Campbell presumed from Matthew 6:12 that "the character of the prayer further eliminates it from the realm of church truth because it is based on law and not upon grace."[516] However, Campbell's assertion is not derived from a solid exegetical and contextual analysis of the Lord's Prayer. Jesus was not preaching a covenant of law-works to His listeners. Rather, He proclaimed a covenant based on grace, for He anticipated the work of the cross that He would eventually perform. In fact, throughout Jesus' earthly ministry, the concept of God's redeeming grace undergirded all His teaching (cf. John 1:17).

As Jesus spoke to His disciples, He instructed them to consider their relationships with others. This truth reflects what is taught in the Decalogue, the last six commandments of which deal with one's obligations to his fellow human beings (Exod. 20:12–17). Clearly, both the Decalogue and the Sermon on the Mount emphasize that one's relationships with others must not be ignored or dishonored.[517] With respect to the Sermon, Jesus stressed that God's forgiveness of His children should be reflected in their willingness to forgive people who wrong them.[518] The idea is that the more aware and appreciative Christians are of God's forgiveness, the more inclined they will be to forgive others.

Next, Christ encouraged His disciples to talk to God about their spiritual well-being. This truth is reflected in the NRSV marginal rendering of Matthew 6:13: "and do not bring us into temptation." On the surface this translation seems to suggest that God is the One who leads His people into temptation.[519] Such a conclusion, however, is theologically unsustainable (cf. Jas. 1:13–15).[520] Most likely, Jesus was stressing the importance of asking God to protect believers from situations that would entice them to sin.[521] Although God would never tempt His people to do evil, He does allow them to be tested in their faithfulness.[522] It is also possible to render Matthew 6:13 as, "and do not bring us to the time of trial" (NRSV main reading). This translation would be a reference to a time of persecution, whether imminent or future (cf. 13:21; 24:9–28).[523] This rendering serves as a reminder that believers should regularly ask God to deliver them from all evil influences, including the father of wickedness, the devil (cf. John 8:44).[524]

Some ancient Greek manuscripts add the following ending to Matthew 6:13: "For the kingdom and the power and the glory are yours forever. Amen" (NRSV, margin). The majority of New Testament text critical scholars consider this ending of late origin and thus seriously doubt its authenticity.[525] That possibility notwithstanding,[526] when the doxology is retained,[527] it provides an appropriate ending to verses 9–13.[528] It encourages believers to recognize that God is deserving of all power, authority, and honor throughout eternity. The disputed ending also fittingly balances the emphasis of Christ's model prayer. The invocation begins by focusing on God, then proceeds to focus on human needs, and ends by once again focusing on God.

Jesus had been stressing the importance of avoiding temptation and being delivered from the evil one.[529] His words served as a reminder that believers daily transgress against God and others (cf. 1 John 2:10). The Greek noun rendered "trespasses" (παράπτωμα, *paráptōma*)[530] conveys the "imagery of one making a false step so as to lose footing."[531] From a moral perspective, the noun denotes the violation of "the will and law of God."[532] Such terms as "offense," "failure," "wrongdoing," and "sin" help to convey this notion.[533] While *paráptōma* could refer to inadvertent misdeeds, the emphasis in Matthew 6:14 is on deliberate acts against God and humankind.[534]

In this verse, Christ taught that His followers would enjoy God's forgiveness to the same extent that they forgave other people for transgressing against them. Also, Jesus said that His disciples would not enjoy God's forgiveness to the same extent that they refused to forgive others for transgressing against them (vs. 15). Based on this verse, some have concluded that "forgiveness of others is a condition for receiving forgiveness from God."[535] But this supposition would contradict the truth that God's pardon of sin is entirely dependent on Jesus' atoning sacrifice.[536] Christ was not teaching that one has to forgive others in order to merit God's absolution. Rather, Jesus was stating that the outworking of the believer's having been forgiven in his daily life was linked to his willingness to forgive others who had wronged him (cf. Eph. 4:32).[537]

Fasting with the proper attitude (Matthew 6:16–18) was the third issue that Jesus discussed. Fasting is abstaining from eating for a period of time for a religious purpose.[538] Throughout history, believers have fasted for a variety of reasons: to express grief (1 Sam. 31:13), to petition God (2 Sam. 12:15–23), to humble oneself before God (1 Kings 21:27–29), to seek God's help (2 Chron. 20:1–4), to confess sins (Neh. 9:1–2), and to prepare oneself spiritually (Matt. 4:1–2). In the law of Moses, only the fast on the Day of Atonement was required (cf. Lev. 16:29, 31; 23:27–32; Num. 29:7; Acts 27:9).[539] However, after God's people returned from captivity in Babylon, they observed four other yearly fasts (cf. Neh. 1:4; Dan. 9:3; Zech. 7:5; 8:19); and in Jesus' day, the religious leaders fasted twice a week, namely, on Mondays and Thursdays (cf. Luke 18:12).[540]

Jesus noted that whenever some individuals fasted, they looked dreary and gloomy.[541] They purposely made themselves appear dismal so that others would know they were fasting. These pretenders wanted people to give them praise for what appeared to be a holy life. Jesus warned His followers not to act this way. He solemnly affirmed that the recognition the imposters received from the public was the only reward they could expect (Matt. 6:16). As in the examples of almsgiving and praying, fasting for self-centered reasons violated the spirit of the first and second commandments of the Decalogue. Instead of focusing one's attention on God and preparing oneself to serve Him better, the hypocrite sought to draw attention away from the Lord and to himself. He was also less effective in serving God with a humble heart. Moreover, the one who fasted for the wrong reasons was deceiving others (a violation of the ninth commandment) and coveting their praise (a violation of the tenth commandment).

Christ stated that when His disciples fasted, they were to anoint, or perfume, their heads with olive oil and wash their face (vs. 17). In ancient times anointing one's head with oil was part of the daily routine—except when fasting (Dan. 10:3)—and symbolized rejoicing (Ps. 23:5; 45:7; 104:15; Isa. 61:3). By anointing themselves when fasting, Jesus' followers would create a refreshed and invigorated appearance.[542] Though others might not know they were fasting, their unseen Father, who knows what was done in private, would eternally reward them for their devotion (Matt. 6:18). From what has been said, it should be evident that fasting is difficult, requiring self-discipline and sacrifice. It gives believers the opportunity to devote more time to spiritual pursuits. It says to God, in effect, "What I seek from You is more important to me even than eating." When believers fast quietly and sincerely, the Lord endows their work in the kingdom with spiritual power.

Shunning greed (Matthew 6:19–24) was the fourth issue that Jesus discussed. Some prominent individuals in Jesus' day sought to amass wealth, for they believed material riches were a sign of God's favor. In contrast, they regarded the absence of wealth as a sign of His displeasure. Such greed and materialism betrayed a spirit of worldliness and represented a violation of the tenth commandment of the Decalogue.[543] Jesus shattered these false notions by declaring that it was misguided to devote one's life to accumulating earthly treasures, for material wealth was subject to decay, destruction, and confiscation (vs. 19).

No one, of course, can escape the fact that everything in this world is subject to ruin.[544] Nevertheless, some people imagine they can prevent this from happening to their material goods. Christ made it clear, however, that everything one owns will one day be destroyed. Thus, it is foolish from an eternal perspective to amass earthly possessions.[545] This truth is reinforced by Jesus' use of the Greek noun translated "rust" (βρῶσις, *brōsis*), which literally means "eating."[546] In this verse it refers not only to the ordinary corrosion of metal, but also to mildew and wood rot.[547] Moreover, the noun could denote "consumption by insects," whose "activity works destructively and therefore prohibits the hoarding and collecting of earthly things."[548]

In first-century Palestine, the poorer inhabitants made their homes out of mud bricks; and it was easy for thieves to break into these dwellings and steal things.[549] Jesus alluded to this fact to point out how easy it was for someone to lose what he owned. Tragically, this did not prevent multitudes of people from continually hoarding greater and greater amounts of earthly treasures. Despite their efforts, this did not bring them real satisfaction. If anything, it filled the greedy rich with increased anxiety, for they were engrossed with preserving their temporal fortunes from being depreciated, lost, or stolen. Their lives became a visible testimony to the foolishness of covetousness and to the wisdom of heeding the tenth commandment of the Decalogue.

Jesus declared that it was far better to accumulate heavenly treasures,[550] for these were immune to decay, destruction, and confiscation. Likewise, the spiritual riches of God's kingdom could never be devalued, lost, or stolen (vs. 20). Other portions of Scripture teach similar truths. For instance, God preserves the believer's inheritance in Christ forever in heaven, allowing nothing to jeopardize God's bestowal of His eternal blessings (cf. 1 Pet. 1:3–5). Christ announced that wherever one's treasure was, that was also where his aspirations and desires were located (Matt. 6:21).[551] Expressed differently, where a person invested his time, talents, and resources was a barometer of what concerned him the most (Luke 12:34). People who spent their time amassing material wealth had their interests and aims anchored on temporal concerns, whereas people who spent their time amassing spiritual treasures had their interests and aims anchored on eternal concerns.

Jesus switched from talking about one body part—the heart—to talking about another—the eye; nevertheless, He was still on the topic of problems associated with greed for worldly wealth.[552] In first-century A.D. Palestine, the setting of the sun meant it was time to light the lamps. Jesus said that just as a lamp spreads a glow in a room at night, so the eye brings light into the body. A person's eyes give his body the ability to see. If one's vision is clear and accurate, his body will be unimpaired in its ability to see. Likewise, God has given believers spiritual vision, that is, the ability to grasp eternal truths.[553] If a believer's spiritual vision is clear and accurate, he will be unimpaired in his ability to discern God's will and effectively serve Him (Matt. 6:22). If a person's physical eyes are damaged, however, his vision will be obscured or even eliminated. Likewise, if someone's spiritual eyes are damaged, his ability to discern God's will and effectively serve Him will be impaired. With blinded or obscured spiritual vision, the darkness or ignorance a person encounters is immeasurably great (Matt. 6:23; cf. Luke 11:34–36).

Jesus' comments had a direct application to the pursuit of wealth.[554] The presence of self-serving goals, desires, and interests can block a person's spiritual vision and impair his ability to see clearly what God wants to do with his life. Thus, if a person's foremost goal is to amass material possessions, his spiritual vision is blocked and he has become misguided. Only God can enable a person in this condition to radically change his life priorities (cf. 1 Tim. 6:9–10, 17–18).

Some people who intellectually grasp the significance of Jesus' comments try to straddle the fence between temporal and eternal interests. Like some individuals living in first-century Palestine, they imagine they can serve God and still hoard material wealth. The Savior, however, asserted that no person can serve two masters. For example, a person's master is either material riches or the Lord. He either loves money and hates God, or hates money and loves God. There is no middle ground. His devotion will be so fixed on one concern that he will think nothing of the other concern. Consequently, no person can be the servant of both God and money (Matt. 6:24; cf. Luke 16:13).

Jesus was urging His followers to decide who was going to be their real master, for He knew that divided loyalties between God and money would plunge them into spiritual turmoil. Jesus' words reflect "the same insistence on undivided loyalty to God that we found in the first of the Ten Commandments."[555] Moreover, Christ realized that selfishness and greed would leave His disciples spiritually blinded. He wanted them to live contentedly with whatever they possessed, for they had chosen what was eternal and lasting. Those who ignored the Savior's teaching on this matter would remain entrapped in their worship of a pseudo-deity. Although they might think they could worship the true God while being the slave of money, they were incorrect. Serving materialistic goals remains forever incompatible with serving the living God. Furthermore, once money is given power, it crowds out everything else and leaves the worship of God as an empty gesture.[556]

It would be mistaken to conclude from Jesus' teaching that riches are inherently evil. The Savior was not condemning wealth, but greed and the hoarding of money. He viewed the desire to accumulate wealth as a substitute for faith.[557] He also saw enslavement to wealth as the root cause of covetousness (a violation of the tenth commandment of the Decalogue) as well as murder (a violation of the sixth commandment), adultery (a violation of the seventh commandment), stealing (a violation of the eighth commandment), and lying (a violation of the ninth commandment).

Forsaking worry (Matthew 6:25–34; Luke 12:22–31) was the fifth issue that Jesus discussed. The vast majority of people in the world are preoccupied with getting more money and possessions. The poor want to become rich and escape their poverty, while the rich want to become wealthier so they can preserve their affluence. Both groups fear being out of control or overwhelmed by life-threatening circumstances. Jesus taught that the believer's outlook on life was to be radically different from that of the unsaved.[558] Christians were not to worry, for it was counterproductive and prevented them from fully trusting God. Jesus was not condemning proper stewardship and forethought; rather, He was censuring anxiety over the future.

In view of that issue, the Savior urged believers not to be panicky about their lives. For instance, the provision of food, drink, and clothes—matters that the unsaved constantly fretted over—were not to preoccupy the thoughts of Jesus' followers. This is because there was more to life than these things (Matt. 6:25). Christ then explained that the lives of believers were of more significance and value than what they wore and ate. He pointed to the wild birds that flew in the sky[559] and stated that these creatures were not involved in planting and harvesting crops; yet the Father in heaven amply supplied their material needs. The point of Jesus' illustration was not idleness, but rather freedom from anxiety.[560]

The birds could find everywhere around them the insects they needed to eat—all provided by God. It stood to reason that the person of faith was of more value to God than a bird (vs. 26). This being the case, God would not fail to provide graciously for His people's needs, just as He never failed to provide for the needs of such creatures as birds. This truth stands in agreement with Exodus 20:6 of the Decalogue, where God promised to show mercy on those who loved Him and kept His commandments.

Sadly, the tendency of believers was to be consumed with worry over the most insignificant details of life. Christ declared that being anxious was powerless and useless, and thus a waste of time.[561] Some Bible scholars think Matthew 6:27 should be translated as it appears in the NRSV: "And can any of you by worrying add a single hour to your span of life?" Others think the verse should be rendered as it appears in the NRSV margin: "And can any of you by worrying add one cubit to your height?" In ancient times a cubit varied in length from eighteen to twenty-one inches.[562] It was the measure taken from the length of a person's arm from the elbow to the tip of his middle finger.[563] Jesus' point comes through clearly in either translation—worry does not change things.[564] It not only was futile to worry about small matters one could not control, but also the larger matters of life that lie even farther beyond one's control.[565]

Those who were excessively concerned about where their clothing, food, and shelter would come from never had any inner peace and rest. This condition is far different from the one Christ offers to believers. He is their source of eternal spiritual rest, a truth reflected in statements of the fourth commandment of the Decalogue. Christ pointed to the lilies of the field[566] and asked His audience to consider how such delicate flowers grew. These plants did not labor to provide covering for themselves; yet the great King Solomon in his entire splendor had not been clothed as magnificently as these flowers (vss. 28–29). To Christ's Jewish audience, Solomon would have been the foremost example of human glory.[567]

It stood to reason that the person of faith was more valuable to God than the lilies of the field. This being the case, God would not fail to provide for His people's needs, just as He never failed to clothe the grass of the field. Through faith in Christ, they could enter into their eternal Sabbath rest (cf. Heb. 4:1–11). Jesus then stated that the life span of grass was very short. One day it was alive and the next day people removed it to burn as fuel in the clay ovens of Palestine.[568] If God was willing to do so much to ensure the growth and development of something as seemingly insignificant as field grass, would He not do unbelievably more for His people?

Jesus assured His listeners that the Lord would provide for the basic needs of His children, individuals who typically were characterized by little (Matt. 6:30). Since God abundantly cared for His lesser creatures, it stood to reason that He would care even more for His highest creatures—human beings. That is why it was irrational to worry even in the face of transitoriness and death.[569] The Savior's comments were intended to enhance the confidence of His followers' trust in God. Since the Lord would always meet His people's needs, they were not to worry about obtaining such essential items as food, drink, and clothing (vs. 31). The more they remained panicky about these things, the less able they would be to serve the Lord effectively. Likewise, as long as they lived in worry, they would miss what true life in Christ was all about.[570]

Jesus next stated that the basic necessities of life were constantly preoccupying the thoughts of the unsaved. Believers, however, were not to be like them, for Christ promised that the Father would supply His people's needs (vs. 32). While the unsaved spent their lives seeking after the things of the world, which were destined to pass away, Jesus urged His followers to make seeking God's kingdom and righteousness their foremost priority. Some think the emphasis in this verse is mainly eschatological and thus understand Jesus to be referring to the future expansion of God's active reign on earth, the vindication of the upright, and the punishment of the wicked.[571] More likely, the connotation is ethical in nature.[572] This means that the principal goal of believers is the establishment of God's rule in their lives and in the lives of the unconverted. Also, the highest aim of any disciple is the manifestation of Jesus' righteousness in the lives of His people and imputed to repentant sinners.

Christians need not fear making heavenly concerns their greatest priority, for the Lord would not neglect their needs (vs. 33). When they truly honored God by their faith, He would honor their dependence on Him by supplying their needs. His children might not become wealthy in earthly treasures, but He would ensure they did not lack anything to serve Him effectively.[573] When God had the foremost place in the life of His children, they would turn to Him first for help, fill their thoughts with His desires, make His character the pattern for their behavior, and obey His moral law. In accordance with the first commandment of the Decalogue, they would worship God exclusively; and in accordance with the second commandment, they would serve Him only. Draper, in commenting on Matthew 6:22–34, stated that the "only call on the Christian is to seek to fulfill the provisions of the Torah as interpreted in Christian halakah."[574]

Since God would meet the needs of His people, they were not to worry about tomorrow. In fact, tomorrow would have anxieties of its own. Moreover, worrying about the future was pointless, for people could not control it. In fact, worrying about the future could never give anyone the ability to control it. Because people could not control the present with its innumerable problems, it was futile to become preoccupied with the concerns of the future. The troubles believers encountered each day were too many to count and beyond their control. This being the case, they were to entrust the present and the future to God (vs. 34). The grace He gave His children was sufficient only for the day; it could not be saved for use at a future time. If Jesus' disciples encountered troubles in the future, God would give them the grace they needed to handle their difficulties.[575]

Ceasing to judge others (Matthew 7:1–6; Luke 6:41–42) was the sixth issue that Jesus discussed. Here we find Jesus turning "from a negative attitude in one's own affairs (worry) to a negative attitude in one's attitude to others (censoriousness)."[576] Some in Jesus' day were experts at criticizing and condemning others in an unfair and hypocritical manner. By using unbiblical presuppositions, they formed distorted opinions about people. For example, they slandered and denounced John the Baptist and Jesus, basing their assumptions on inaccurate observations and conclusions. Such actions represented a fundamental violation of the fifth commandment of the Decalogue, for they had failed to affirm the dignity and worth of others.

The Savior countered such abuses of power and authority by stating that believers should pass no judgment on others, unless they also wanted to be judged in the same way (Matt. 7:1). One group interprets this verse to mean that other people would do the judging, while a second group says Christ was referring to God. According to the latter view, the judgmental person would be called by God to give an account for his censorious ways. Regardless of which option is preferred, the reason for Jesus' warning was simple and clear. Just as a person criticized and condemned others, in the same way he would be criticized and condemned. This judgment would be in accordance with the same moral standard that the original person used against others (vs. 2). Since that standard of measure was typically unfair and preposterous, any person being measured by it would feel that injustice was taking place.

The harsh, judgmental attitude that Jesus was condemning ran counter to the spirit of the ninth commandment of the Decalogue. Those who made unfair and preposterous judgments of others were distorting the truth and embracing a deceitful attitude. Jesus accordingly urged His followers to exchange a critical and harsh spirit for one that was merciful and generous to others. He noted that, if people knew how much blame they deserved to receive, they would be much less inclined to censure others. Likewise, if people took to heart their own faults, they would be much less eager to judge others for their shortcomings.[577] The true children of God endeavor not to denigrate others with severe and unfair criticism. Instead, they aim to be sympathetic and understanding of others when they fail.[578]

It would be incorrect to assume from Jesus' comments that one can eliminate the necessity of observing and evaluating the actions of others, especially in the spiritual realm.[579] For example, church leaders should ensure that God's people are not being led astray by counterfeit teachers and preachers (cf. 1 Thess. 5:21; 1 John 4:1). The method of observation and evaluation, however, is fair and objective. It is based on solid and factual evidence, not conjecture, gossip, and rumor. The goal is neither to criticize and condemn others nor to protect a particular power base of individuals. Likewise, the intent is not to destroy or to defame potential threats to the core group of leaders. Instead, one aim is to protect believers from spiritual impostors by alerting them to the presence of danger. Another objective is to lead the unsaved to a knowledge of the truth and salvation in Christ.

Some living in first-century Palestine did not have these biblical goals in mind when they criticized and condemned others. They sought to protect their power base by defaming and destroying any potential threats. Jesus told His disciples that such motives and actions were wrong. By His statements, He directed His followers not to criticize and condemn other people unfairly. The Savior followed this up by questioning how someone could criticize another person for a small particle of sawdust in his eye,[580] when the detractor failed to censure himself for the timber beam[581] in his own eye (Matt. 7:3). This is an example of rhetorical overstatement, and Christ used it to make His point.[582] He declared that people tended to exaggerate the flaws of others and overlook their own glaring problems.[583]

Jesus' line of reasoning is that it was hypocritical for someone to offer to remove the minute problem from another person's life, yet ignore or deny the existence of a major problem in his own life (vs. 4). That is why Jesus condemned all forms of unfair criticism. He told the frauds to deal honestly with and resolve the major problems in their own lives before they even tried to remove the minor problems in lives of others (vs. 5). Otherwise, when someone disregards his sins and capitalizes on the sins of others, he is trying to control and manipulate them to his advantage. He knows how easy it is to ignore ethical and spiritual deficiencies in his own life and stand in judgment over minor flaws that he sees in other people. In fact, doing this gives him a false sense of moral superiority and influence. But James 4:12 says there is only one Lawgiver and Judge—God. Consequently, those who try to usurp Him in this role are assuming a divine prerogative, and this represents a fundamental violation of the first commandment of the Decalogue.

Christ knew that many would not accept or appreciate His teaching and the future teaching ministries of His disciples. Moreover, He and His followers would face rejection and persecution. The Savior therefore urged His disciples to exercise discernment and caution as they ministered the truth.[584] They were to invest their time and resources in people who had a genuine desire to learn God's Word and spiritually grow. The selectivity Christ advocated did not mean believers should avoid evangelizing the unsaved and discontinue teaching them spiritual truths. Jesus' point was that the verities of God's holy Word should not be entrusted to depraved individuals, who only cared to reject the truth and attack believers.

The Messiah realized it was senseless to waste one's time trying to teach people who would disdain Scripture and detest God's children (cf. Acts 13:44–51; 18:5–6; 28:17–28). The unappreciative ingrates were like wild, unclean dogs that roamed the streets of Jerusalem in a dispassionate manner as they scavenged for food (cf. 2 Sam. 17:43; 24:14; 1 Kings 14:11; 21:19; 2 Kings 8:13; Prov. 26:11).[585] These individuals were also as insensitive as vicious swine.[586] Just as pigs, which were ceremonially unclean (cf. Deut. 14:8),[587] would trample and crush precious pearls, so too some individuals only wanted to tear apart what believers had to say (Matt. 7:6).[588]

Praying persistently (Matthew 7:7–12; Luke 11:9–13) was the seventh issue that Jesus discussed. In moments of discouragement or distress, believers can receive consolation and encouragement from their heavenly Father. Although He is the all-powerful and sovereign Lord, they should not be timid or fearful about praying to Him, for Jesus will intercede on their behalf (cf. Heb. 4:14–16; 1 John 2:1). Likewise, believers should not worry about petitioning God in a religiously acceptable manner or framing their words in exactly the proper way, for the Spirit will help them to communicate with God (cf. Rom. 8:26–27).

Thus, it was fitting for Jesus to encourage His disciples to pray. He stated that when they asked the Father for something, it would be given to them. This meant He delighted to hear and answer their requests. It also meant the disciples were totally dependent on the Lord. The more they looked to God to meet their needs, the less inclined they would be to covet what others had (which would be a violation of the tenth commandment of the Decalogue). Whatever Christians sought from God would be found, and whatever door of ministry opportunity they accessed in His will would be opened to them (Matt. 7:7). The idea of knocking suggests that a certain urgency should accompany the disciples' praying. The Savior explained that His followers need not fear being rejected or ignored, for God would answer their petitions (vs. 8).

The tense of the Greek verb used in this verse (present active imperative) indicates continuous action—keep on asking, keep on seeking, and keep on knocking.[589] The Savior's comments implied that His followers were to persist until the answer came. Perseverance in prayer would produce tangible results, for no prayer went unheard or unanswered by God (cf. Luke 18:1). The Lord would neither disregard the petitions of His people nor treat them as insignificant. In fact, the prayers of His children were important and would get His personal attention.

It would be mistaken to assume from what Christ said that God would fulfill unbiblical requests. In that regard, Matthew 7:7 and 8 are not like a blank check that God issues to people for them to fill in as they please.[590] Before the Lord will answer a believer's request, he should be seeking to live and pray in His will. Also, the believer's requests have to reflect the Lord's desires and be in agreement with the moral law. Otherwise, if a Christian is selfish or self-serving in his requests, he cannot expect God to comply with them (Jas. 4:3). Likewise, if he approaches the Lord with doubt and skepticism, God will not fulfill his petitions. Moreover, if the believer asks the Lord for something that is sinful and contrary to Scripture, he will not receive it.

Ultimately, Jesus intended His comments to encourage, not discourage, His followers to pray. The Savior illustrated His Father's eagerness to fulfill the requests of His children by referring to the sensible practices of all parents. Normally, when a child asked his parent for a loaf of bread, he would not get something as useless and inappropriate as a stone. Moreover, if the child asked for a fish, a reasonable parent would not hand him a snake, for that would be cruel and insensitive (Matt. 7:9–10).[591] Similarly, God was not cruel and insensitive toward His children; rather, He was sensible and reasonable in handling their requests.

Human beings, who are fallen and inclined to do evil, understood how to give beneficial and appropriate things to their children. This being true, believers were to consider how much more their heavenly Father would do for them when they brought their requests to Him. He would always give them what was sensible and appropriate to meet their needs for that moment. This would include such virtues as righteousness, purity, and wisdom (Matt. 7:11; Jas. 1:5). Luke 11:13 specifies that the Holy Spirit is the ultimate good gift one can receive from God.

Christ's teaching unveiled the heart of God. The Savior revealed that the Father was not stingy, selfish, or begrudging. Thus, His children did not have to grovel and beg as they brought Him their requests. They knew He was a compassionate Father, who understood their needs and cared deeply for them. If human parents could be kind to their children, God, the heavenly Father of believers, was infinitely more considerate in hearing their petitions and meeting their needs.

Christ's teaching serves as a reminder of the true nature of God. He is not a reluctant stranger who has to be coaxed and harassed into bestowing His gifts; nor is He a malicious tyrant who takes vicious glee in playing tricks on others. God is not even like an indulgent grandparent who provides whatever one asks of him. Rather, God is the believer's heavenly Father and the Lord of an eternal kingdom. He is also the One who graciously and willingly bestows the good gifts of His kingdom in answer to prayer.[592]

In analyzing Matthew 7:11, Campbell asserted the following:[593]

> The distinctive character of this instruction on prayer is important. That this is not grace teaching is evident from the fact that prayer is not made in the name of Christ. ... The basis of appeal in the praying just considered is the faithfulness of the Father to His children, whereas the basis of appeal under grace is the believer's identification and union with Christ. Accordingly these verses have special relationship to the three periods often mentioned in this work: the first portion of Christ's earthly ministry while the kingdom was being offered, the tribulation period when the offer will again be renewed, and the kingdom itself, Christ's thousand-year reign upon the earth.

Despite the novelty of Campbell's view, it is incorrect for several reasons. First, the Bible does not restrict New Testament believers to praying only in Jesus' name. Prayer is typically addressed to the Father (Matt. 6:9–13; Luke 11:2–4; John 16:23; 17:1ff.; Eph. 1:16–17; Phil. 1:3; Col. 1:3), through the Son (John 16:24; Heb. 4:14–16; 7:25; 1 John 2:1), and by the power and provision of the Spirit (Rom. 8:26–27; Eph. 5:16), all of which is in accordance with His promptings (Jude 1:20).

Second, it is true that Christ encouraged believers to pray in His name (John 14:13; cf. Acts 7:59; 1 Cor. 1:2; 2 Cor. 12:8). Despite Campbell's assertions, however, this does not mean that Jesus banned Christians from praying in the name of the Father. Jesus' name is not a special, magical formula added onto the end of each prayer to guarantee God's answer. Rather, it signifies that one desires the same things Christ would desire to be accomplished (cf. John 15:7). Thus, the requests are made in the authority that His person represents.

Third, Campbell made a sharp distinction between appealing in prayer to the faithfulness of the Father to His children and appealing in prayer to the believer's identification and union with Christ. However, there does not seem to be any theological or exegetical basis for such a differentiation. Thus, it is groundless to suppose that Matthew 7:11 is not grace teaching. In fact, Christ was addressing His disciples, and through them, the future church, all of whom would be the recipients of His grace (cf. Eph. 4:8–9). This being the case, Campbell is incorrect to assert that either Matthew 7:11, the Lord's Prayer, or the entire Sermon on the Mount have nothing to do with the church.

In His discourse, Christ was encouraging His followers to pray persistently to God with the assurance of knowing that He would answer their requests. Jesus also stressed the importance of His disciples modeling the behavior of their heavenly Father. Like Him, they needed to be generous and gracious to others. Believers also needed to be sensible and reasonable in how they responded to the requests of those in need. In short, Christians were to do what was beneficial and appropriate, not what was cruel or insensitive.

Given that, Jesus urged His followers to do for others what they wanted others to do for them (Matt. 7:12). Philosophers have called this truth the Golden Rule.[594] This maxim is found in negative form in the ethical teachings of ancient Greeks, Romans, Jews, Hindus, Buddhists, and Confucianists.[595] Among ancient non-Christian thinkers, the Golden Rule went something like this: "Do not do to others what you do not want done to you."[596] This formulation is restrictive in nature and premised on the fear of retaliation. Jesus, however, made the truth a positive obligation, one that was inclusive, not exclusive, in nature.[597] By formulating it this way and placing it at the end a major section of His teaching, the Savior enabled the "ethical maxim" to take on "new meaning."[598] Likewise, Jesus "demands that the person addressed take the initiative."[599] Christ's statement is based on the generosity, forbearance, and forgiveness of God. Believers were to follow the example of their heavenly Father in the hope that others whom they treated kindly would respond with kindness.[600]

Jesus' declaration implied that He did not want His followers to be preoccupied with protecting themselves from outside harm. Rather, He wanted them to concentrate on actively helping others in need.[601] It may be a loving gesture to refrain from killing one's enemy. However, the ultimate act of love is to give one's life for one's enemy (cf. John 15:13).[602] What Christ said, as articulated in the Golden Rule of Matthew 7:12 (cf. Luke 6:31), encapsulated the teaching of the Law and the Prophets (that is, the entire Old Testament; cf. Exod. 23:4; Lev. 19:18; Deut. 15:7–8; Prov. 24:17; 25:21).[603] Expressed differently, this timeless truth did not do away with and replace the Torah, but rather fulfilled it. The Golden Rule served as an integrating hermeneutical principle for understanding the Old Testament. Although the Golden Rule was not explicitly stated in the Hebrew Scriptures, it was implicitly contained in them and thus was a key to their proper interpretation.

The phrase "the Law and the Prophets" in Matthew 7:12 bracket off the preceding verses (beginning at 5:17) from the rest of the Sermon on the Mount.[604] Christ's intent in this section of Scripture was to relate His teaching and redemptive work to the moral law.[605] This is substantiated by the fact that the content analysis of 5:17–7:12 contains repeated references and allusions to the Decalogue. By contrasting Christian righteousness with legalistic righteousness,[606] Jesus decreed that only God could enable His people to fulfill the moral law and the nature of its absolute requirements.

The Direction, Lifestyle, and Spiritual Foundation of Christ's Followers (Matthew 7:13-27)

Matthew 7:13–27 explains the direction, lifestyle, and spiritual foundation of Christ's followers. These verses are parallel to 5:2b–16 and with them form the secondary emphasis of the Sermon on the Mount. Both these outlying frames of text concern the relationship of Jesus' followers to the moral law. One learns that when believers are properly related to the moral law, their lives will be filled with joy, purpose, and eternal hope. The antithesis of this is that those who are improperly related to the moral law will experience sorrow, futility, and despair in their lives. Christ's followers are on the path that leads into the kingdom of heaven (7:13–14). The genuineness of their conversion and commitment to Him is demonstrated by what they think, say, and do (vss. 15–23). Also, their lives are founded on the Savior, His teaching, and His redeeming work, not on themselves or others (vss. 24–27). Verses 13–23 are characterized by ethical admonitions, whereas verses 24–27 are presented in the form of a short parable.

The Two Ways (Matthew 7:13–14). Not every person who claimed to be a follower of Christ would be caring and compassionate. Also, not every person who insisted that he represented God would be obedient to the teachings of His Word. This was true in Jesus' day of all unsaved people. For example, some tried to merit God's favor by doing good works. Likewise, they believed their pious activities could earn them a spot in heaven (cf. Rom. 9:30–33). In contrast, others typically thought that anyone could get into heaven. They also reasoned that a God of love would not reject or condemn people He created, for supposedly that would be unfair and cruel.[607]

Jesus shattered the contemporary myths surrounding salvation by declaring that the entrance into eternal life was narrow. In contrast, the entrance into eternal destruction was wide and its pathway was broad or spacious. The road to eternal ruin was also convenient and acceptable to the unsaved. There were no obstacles or annoyances to discourage people from traveling down its path. That was why so many people entered through its gate (Matt. 7:13). Most scholars think Jesus was talking about issues relating to salvation and eternal life. Campbell, however, maintained that Jesus was speaking to first century Jews about their entrance into an earthly millennial kingdom centered in Jerusalem.[608]

This assertion stands in contrast to what was said in the previous chapter regarding the kingdom of God. In brief, the focus in Jesus' Sermon is on the royal reign of God and the fact of His ruling, not on a particular place (such as Jerusalem), a political entity such as the nation of Israel, or a special period of time (such as the so-called millennium).[609] These observations indicate that Campbell is mistaken in his claims about Matthew 7:13 and 14. Jesus was not speaking to Jews about entrance into an earthly, Davidic, millennial kingdom. Rather, Christ was talking about the way of salvation. When He spoke about the wide, easy road, He was referring to the path leading to hell, not exclusion from a classical and revised dispensationalist concept of the kingdom. Likewise, when He talked about the narrow, hard road, He was referring to the path leading to eternal life, not entrance into a literal ethnic Israel that was situated in Palestine and had Jerusalem as its capital.

In terms of Jesus' Sermon, He taught that people who criticized and condemned others or treated them in a harsh and insensitive manner would represent the types of individuals one would find on the path of destruction. They might have insisted they were good or pious individuals who had never done anything wrong; however, they were blinded to their spiritual need and how to meet it. Through the work of the law in one's life, a person sees that all have sinned and fall short of God's supreme standard of righteousness

(Rom. 3:23). One also learns that he needs divine pardon and stands in danger of being eternally damned. Tragically, some in Jesus' day had not allowed the moral law to do its work in their hearts. They may have had an expert knowledge of the Decalogue, but their pride and smugness blinded them to their need for redemption through faith in Christ.

Along the broad path that leads to destruction, people need not concern themselves with obeying God or loving others. Such freedom, however, was really a camouflage for slavery to sin. Although being on this path may have seemed fashionable and enjoyable, its destination brought unending anguish and suffering. In contrast, the entrance leading to eternal life was narrow, or small, and its road was constricted. This path on which believers travel might be compared to a difficult pass between two cliffs that is hemmed in from both sides.[610] The entrance into the divine kingdom is constricted for two related reasons. First, Jesus provides the only means for obtaining eternal life. This implies that a person is saved only through faith in Him. Second, all forms of sin must be abandoned. The implication is that a true citizen of heaven does not live in rebellion against God.

Along the pathway to life the traveler encounters many obstacles and hardships. For example, he might be struggling with sin, the flesh, the world, and the devil; or he might be criticized and condemned by other people; or he might be treated harshly and insensitively, and even experience persecution. These are the sorts of reasons why so few people travel along this road (Matt. 7:14). Furthermore, throughout life people are faced with making decisions concerning whom they will marry, where they will live and work, and what they will buy. More important than any other decision they make is the one concerning eternal life. Will they choose the path of life or the path of ruin? While it might be more popular to choose destruction, picking deliverance through faith in Christ is far wiser. Despite the conflicts the believer might experience, God will bless him with His eternal riches (cf. 2 Cor. 4:16–17).

The Two Fruits (Matthew 7:15–23). Christ warned His followers to be on the look out for spiritual frauds. These were bogus prophets or pseudo-spokespersons for God who claimed they were His authorized representatives. In reality they were like savage wolves disguised as harmless sheep. They might have appeared to be gentle and caring, but they were cruel and insensitive (Matt. 7:15; cf. John 10:12; Acts 20:29). The duplicity of these individuals indicated they had not taken to heart the spiritual intent behind the ninth commandment of the Decalogue. Also, their harsh demeanor revealed they were calloused to the spiritual implications of the fifth commandment. They may have thought they were lawkeepers, but their attitudes and actions indicated they were lawbreakers (cf. Jas. 2:10).

Jesus said the pious charlatans could be recognized by the spiritual yield they produced. Some of the fruits of these swindlers are mentioned in the New Testament: controversies (1 Tim. 1:3), divisions (6:3–5), destruction of faith (2 Tim. 2:18), and self-destruction by heresy (2 Pet. 2:1). To illustrate His point, the Savior noted that grapes were not harvested from thorn bushes or briars. Likewise, figs were not harvested from thistles (Matt. 7:16). In Christ's day grapes and figs were valuable food crops. In contrast, thorn bushes and thistles were worthless and irritating plants, whose presence could threaten the growth and development of valuable plants.

Jesus stated that a healthy, or sound, tree would always produce acceptable fruit, whereas a sickly, or worthless, tree would always produce unacceptable fruit. Likewise, a healthy tree could not produce worthless fruit and a sickly tree could not produce worthwhile fruit. In Bible times, farmers eventually chopped down and burned sickly trees that bore worthless fruit (vss. 17–19). Jesus again emphasized in verse 20 that religious frauds could be recognized by the spiritual fruits they produced. Genuine believers produced spiritual fruit that was acceptable, while self-righteous frauds produced fruit that was unacceptable.

There were two basic areas one had to consider: a person's beliefs and his behavior. For example, did he teach false doctrine or God's Word? Also, was he characterized by moral purity or impurity? Moreover, did he exalt himself or the Lord? Answering these sorts of questions would help one examine the motives of a self-proclaimed religious teacher, the direction of his life, and the outcome of his actions. Jesus explained that one day God would judge spiritual fakes and condemn them to eternal punishment in hell. The Savior undoubtedly had in mind people who believed they were right with God and yet were not. They imagined their devout activities met with His approval and merited His favor. In reality, what they said and did met with His disapproval and could never earn His favor. Concerning these individuals, Draper noted that they are "rejected as those who do lawlessness."[611] This denotes "the act of rejecting the Torah, which is described in 5:17–20."

Perhaps these lawbreakers were convinced they had a personal relationship with God; however, nothing could be farther from the truth. The Savior declared that not every person who repeatedly addressed Him as "Lord" (7:21) would get into the heavenly kingdom.[612] The Greek noun rendered "Lord" (κύριος, *kýrios*)[613] denoted a person who was "in a position of authority."[614] The word was also a "title of respect used in addressing or speaking of a man."[615] Throughout the New Testament, *kýrios* is used "of Yahweh/God."[616] This undoubtedly is due to the fact that, in the Septuagint, the noun "replaces the [Hebrew] proper name of God, the tetragrammaton YHWH."[617] When applied to Jesus, *kýrios* is used as "a royal and messianic title,"[168] indicating that the risen and exalted Savior is co-equal with the Father.[619]

Betz seems to advocate an alternate position. He maintains that while the title "Lord" assuredly "presupposes a christology, it is a christology which the Jesus of the [Sermon on the Mount] rejects."[620] This assertion, however, is not in harmony with the biblical text. As Kingsbury notes, "Matthew employs *kyrios*" as an "auxiliary christological title" with the intent of attributing "divine authority to Jesus in his capacity as the 'Christ'."[621] Moreover, Jesus did not rebuff some for being "deluded by their christology."[622] Instead, the Savior's point was that just because an individual sounded pious did not mean he was genuinely upright in his conduct. The true citizens of the divine kingdom were people who trusted and obeyed their heavenly Father (Matt. 7:21; cf. Luke 6:46). Betz also maintains that in Matthew 7:21–23, "Jesus does not figure as judge but as advocate of his disciples."[623] This claim, however, does not seem in accord with the text, in which the Messiah "appears as the eschatological judge"[624] who "exercises dominion on authority derived from God himself."[625]

With respect to the day of reckoning, many would claim and perhaps even argue with Christ that they did many wonderful deeds in His name.[626] These works included prophesying, casting out demons, and performing miracles (Matt. 7:22). But much to the surprise of these people, Jesus would declare that He never knew them in an intimate and personal way.[627] The implication is that they were not truly saved. In fact, the Lord would consider their vaunted deeds to be unacceptable. He would command them to depart from His presence, for they were practitioners of evil, not good (vs. 23). It is clear from this verse that Jesus, as the sovereign Master and Judge of the universe, would not tolerate practitioners of wickedness, or lawlessness, to dwell in His presence.

If pious frauds had compared their attitudes and actions with the stipulations of the Decalogue, they would have realized they were morally depraved. For example, in violation of the first and second commandments, they worshiped and served the false gods of popularity, power, and pride. In violation of the second commandment, they blasphemed the name of the Lord by their corrupt lives. In violation of the third commandment, the religious charlatans allowed disobedience and unbelief to prevent them from entering God's eternal Sabbath rest. In violation of the fifth commandment, they despised others who did not heed their humanly devised traditions. In violation of the sixth commandment, they cultivated hateful thoughts toward those who opposed them. In violation of the ninth commandment, they deceived others into thinking they were pious. Finally, in violation of the tenth commandment, they coveted the material wealth of others.

The problem of false conversions is still present today. Many well-intentioned people who engage in upstanding religious activities deceive themselves and others that they are saved, even though they are lost in sin. They imagine their noble deeds will earn them God's favor. The Lord, however, will reject their self-righteous ways, for they never learned the importance of trusting and obeying Him. Sadly, these people try to get to God on their own terms and in their own ways. They will one day discover that all self-motivated righteousness is unacceptable to the Lord, for it reveals an attitude of arrogance and independence, not humility and dependence on Him.

The Two Foundations (Matthew 7:24–27; Luke 6:47–49). Some prominent individuals in first-century Palestine took pride in their achievements. They proved by their attitude and actions that they did not need God. In this way, they had violated the first commandment of the Decalogue. Regrettably, their spiritual future was built on a foundation they had constructed. Because of this, they had failed to appropriate God's Sabbath rest, and thus violated the fourth commandment. Jesus declared that His true followers not only listened to His teachings but also put them into practice.[628] What He taught was based on the Decalogue and reflected its true spiritual implications.[629] Christ knew that some in His day refused to heed His instructions. They not only had rejected His claims to be the Messiah, but also had spurned His teachings. In the end they were foolish, even though they imagined themselves to be wise (cf. Rom. 1:22).

The genuine follower of Christ—that is, the one who trusted and obeyed Him—could be compared to a wise person who constructed his house on a foundation of solid bedrock (Matt. 7:24). The house represented the believer and his life, while the rock represented Jesus and His teachings.[630] The authentic child of God trusted in Jesus for salvation and built his life on the Savior's doctrine.[631] In Jesus' illustration the wise person's house successfully weathered severe rain storms. Though the rains descended, the rivers or flood waters rose, and the winds blew violently against the house, it remained standing, for it was founded on solid bedrock (vs. 25). Likewise the person who has faith in Christ and whose life is founded on His teachings would not only survive the storms of life but also enter the kingdom of God. Regardless of how rough life might have seemed at times, the believer was assured of being in Jesus' presence. The follower of Christ trusted and obeyed his Master, and his Master watched over him in this present life and in the life to come.

In contrast with the upright, the unregenerate spurned Jesus' teachings. They did not trust in Him for salvation, and they failed to apply His words to their lives. They were comparable to a foolish person who constructed his house on sand (vs. 26). Sand is a poor foundation for any structure because it provides an unstable and constantly shifting base. Likewise, founding one's life on the mere opinions of people leads to instability and ultimately ruin. When severe rain storms came, including tremendous floods and violent winds, the water washed away the sand. The person's house that was built on this unsure foundation quickly fell with a great crash (vs. 27). This means the collapse was complete and devastating. Similarly, the person who rejected Christ and His teachings would not successfully weather the storms of life. He had no guarantee of being with Christ either in the present or the future. On judgment day, the foolishness of his decision to live for himself would become apparent.

Regrettably, the unsaved's foundation was his own merit and worth. He guided his life on what he imagined was proper, and he staked his future on the goodness of his religious deeds. Despite his pious activities, he was devoid of eternal life and the Spirit's presence. On judgment day, Jesus would reject this person's self-righteous ways and condemn him to eternity in hell.

The unsaved had chosen to live in independence and defiance of God. In eternity, his self-imposed separation from the Lord would become an irreversible reality.

Epilogue (Matthew 7:28-29)

Matthew 7:28 and 29 form the epilogue of the Sermon on the Mount. Just as the prologue (5:1–2a) introduced Jesus' discourse, so the epilogue brought His message to a close. Christ's audience was favorably impressed with His teachings. In fact, when He had finished His preaching, the crowds were astounded and perhaps somewhat perplexed (7:28). Here was someone who had not received the formal religious training that other leaders of His day had obtained; yet, despite His lack of the proper credentials, He taught with distinctive power and persuasiveness.[632]

The legal experts of the day typically cited other scholars to support their statements (vs. 29).[633] But when Jesus taught, His spoke as the Son of God.[634] This meant His authority, which was divine, not only exceeded that of the legalists of His day,[635] but also that of Moses, the great lawgiver.[636] In fact, Jesus exercised the authority of "the One who will judge humanity in the final day"[637] (cf. vss. 21–23). Luz fittingly noted that this "authority shows first of all in [Jesus'] teaching."[638] It will also "be shown in his deeds in what follows." Moreover, in 10:1, Christ's authority is "transferred to the disciples." This episode anticipates "the universal authority which is given to the one who is exalted above heaven and earth" (cf. 28:18). Consequently, "for the believer, there shines in the Sermon on the Mount a glimpse of the glory and power of the heavenly Lord."

Matthew 7:28 and 29 imply that what Jesus preached must be heeded and applied by His followers. This is because the Savior's teachings are the expression of God's will and possess the supreme and absolute right to define what one believes and how he behaves.[639] This statement is an affirmation of the truth that the Sermon on the Mount applies to all believers, whether the followers of Christ's day or those of the whole church today. Expressed differently, Jesus' discourse provides guidance for regenerate persons (namely, Christians) living in an unregenerate world throughout church history.

Conclusion

In this chapter a content analysis of the Sermon on the Mount was conducted. Each major section was examined, and the conclusions reached in the preceding chapters were repeatedly drawn upon as Jesus' discourse was investigated. The study has shown unequivocally that the moral law of God and the nature of its absolute requirements are of central importance to understanding the overall thrust of Jesus' Sermon. Draper concludes his research on Jesus' discourse with this apt observation: "Its focus is, from start to finish, the question of the role of the Torah in the Christian community, and of true leadership and teaching consistent with that."[640]

The information obtained from the content analysis of the Sermon on the Mount, along with the information presented in the preceding chapters, makes it possible to address the five key questions that were broached at the beginning of this study. In turn, dealing with these issues will enable us to bring closure to the goal of this work, namely, to determine the nature of the relationship between the Decalogue and the Sermon and how that relationship affects the extent to which the moral law has ongoing pertinence for the Christian church today.

Chapter 7

Affirming the Moral Law's Enduring Relevance

The findings of chapters 2 through 6 make it possible to answer the five key questions introduced in chapter 1. Also, the observations and conclusions drawn from investigating these questions will make it possible to determine the nature of the relationship between the Decalogue and the Sermon on the Mount. A clear understanding of that relationship will indicate the extent to which the moral law has continuing relevance as a rule or guide of life for the church today.

The Biblical and Theological Relationship between the Decalogue and the Sermon on the Mount

The content analysis of the Sermon on the Mount indicates there is a strong biblical relationship between the Decalogue and Jesus' discourse. This is evident in the way the Sermon makes repeated direct and indirect reference to the commandments of the Decalogue. Beginning with the *first commandment*, it required the Israelites to worship no other god but the Lord (Exod. 20:2; cf. Deut. 5:7). The Sermon likewise emphasized the importance of making God the believer's only master (Matt. 6:24). Jesus also told His followers to set their minds on God's kingdom and His righteousness before everything else (vs. 33). They were worshiping the Lord exclusively when they did His will (7:21) and heeded what He taught (vs. 24).

The *second commandment* of the Decalogue directed the Israelites not to make for themselves a carved image of any likeness that is in creation (Exod. 20:4; cf. Deut. 5:8). They were neither to bow down to these images nor serve them (Exod. 20:5). The Sermon also emphasized the importance of giving exclusive service to God. Believers were to store up for themselves treasures in heaven by faithfully doing the Lord's will and work (Matt. 6:19–21). Jesus' followers were also to shun one of the world's most prominent idols—wealth (vs. 24). Instead of reverencing money, as many people did, believers were to give their hearts and lives to God.

The *third commandment* of the Decalogue directed the Israelites not to the take the name of the Lord in vain (Exod. 20:7; cf. Deut. 5:11). The Sermon likewise emphasized the importance of not treating God's name in an empty or meaningless way. For example, Jesus told His followers not to profane the name of the Lord in the taking of oaths (Matt. 5:33–37). He wanted them to treat the Lord's name—to which heaven, earth, and Jerusalem pointed—with the highest respect, honor, and reverence.

The *fourth commandment* of the Decalogue directed the Israelites to observe the Sabbath faithfully (Exod. 20:8–11; cf. Deut. 5:12). During this special time, they rested from their works so they could focus their attention exclusively on the Lord and make a determined effort to commune with Him. For example, by ceasing from their normal daily activities, they had an opportunity to meditate on His Word and worship Him in prayer. Calvin interpreted the Sabbath as a type of the believers' resting in Christ, that is, a ceasing from their own works.[1] Jesus had this concept of salvation-rest in mind when He said to His disciples, "strive first for the kingdom of God and his righteousness, and all these things will be given to you as well" (Matt. 6:33). In view of that, as the believer finds his eternal rest in Christ, he can cease from his works and allow God to work in him. The believer can also stop worrying about tomorrow (vs. 34), for he knows that God will supply whatever he needs to be faithful in his service.

The *fifth commandment* of the Decalogue directed the Israelites to honor their parents (Exod. 20:12; cf. Deut. 5:16). At the heart of this injunction is the obligation to respect and esteem one's parents. This includes affirming the dignity and worth of all people. In fact, by learning to honor one's parents, a person discovers the importance of appreciating all people. The Sermon also emphasized the importance of treating all people with dignity. For instance, Christ encouraged His followers to be merciful, for they were the beneficiaries of God's mercy (Matt. 5:7). Jesus taught His disciples to be peacemakers and thus demonstrate how God's children can be a force for harmony and reconciliation in the world (vs. 9). The Savior underscored the importance of not seeking revenge on those who mistreated them. Instead, believers were to be kind and conciliatory even toward their enemies (5:38–42). In fact, Christians were to love and pray for those who hated and mistreated them (vss. 43–48).

The *sixth commandment* of the Decalogue directed the Israelites not to murder (Exod. 20:13; cf. Deut. 5:17). Likewise, in Matthew 5:21, Christ made specific reference to this injunction. He went to the heart of the matter by stressing that even the presence of malice against someone else was a violation of this commandment. He also declared that God did not tolerate either those who verbally abused others or those who refused to forgive people who had wronged them in some way (vss. 22–26).

The *seventh commandment* of the Decalogue directed the Israelites not to commit adultery (Exod. 20:14; cf. Deut. 5:18). Likewise, in Matthew 5:27, Christ made specific reference to this injunction. He went to the heart of the matter by stressing that a man who looked at a woman with lust had already committed adultery in his heart with her. Jesus also emphasized the importance of eliminating all sources of sin in a person's life (vss. 28–30). Adultery was not the only transgression that undermined the marriage relationship. Divorce was another sin that could destroy marital union, fidelity, and stability (vs. 31). Jesus declared that divorce for any reason other than sexual immorality—namely, any form of marital unfaithfulness or unchastity—caused the rejected spouse to commit adultery. Likewise marriage to an improperly divorced person was an act of adultery (vs. 32).

The *eighth commandment* of the Decalogue directed the Israelites not to steal (Exod. 20:15; cf. Deut. 5:19). The Hebrew verb rendered "steal" (גָּנַב, *gānab*) is a primary Hebrew root that refers to any form of thievery, from kidnapping to burglary. In the Sermon on the Mount, Jesus affirmed the abiding validity of the eighth commandment when He stressed the importance of being generous in spirit and kindhearted toward others. When these two virtues are cultivated, they help mitigate against the presence of thievery in society.

The Savior, for instance, communicated His approval of those who were poor in spirit (Matt. 5:3). Because such individuals were genuinely unpretentious, they would be the least likely to entertain thoughts of stealing from others. Christ also commended those who mourn over their own ethical depravity (vs. 4). Like the poor in spirit, these believers would not be inclined to pilfer from others. Similarly, those who hunger and thirst for righteousness, who are pure in heart, who are peacemakers, or who willingly endure persecution (vss. 5–11) are not likely to rob others. Stealing, of course, can take many forms. One is guilty of thievery when he robs others of life by murdering them, when he deprives his wife of a happy marriage by either committing adultery or unlawfully divorcing her, when he tries to take away the honor associated with God's name by swearing falsely, when he refuses to give to others the joy of knowing that he forgives them for wronging him, and when he repudiates the idea of showing God's love to his enemies. These are all issues that Christ addressed in His Sermon (6:21–48).

The *ninth commandment* of the Decalogue directed the Israelites not to bear false witness against their neighbor (Exod. 20:16; cf. Deut. 5:20). Telling the truth and shunning all forms of deceitfulness are at the heart of this injunction. The Sermon on the Mount addressed these issues in several ways. For instance, Christ urged His followers to be pure in heart (Matt. 5:8), which means they were to be characterized by genuineness and honesty in all their dealings. When Jesus told His disciples that they were to be the salt of the earth (vs. 13), He was urging them to be people characterized by moral rectitude. Similarly, when He reminded them that they were the light of the world (vs. 14), He was encouraging them to be characterized by truth, virtue, and goodness. Furthermore, when Christ issued His prohibition of oaths, He was stressing the importance of maintaining integrity of speech (vss. 33–37).

In His discourse, Jesus noted that some prominent individuals were hypocritical in their pious actions, whether these involved charitable giving, praying, or fasting (6:2–17). Christ urged His followers to be people of honesty and integrity in all they did for the Lord. Jesus also stated that good deeds should be done with no thought of being noticed or praised by anyone. When engaging in religious activities, one's motives should remain pure and free from any self-serving tendencies (vs. 1). Jesus thus censured those who were experts at criticizing and condemning others in an unfair and hypocritical manner. They had formed distorted opinions about people by using unbiblical presuppositions. In the Sermon, Jesus told His followers not to make unfair and preposterous judgments of others (7:1–5). Instead, they were to be generous and fair in their evaluation of people.

The *tenth commandment* of the Decalogue directed the Israelites not to covet anyone's house, wife, servants, or domesticated animals (Exod. 20:17; cf. Deut. 5:21). At issue here was the harboring of inordinate, ungoverned, and selfish desires. The Sermon addressed this matter by emphasizing moral virtues that ran counter to the disposition of greed. For instance, the presence of such qualities as humility, meekness, uprightness, and mercifulness in a believer's life would help to combat the presence of avarice and selfishness (cf. Matt. 5:3, 5–9). Jesus attacked the sin of greed by telling His disciples not to store up for themselves treasures on earth (6:19). He also reminded them that they could not have both God and wealth as their masters (vs. 20). Furthermore, the Savior encouraged His followers to trust God exclusively to provide for their needs and thereby undercut any rapacious tendencies they might have (vss. 25–34).

The Decalogue and the Sermon on the Mount are not just biblically related, but also theologically related. A major finding of the structural analysis of the Decalogue was that the Ten Commandments contained the basic elements of a suzerainty pact, especially Hittite state treaties. The Decalogue begins with a preamble in which the great King identifies Himself (Exod. 20:1–2a; Deut. 5:6a). The preamble of the Decalogue is followed by a brief historical prologue. In this section, Yahweh summarized the gracious acts that He displayed toward His covenant people (Exod. 20:2b; Deut. 5:6b). Finally, the Lord delineated the stipulations of the covenant He was making with His people. God expected His subjects to obey these directives, which were ten in number (Exod. 20:3–17; Deut. 5:1–3, 7–21).

As in the Decalogue, covenantal ideas are present throughout Jesus' discourse. For example, the concept of God's rule over His people is bound up in the phrase "kingdom of heaven," which appears in Matthew 5:3, 10, 19, 20, and 7:21. Likewise, in the Beatitudes Jesus repeatedly emphasized the notion of receiving eternal blessings from God for living in a way that pleases Him (5:3–11). The reality of the relationship between God and His people is a covenantal idea emphasized numerous times in the Sermon. Believers are to give glory to their Father in heaven by the good works they did (5:16). They were to love and pray for their enemies and thus show that they were children of their heavenly Father (vs. 45). In every area of life, believers were to adhere to their Father's perfect moral standard (vs. 48).

Christ urged His disciples to practice their piety before people in an appropriate manner; otherwise, they would receive no reward from their Father in heaven (6:1). For instance, when they gave alms, prayed, or fasted in a proper way, their Father would see and eternally reward them (vss. 4, 6, 18). The Lord's Prayer encourages believers to refer to God as their heavenly Father (vs. 8). Christ urged His disciples to forgive those who wronged them so that they might fully enjoy the forgiveness of their Father in heaven (vss. 14–15). Jesus reminded His followers that their heavenly Father provides for the birds of the air (vs. 26) and that He knows what His spiritual children need to exist (vs. 32). The Savior reassured His disciples that their Father in heaven gives what is good to those who ask Him (7:11).

The importance of obeying the Lord is another covenantal idea emphasized in the Sermon. Christ said that one can tell a true follower of His by the spiritual fruit he bore in his life (7:15–20). Those who were characterized by such virtues as integrity, honesty, love, and mercy were the ones bearing genuine fruit for God. Jesus warned that only those who did the will of His heavenly Father would enter the kingdom of heaven (vs. 21). Not even crying out "Lord, Lord" or claiming to have done miraculous deeds in His name could fool God (vs. 22). Christ would refuse to acknowledge those who asserted to be His but chose not to trust in Him and obey His directives (vs. 23). Jesus stressed the wisdom of heeding His teachings and the folly of ignoring or rejecting them (vss. 24–27). It was only the person who paid attention to what the Savior taught and who acted on His teachings who could count on withstanding the challenges to his faith. He would be the one who would endure to the end as a faithful follower of Christ.

The Decalogue's Structure and the Arrangement of the Sermon on the Mount

A key finding of this study is that the Sermon follows a literary chiastic arrangement, with the central section—Matthew 5:17–7:12—forming the crucial portion of the text. This organizational scheme indicates that the moral law and the nature of its absolute requirements are of foremost importance to understanding the overall thrust of the Sermon on the Mount. The outlying frames of text indicate that when the followers of Christ are rightly related to the law, their lives will be filled with joy, purpose, and eternal hope. The antithesis of this is that those who are improperly related to the law will experience sorrow, futility, and despair in their lives.

Hence, the chiastic arrangement of the Sermon is a vital piece of information, for it spotlights how centrally important the moral law of God was to Jesus' discourse. The inherent structure of the Sermon indicates that the moral law is not something passé. Rather, it is of prime importance to the lives of those who are disciples of the Savior. Thus, the moral law should neither be taken lightly nor ignored by them as they seek to live for the Lord.

With respect to the Ten Commandments, its traditional classification into four laws having to do with obligations to God (Exod. 20:2–11), followed by six laws having to do with obligations to fellow human beings (Exod. 20:12–17) seems to do the best job of reflecting the emphasis and scope found in the Decalogue. It is a useful thematic model by which to analyze the Ten Commandments.

A candid analysis of the data indicates that the Sermon on the Mount cannot be neatly broken down in the same way. Also, when the literary structure of the Decalogue and the literary structure of Jesus' Sermon are compared, it is clear that the arrangement of the former did not directly influence the arrangement of the material in the Sermon on the Mount. This does not mean that the relationship between these two passages of Scripture is weak or shallow, for there are other ways to establish a fundamental connection between the two. For instance, the truths Jesus taught and the directives He emphasized concern both humanity's moral obligations toward God and toward one another. They appear intermingled throughout the body of His discourse, rather than in neatly discernible and separate sections as one finds in the Decalogue.

Furthermore, the biblical and theological ties between the Decalogue and the Sermon on the Mount are the main way these two passages are fundamentally connected. This means that the primary relationship between them is biblical and theological, rather than structural. The nature of this relationship has a direct bearing on the question of whether the moral law has continuing relevance as a rule or guide of life for the New Testament church. The discussion that follows will make it clear that because of the fundamental relationship between the Decalogue and Jesus' Sermon, Christians are obligated to obey the moral law.

The Extent to which the Church Is Obligated to Obey the Sermon on the Mount

Because Jesus' call to moral and ethical living is quite high, scholars have taken a variety of divergent views regarding the degree to which the Sermon should be interpreted and applied. Some have maintained that Jesus' discourse has no application for believers today. For example, Pentecost argued that the Sermon is to be related to the future earthly messianic kingdom of Christ.[3] Supposedly Jesus' discourse, in its primary interpretation, is directly applicable only to those of Christ's day who, by their profession in John's baptism, were anticipating the coming of Messiah in His millennial kingdom.[4] However, in chapter 5 it was maintained that the Gospel of Matthew was written for the benefit of all New Testament believers, not just God's people who will be living in a future kingdom age, regardless of the nature of that kingdom.[5] Furthermore, though Jesus directed His message to His original disciples, He also had future disciples in mind (cf. Matt. 10:5–15; 16:17–19; 28:18–20).[6]

Some dispensationalists such as Pentecost have claimed that the Sermon has only secondary application for believers today.[7] However, in chapter 5 it was concluded that such a notion can leave the Christian with the impression that he is not really responsible to heed Jesus' specific injunctions. Likewise, the importance and urgency of Jesus' statements are removed by such a view. Others have fully applied the Sermon only to special classes of Christians (such as clergy).[8] However, in chapter 5 it was concluded that these clergy-laity distinctions are artificial and contrived, without having any solid scriptural or theological support. There is no credible reason why God would hold some Christians to one moral standard which is supposedly higher, and the rest to another standard which is supposedly lower. Likewise, there is no sensible basis for asserting that God would demand that certain groups of believers adhere to a stringent code of ethics, but permit the rest to follow a more lenient body of law.

Based on what has just been said, it is concluded that the Sermon on the Mount applies to all believers, whether the followers of Christ's day or those of the entire church today. It is also concluded that believers are duty bound to obey every aspect of the Sermon, for Jesus' discourse represents His instructions to us to be godly people in this present fallen world. Furthermore, the Sermon addresses both inward motives and outward conduct (cf. Matt. 5:21, 22, 27, 28). Thus, it would be mistaken to say that only one or the other was being stressed by Christ. It is valid to say that the demands Jesus' made are so strict that no one can perfectly obey them (cf. vs. 48). It would be incorrect, however, to limit in some way either the interpretation or application of these demands, for Jesus wanted His listeners to accept the full force of what He was saying.

Consequently, it is best to take the injunctions in the Sermon of the Mount at face value. Such literary conventions as poetry, ethical admonitions, and hyperbole should be recognized and handled accordingly. They should neither be over-interpreted nor under-interpreted. Rather, the ethical or moral values being stressed through these literary conventions should be detected and fully embraced. These findings reinforce the conclusion that believers are fully obligated to obey the entire Sermon on the Mount. Because such moral virtues as self-control, integrity, honesty, kindness, and compassion transcend all time and cultures, it is best to see the Sermon as having direct applicability to God's people in all ages. Its moral precepts are timeless in their relevance, and its truths are worthy of consideration and practice by God's people regardless of where or when they live.

The Relevancy of the Moral Law for the Church

As the study of Jesus' discourse was conducted, the substantive relationship between it and the Decalogue was repeatedly noted and discussed. The strength of this biblical and theological relationship indicates that the Savior considered the moral law to have continuing relevancy for the church. Moreover, it was noted that the Sermon follows a literary chiastic arrangement, with the central section—Matthew 5:17–7:12—forming the crucial portion of the text. This approach to sequencing the material indicates that the law of God and the nature of its absolute requirements are of continuing relevance as a rule or guide of life for the church. Since Jesus placed such a strong emphasis on the moral law, His fulfillment of it, and His believers' obligation to heed it, they cannot ignore or reject it.

It has already been maintained that Christians are fully obligated to obey the Sermon on the Mount. Since Jesus' discourse predominantly concerns the moral law, it is reasonable to infer from this that the Decalogue also has full and continuing relevance for the church. After all, by acknowledging that the believer has an obligation to heed all that Jesus taught in the Sermon, one is conceding that the Decalogue has full and continuing relevance for believers today. This conclusion is based on the fact that the Sermon and the Decalogue are biblically and theologically related to one another.

Scholars, of course, are divided in their views on the relationship that Jesus had to the law. The discussion in chapters 5 and 6 makes it clear that Christ did not abrogate the law, supersede or replace it, intensify its demands beyond what they originally meant, introduce new demands of His own, or point His followers in a different ethical direction than that emphasized by the law. Rather, He affirmed the abiding validity of the Decalogue. Through His preaching and teaching ministry He declared the true meaning of the moral law, which had been obscured by some in His day.

The preceding analysis indicates that the moral law is of prime importance to the lives of Christians. At the least the investigation suggests they can neither disregard the moral law nor be inattentive to its injunctions. Instead, they need to affirm and take to heart the law's full and continuing relevance for them today. The moral law should be their guide for upright living as children of God in a corrupt and fallen world.

The Extent to which Christians Are Obligated to Obey the Moral Law

The structure of the Sermon indicates that the moral law was at the heart of Christ's lengthy discussion. He stressed that He came to fulfill the law, not abolish it (Matt. 5:17). As the greatest expositor of the Torah, Jesus upheld the moral law, showing obedience to all of its commands and demonstrating its original intent by His teaching. Christ's profound statement regarding His relationship to the moral law makes it clear that the Decalogue was not irrelevant for the church. In fact, based on what He asserted in verses 18–20, it was determined that He expected His followers to practice and teach all that was written in the Decalogue. Christ also expected His people to heed the least important command found in the law and to teach others to do the same.

The assertion that Christians are obligated to obey all the moral law because of the relationship between the Decalogue and the Sermon on the Mount is further reinforced in the series of statements recorded in Matthew 5:21–48. In this passage, Jesus contrasted His ethical teachings with those of the legalistic traditions of the Jews. The Savior maintained that it was a sham to keep some of the laws externally, yet violate them internally. By making direct and indirect allusions to the Decalogue, Jesus discussed some of the ways He expected His followers to obey all of the moral law.

An analysis of Matthew 6:1–7:12 provides further support for the conclusion that Christians are obligated to obey all of the moral law. In this passage Jesus dealt with a variety of biblical and theological subjects that appeared in the Decalogue. As He discussed each topic, the Savior indicated how all of the moral law was to be heeded properly. Christ focused on specific aspects of the law that some in His day had misapplied and that needed to be handled correctly. Jesus instructed His listeners not to perform righteous acts so as to gain attention from people. He explained how these good deeds were to be performed and what rewards would flow from doing them. Jesus' intent was to indicate how His disciples could properly obey all of God's moral law.

An analysis of Matthew 7:13–27 provides additional support that Christians are obligated to obey all of the moral law. In this passage Jesus dealt with a variety of biblical and theological subjects that appeared in the Decalogue. The research indicated that when the followers of Christ are rightly related to the law, their lives will be filled with joy, purpose, and eternal hope. The antithesis of this is that those who are improperly related to the law will experience sorrow, futility, and despair in their lives.

Some might argue that Christians are only duty bound to obey part of the moral law. This conclusion, however, cannot be supported by the biblical evidence. When Christ declared that He came to fulfill the law (Matt. 5:17), He did not place any qualifiers or restrictions on the nature of His fulfillment. He also did not water down or reduce the obligation of His followers to heed the moral law. Even the least of the commandments was binding (vs. 18). In fact, whoever was guilty of rejecting the least important command in the moral law would be considered least important in God's kingdom. The corollary was also true. Whoever practiced and taught even the smallest injunction of Scripture would be considered great in the divine kingdom (vs. 19). Thus Christians are duty bound to obey all of the moral law, as it is expressed in the Decalogue.

This conclusion need not be based solely on the relationship between the Sermon and the Decalogue. This assertion can also be upheld on theological grounds. For instance, God's moral law is absolute, perfect, unchanging, and eternal in nature. The Lord and His holy character, as reflected in His universal moral law, is the abiding standard for how people of all ages should live (cf. Matt. 5:48; Rom. 8:29; 2 Cor. 3:18; Eph. 4:13; Col. 3:10; 1 Pet. 1:15–16). This means the moral law is relevant for Christians, regardless of the age or society in which they live.

Neither Jesus nor Paul set the believer free from obeying the moral law. Rather, Christ, through His redemptive work, enables His people to heed the moral law in ways and to degrees that were impossible before their salvation. This is confirmed by what Paul said in Romans 8:4: "so that the just requirement of the law might be fulfilled in us, who walk not according to the flesh but according to the Spirit."

The Nature and Extent of the Moral Law's Continuing Relevance for the Church

An in-depth analysis and comparison of the Decalogue and the Sermon on the Mount has been done to determine the nature of the relationship between the two and to determine whether and to what extent the moral law has continuing relevance as a rule or guide of life for the church today. It has been determined that these two passages of Scripture are closely related biblically and theologically.

It was also concluded that the structure of the Decalogue did not influence the way the material in the Sermon on the Mount has been sequenced. Nevertheless, the literary chiastic arrangement of Jesus' discourse indicates that the moral law of God and the nature of its absolute requirements are of foremost importance to understanding the overall thrust of the Sermon. The inherent structure of Jesus' discourse indicates that the moral law is of prime importance to the lives of those who are Christians. It was further determined that the church is duty bound to obey all of the Sermon on the Mount. Consequently, it would be incorrect to maintain either that Jesus' discourse has no application for believers today, has only secondary application, or fully applies only to special classes of Christians.

On the basis of the information presented, a definitive conclusion can be reached concerning the primary question raised in this work. The references and allusions in the Sermon on the Mount to the Decalogue indicate that the moral law has full and continuing relevance as a rule or guide of life for the church. Because of the strong biblical and theological relationship between these two great bodies of Scripture, Christians are obligated to obey all of the moral law. They can neither disregard the Decalogue nor be inattentive to its injunctions.

Areas for Future Research

There are three major areas for future research worth mentioning. First, the content analysis of the Decalogue was not restricted to either Exodus 20:1–17 or Deuteronomy 5:6–21. Rather, other portions of the Old and New Testaments were briefly considered to see what God's Word in its entirety had to say about the topics introduced by each of the Ten Commandments. The information obtained from this investigation suggests that the Decalogue not only has a strong biblical and theological relationship with the Sermon on the Mount but also with other portions of Scripture. Does the fact that the writers of the New Testament make repeated direct and indirect reference to the commandments of the Decalogue imply that they considered this body of literature to be relevant and binding on the church today? This would be an important question to investigate further.

Second, it is evident from the research conducted in this work that Matthew 5:17–20 is a key passage to exegete and interpret when addressing the issue of the continuing relevancy of the moral law and the believer's ongoing obligation to obey it. Another key passage to explore fully is Romans 10:4. In fact, it would be beneficial to do a thorough study of these two passages together to see whether they are in essential agreement in what they teach about the continuing relevancy of the moral law. Also, the findings of such a study would be immensely useful as one examined how the rest of the New Testament made repeated use of the Decalogue.

Third, the writer of Hebrews had much to say about Christ and His relationship to the Mosaic covenantal system. It would be helpful to do a comprehensive examination of what the author of the letter taught concerning the continuity and discontinuity between the testaments and how this impacts the issue of the moral law and its continuing relevancy for the church. One might also want to correlate the findings of this study with those obtained from a comparative analysis of Matthew 5:17–20 and Romans 10:4.

Notes

Chapter 1: The Enduring Relevance of the Moral Law

1. With respect to the latter, R. A. Guelich ("Interpreting the Sermon on the Mount," *Interpretation*, vol. 41, no. 2 [1987], 117–118) opined that the vast "sea of literature on the Sermon demonstrates that the meaning of the Sermon is anything but self-evident."
2. The validity of these statements is reflected in the comments made by G. N. Stanton ("Sermon on the Mount/Plain," in *Dictionary of Jesus and the Gospels*, eds. J. B. Green, S. McKnight, & I. H. Marshall [Downers Grove, IL: InterVarsity, 1992], 737) as he discussed the different and sometimes conflicting ways interpreters such as Augustine tried to make sense of Matthew 5:17–48: "Augustine may have been inconsistent, but the issue is still with us today. To what extent and in what ways is the ethical teaching of the OT still important today? How 'new' is the teaching of Jesus, and does it have priority over Scripture? Do we retain the parts of Scripture to which Jesus refers, and ignore or reject the rest?" Cf. also the introductory remarks made by W. Eichrodt in "The Law and the Gospel: The Meaning of the Ten Commandments in Israel and for Us" (trans. C. F. McRae, *Interpretation*, vol. 11 [1957], 23).
3. E. P. Sanders, "Torah and Christ," *Interpretation*, vol. 29 (1975), 372; cf. S. Motyer, "The Old Testament in the New Testament," in *Evangelical Dictionary of Biblical Theology*, ed. W. A. Elwell (Grand Rapids: Baker, 1996), 582; C. H. Bullock, "Old Testament Theology," in *Evangelical Dictionary of Theology* (2nd ed.), ed. W. A. Elwell (Grand Rapids: Baker Book House, 2001), 861–862.
4. R. Bultmann, "The Significance of the Old Testament for the Christian Faith," in *The Old Testament and Christian Faith: A Theological Discussion*, ed. B.W. Anderson (New York: Harper & Row, 1964), 8–35.
5. W. Zimmerli, "Promise and Fulfillment," *Interpretation*, vol. 15 (1961), 310–338.
6. F. Baumgärtel, *Zur Frage des evangelischen Verständnisses des Alten Testaments* (Gütersloh: Bertelsmann Verlag, 1952), 92.
7. F. Hesse, *Das Alte Testament als Buch der Kirche* (Gütersloh: Mohn, 1966), 82.
8. K. Schwarzwäller, "Das Verhältnis Altes Testament—Neues Testament in Lichte der gegenwärtigen Bestimmungen," *Evangelische Theologie*, vol. 29 (1969), 305.
9. W. Vischer, *Das Christuszeugnis des Alte Testament* (Zurich: 1934). Translated *The Witness of the Old Testament to Christ* (London: Lutterworth, 1949), 7–8.
10. A. A. Van Ruler, *The Christian Church and the Old Testament* (Grand Rapids: Eerdmans, 1971), 72.
11. W. Eichrodt, "Is Typological Exegesis an Appropriate Method?" in *Essays on Old Testament Hermeneutics*, ed. C. Westermann (Richmond: John Knox Press, 1963), 224–245.
12. G. Von Rad, "Typological Interpretation of the Old Testament," in *Essays on Old Testament Hermeneutics*, ed. C. Westermann (Richmond: John Knox Press, 1963), 364–374.
13. R. Lucas, "Considerations of Method in Old Testament Hermeneutics," *The Dunwoodie Review*, vol. 6 (1966), 35.
14. R. E. Murphy, "The Relationship Between the Testaments," *Catholic Biblical Quarterly*, vol. 26 (1964), 349–359.
15. G. F. Hasel, *Old Testament Theology: Basic Issues In the Current Debate*, 4th ed. (Grand Rapids: Eerdmans, 1991), 183–185.
16. Ibid., 191–193; cf. Motyer ("The Old Testament in the New Testament," 583–585),

who discusses five New Testament patterns of use with respect to the Old Testament: the confirmation of Old Testament theology; the fulfillment of Old Testament prophecy; the rereading of Old Testament history; the expansion of Old Testament people; and the renewal of Old Testament religion. Furthermore, Motyer sees a circular relationship and process in which the "New Testament authors both use the Old Testament to explain Jesus and use Jesus to explain the Old Testament" (583).

17. For example, theonomic, covenantal, Lutheran, Anabaptist, and dispensational (to name a few).

18. Cf. Bullock ("Old Testament Theology," 862), who notes that the issue of a theological center of the Old Testament retains "great importance because how one answers this question will affect both method and structure of OT theology."

19. W. A. VanGemeren, "Systems of Continuity," in *Continuity and Discontinuity: Perspectives on the Relationship Between the Old and New Testaments*, ed. J. S. Feinberg (Westchester, IL: Crossway Books, 1988), 37–62.

20. As C. Blaising ("Dispensation, Dispensationalism," in *Evangelical Dictionary of Theology* [2nd ed.], ed. W. A. Elwell [Grand Rapids: Baker Book House, 2001], 344–345) has noted, dispensationalism is not a philosophical monolith, but rather is distinguished by such strains as classical, ultra, revised (or traditional), and progressive dispensationalism; cf. K. Ahn, *The Sinaitic Covenant and Law in the Theology of Dispensationalism* (Ph.D. dissertation, Berrien Springs, MI: Andrews University, Seventh-day Adventist Theological Seminary, 1989), 45–46; C. Ryrie, "Dispensationalism," in *Dictionary of Premillennial Theology*, ed. M. Couch (Grand Rapids: Kregel, 1996), 96–98; R. P. Lightner, "Progressive Dispensationalism," *Conservative Theological Journal*, vol. 4, no. 11 (2000), 47, 49–50. The broad strands of classical and revised dispensationalism are well represented within evangelical circles (e.g. The Master's Seminary [http://www.tms.edu/], Baptist Bible College and Seminary [http://www.bbc.edu/], Grand Rapids Baptist Seminary [http://grbs.cornerstone.edu/], Chafer Theological Seminary [http://www.chafer.edu/], et al.). Throughout the remainder of this study, particular attention will be given to what these two forms of dispensational thinking have to say about matters being addressed; cf. H. H. Rowdon, "Dispensational Theology," in *New Dictionary of Theology*, eds. S. Ferguson, D. F. Wright, & J. I. Packer (Downers Grove, IL: InterVarsity Press, 1988), 200–201; P. Heideman, "Dispensational Theology," *Chafer Theological Seminary Journal*, vol. 4, no. 3 (1998), 31–33.

21. J.S. Feinberg, "Systems of Discontinuity," in *Continuity and Discontinuity: Perspectives on the Relationship Between the Old and New Testaments*, ed. J. S. Feinberg (Westchester, IL: Crossway Books, 1988), 63–86.

22. Blaising, "Dispensation, Dispensationalism," 344–345.

23. C. Ryrie, *Dispensationalism Today* (Chicago: Moody Press, 1965), 132–176.

24. For example, W. Kaiser (*Toward Old Testament Ethics* [Grand Rapids: Zondervan, 1983], 33) observed the following: "The Old Testament commands and its injunctions cannot be jettisoned in a cavalier manner by contemporary Christians without denying or rewriting our history of salvation—a stance which most Christians are loathe (fortunately) to take....The ethics of the Old Testament are an absolute necessity for formulating New Testament ethics or any kind of Christian ethics, for only in the Old Testament can the proper foundations be laid for all biblical, theological, or Christian theory or action."

25. For example, D. A. Carson, D. J. Moo, and L. Morris (*An Introduction to the New Testament* [Grand Rapids: Zondervan, 1992], 84) gave this assessment: "Matthew preserves large blocks of Jesus' teaching, in the discourses already enumerated. Doubtless that was one of the major reasons this gospel was so popular in the early church. However, they came to be preserved in this form, there can be no doubt that the church would be greatly impoverished without the Sermon on the Mount, Matthew's list of parables, his version of the eschatological discourse, and so forth."
26. J. M. Lochman, *Signposts to Freedom: The Ten Commandments and Christian Ethics*, trans. D. Lewis (Minneapolis, MN: Augsburg Publishing House, 1982), 16; D. G. Bloesch, *Freedom for Obedience: Evangelical Ethics in Contemporary Times* (San Francisco: Harper & Row, Publishers, 1987), 7, 129; J. Douma, *The Ten Commandments: Manual for the Christian Life*, trans. N. D. Kloosterman (Phillipsburg, NJ: P. & R. Publishing, 1996), xi.
27. A. Gearey, "The Bible, Law and Liberation: Towards a Politico-Legal Hermeneutics of the Sermon on the Mount," in eds. *Law and Literature: Current Legal Issues 1999, Volume 2*, M. Freeman and A. D. E. Lewis (Oxford: Oxford University Press, 1999), 264.
28. D. G. Bloesch, "Law and Gospel in Reformed Perspective," *Grace Theological Journal*, vol. 12, no. 2 (1991), 186.
29. For example, D. C. Jones makes this point, and notes that the early church used the Ten Commandments for instruction in the Christian way of life (*Biblical Christian Ethics* [Grand Rapids: Baker, 1994], 105): "The Ten Commandments or the Decalogue are listed first in Exodus 20 and repeated (with some variation of details) in Deuteronomy 5. Their unique place in the history of special revelation is formally recognized in the liturgical and catechetical traditions of both Judaism and Christianity." Also, cf. the remarks of R. H. Fuller, "The Decalogue in the New Testament," *Interpretation*, vol. 43, no. 3 (1989), 243, 255; W. R. Estep, "Law and Gospel in the Anabaptist/Baptist Tradition," *Grace Theological Journal*, vol. 12, no. 2 (1991), 214; R. C. Barcellos, *In Defense of the Decalogue: A Critique of New Covenant Theology* (Enumclaw, WA: WinePress Publishing, 2001, 19–20). These sentiments are contra R. L. Aldrich ("The Mosaic Ten Commandments Compared To Their Restatements In The New Testament," *Bibliotheca Sacra*, vol. 118 [1961], 251), who states the following: "The moral law is the basis of the Mosaic law, but the two should not be confused. Christians and all of God's intelligent creatures are under His eternal moral law, but only Israel was ever under the Mosaic pattern of the moral law."
30. For example, Carl Henry wrote the following about the Sermon on the Mount (*Christian Personal Ethics* [Grand Rapids: Eerdmans, 1957], 278): "Without question, the best known fact about Jesus Christ is that he gave the Sermon on the Mount....Actually it is his fullest treatment of morality....It has exercised enormous influence both inside and outside organized Christianity because of the revolutionary character of the ethics it contains." Also, cf. the remarks of S. Freyne, "The Ethic of Jesus: The Sermon on the Mount Then and Now," in *Ethics and the Christian*, ed. S. Freyne (Dublin: The Columba Press, 1991), 44.
31. Cf. R. T. Clutter, "Law and Gospel in the Brethren Tradition," *Grace Theological Journal*, vol. 12, no. 2 (1991), 231.
32. For example, Greg L. Bahnsen and Kenneth L. Gentry (*House Divided: The Break-Up Of Dispensational Theology* [Tyler, TX: Institute for Christian Economics, 1989], 3) make the following comment: "The authors...believe that the entire Bible is ethically

normative for us today, including the Mosaic law. They believe that the kingdom of Jesus Christ was established at His first advent, and that the Great Commission will see marvelous success before Christ returns. These two convictions lead them to expect and to seek the transformation of every area of life, including society and politics, according to the word of God."

33. For example, Gary North and Gary DeMar (*Christian Reconstruction: What It Is, What It Isn't* [Tyler, TX: Institute for Christian Economics, 1991], 78) noted the following: "The legal and moral principles of the gospel must be applied plainly and specifically to every area of life; the church must therefore speak prophetically. Just as the prophets of old came to the kings and people of ancient Israel, so do Christian Reconstructionists come to Christians today and non-Christians: to remind them of the four covenants of God. We are inescapably under God's comprehensive covenant sanctions. Better to be under His positive sanctions than His negative sanctions, both in history and in eternity."

34. Ahn, *The Sinaitic Covenant and Law in the Theology of Dispensationalism,* 5–6, 185, 191, 219, 288, 306; cf. H. D. Kim, *The Mosaic Law in the Old Testament and the New Testament* (M.A. thesis, South Hamilton, MA: Gordon-Conwell Theological Seminary, 2003), 5. By way of example, Lewis S. Chafer (*Chafer's Systematic Theology* [Dallas: Dallas Seminary Press, 1978], 4:208–209) maintained the following: "The moral commandments of the Decalogue are almost universally imposed upon the church by...legalists. In justification of this imposition, the plea is usually made that apart from the direct application of the Decalogue there could be no divine authority or government in the earth. In no sense does this question involve the issues of world government; for God has never addressed either the teachings of the law or the teachings of grace to the whole world."

35. It is worth noting that, in contrast to classical and revised dispensationalists, such progressive dispensationalists as Saucy see the application of the Sermon on the Mount "as continuing throughout this age" (*The Case for Progressive Dispensationalism: The Interface Between Dispensational and Non-Dispensational Theology* [Grand Rapids: Zondervan, 1993], 18). Furthermore, Saucy affirms that "the pattern of life set forth by Jesus in the Sermon applies directly to [believers] during this age." Not surprisingly, classical and revised dispensationalists such as Thomas take issue with this view ("The Hermeneutics of Progressive Dispensationalism," *The Master's Seminary Journal*, vol. 6, no. 1 [1995], 87–88).

36. T. D. Bonham, *A Study of the Relevance of the Sermon on the Mount in Matthew 5–7* (Th.D. dissertation, Fort Worth, TX: Southwestern Baptist Theological Seminary, 1963), 2, 57, 61, 72, 80, 86–87; Ahn, *The Sinaitic Covenant and Law in the Theology of Dispensationalism,* 8, 201–202, 220, 324, 333, 368, 372. By way of example, Pentecost ("The Purpose of the Sermon on the Mount," *Bibliotheca Sacra,* vol. 115 [1958], 132–133) offered this assessment: "Without doubt the commonly accepted view of those who espouse the literal and dispensational method of interpretation is that this discourse is to be related to the future Messianic or earthly kingdom of our Lord. This is the outgrowth of the proposition that Christ offered Israel a kingdom at His first advent, which was rejected by that nation, and therefore postponed. Our Lord in the Sermon on the Mount, it is contended, made this pronouncement in connection with the offer of the kingdom, and is to be interpreted as a description of that kingdom, its character, constitution, and constituents."

37. Douma, *The Ten Commandments: Manual for the Christian Life,* 12. For example, Jones (*Biblical Christian Ethics,* 107–108) noted the following: "That the ten words are still operative appears also from Jesus' exposition of the moral law in the Sermon on the Mount. In this royal proclamation of kingdom righteousness, Jesus cites directly the sixth and seventh commandments, 'Do not murder' (Matt. 5:21) and 'Do not commit adultery' (Matt. 5:27), and brings out their full import and reach to the thoughts and intents of the heart. The authority of the Decalogue is thus presupposed in Jesus' teaching."
38. E.g. as reflected by the listings in the bibliography.
39. E.g. the study conducted by M. W. Baird, *Jesus' Use of the Decalogue in the Synoptics: An Exegetical Study* (Ph.D. dissertation, Fort Worth, TX: Southwestern Baptist Theological Seminary, 1982). Jones (*Biblical Christian Ethics,* 106–107) provided this helpful analysis: "The continuing relevance of the Ten Commandments to the people of God may be determined by observing how they function in the New Testament. In a number of places the Ten Commandments are cited directly where the context requires a summary of the revealed will of God (Matt. 19:18–19; Rom. 13:8–10; James 2:8–11). In other places the Ten Commandments, though not cited directly, provide the framework for moral analysis and exhortation."
40. Cf. the discussion in chapter 7, which recaps each of these issues in detail.
41. Cf. the discussion of E. W. Nicholson, "Decalogue as the Direct Address of God," *Vetus Testamentum,* vol. 27, no. 4 (1977), 424; M. E. Tate, "Legal Traditions of the Books of Exodus," *Review & Expositor*, vol. 74 (1977), 484.
42. E.H. Merrill, "A Theology of the Pentateuch," in *A Biblical Theology of the Old Testament,* eds. R. B. Zuck, E. H. Merrill, and D. L. Bock (Chicago: Moody Press, 1991), 8; R. W. Dalman, *Sojourners in the Promise: Genesis and the Origin of Abraham's Faith* (New Hope, MN: Rodger W. Dalman, 2002), 1, 14.
43. R. K. Harrison, "Book of Exodus," in *The International Standard Bible Encyclopedia,* ed. G. W. Bromiley (Grand Rapids: Eerdmans, 1982), 2:226–227.
44. A. D. H. Mayes, *New Century Bible Commentary: Deuteronomy* (Grand Rapids: Eerdmans, 1981), 161–162.
45. R. E. Friedman, "Torah (Pentateuch)," in *The Anchor Bible Dictionary,* ed. D. N. Freedman (New York: Doubleday, 1992), 6:608–609.
46. B. S. Childs, *The Book of Exodus: A Critical, Theological Commentary* (Philadelphia: Westminster, 1974), 391.
47. C. M. Carmichael, *Law and Narrative in the Bible: The Evidence of the Deuteronomic Laws and the Decalogue* (Ithaca, NY: Cornell University Press, 1985), 313; I. Cairns, *Word and Presence: A Commentary on the Book of Deuteronomy* (Grand Rapids: Eerdmans, 1992), 69–70.
48. J. A. Thompson, "Deuteronomy: An Introduction and Commentary," in *Tyndale Old Testament Commentaries,* ed. D. J. Wiseman (Downers Grove, IL: InterVarsity, 1974), 29.
49. R. K. Harrison, "Law in the OT," in *The International Standard Bible Encyclopedia,* ed. G. W. Bromiley (Grand Rapids: Eerdmans, 1986), 3:81.
50. Childs, *The Book of Exodus: A Critical, Theological Commentary,* 398–399.
51. V. Hamilton, *Handbook on the Pentateuch* (Grand Rapids: Baker, 1982), 377–378.
52. M. C. Tenny, *New Testament Survey* (Grand Rapids: Eerdmans, 1961), 142.
53. D. Greenwood, "Moral Obligation in the Sermon on the Mount," *Theological Studies,* vol. 31 (1970), 301; H. D. Betz, *The Sermon on the Mount* (Minneapolis, MN: Fortress Press, 1995), 4–5.

54. J. O. Buswell, "Sermon on the Mount," in *The Zondervan Pictorial Bible Dictionary*, ed. M. C. Tenny (Grand Rapids: Zondervan, 1963), 773.
55. R. H. Mounce, "Sermon on the Mount," in *The International Standard Bible Encyclopedia*, ed. G.W. Bromiley (Grand Rapids: Eerdmans, 1988), 4:411.
56. G. T. Burke, "Sermon on the Mount," in *Evangelical Dictionary of Theology* (2nd ed.), ed. W. A. Elwell (Grand Rapids: Baker, 2001), 1094.
57. S. Zeitlin, "Prolegomenon," in *The Jewish Sources of the Sermon on the Mount*, ed. G. Friedlander (New York: KTAV Publishing House, 1969), xv–xvi.
58. D. E. Lanier, "The Lord's Prayer: Matt 6:9–13—A Thematic and Semantic-Structural Analysis," *Criswell Theological Review*, vol. 6, no. 1 (1992), 57.
59. Ibid. Admittedly, Lanier's remarks pertain specifically to Jesus' discourse. Nevertheless, they also remain true for the Decalogue and thus are applied to it here.
60. E.g. D. Stoutenburg (*With One Voice: The Sermon on the Mount and Rabbinic Literature* [San Francisco: International Scholars Publications, 1996], 97–98), who makes the following claim: "The critical study of the SM, and the whole NT, requires an objectivity that has often been lacking in past publications by scholars who operate from a faith-affirming supposition. Such is the reality of most evangelical expositional and exegetical commentaries that assume what is necessary to validate their theological presuppositions."
61. J. C. Anderson, *Matthew's Narrative Web: Over, and Over, and Over Again* (Sheffield, England: Sheffield Academic Press, 1994), 8.
62. G. P. Johnson, *A Semantic and Discourse Analysis of Matthew 5:17–20* (Th.M. thesis, Portland, OR: Western Conservative Baptist Seminary, 1984), 3.
63. J. G. Williams, "Paraenesis, Excess, and Ethics: Matthew's Rhetoric in the Sermon on the Mount," *Semeia*, vol. 50 (1990), 167.
64. G. A. Tuttle, "The Sermon On The Mount: Its Wisdom Affinities And Their Relation To Its Structure," *Journal of the Evangelical Theological Society*, vol. 20, no. 3 (1997), 218–219.
65. D. J. Moo, "Jesus and the Authority of the Mosaic Law," *Journal for the Study of the New Testament*, vol. 20 (1984), 24.
66. Anderson, *Matthew's Narrative Web: Over, and Over, and Over Again*, 7.
67. J. Meier, *Law and History in Matthew's Gospel: A Redactional Study of Mt. 5:17–58* (Rome: Biblical Institute Press, 1976), 1.
68. Cf. E. Linnemann, *Historical Criticism of the Bible: Methodology or Ideology? Reflections of a Bultmannian Turned Evangelical* (Grand Rapids: Baker, 1990), 107.
69. Cf. Ibid., 52–53, 64, 85, 142–144, 147, 149, 152, 154, 155, 157.
70. Cf. E. Linnemann, *Is There a Synoptic Problem? Rethinking the Literary Dependence of the First Three Gospels* (Grand Rapids: Baker, 1992), 21–22.
71. Cf. Linnemann, *Historical Criticism of the Bible: Methodology or Ideology? Reflections of a Bultmannian Turned Evangelical*, 88.
72. Cf. Linnemann, *Is There a Synoptic Problem? Rethinking the Literary Dependence of the First Three Gospels*, 159, 178, 185–191.
73. Cf. Ibid., 162, 178, 185–191.

Chapter 2: The Biblical Concept of Law

1. R. Banks, *Jesus and the Law in the Synoptic Tradition* (London: Cambridge University Press, 1975), 39.

2. S. Wager, "*yārâ*," in *Theological Dictionary of the Old Testament,* G. J. Botterweck & H. Ringgren, eds., D. E. Green, trans. (Grand Rapids: Eerdmans, 1990), 6:330.
3. L. Koehler & W. Baumgartner, *The Hebrew and Aramaic Lexicon of the Old Testament,* Study Edition, trans. M. E. J. Richardson (Leiden, the Netherlands: Koninklijke Brill NV, 2001), 2:1710.
4. M. J. Selman, "Law," in *Dictionary of the Old Testament: Pentateuch,* eds. T. D. Alexander & D. W. Baker (Downers Grove, IL: InterVarsity, 2003), 498.
5. F. Brown, *The New Brown-Driver-Briggs-Gesenius Hebrew and English Lexicon with an Appendix Containing the Biblical Aramaic* (Christian Copyrights, 1983), 435.
6. J. E. Hartley, "*tôrâ*," in *Theological Wordbook of the Old Testament,* eds. R. L. Harris, G. L. Archer, & B. K. Waltke (Chicago: Moody Press, 1980), 1:403–404.
7. R. K. Harrison, "Law in the OT," in *The International Standard Bible Encyclopedia,* ed. G. W. Bromiley (Grand Rapids: Eerdmans, 1986), 3:76.
8. P. Enns, "*tôrâ*," in *New International Dictionary of Old Testament Theology & Exegesis,* ed. W. A. VanGemeren (Grand Rapids: Eerdmans, 1997), 4:893.
9. E. P. Sanders, "Torah and Christ," *Interpretation,* vol. 29 (1975), 372.
10. M. E. Tate, "Legal Traditions of the Books of Exodus," *Review & Expositor,* vol. 74 (1977), 503.
11. J. M. Sprinkle, "Law," in *Evangelical Dictionary of Biblical Theology,* ed. W. A. Elwell, (Grand Rapids: Baker, 1996), 467.
12. Selman, "Law," 498–499; cf. C. T. Brown, *Beyond Obedience: Jesus and the Law in Matthew 5:17–20* (M.A. thesis, Chicago, IL: The Catholic Theological Union, 1991), 5, 83.
13. Koehler & Baumgartner, *The Hebrew and Aramaic Lexicon of the Old Testament,* 1:234.
14. G. A. Lint, ed., *The Old Testament Hebrew-English Dictionary: Gimel–Zayin* (Springfield, Missouri: World Library Press, 1996), 276.
15. R. Schultz, "*shāphat*," in *New International Dictionary of Old Testament Theology & Exegesis,* ed. W. A. VanGemeren (Grand Rapids: Eerdmans, 1997), 4:213.
16. W. L. Holladay, ed. *A Concise Hebrew and Aramaic Lexicon of the Old Testament* (Leiden, the Netherlands: E.J. Brill, 1988), 221.
17. R. D. Culver, "*mishpāt*," in *Theological Wordbook of the Old Testament,* eds. R. L. Harris, G. L. Archer, & B. K. Waltke (Chicago: Moody Press, 1980), 948–949. U. C. Rule ("Law in the OT," in *The International Standard Bible Encyclopedia,* ed. J. Orr [Grand Rapids: Eerdmans, 1955], 3:1852) offered this assessment: "[It] is a term constantly used in connection with, and distinction from, *statutes,* to indicate laws of a particular kind, viz. laws which, though forming part of the *torah* by virtue of Divine sanction, originated in decisions of judges upon cases brought before them for judgment" (emphasis in the original).
18. H. Ringgren, "*chāqâ*," in *Theological Dictionary of the Old Testament,* eds. G. J. Botterweck & H. Ringgren, trans. D. E. Green (Grand Rapids: Eerdmans, 1986), 5:141.
19. Brown, *The New Brown-Driver-Briggs-Gesenius Hebrew and English Lexicon with an Appendix Containing the Biblical Aramaic,* 349.
20. P. Enns, "*chōq*," in *New International Dictionary of Old Testament Theology & Exegesis,* ed. W. A. VanGemeren (Grand Rapids: Eerdmans, 1997), 2:250.
21. J. Lewis, "*chōq,*" in *Theological Wordbook of the Old Testament,* eds. R. L. Harris, G. L. Archer, & B. K. Waltke (Chicago: Moody Press, 1980), 1:317.
22. G. Gerleman, "*dābār,*" in *Theological Lexicon of the Old Testament,* eds. E. Jenni &

C. Westermann, trans. M. E. Biddle (Peabody, MA: Hendrickson Publishers, 1997), 1:325.

23. Lint, *The Old Testament Hebrew-English Dictionary: Gimel–Zayin*, 176.
24. W. H. Schmidt, "*dābhar*," in *Theological Dictionary of the Old Testament*, eds. G. J. Botterweck & H. Ringgren, trans. J. T. Willis, G. W. Bromiley, & D. E. Green (Grand Rapids: Eerdmans, 1978), 3:104.
25. Harrison, "Law in the OT," 3:77.
26. E. S. Kalland, "*dābār*," in *Theological Wordbook of the Old Testament*, eds. R. L. Harris, G. L. Archer, & B. K. Waltke (Chicago: Moody Press, 1980), 1:180.
27. Brown, *The New Brown-Driver-Briggs-Gesenius Hebrew and English Lexicon with an Appendix Containing the Biblical Aramaic*, 728.
28. C. van Leeuwen, "*'ēd*," in *Theological Lexicon of the Old Testament*, eds. E. Jenni & C. Westermann, trans. M. E. Biddle (Peabody, MA: Hendrickson Publishers, 1997), 2:839.
29. R. B. Chisholm, "*'wd*," in *New International Dictionary of Old Testament Theology & Exegesis*, ed. W. A. VanGemeren (Grand Rapids: Eerdmans, 1997), 3:335.
30. Koehler & Baumgartner, *The Hebrew and Aramaic Lexicon of the Old Testament*, 1:790.
31. H. Simian-Yofre, "*'wd*," in *Theological Dictionary of the Old Testament*, eds. G. J. Botterweck, H. Ringgren, and H. J. Fabry, trans. D. W. Scott (Grand Rapids: Eerdmans, 1999), 10:497.
32. C. Schultz, "*'ûd*," in *Theological Wordbook of the Old Testament*, eds. R. L. Harris, G. L. Archer, & B. K. Waltke (Chicago: Moody Press, 1980), 2:649–650; E. Lohse, *Theological Ethics of the New Testament*, trans. M. B. Boring (Minneapolis: Fortress Press, 1991), 8.
33. Rule, "Law in the OT," 3:1852.
34. Holladay, *A Concise Hebrew and Aramaic Lexicon of the Old Testament*, 304.
35. Koehler & Baumgartner, *The Hebrew and Aramaic Lexicon of the Old Testament*, 1:622.
36. Brown, *The New Brown-Driver-Briggs-Gesenius Hebrew and English Lexicon with an Appendix Containing the Biblical Aramaic*, 846.
37. J. E. Hartley, "*tsāwâ*," in *Theological Wordbook of the Old Testament*, eds. R. L. Harris, G. L. Archer, & B. K. Waltke (Chicago: Moody Press, 1980), 2:757.
38. Harrison, "Law in the OT," 3:77.
39. S. B. Ferguson, *Kingdom Life In A Fallen World: Living Out the Sermon on the Mount* (Colorado Springs, CO: Nav Press, 1986), 96.
40. F. W. Danker, ed., *A Greek-English Lexicon of the New Testament and Other Early Christian Literature*, 3rd ed. (Chicago, IL: The University of Chicago Press, 2000), 677.
41. J. P Louw & E. A. Nida, eds., *Greek-English Lexicon of the New Testament: Based on Semantic Domains*, 2nd ed., vol. 1: Introduction and Domains, vol. 2: Indices (New York, New York: United Bible Societies, 1989), 1:426.
42. W. Gutbrod, "*nómos*," in *Theological Dictionary of the New Testament*, G. Kittel, ed., G.W. Bromiley, trans. (Grand Rapids, Michigan: Eerdmans, 1999), 4:1059.
43. A. J. McClain, "What Is 'the Law'?" *Bibliotheca Sacra*, vol. 110, no. 440 (1953), 333–334.
44. H. H. Esser, "*nómos*," in *New International Dictionary of New Testament Theology*, ed. C. Brown (Grand Rapids, Michigan: Zondervan, 1986), 2:439.
45. D. J. Moo, "Law," in *Dictionary of Jesus and the Gospels*, J. B. Green, S. McKnight,

& I. H. Marshall, eds. (Downers Grove, IL: InterVarsity, 1992), 451.

46. E. Sanders, "Law in Judaism of the NT Period," in *The Anchor Bible Dictionary*, D. N. Freedman, ed. (New York: Doubleday, 1992), 4:254–255.
47. H. Hübner, "*nómos*," in *Exegetical Dictionary of the New Testament*, eds. H. Balz & G. Schneider, trans. J. W. Thompson & J. W. Medendorp (Grand Rapids: Eerdmans, 1991), 2:473.
48. Danker, *A Greek-English Lexicon of the New Testament and Other Early Christian Literature*, 676.
49. Louw & Nida, *Greek-English Lexicon of the New Testament: Based on Semantic Domains*, 1:427.
50. Gutbrod, "*nómos*," 4:1089.
51. Danker, *A Greek-English Lexicon of the New Testament and Other Early Christian Literature*, 567–568; cf. Louw & Nida, *Greek-English Lexicon of the New Testament: Based on Semantic Domains*, 1:359, 362–364, 366, 555–556; M. Rissi, "*krínō*," in *Exegetical Dictionary of the New Testament*, eds. H. Balz & G. Schneider, trans. J. W. Thompson & J. W. Medendorp (Grand Rapids: Eerdmans, 1991), 2:318.
52. F. Büchsel, "*krínō*," in *Theological Dictionary of the New Testament*, ed. G. Kittel, trans. G. W. Bromiley (Grand Rapids, Michigan: Eerdmans, 1999), 3:923; cf. W. Schneider, "*kríma*," in *New International Dictionary of New Testament Theology*, ed. C. Brown (Grand Rapids, Michigan: Zondervan, 1986), 2:362.
53. Louw & Nida, *Greek-English Lexicon of the New Testament: Based on Semantic Domains*, 1:427–428.
54. Danker, *A Greek-English Lexicon of the New Testament and Other Early Christian Literature*, 337; cf. H. Balz, "*énnomos*," in *Exegetical Dictionary of the New Testament*, eds. H. Balz & G. Schneider, trans. V.Howard & J.W. Thompson (Grand Rapids: Eerdmans, 1990), 1:455.
55. Gutbrod, "*nómos*," 4:1087; cf. Esser, "*nómos*," 2:446.
56. Danker, *A Greek-English Lexicon of the New Testament and Other Early Christian Literature*, 675–676; cf. Louw & Nida, *Greek-English Lexicon of the New Testament: Based on Semantic Domains*, 1:427.
57. Gutbrod, "*nómos*," 4:1088; cf. H. Hübner, "*nomikós*," in *Exegetical Dictionary of the New Testament*, eds. H. Balz & G. Schneider, trans. J. W. Thompson & J. W. Medendorp (Grand Rapids: Eerdmans, 1991), 2:471.
58. Louw & Nida, *Greek-English Lexicon of the New Testament: Based on Semantic Domains*, 1:427.
59. Danker, *A Greek-English Lexicon of the New Testament and Other Early Christian Literature*, 676.
60. Gutbrod, "*nómos*," 4:1090.
61. J. D. Charles, "The Greatest Or The Least In The Kingdom?: The Disciple's Relationship To The Law (Matt 5:17–20)," *Trinity Journal*, vol. 13, no. 2 (1992), 140.
62. H. C. Thiessen, *Lectures in Systematic Theology*, rev. ed. (Grand Rapids: Eerdmans, 1979), 169.
63. R. Mohrlang, *Matthew and Paul: A Comparison of Ethical Perspectives* (Cambridge: Cambridge University Press, 1984), 7; B. H. Young, *Jesus the Jewish Theologian* (Peabody, MA: Hendrickson Publishers, 1995), 265–266; M. J. Erickson, *Christian Theology*, 2nd ed. (Grand Rapids: Baker, 1998), 313.
64. T. G. Bunch, *The Ten Commandments: The Law of Liberty* (Washington, DC: Review and Herald, 1944), 16–17.
65. V. Hamilton, *Handbook on the Pentateuch* (Grand Rapids: Baker, 1982), 197.

66. *The Westminster Confession of Faith*, 3rd ed. (Atlanta, GA: Committee for Christian Education & Publications, Presbyterian Church in America, 1990).
67. Ibid., 55.
68. Ibid., 55–56.
69. J. H. Gerstner, "Law in the NT," in *The International Standard Bible Encyclopedia*, ed. G. W. Bromiley (Grand Rapids: Eerdmans, 1986), 3:85; S. Bolton, "The Moral Law: A Rule of Obedience" ([Web:] http://www.the-highway.com/articleFeb00.html. [Date of access: 27 November 2003]. 2000); E. Kevan, "The Moral Law and its Relation to Believers" ([Web:] http://www.the-highway.com/articleSept02.html. [Date of access: 26 November 2003], 2002); B. Schwertley, "God's Law for Modern Man" ([Web:] http://www.reformed.com/pub/law.htm#f4. [Date of access: 26 November 2003], 2003).
70. J. A. Motyer, "Law, Biblical Concept of," in *Evangelical Dictionary of Theology*, ed. W. Elwell (Grand Rapids: Baker, 2001), 675.
71. McClain, "What Is 'the Law'?", 334; McClain, *Law and Grace* (Winona Lake, IN: BMH Books, 1973), 8–9; cf. R. L. Aldrich, "Has the Mosaic Law Been Abolished?", *Bibliotheca Sacra*, vol. 116, no. 464 (1959), 322, 325; F. G. Zaspel, "The Continuing Relevance of Divine Law," in *Evangelical Theological Society*, paper read at the Eastern Regional Evangelical Theological Society in Lanham, Maryland on 3 April 1992 (Portland, OR: Theological Research Exchange Network, 1992), 5–6; A. Fruchtenbaum, "Israelology: Part 3 of 6," *Chafer Theological Seminary Journal*, vol. 5, no. 4 (1999), 27–29, 33, 36.
72. Contra, Dorsey ("The Law of Moses and the Christian: A Compromise," *Journal of the Evangelical Theological Society*, vol. 34, no. 3 [1991], 330), who asserts that the New Testament "speaks of the law in quite monolithic terms."
73. L. I. Hodges, "A Defense of the Tripartite Understanding of the Law Articulated in the 'The Westminster Confession,'" in *Evangelical Philosophical Society*, paper read at the meeting held during November 1990 (Portland, OR: Theological Research Exchange Network, 1990), 2–3; W. C. Kaiser, "God's Promise Plan and His Glorious Law," *Journal of the Evangelical Theological Society*, vol. 33, no. 3 (1990), 290, 300.
74. Cf. R. Alderson, "The Law–Civic, Ceremonial, and Moral," in *No Holiness, No Heaven!: Antinomianism Today*, R. Alderson (Carlisle, PA: Banner of Truth Trust, 1986) [Web:] http://www.the-highway.com/law1_Alderson.html. [Date of access: 27 November 2003]. E. C. Reisinger (*The Law and the Gospel* [Phillipsburg, NJ: P. & R. Publishing, 1997], 49) issued this cautionary note: "[I]n any serious study of the law it is absolutely necessary to make a proper distinction between the moral, ceremonial, and civil laws. Failure to make clear and proper distinctions will always lead to either legalism or antinomianism."
75. Cf. Kevan, "The Moral Law and its Relation to Believers." *The Westminster Confession of Faith* contains a classic statement on the tripartite division of the Mosaic law (XIX, 3–4): "3. Besides this law, commonly called moral, God was pleased to give to the people of Israel, as a church under age, ceremonial laws, containing several typical ordinances, partly of worship, prefiguring Christ, His graces, actions, sufferings, and benefits; and partly, holding forth divers instructions of moral duties. All which ceremonial laws are now abrogated, under the new testament. 4. To them also, as a body politic, He gave sundry judicial laws, which expired together with the state of that people; not obliging any other now, further than the general equity thereof may require."
76. Hodges, "A Defense of the Tripartite Understanding of the Law Articulated in the

'The Westminster Confession,'" 1.

77. R. McQuilkin, *An Introduction to Biblical Ethics*, 2nd. ed. (Wheaton, IL: Tyndale House Publishers, 1995), 51.
78. Cf. similar remarks made by Aldrich, "Has the Mosaic Law Been Abolished?", 322–324; Dorsey, "The Law of Moses and the Christian: A Compromise," 329–330; Zaspel, "The Continuing Relevance of Divine Law," 5; J. D. Hays, "Applying the Old Testament Law Today," *Bibliotheca Sacra*, vol. 158, no. 629 (2001), 22–24.
79. Kaiser, "God's Promise Plan and His Glorious Law," 290–291.
80. McQuilkin, *An Introduction to Biblical Ethics*, 53; cf. P. R. Schmidtbleicher, "Balancing The Use Of The Old Testament," *Chafer Theological Seminary Journal*, vol. 8, no. 3 (2002), 42, 44, 60.
81. Cf. Selman, "Law," 509, who advocates for the unity of the law, though he does not favor the division of it into "moral, ritual and civil law."
82. W. Kaiser, *Toward Old Testament Ethics* (Grand Rapids: Zondervan, 1983), 46.
83. L. O. Richards, *Zondervan Expository Dictionary of Bible Words*, 1st ed. (Grand Rapids, Zondervan, 1991), 390.
84. Cf. the discussion in chapters 5 and 6 regarding Matthew 5:17–20.
85. Kaiser, *Toward Old Testament Ethics*, 46.
86. G. Wenham, *The Book of Leviticus* (Grand Rapids: Eerdmans, 1979), 32.
87. McQuilkin, *An Introduction to Biblical Ethics*, 50–53.
88. Hays, "Applying the Old Testament Law Today," 30–31.
89. Contra Hays, 35.
90. T. Tiessen, "Toward A Hermeneutic For Discerning Universal Moral Absolutes," *Journal of the Evangelical Theological Society*, vol. 36, no. 2 (1993), 189.
91. Ibid., 192.
92. Ibid.
93. Ibid., 193, 194, 198, 200, 203, respectively; cf. the less helpful five-step approach suggested by Hays, "Applying the Old Testament Law Today," 31–35.
94. N. Geisler, *Christian Ethics: Options and Issues* (Grand Rapids: Baker, 1989), 117.
95. Wenham, *The Book of Leviticus*, 32–33.
96. R. Lightner, "Theological Perspectives on Theonomy; Part 3: A Dispensational Response to Theonomy," *Bibliotheca Sacra*, vol. 143 (1986), 237.
97. Kaiser, "God's Promise Plan and His Glorious Law," 291.
98. Lightner, "Theological Perspectives on Theonomy; Part 3: A Dispensational Response to Theonomy," 236.
99. In a similar vein, L. S. Chafer (*Grace* [Grand Rapids: Zondervan, 1922], 215, 239) wrote: "[The Scriptures of the New Testament] both assume and directly teach that the law is done away. Consequently, it is not in force in the present age in any sense whatsoever....The Old Testament system of law is absolutely superseded by the new system under grace. Christians are not under law either for justification or for sanctification."
100. Unless otherwise noted, all Scripture quotations are taken from the New Revised Standard Version of the Bible.
101. This probably was a reference to the Savior's teachings and injunctions; cf. F. W. Grosheide, *The First Epistle to the Corinthians* (Grand Rapids: Eerdmans, 1953), 213; W. Hendriksen, *New Testament Commentary: Exposition of Galatians* (Grand Rapids: Baker 1968), 232–233; A. W. Pink, "The Law and the Saint" ([Web:] http://www.the-highway.com/Law_Pink.html. [Date of access: 27 November 2003], 2003).
102. N. Geisler, *Christian Ethics: Options and Issues* (Grand Rapids: Baker, 1989), 206.
103. C. Ryrie, *Basic Theology: A Popular Systematic Guide To Understanding Biblical*

Truth (Wheaton, IL: Victor Books, 1986), 304; cf. Thiessen, *Lectures in Systematic Theology*, 170.

104. E. Hughes, *Paul's Second Epistle to the Corinthians* (Grand Rapids: Eerdmans, 1962), 96–106).
105. Geisler, *Christian Ethics: Options and Issues*, 206.
106. Kaiser, *Toward Old Testament Ethics*, 310.
107. W. Hendriksen, *New Testament Commentary: Exposition of Ephesians* (Grand Rapids: Baker, 1967), 134–135.
108. Geisler, *Christian Ethics: Options and Issues*, 207; cf. similar remarks made by Zaspel, "The Continuing Relevance of Divine Law," 6.
109. W. Hendriksen, *New Testament Commentary: Exposition of Galatians* (Grand Rapids: Baker, 1968), 147–148.
110. Geisler, *Christian Ethics: Options and Issues*, 207.
111. S. J. Kistemaker, *New Testament Commentary: Exposition of Hebrews* (Grand Rapids: Baker, 1984), 192–231; cf. J. N. Oswalt, "Ten Commandments," in *Evangelical Dictionary of Biblical Theology*, ed. W. A. Elwell (Grand Rapids: Baker, 1996), 763.
112. Geisler, *Christian Ethics: Options and Issues*, 207.
113. C. F. Henry, *Christian Personal Ethics* (Grand Rapids: Eerdmans, 1957), 355; Pink, "The Law and the Saint."
114. Hendriksen, *New Testament Commentary: Exposition of Galatians*, 126–127.
115. For example, G. L. Bahnsen (*By This Standard: The Authority Of God's Law Today* [Tyler, TX: Institute for Christian Economics, 1985], 310) remarked: "Since God himself is ever the same (immutable in character), the moral principles expressive of his nature are universal in validity, applying to all men in all places at all times." Bahnsen ("The Authority of God's Law," *The Presbyterian Journal*, vol. 6 [1978], 11) also wrote: "The law is a transcript—a writing out of the details—of God's moral perfection (Matt. 5:48; Ps. 19:7). As such, the law can no more be changed, abrogated, or improved upon than can God's perfection (Deut. 12:32; Ps. 119:160)."
116. D. E. Chismar & D. A. Rausch, "Regarding Theonomy: An Essay of Concern," *Journal of the Evangelical Theological Society*, vol. 27 (1984), 321.
117. For example, Bahnsen (*By This Standard: The Authority Of God's Law Today*, 141) wrote: "The principles of God's law are perpetual because they reflect the character of God, who is unchanging."
118. Cf. Ibid., 135–136, 316.
119. D. C. Jones, *Biblical Christian Ethics* (Grand Rapids: Baker, 1994), 113.
120. Bahnsen, *By This Standard: The Authority Of God's Law Today*, 135.
121. G. L. Bahnsen, *Theonomy in Christian Ethics*, 2nd ed. (Phillipsburg, NJ: Presbyterian and Reformed, 1984), xvii.
122. Bahnsen, *By This Standard: The Authority Of God's Law Today*, 271; emphasis in the original; cf. H. D. Kim, *The Mosaic Law in the Old Testament and the New Testament* (M.A. thesis, South Hamilton, MA: Gordon-Conwell Theological Seminary, 2003), 5–6.
123. Bahnsen, *Theonomy in Christian Ethics*, 317. In *By This Standard: The Authority Of God's Law Today* (271), he gave the following examples of unabrogated laws that society should enforce as universally binding policy directives on classes of individuals: "Thieves should be made to offer restitution, rapists should be executed, perjurers should suffer the penalty they would have inflicted on the accused, etc."
124. For example, Bahnsen (*By This Standard: The Authority Of God's Law Today*, 323) remarked, "What is proposed here is that all civil governments, whatever their struc-

ture, should be encouraged to submit to and apply the standing laws of the Old Testament Israel."

125. Ibid., 320–322.
126. Jones, *Biblical Christian Ethics*, 115.
127. Cf. Dorsey, "The Law of Moses and the Christian: A Compromise," 331.
128. *The Westminster Confession of Faith* reflected this position when it affirmed, "To them [the people of Israel] also, as a body politic, He gave sundry judicial laws, which expired together with the state of that people; not obliging any other now, further than the general equity thereof may require" (XIX, 4; cf. Exod. 21; 22:1–29).
129. Jones, *Biblical Christian Ethics*, 115; contra Schwertley, "God's Law for Modern Man."
130. Jones, *Biblical Christian Ethics*, 81–82.
131. Cf. Ferguson, *Kingdom Life In A Fallen World: Living Out the Sermon on the Mount*, 99; W. C. Kaiser, "Exodus," in *The Expositor's Bible Commentary*, ed. F. E. Gabelein, (Grand Rapids: Zondervan, 1990), 2:420.
132. A. M'Caig, "Law in the NT," in *The International Standard Bible Encyclopedia*, ed. J. Orr (Grand Rapids: Eerdmans, 1955), 3:1848.
133. W. R. Estep, "Law and Gospel in the Anabaptist/Baptist Tradition," *Grace Theological Journal*, vol. 12, no. 2 (1991), 196–197; J. Douma, *The Ten Commandments: Manual for the Christian Life*, trans. N. D. Kloosterman (Phillipsburg, NJ: P. P. & R. Publishing, 1996), 10.
134. S. Osborne, "The Christian and the Law," *Bibliotheca Sacra*, vol. 109, no. 435 (1952), 242, 247; McClain, *Law and Grace*, 25.
135. Bunch, *The Ten Commandments: The Law of Liberty*, 20–21.
136. A. D. H. Mayes, "The Decalogue of Moses: An Enduring Ethical Programme?," *Ethics and the Christian*, ed. in S. Freyne (Dublin: The Columba Press, 1991), 25.
137. M'Caig, "Law in the NT," 3:1850; Reisinger, *The Law and the Gospel*, 41; Kim, *The Mosaic Law in the Old Testament and the New Testament*, 40.
138. D. P. Scaer ("The Law and the Gospel in Lutheran Theology," *Grace Theological Journal*, vol. 12, no. 2 [1991], 164) refers to the Torah not only as "the written law" but also as "the promise of salvation."
139. Cf. G. Ladd, *A Theology of the New Testament: Revised Edition*, ed. D. A. Hagner (Grand Rapids: Eerdmans, 1993), 546.
140. J. J. Davis, *Evangelical Ethics: Issues Facing the Church Today*, 2nd ed. (Phillipsburg, PA: P. P. & R., 1993), 3; cf. D. W. Dayton, "Law and Gospel in the Wesleyan Tradition," *Grace Theological Journal*, vol. 12, no. 2 (1991), 240–241.
141. Cf. the stipulations in the Decalogue.
142. W. Barclay, *The Old Law and the New Law: The Ten Commandments and the Sermon on the Mount* (Edinburgh: The Saint Andrew Press, 1991), 3.
143. D. G. Bloesch, *Freedom for Obedience: Evangelical Ethics in Contemporary Times* (San Francisco: Harper & Row, Publishers, 1987), 128; D. G. Bloesch, "Law and Gospel in Reformed Perspective," *Grace Theological Journal*, vol. 12, no. 2 (1991), 180. Reisinger (*The Law and the Gospel*, 44) aptly noted that the moral law "*provides a real standard for direction in the way of holiness*" (emphasis his).
144. Ladd, *A Theology of the New Testament: Revised Edition*, 553.
145. Ibid., 554.
146. M'Caig, "Law in the NT," 3:1846.
147. J. Murray, *Principles of Conduct: Aspects of Biblical Ethics* (Grand Rapids: Eerdmans, 1957), 226–227.

148. Ferguson, *Kingdom Life In A Fallen World: Living Out the Sermon on the Mount*, 98; Bolton, "The Moral Law: A Rule of Obedience."
149. Alderson, "The Law–Civic, Ceremonial, and Moral"; Reisinger, *The Law and the Gospel*, 104–105.
150. Jones, *Biblical Christian Ethics*, 109; E. Kevan, "The Law not Abrogated by Christ to Believers" ([Web:] http://www.the-highway.com/law_Kevan.html. [Date of access: 27 November 2003], 2003).
151. Murray, *Principles of Conduct: Aspects of Biblical Ethics*, 151; Alderson, "The Law–Civic, Ceremonial, and Moral."
152. Kevan, "The Law not Abrogated by Christ to Believers."
153. Henry, *Christian Personal Ethics*, 351.
154. W. C. Kaiser, "Response to Douglas Moo," in *The Law, the Gospel, and the Modern Christian: Five Views*, ed. W. G. Strickland (Grand Rapids: Zondervan, 1993), 198.
155. Jones, *Biblical Christian Ethics*, 110.
156. Harrison, "Law in the OT," 3:79.
157. Henry, *Christian Personal Ethics*, 269; Kevan, "The Moral Law and its Relation to Believers"; Kevan, "The Law not Abrogated by Christ to Believers." Concerning the enduring relevancy of the Ten Commandments, P. D. Miller ("The Place of the Decalogue in the Old Testament and Its Law," *Interpretation*, vol. 43 [1989], 229–230) offered these cogent thoughts: "Whatever uncertainties and ambivalences we may have as Christians about the place of law in the Christian life, most of us understand that the Ten Commandments are basic and not abrogated in any final way by the Christ event. While we may not always know what they mean for our conduct or how literally or strictly they are to be obeyed, there is some sense that they transcend the normal limitations, restraints, and temporality of most of what we call law, within the Scriptures and beyond."
158. Alderson, "The Law–Civic, Ceremonial, and Moral"; Reisinger, *The Law and the Gospel*, xviii; Bolton, "The Moral Law: A Rule of Obedience."
159. E. H. Merrill, *The New American Commentary: An Exegetical and Theological Exposition of Holy Scripture–Deuteronomy* (Nashville, TN: Broadman & Holman Publishers, 1994), 145.
160. Jones, *Biblical Christian Ethics*, 116; Pink, "The Law and the Saint"; contra McClain, *Law and Grace*, 48–49.
161. Douma, *The Ten Commandments: Manual for the Christian Life*, xi.
162. Gerstner, "Law in the NT," 3:88.
163. R. S. Wallace, *The Ten Commandments: A Study of Ethical Freedom* (Grand Rapids: Eerdmans, 1965), ix; Hodges, "A Defense of the Tripartite Understanding of the Law Articulated in the 'The Westminster Confession,'" 16.
164. J. M. McBain, *The Ten Commandments in the New Testament* (Nashville: Broadman Press, 1977), 14; K. Ahn, *The Sinaitic Covenant and Law in the Theology of Dispensationalism* (Ph.D. dissertation, Berrien Springs, MI: Andrews University, Seventh-day Adventist Theological Seminary, 1989), 314.
165. Cf. Schmidtbleicher, "Balancing The Use Of The Old Testament," 48.
166. Kevan, "The Law not Abrogated by Christ to Believers"; Pink, "The Law and the Saint."
167. Douma, *The Ten Commandments: Manual for the Christian Life*, 5.
168. Davis, *Evangelical Ethics: Issues Facing the Church Today*, 2.
169. Wallace, *The Ten Commandments: A Study of Ethical Freedom*, 7.
170. Ibid.

Chapter 3: An Overview of the Decalogue

1. J. P. Hyatt (*New Century Bible Commentary: Exodus* [Grand Rapids: Eerdmans, 1980], 207) noted that the Ten Commandments are "sometimes called the ethical decalogue to distinguish it from a supposed 'ritual decalogue' of [Exod.] 34:17–26."
2. G. A. F. Knight, *Theology as Narration: A Commentary on the Book of Exodus* (Grand Rapids: Eerdmans, 1976), 134–135.
3. J. M. Lochman, *Signposts to Freedom: The Ten Commandments and Christian Ethics*, trans. D. Lewis (Minnepolis, MN: Augsburg Publishing House, 1982), 18; emphasis in the original.
4. N. M. Sarna, *Studies in Biblical Interpretation* (Philadelphia: The Jewish Publication Society, 2000), 229.
5. H. D. Preuss, *Old Testament Theology: Volume 1*, trans. L. G. Perdue (Louisville, KY: Westminster John Knox Press, 1995), 100. D. L. Christensen (*Deuteronomy 1:1–21:9, Word Biblical Commentary* [Dallas: Word Books, 2001], 105) theorizes that "the number ten was selected to enumerate the basic commandments because of the simple fact that we have ten digits, five on each hand, which facilitate the process of memorization and recitation, especially within catechetical contexts."
6. J. H. Sailhamer, *The Pentateuch as Narrative: A Biblical-Theological Commentary* (Grand Rapids: Zondervan, 1992), 283; A. M. Harman, "Decalogue (Ten Commandments)," in *New International Dictionary of Old Testament Theology & Exegesis*, ed. W. A. VanGemeren (Grand Rapids: Eerdmans, 1997), 4:513.
7. J. Douma, *The Ten Commandments: Manual for the Christian Life*, trans. N. D. Kloosterman (Phillipsburg, NJ: P. & R. Publishing, 1996), 4.
8. F. W. Farrar, *The Voice from Sinai: The Eternal Bases of the Mosaic Law* (London: Isbister and Company, 1896), 8; N. M. Sarna, *The JPS Torah Commentary: Exodus* (Philadelphia: The Jewish Publication Society, 1991), 107.
9. T. G. Bunch, *The Ten Commandments: The Law of Liberty* (Washington, DC: Review and Herald, 1944), 24.
10. D. C. Jones, *Biblical Christian Ethics* (Grand Rapids: Baker, 1994), 103.
11. M. Weinfield, "The Decalogue: Its Significance, Uniqueness, and Place in Israel's Tradition," in *Religion and Law: Biblical-Judaic and Islamic Perspectives*, eds. E. B. Firmage, B. G. Weiss, & J. W. Welch, (Winona Lake, IL: Eisenbrauns, 1990), 10. The Shema was the Jewish confession of faith made up of Deuteronomy 6:4–9, 11:13–21, and Numbers 15:37–41.
12. Ibid., 10.
13. Ibid., 34. Phylacteries were small square leather boxes that contained slips inscribed with scriptural passages. Jewish men traditionally wore phylacteries on the left arm and on the head during morning weekly prayers (R. S. Fagen, "Phylacteries," in *The Anchor Bible Dictionary*, ed. D. N. Freedman [New York: Doubleday, 1992], 5:368).
14. Jones, *Biblical Christian Ethics*, 104.
15. C. J. H. Wright, "Ten Commandments," in *The International Standard Bible Encyclopedia*, ed. G. W. Bromiley (Grand Rapids: Eerdmans, 1988), 4:786; P. D. Miller, *Deuteronomy–Interpretation, A Bible Commentary for Teaching and Preaching* (Louisville, KY: John Knox Press, 1990), 71.
16. Jones, *Biblical Christian Ethics*, 104.
17. Douma, *The Ten Commandments: Manual for the Christian Life*, 1.
18. Cf. Ibid., 12.
19. Cf. J. H. Hertz, *The Pentateuch and Haftorahs*, 2nd ed. (London: Soncino Press,

1981), 295; U. Cassuto, *A Commentary on the Book of Exodus* (Jerusalem: Magnes Press, 1983), 239.

20. Philo of Alexandria in Egypt was a well-known representative of Hellenistic Judaism at the time of Christ (Weinfield, "The Decalogue: Its Significance, Uniqueness, and Place in Israel's Tradition," 30).
21. Hyatt (*New Century Bible Commentary: Exodus*, 208) seems to echo this sentiment when he maintains that the "Ten Commandments do not deal with individual acts and their punishment, but rather with general principles."
22. Philo, "On the Decalogue, On the Special Laws, On the Virtues," in *The Loeb Classical Library,* ed. E. H. Warmington, trans. F. H. Colson (Cambridge: Harvard University, 1937), 50–51.
23. Ibid., 110.
24. R. M. Grant, "The Decalogue in Early Christianity," *Harvard Theological Review*, vol. 40 (1947), 1–17.
25. D. Kidner, "Ten Commandments," in *The Zondervan Pictorial Encyclopedia of the Bible,* ed. M. C. Tenny (Grand Rapids: Zondervan, 1976), 5:673.
26. Jones, *Biblical Christian Ethics*, 104.
27. J. B. Coffman, *Commentary on Exodus: The Second Book of Moses* (Abilene, TX: Abilene Christian University Press, 1985), 267.
28. Cf. B. Jacob, *The Second Book of the Bible: Exodus,* trans. W. Jacob (Hoboken, NJ: KTAV Publishing House, 1992), 544–545.
29. A. A. MacRae, "Book of Exodus," in *The Zondervan Pictorial Encyclopedia of the Bible,* ed. M. C. Tenney (Grand Rapids: Zondervan, 1976), 2:446.
30. Sarna, *The JPS Torah Commentary: Exodus*, 108.
31. E. H. Merrill, *The New American Commentary: An Exegetical and Theological Exposition of Holy Scripture–Deuteronomy* (Nashville, TN: Broadman & Holman Publishers, 1994), 143; Harman, "Decalogue (Ten Commandments)," 4:516; cf. the discussion to follow concerning suzerainty royal treaties.
32. Sarna, *Studies in Biblical Interpretation* (Philadelphia: The Jewish Publication Society, 2000), 235.
33. P.C. Craigie, "Ten Commandments," in *Evangelical Dictionary of Theology* (2nd ed.), ed. W. A. Elwell (Grand Rapids: Baker, 2001), 1171–1172.
34. G. E. Mendenhall & G. A. Herion, "Covenant," in *The Anchor Bible Dictionary,* ed. D. N. Freedman (New York: Doubleday, 1992), 1:1184; emphasis in the original.
35. Douma, *The Ten Commandments: Manual for the Christian Life*, 35; C. H. Bullock, "Old Testament Theology," in *Evangelical Dictionary of Theology* (2nd ed.), ed. W. A. Elwell (Grand Rapids: Baker Book House, 2001), 860.
36. J. E. Park, "The Book of Exodus," in *The Interpreter's Bible,* ed. G. A. Buttrick (New York: Abingdon Press, 1952), 1:980.
37. Farrar, *The Voice from Sinai: The Eternal Bases of the Mosaic Law*, 25.
38. Ibid., 25–26.
39. W. C. Kaiser, *Toward an Old Testament Theology* (Grand Rapids: Zondervan, 1978), 115.
40. Cf. Christensen, *Deuteronomy 1–11, Word Biblical Commentary*, 106.
41. Cf. the discussion later in this chapter regarding the ongoing relevance and applicability of the fourth commandment.
42. J. S. Spong & D. G. Haines, *Beyond Moralism: A Contemporary View Of The Ten Commandments* (San Francisco: Harper & Row, 1986), 19.
43. R. Brown, *The Message of Deuteronomy: Not by Bread Alone* (Downers Grove, IL: InterVarsity, 1993), 82.

44. W. Eichrodt ("The Law and the Gospel: The Meaning of the Ten Commandments in Israel and for Us," trans. C. F. McRae, *Interpretation,* vol. 11 [1957], 27), not only noted "that the Decalogue series does not show a uniform sentence structure and metric consonance," but also observed that "the sentences vary in length, in the number of their words and in their structure—now transitive, now instransitive, now with, now without an object."
45. The comments of B. S. Childs (*The Book of Exodus: A Critical, Theological Commentary* [Philadelphia: Westminster, 1974], 398) would be typical of the views espoused by certain scholars: "The variation of the Deuteronomic rescession amply illustrates the tendency to alter and expand elements within the commandments. Moreover, the different styles of writing attributed to a Deuteronomic or Priestly editor would further confirm the presence of several layers of historical development within the present form."
46. P. D. Miller, "The Place of the Decalogue in the Old Testament and Its Law," *Interpretation,* vol. 43 (1989), 231.
47. Ibid.
48. J. A. Thompson, "Deuteronomy: An Introduction and Commentary," in *Tyndale Old Testament Commentaries* (vol. 5), ed. D. J. Wiseman (Downers Grove, IL: Inter-Varsity, 1974), 29.
49. R. K. Harrison, "Law in the OT," in *The International Standard Bible Encyclopedia,* ed. G. W. Bromiley (Grand Rapids: Eerdmans, 1986), 3:81.
50. O. T. Allis, *God Spake By Moses: An Exposition of the Pentateuch* (Phillipsburg, NJ: Presbyterian and Reformed, 1951), 135–136.
51. Miller, *Deuteronomy–Interpretation, A Bible Commentary for Teaching and Preaching,* 73.
52. J. H. Tigay, *The JPS Torah Commentary: Deuteronomy* (Philadelphia: The Jewish Publication Society, 1996), 62; cf. M. Noth, *Exodus: A Commentary,* trans. J. S. Bowden (Philadelphia: The Westminster Press, 1962), 168.
53. A. D. H. Mayes, "The Decalogue of Moses: An Enduring Ethical Programme?," *Ethics and the Christian,* ed. in S. Freyne (Dublin: The Columba Press, 1991), 29.
54. Noth, *Exodus: A Commentary,* 160. C. F. Keil & F. Delitzsch ("The Second Book of Moses [Exodus]," in *Biblical Commentary on the Old Testament,* trans. J. Martin [Grand Rapids: Eerdmans, 1981], 2:114) maintained that "nearly all the commandments are couched in the negative form of prohibition, because they presuppose the existence of sin and evil desires in the human heart." Weinfield ("The Decalogue: Its Significance, Uniqueness, and Place in Israel's Tradition," 10–11) similarly asserted that "even the 'positive' commandments...are in fact prohibitives." But Kaiser (*Toward an Old Testament Theology,* 114–115) offered this alternative explanation: "This has nothing to do with either the tone or aim of that law. It was simply easier to express a believer's restrictions in a few words, for his freedom was so vast. Besides, all morality is double sided anyway—every moral act is at one and the same time a refraining from a contrary mode of action and the adoption of its opposite. It would make no difference if that law were stated negatively or positively."
55. F. R. Harm, "Sabbatarianism," in *Evangelical Dictionary of Theology* (2nd ed.), ed. W. Elwell (Grand Rapids: Baker, 2001), 1045. Schaff (*History of the Christian Church* [Grand Rapids: Eerdmans 1979], 6:494) traced the origin of the sabbatarian view to the Puritans at the close of the sixteenth century.
56. J. S. Spong & D. G. Haines, *Beyond Moralism: A Contemporary View Of The Ten*

Commandments (San Francisco: Harper & Row, 1986), 49–51; W. Barclay, *The Old Law and the New Law: The Ten Commandments and the Sermon on the Mount* (Edinburgh: The Saint Andrew Press, 1991), 21–22. The Christian Sabbath view is appealing to some, for it proposes a biblical reason for the observance of Sunday by basing this practice on the fourth commandment of the Decalogue.

57. C. Hodge, *Systematic Theology* (Grand Rapids: Eerdmans, 1981), 329–330. Merrill (*The New American Commentary: An Exegetical and Theological Exposition of Holy Scripture–Deuteronomy*, 152) seems sympathetic to this view when he states that "by example if not by explicit command Jesus and the apostles mandated the observance of the first day of the week as commemorative of his triumphant victory over death." Also, cf. J. C. Slemp, *Twelve Laws of Life: A Study of the Ten Commandments and Related Teachings of Jesus* (Philadelphia: The Judson Press, 1950), 45; J. M. McBain, *The Ten Commandments in the New Testament* (Nashville: Broadman Press, 1977), 43–44.
58. R. S. Wallace, *The Ten Commandments: A Study of Ethical Freedom* (Grand Rapids: Eerdmans, 1965), 81.
59. W. F. Crafts, *The Sabbath for Man* (New York: Funk and Wagnalls, 1885), 366.
60. S. Bacchiocchi, *From Sabbath to Sunday: A Historical Investigation of the Rise of Sunday Observance in Early Christianity* (Rome: Pontifical Gregorian University Press, 1977), 56.
61. Ibid., 212.
62. D. K. Lowery, "Lord's Day," In *Evangelical Dictionary of Theology* (2nd ed.), ed. W. Elwell (Grand Rapids: Baker, 2001), 700.
63. Waterman, "Sabbath," 5:188; A. Fruchtenbaum, "Israelology: Part 3 of 6," *Chafer Theological Seminary Journal*, vol. 5, no. 4 (1999), 37.
64. F. W. Danker, ed., *A Greek-English Lexicon of the New Testament and Other Early Christian Literature,* 3rd ed. (Chicago, IL: The University of Chicago Press, 2000), 909–910.
65. Cf. W. Hendriksen, *New Testament Commentary: The Gospel of Matthew* (Grand Rapids: Baker, 1973), 987; D.A. Carson, "Matthew," in *The Expositor's Bible Commentary,* ed. F. E. Gaebelein (Grand Rapids: Zondervan, 1984), 8:587.
66. R. H. Worth, *The Sermon on the Mount: Its Old Testament Roots* (New York: Paulist Press, 1997), 43.
67. Douma, *The Ten Commandments: Manual for the Christian Life*, 111.
68. Many of the arguments that follow appear in the Seventh-day Adventist publication *Questions in Doctrine: An Explanation of Certain Major Aspects of Seventh Day Adventist Leaders, Bible Teachers and Editors*, by F. D. Nichol (Washington, DC: Review and Herald Publishing Association, 1957).
69. Ibid., 149.
70. A. L. Baker, *Belief and Work of Seventh-Day Adventists* (Washington, DC: Review and Herald Publishing Association, 1919), 74; R. Gane, "Sabbath and the New Covenant," *Journal of the Adventist Theological Society*, vol. 10, nos. 1–2 (1999), 311, 331; N. R. Gulley, "Basic Issues between Science and Scripture: Theological Implications of Alternative Models and the Necessary Basis for the Sabbath in Genesis 1–2," *Journal of the Adventist Theological Society*, vol. 14, no. 1 (2003), 223, 225.
71. E.g. Gane, "Sabbath and the New Covenant," et al.
72. Baker, *Belief and Work of Seventh-Day Adventists*, 73–74.
73. E. G. White, *The Great Controversy* (Washington, DC: Review and Herald Publishing Association, 1926), 58–59.

74. W. M. Martin, *The Kingdom of the Cults: An Analysis of the Major Cult Systems in the Present Christian Era* (Minneapolis, MN: Bethany Fellowship Publishers, 1977), 398–399.
75. Waterman, "Sabbath," 5:188.
76. Douma, *The Ten Commandments: Manual for the Christian Life*, 111.
77. Carson, "Matthew," 8:501.
78. E.g. J. F. Walvoord, *The Revelation of Jesus Christ* (Chicago: Moody Press, 1966), 42; Bacchiocchi, *From Sabbath to Sunday: A Historical Investigation of the Rise of Sunday Observance in Early Christianity*, 123.
79. E. Hughes, *The Book of Revelation: A Commentary* (Grand Rapids: Eerdmans, 1990), 24–25.
80. R. H. Mounce, *The Book of Revelation* (Grand Rapids: Eerdmans, 1977), 76.
81. R. L. Aldrich, "The Mosaic Ten Commandments Compared To Their Restatements In The New Testament," *Bibliotheca Sacra*, vol. 118 (1961), 253; Martin, *The Kingdom of the Cults: An Analysis of the Major Cult Systems in the Present Christian Era*, 395.
82. M. A. Smith, "Worship and the Christian Year," in *Eerdman's Handbook to the History of Christianity*, ed. Tim Dowley (Grand Rapids: Eerdmans, 1977), 9; e.g. *Didache 14:1*; *Barnabas 15:1; 15:8; 15:9.*
83. For example, Part Five of Martin Luther's Large Catechism (1529); Question and Answer 103 of the Heidelburg Catechism (1563); Questions and Answers 63–68 of Benjamin Keach's Catechism (1677); and Chapter 22 of the London Baptist Confession (1689).
84. Waterman, "Sabbath," 5:189.
85. J. Calvin, *Institutes of the Christian Religion* (Grand Rapids: Zondervan, 1981), 1:341.
86. Bacchiocchi, *From Sabbath to Sunday: A Historical Investigation of the Rise of Sunday Observance in Early Christianity*, 63–64.
87. Douma, *The Ten Commandments: Manual for the Christian Life*, 110.
88. Bacchiocchi, *Divine Rest for Human Restlessness: A Theological Study of the Good News of the Sabbath for Today*, 19–20.
89. Calvin, *Institutes of the Christian Religion*, 1:342.
90. Douma, *The Ten Commandments: Manual for the Christian Life*, 122.
91. Waterman, "Sabbath," 5:184.
92. Shead, "Sabbath," 750.
93. Hodge, *Systematic Theology*, 3:322.
94. This most likely corresponded with the Mosaic period (Wright, "Ten Commandments," 4:787).
95. G. von Rad, *Old Testament Theology* (New York: Harper and Row, 1962), 1:132.
96. Kidner, "Ten Commandments," 5:673; R. W. Dalman, *Sojourners in the Promise: Genesis and the Origin of Abraham's Faith* (New Hope, MN: Rodger W. Dalman, 2002), 28.
97 G. E. Mendenhall, "Covenant Forms in Israelite Tradition," *Biblical Archaeologist*, vol. 17, no. 3 (1954), 50–76.
98. M. G. Klein, *Treaty of the Great King* (Grand Rapids: Eerdmans, 1963).
99. A. Phillips, *Ancient Israel's Criminal Law: A New Approach to the Decalogue* (New York: Schocken Books, 1970), 1; Harman, "Decalogue (Ten Commandments)," 4:514; *The Net Bible* (Garland, Texas: Biblical Studies Press, L.L.C., and the authors [Web:] http://www.bible.org/netbible/index.htm. [Date of access: 13 March 2003], 2001).
100. R. K. Harrison, "Book of Exodus," in *The International Standard Bible Encyclopedia*, ed. G. W. Bromiley (Grand Rapids: Eerdmans, 1982), 2:229.

101. Wright, "Ten Commandments," 4:787.
102. Mendenhall & Herion, "Covenant," 1:1180–1181.
103. Sarna, *Studies in Biblical Interpretation* (Philadelphia: The Jewish Publication Society, 2000), 236.
104. Wright, "Ten Commandments," 4:788.
105. For example, the provision for deposit and periodic reading, the list of witnesses, and the curses and blessings.
106. Mendenhall & Herion, "Covenant," 1:1184. They go on to explain: "Even if all the LB elements are not attested in the first 17 verses of Exodus 20 (they are not even all attested in many LB treaties!), virtually all of them are nevertheless reflected in the later elaboration of traditions associated with the Sinai covenant....If these elements were truly absent from the complex of traditions about the very founding of the ancient Israelite community, it is indeed strange that in later times (when most of these elements had been completely forgotten in the process of ANE treaty enactments) some biblical scribes felt it necessary to add them to the complex of the Mosaic tradition."
107. Mendenhall & Herion, "Covenant," 1:1181.
108. Ibid., 1:1184.
109. J. W. Marshall, "Decalogue," in *Dictionary of the Old Testament: Pentateuch*, eds. T. D. Alexander & D. W. Baker (Downers Grove, IL: InterVarsity, 2003), 174.

Chapter 4: A Content Analysis of the Decalogue

1. S. R. Driver, *The International Critical Commentary: A Critical and Exegetical Commentary on Deuteronomy* (New York: Charles Scribner's Sons, 1902), 82; J. Hsu, *The Decalogue and Moral Conscience in the Ancient Near East: A Comparative Study* (Th.M. thesis, Deerfield, IL: Trinity Evangelical Divinity School, 1986), 5; R. W. Dalman, *Sojourners in the Promise: Genesis and the Origin of Abraham's Faith* (New Hope, MN: Rodger W. Dalman, 2002), 32.
2. Hsu, *The Decalogue and Moral Conscience in the Ancient Near East: A Comparative Study*, 6.
3. A. Phillips, *Ancient Israel's Criminal Law: A New Approach to the Decalogue* (New York: Schocken Books, 1970), 4; N. M. Sarna, *Studies in Biblical Interpretation* (Philadelphia: The Jewish Publication Society, 2000), 232.
4. C. F. Keil & F. Delitzsch, "The Second Book of Moses (Exodus)," in *Biblical Commentary on the Old Testament*, trans. J. Martin (Grand Rapids: Eerdmans, 1981), 2:113–114.
5. A. M. Silbermann, *Chumash with Targum Onkelos, Haphtaroth and Rashi's Commentary: Shemoth* (Jerusalem: Feldheim Publishers, 1988), 102.
6. F. Brown, *The New Brown-Driver-Briggs-Gesenius Hebrew and English Lexicon with an Appendix Containing the Biblical Aramaic* (Christian Copyrights, 1983), 43.
7. L. Koehler & W. Baumgartner, *The Hebrew and Aramaic Lexicon of the Old Testament*, Study Edition, trans. M. E. J. Richardson (Leiden, the Netherlands: Koninklijke Brill NV, 2001), 1:52.
8. H. Ringgren, "*'ĕlōhîm*," in *Theological Dictionary of the Old Testament*, eds. G. J. Botterweck & H. Ringgren, trans. J. T. Willis (Grand Rapids: Eerdmans, 1974), 1:272; M. Rose, "Names of God in the OT," in *The Anchor Bible Dictionary*, ed. D. N. Freedman (New York: Doubleday, 1992), 4:1006.
9. J. B. Scott, "*'ĕlōhîm*," in *Theological Wordbook of the Old Testament*, eds. R. L. Har-

ris, G. L. Archer, & B. K. Waltke (Chicago: Moody Press, 1980), 1:44.

10. T. E. Fretheim, "'*ělōhîm*," in *New International Dictionary of Old Testament Theology & Exegesis*, ed. W. A. VanGemeren (Grand Rapids: Eerdmans, 1997), 1:405.
11. G. A., Lint, ed. *The Old Testament Hebrew-English Dictionary: Aleph-Beth* (Springfield, Missouri: World Library Press, 1995), 244–245.
12. W. H. Schmidt, "'ĕlōhîm," in *Theological Lexicon of the Old Testament*, eds. E. Jenni & C. Westermann, trans. M. E. Biddle (Peabody, MA: Hendrickson Publishers, 1997), 1:115–116.
13. D. W. Baker, "God, Names of," in *Dictionary of the Old Testament: Pentateuch*, eds. T. D. Alexander & D. W. Baker (Downers Grove, IL: InterVarsity, 2003), 362.
14. H. B. Kuhn, "Names of God," in *The Zondervan Pictorial Encyclopedia of the Bible*, ed. M. C. Tenney (Grand Rapids: Zondervan, 1976), 2:763.
15. R. J. Wyatt, "Names of God," in *The International Standard Bible Encyclopedia*, ed. G. W. Bromiley (Grand Rapids: Eerdmans, 1982), 2:506
16. Brown, *The New Brown-Driver-Briggs-Gesenius Hebrew and English Lexicon with an Appendix Containing the Biblical Aramaic*, 217.
17. Baker, "God, Names of," 362.
18. M. E. Tate, "Legal Traditions of the Books of Exodus," *Review & Expositor*, vol. 74 (1977), 486; Rose, "Names of God in the OT," 4:1003; R. L. Smith, *Old Testament Theology: Its History, Method, and Message* (Nashville, TN: Broadman & Holman, Publishers, 1993), 120.
19. G. L. Bray, "God," in *New Dictionary of Biblical Theology*, eds. T. D. Alexander, B. S. Rosner, D. A. Carson, & G. Goldsworthy (Downers Grove, IL: InterVarsity, 2000), 513.
20. The subsequent material is a distillation of information presented by the following authors: J. B. Payne, "*hāwâ*," in *Theological Wordbook of the Old Testament*, eds. R. L. Harris, G. L. Archer, & B. K. Waltke (Chicago: Moody Press,1980), 1:210–212; D. N. Freedman & M. O'Connor, "*yhwh*," in *Theological Dictionary of the Old Testament*, eds. G. J. Botterweck & H. Ringgren, trans. D. E. Green (Grand Rapids: Eerdmans, 1986), 5:500–521; H. D. Preuss, *Old Testament Theology: Volume 1*, trans. L. G. Perdue (Louisville, KY: Westminster John Knox Press, 1995), 140–141; T. Fretheim, "*yahweh*," in *New International Dictionary of Old Testament Theology & Exegesis*, ed. W. A. VanGemeren (Grand Rapids: Eerdmans, 1997), 4:1295–1300; E. Jenni, "*yhwh*," in *Theological Lexicon of the Old Testament*, eds. E. Jenni & C. Westermann, trans. M. E. Biddle, (Peabody, MA: Hendrickson Publishers, 1997), 2:522–526; Koehler & Baumgartner, *The Hebrew and Aramaic Lexicon of the Old Testament*, 1:394–395.
21. Cf. the discussion of G. Quell ("*kýrios*," in *Theological Dictionary of the New Testament*, ed. G. Kittel, trans. G. W. Bromiley [Grand Rapids, MI: Eerdmans, 1999], 3:1067–1069, 1081), who notes that, "even in respect of the form of the name there are difficulties in the tradition which prevent us, or largely prevent us, from reading the word in its full phonetic form with no possibility of objections" (3:1067).
22. C. R. Gianotti, "The Meaning of the Divine Name YHWH," *Bibliotheca Sacra*, vol. 142, no. 165 (1985), 39; cf. Tate, "Legal Traditions of the Books of Exodus," 486; D. G. Bloesch, *Freedom for Obedience: Evangelical Ethics in Contemporary Times* (San Francisco: Harper & Row, Publishers, 1987), 65.
23. Gianotti, "The Meaning of the Divine Name YHWH," 48; cf. A. B. Davidson, *The Theology of the Old Testament* (Edinburgh: T. & T. Clark, 1904), 54–57; H. F. Stevenson, *Titles of the Triune God* (Westwood, NJ: Revell, 1956), 21. Quell ("*kýrios*," 3:1062) echoes this sentiment when he writes as follows: "The OT belief in God is grounded in historical experience and it developed in continuing contact with history.

The most meaningful expression of this fact is the use of the name Yahweh in statements about God and in calling upon Him."

24. E. A. Martens, "God, Names of," in *Evangelical Dictionary of Biblical Theology*, ed. W. A. Elwell (Grand Rapids: Baker, 1996), 298; cf. W. J. Schröeder ("Deuteronomy or The Fifth Book of Moses," in *Commentary on the Holy Scriptures: Critical, Doctrinal, and Homiletical*, ed. J. P. Lange, trans. P. Schaff & A. Gosman, [Grand Rapids: Zondervan, 1978], 2:88), who refers to Yahweh as "the only or self-existent being."
25. Cf. T. G. Bunch, *The Ten Commandments: The Law of Liberty* (Washington, DC: Review and Herald, 1944), 12.
26. T. E. McComiskey, "God, Names of," in *Evangelical Dictionary of Theology* (2nd ed.), ed. W. A. Elwell (Grand Rapids: Baker, 2001), 507.
27. J. I. Packer, "God," in *New Dictionary of Theology*, eds. S. Ferguson, D. F. Wright, & J. I. Packer (Downers Grove, IL: InterVarsity Press, 1988), 274–275.
28. F. W. Farrar, *The Voice from Sinai: The Eternal Bases of the Mosaic Law* (London: Isbister and Company, 1896), 15.
29. W.A. VanGemeren, "Tetragammaton," in *Evangelical Dictionary of Theology* (2nd ed.), ed. W. A. Elwell (Grand Rapids: Baker, 2001), 1177.
30. A brief observation is in order regarding the Hebrew term הוֹצֵאתִיךָ (literally rendered, "has brought out you"). The primary root is יָצָא (*yātsā'*), which means "to come out," "to come forth," or "to proceed" (Koehler & Baumgartner, *The Hebrew and Aramaic Lexicon of the Old Testament*, 1:425). The verb appears in the Hiphil perfect, first person common singular form. It also has a second person masculine singular suffix. As *The Net Bible* (Garland, Texas: Biblical Studies Press, L.L.C., and the authors [Web:] http://www.bible.org/ netbible/index.htm. [Date of access: 13 March 2003], 2001) notes, the intent of the masculine form is not to exclude the female gender. On the one hand, God "is addressing [all the Israelites] as his people." On the other hand, "he is addressing them individually for their obedience."
31. I. Cairns, *Word and Presence: A Commentary on the Book of Deuteronomy* (Grand Rapids: Eerdmans, 1992), 71.
32. J. H. Sailhamer, *The Pentateuch as Narrative: A Biblical-Theological Commentary* (Grand Rapids: Zondervan, 1992), 285.
33. W. G. Plaut, *The Torah: A Modern Commentary* (New York: Union of American Hebrew Congregations, 1981), 539.
34. P. D. Miller, *Deuteronomy–Interpretation, A Bible Commentary for Teaching and Preaching* (Louisville, KY: John Knox Press, 1990), 75.
35. A. M. Harman, "Decalogue (Ten Commandments)," in *New International Dictionary of Old Testament Theology & Exegesis*, ed. W. A. VanGemeren (Grand Rapids: Eerdmans, 1997), 4:516.
36. R. A. MacKenzie, "The Formal Aspect of Ancient Near Eastern Law," in *The Seed of Wisdom: Essays in Honor of T. J. Meek*, ed. W. S. McCollough (Toronto: University of Toronto Press, 1964), 39.
37. W. Eichrodt, "The Law and the Gospel: The Meaning of the Ten Commandments in Israel and for Us," trans. C. F. McRae, *Interpretation*, vol. 11 (1957), 24; Noth, *Exodus: A Commentary*, 160; Preuss, *Old Testament Theology: Volume 1*, 102.
38. J. Blenkinsopp, *The Pentateuch: An Introduction to the First Five Books of the Bible* (New York: Doubleday, 1992), 204.
39. J. W. Marshall, "Decalogue," in *Dictionary of the Old Testament: Pentateuch*, eds. T. D. Alexander & D. W. Baker (Downers Grove, IL: InterVarsity, 2003), 174.
40. M. Weinfield, "The Decalogue: Its Significance, Uniqueness, and Place in Israel's Tradition," in *Religion and Law: Biblical-Judaic and Islamic Perspectives*, eds. E. B.

Firmage, B. G. Weiss, & J. W. Welch, (Winona Lake, IL: Eisenbrauns, 1990), 15.

41. B. S. Childs, *The Book of Exodus: A Critical, Theological Commentary* (Philadelphia: Westminster, 1974), 395.
42. D. E. Gowan, *Theology in Exodus: Biblical Theology in the Form of a Commentary* (Louisville, KY: Westminster John Knox Press, 1994), 182. With respect to the apodictic law appearing in the Decalogue, E. S. Kalland ("Deuteronomy," in *The Expositor's Bible Commentary,* ed. F. E. Gabelein [Grand Rapids: Zondervan, 1992], 3:53) describes it as "fiat, divine commands—commands that come directly from the Lord."
43. J. H. Tigay, *The JPS Torah Commentary: Deuteronomy* (Philadelphia: The Jewish Publication Society, 1996), 62.
44. Ibid.; cf. M. Noth, *Exodus: A Commentary,* trans. J. S. Bowden (Philadelphia: The Westminster Press, 1962), 167.
45. W. Kaiser, *Toward Old Testament Ethics* (Grand Rapids: Zondervan, 1983), 85. Contra Keil & Delitzsch, "The Second Book of Moses (Exodus)," 2:114.
46. N. M. Sarna, *The JPS Torah Commentary: Exodus* (Philadelphia: The Jewish Publication Society, 1991), 109; Gowan, *Theology in Exodus: Biblical Theology in the Form of a Commentary,* 180.
47. E. H. Merrill, *The New American Commentary: An Exegetical and Theological Exposition of Holy Scripture–Deuteronomy* (Nashville, TN: Broadman & Holman Publishers, 1994), 146; R. W. Dalman, *A People Come Out of Egypt: A Study of the Books of Exodus, Deuteronomy, and Judges* (Concord, MT: Send the Light Press, 2002), 163–164.
48. Cf. J. P. Lange, "Exodus or the Second Book of Moses," in *Commentary on the Holy Scriptures: Critical, Doctrinal, and Homiletical,* ed. J. P. Lange, trans. P. Schaff & C. M. Mead (Grand Rapids: Zondervan, 1978), 1:74–75.
49. J. H. Walton, V. H. Matthews, & M. K. Chavalas, *The IVP Bible Background Commentary: Old Testament* (Downers Grove, IL: InterVarsity, 2000), 95.
50. D. P. Scaer, "The Law and the Gospel in Lutheran Theology," *Grace Theological Journal,* vol. 12, no. 2 (1991), 171.
51. K. Bailey, "Decalogue as Morality and Ethics," *Theology Today,* vol. 20, no. 2 (1963), 189; C. J. H. Wright, *New International Biblical Commentary: Deuteronomy* (Peabody, MA: Hendrickson Publishers, 1996), 68. Monotheism may be defined as the belief in one eternal, infinite, personal God (N. L. Geisler, *False Gods of Our Time: A Defense of the Christian Faith* [Eugene, OR: Harvest House, 1985], 196).
52. J. M. McBain, *The Ten Commandments in the New Testament* (Nashville: Broadman Press, 1977), 15.
53. R. Youngblood, "Monotheism," in *Evangelical Dictionary of Theology* (2nd ed.), ed. W. Elwell (Grand Rapids: Baker, 2001), 788–789.
54. N. Leibowitz, *Studies in Shemot: Exodus* (Jerusalem: Homanim Press, 1981), 318–319.
55. R. Patai, *The Jewish Mind* (New York: Charles Scribner's Sons, 1977), 10.
56. Ibid., 11.
57. Jewett, "Monotheism," in *The Zondervan Pictorial Encyclopedia of the Bible,* ed. M. C. Tenney (Grand Rapids: Zondervan, 1976), 4:271.
58. Youngblood, "Monotheism," 788.
59. Ibid.
60. Ibid.
61. Jewett, "Monotheism," 2:271.
62. Cf. C. E. B. Cranfield, *A Critical and Exegetical Commentary on the Epistle to the*

Romans (Edinburgh: T. & T. Clark, 1975), 1:113–120.

63. J. C. Slemp, *Twelve Laws of Life: A Study of the Ten Commandments and Related Teachings of Jesus* (Philadelphia: The Judson Press, 1950), 19.
64. Leibowitz, *Studies in Shemot: Exodus*, 321.
65. Merrill (*The New American Commentary: An Exegetical and Theological Exposition of Holy Scripture–Deuteronomy*, 147) notes that this "three-tiered notion of the universe as above, on, and below the earth was...common to ancient Near Eastern cosmology."
66. Bunch, *The Ten Commandments: The Law of Liberty*, 35.
67. Ibid.
68. Koehler & Baumgartner, *The Hebrew and Aramaic Lexicon of the Old Testament*, 949; cf. the discussion of C. Dohmen ("*pāsîl*," in *Theological Dictionary of the Old Testament*, eds. G. J. Botterweck, H. Ringgren, & H. J. Fabry, trans. D. W. Stott [Grand Rapids: Eerdmans, 2003], 12:33).
69. R. C. Van Leeuwen, "Form, Image," in *New International Dictionary of Old Testament Theology & Exegesis*, ed. W. A. VanGemeren (Grand Rapids: Eerdmans, 1997), 4:646.
70. Keil & Delitzsch, "The Second Book of Moses (Exodus)," 2:114–115; W. L. Holladay, ed. *A Concise Hebrew and Aramaic Lexicon of the Old Testament* (Leiden, the Netherlands: E.J. Brill, 1988), 294; B. Jacob, *The Second Book of the Bible: Exodus*, trans. W. Jacob (Hoboken, NJ: KTAV Publishing House, 1992), 547.
71. Craigie, "Idolatry," in *Evangelical Dictionary of Theology* (2nd ed.), ed. W. A. Elwell (Grand Rapids: Baker, 2001), 588–589.
72. J. L. Kelso, "Idol Makers," in *The Zondervan Pictorial Encyclopedia of the Bible*, ed. M. C. Tenny (Grand Rapids: Zondervan, 1976), 2:242.
73. Cf. Beauchamp, "*mîn*," in *Theological Dictionary of the Old Testament*, eds. G. J. Botterweck & H. Ringgren, trans. D. W. Scott (Grand Rapids: Eerdmans, 1997), 8:288–289.
74. Brown, *The New Brown-Driver-Briggs-Gesenius Hebrew and English Lexicon with an Appendix Containing the Biblical Aramaic*, 568.
75. W. C. Kaiser, "*myn, mwn*," in *Theological Wordbook of the Old Testament*, eds. R. L. Harris, G.L. Archer, & B.K. Waltke (Chicago: Moody Press, 1980), 1:504. P. L. Garber and R. J. Wyatt ("Idol," in *The International Standard Bible Encyclopedia*, ed. G. W. Bromiley [Grand Rapids: Eerdmans, 1982], 2:795) made this observation: "The familiarity of the Hebrews with the forms of foreign deities is due not only to the geography of Palestine in OT times, but also to the pagan background from which the Israelite nation emerged. Israel was in close political, social, and economic contact with Syria, Phoenicia, Philistia, and Canaan, and thus was widely exposed to foreign gods. Also, Israel was situated on the main route between Egypt and the rest of the Near East, so that the Hittites, Assyrians, Babylonians, and Egyptians had frequent contact with Israel. The Mesopotamian background of the patriarchs is well known, and coupled with Israel's sojourn in Egypt, it exposed the early Israelites to a variety of idolatries."
76. Cf. W. C. Kaiser, "Exodus," in *The Expositor's Bible Commentary*, ed. F. E. Gabelein, (Grand Rapids: Zondervan, 1990), 2:426.
77. Plaut, *The Torah: A Modern Commentary*, 539.
78. R. F. Collins, "Ten Commandments," in *The Anchor Bible Dictionary*, ed. D. N. Freedman (New York: Doubleday, 1992), 6:385.
79. Hsu, *The Decalogue and Moral Conscience in the Ancient Near East: A Comparative*

Study, 9–10.

80. E. W. Nicholson, "Decalogue as the Direct Address of God," *Vetus Testamentum*, vol. 27, no. 4 (1977), 426; J. Douma, *The Ten Commandments: Manual for the Christian Life*, trans. N. D. Kloosterman (Phillipsburg, NJ: P. & R. Publishing, 1996), 45.
81. Ibid., 48–49.
82. Craigie, "Idolatry," 589. T. E. McComiskey ("Idolatry," in *The International Standard Bible Encyclopedia*, ed. G. W. Bromiley [Grand Rapids: Eerdmans, 1982], 797) provided the following theological clarification: "The command does not preclude the pursuit of art, nor the use of certain representations in worship, such as the cherubim on the ark of the covenant, but that one is not to worship an image or venerate it by bowing down before it. Thus the Israelites were to make no symbolic representations of Yahweh in any form (Dt. 4:15–18). This commandment made Israel's faith unique among the nations of the ancient world."
83. R. McQuilkin, *An Introduction to Biblical Ethics*, 2nd. ed. (Wheaton, IL: Tyndale House Publishers, 1995), 154.
84. G. Sauer, "*qin'â*," in *Theological Lexicon of the Old Testament*, eds. E. Jenni & C. Westermann, trans. M. E. Biddle (Peabody, MA: Hendrickson Publishers, 1997), 3:1145.
85. L. J. Coppes, "*qānā'*," in *Theological Wordbook of the Old Testament*, eds. R. L. Harris, G. L. Archer, & B. K. Waltke (Chicago: Moody Press, 1980), 2:802.
86. Koehler & Baumgartner, *The Hebrew and Aramaic Lexicon of the Old Testament*, 1109–1110.
87. Jacob, *The Second Book of the Bible: Exodus*, 553.
88. Gowan, *Theology in Exodus: Biblical Theology in the Form of a Commentary*, 181.
89. Cf. Sarna, *The JPS Torah Commentary: Exodus*, 110.
90. G. A. F. Knight, *Theology as Narration: A Commentary on the Book of Exodus* (Grand Rapids: Eerdmans, 1976), 136.
91. D. Kidner, "Ten Commandments," in *The Zondervan Pictorial Encyclopedia of the Bible*, ed. M. C. Tenny (Grand Rapids: Zondervan, 1976), 5:674; Smith, *Old Testament Theology: Its History, Method, and Message*, 208.
92. Kaiser, "Exodus," 2:423.
93. G. von Rad, *Old Testament Theology* (New York: Harper and Row, 1962), 207–208.
94. Brown, *The New Brown-Driver-Briggs-Gesenius Hebrew and English Lexicon with an Appendix Containing the Biblical Aramaic*, 823; Koehler & Baumgartner, *The Hebrew and Aramaic Lexicon of the Old Testament*, 955.
95. V. Hamilton, "*pāqad*," in *Theological Wordbook of the Old Testament*, eds. R. L. Harris, G. L. Archer, & B. K. Waltke (Chicago: Moody Press, 1980), 2:731.
96. Ibid.
97. T. F. Williams, "*pqd*," in *New International Dictionary of Old Testament Theology & Exegesis*, ed. W. A. VanGemeren (Grand Rapids: Eerdmans, 1997), 3:660; G. André, "*pāqaḏ*," in *Theological Dictionary of the Old Testament*, eds. G. J. Botterweck, H. Ringgren, & H. J. Fabry, trans. D.W. Stott (Grand Rapids: Eerdmans, 2003), 12:59.
98. Koehler & Baumgartner, *The Hebrew and Aramaic Lexicon of the Old Testament*, 796–797. Brown (*The New Brown-Driver-Briggs-Gesenius Hebrew and English Lexicon with an Appendix Containing the Biblical Aramaic*, 730) surmises that there are actually two roots for *'āwâ*, one meaning "to bend" or "to twist" and the other having the idea of "erring from the way." Recent scholars, though, think there is "more probability" of "only one Hebrew root" (C. Schultz, "*'āwâ*," in *Theological Wordbook of the Old Testament*, eds. R. L. Harris, G. L. Archer, & B. K. Waltke [Chicago: Moody

Press, 1980], 2:650).

99. E. A. Martens, "Sin, Guilt," in *Dictionary of the Old Testament: Pentateuch,* eds. T. D. Alexander & D. W. Baker (Downers Grove, IL: InterVarsity, 2003), 767.
100. K. Koch, "*'āwōn,*" in *Theological Dictionary of the Old Testament,* eds. G. J. Botterweck, H. Ringgren, & H. J. Fabry, trans. D. W. Scott (Grand Rapids: Eerdmans, 1999), 10:546.
101. R. C. Cover, "Sin, Sinners (OT)," in *The Anchor Bible Dictionary,* ed. D. N. Freedman (New York: Doubleday, 1992), 6:32.
102. R. Knierim, "*'āwōn,*" in *Theological Lexicon of the Old Testament,* eds. E. Jenni & C. Westermann, trans. M. E. Biddle (Peabody, MA: Hendrickson Publishers, 1997), 2:863.
103. A. Luc, "*'āwōn,*" in *New International Dictionary of Old Testament Theology & Exegesis,* ed. W. A. VanGemeren (Grand Rapids: Eerdmans, 1997), 3:351.
104. In Exodus 20:5, the verb appears as a Qal participle in the masculine plural form with a first person common singular suffix.
105. A.H. Konkel, "*śn',*" in *New International Dictionary of Old Testament Theology & Exegesis,* ed. W. A. VanGemeren (Grand Rapids: Eerdmans, 1997), 3:1256, 1260; Koehler & Baumgartner, *The Hebrew and Aramaic Lexicon of the Old Testament,* 2:1338–1339.
106. E. Jenni, "*śn',*" in *Theological Lexicon of the Old Testament,* eds. E. Jenni & C. Westermann, trans. M. E. Biddle (Peabody, MA: Hendrickson Publishers, 1997), 3:1277–1278.
107. G. Van Groningen, "*śānē',*" in *Theological Wordbook of the Old Testament,* eds. R. L. Harris, G. L. Archer, & B. K. Waltke (Chicago: Moody Press, 1980), 2:880.
108. Ibid.
109. Kalland, "Deuteronomy," 3:54.
110. *The Net Bible.*
111. Wright, *New International Biblical Commentary: Deuteronomy,* 72.
112. J. H. Hertz, *The Pentateuch and Haftorahs,* 2nd ed. (London: Soncino Press, 1981), 296.
113. Douma, *The Ten Commandments: Manual for the Christian Life,* 56–57; Walton, Matthews, & Chavalas, *The IVP Bible Background Commentary: Old Testament,* 95.
114. U. Cassuto, *A Commentary on the Book of Exodus* (Jerusalem: Magnes Press, 1983), 243.
115. W. G. Plaut (*The Torah: A Modern Commentary* [New York: Union of American Hebrew Congregations, 1981], 542) gave this assessment: "The text expresses the principle of retribution in terms of ancient society, with its close familial patterns, where children were indeed part of their parents' ambience, where deeds or misdeeds of one member of the family involved the whole family. The commandment should therefore not be understood as providing for individual retribution; nor does it address itself to questions of criminal law."
116. H. J. Stoebe ("*chesed,*" in *Theological Lexicon of the Old Testament,* eds. E. Jenni & C. Westermann, trans. M. E. Biddle [Peabody, MA: Hendrickson Publishers, 1997], 2:449) notes that the etymology for חֶסֶד is obscure.
117. Koehler & Baumgartner, *The Hebrew and Aramaic Lexicon of the Old Testament,* 1:336.
118. D.K. Stewart, "Steadfast Love," in *The International Standard Bible Encyclopedia,* ed. G.W. Bromiley (Grand Rapids: Eerdmans, 1988), 4:613.
119. Brown, *The New Brown-Driver-Briggs-Gesenius Hebrew and English Lexicon with an*

Appendix Containing the Biblical Aramaic, 338–339.

120. E. A. Heath, "Grace," in *Dictionary of the Old Testament: Pentateuch*, eds. T. D. Alexander & D. W. Baker (Downers Grove, IL: InterVarsity, 2003), 372.
121. W. A. VanGemeren, "Lovingkindness," in *Evangelical Dictionary of Theology* (2nd ed.), ed. W. Elwell (Grand Rapids: Baker, 2001), 713.
122. D. A. Baer P. & R. Gordon, "*chesed*," in *New International Dictionary of Old Testament Theology & Exegesis*, ed. W. A. VanGemeren (Grand Rapids: Eerdmans, 1997), 2:211; cf. R. Brown, *The Message of Deuteronomy: Not by Bread Alone* (Downers Grove, IL: InterVarsity, 1993), 80; Christensen, *Deuteronomy 1:1–21:9, Word Biblical Commentary* (Dallas: Word Books, 2001), 114.
123. Ibid., 213. H. J. Zoebel ("*chesed*," in *Theological Dictionary of the Old Testament*, eds. G. J. Botterweck & H. Ringgren, trans. D. E. Green [Grand Rapids: Eerdmans, 1986], 5:62) similarly noted that the covenant community responded to Yahweh "in worship, praising his kindness in hymns, confessing it, expressing their confidence and thanksgiving or pleading in laments for a new demonstration of this divine kindness."
124. In Exodus 20:6, the verb appears as a Qal participle in the masculine plural form with a first person common singular suffix.
125. Lint, *The Old Testament Hebrew-English Dictionary: Aleph-Beth*, 87.
126. E. Jenni, "*'hb*," in *Theological Lexicon of the Old Testament*, eds. E. Jenni & C. Westermann, trans. M. E. Biddle (Peabody, MA: Hendrickson Publishers, 1997), 1:46.
127. G. A. Turner, "Love," in *The International Standard Bible Encyclopedia*, ed. G. W. Bromiley (Grand Rapids: Eerdmans, 1986), 3:173.
128. K. D. Sakenfeld, "Love (OT)," in *The Anchor Bible Dictionary*, ed. D. N. Freedman (New York: Doubleday, 1992), 4:376.
129. J. J. S. Els, "*'hb*," in *New International Dictionary of Old Testament Theology & Exegesis*, ed. W. A. VanGemeren (Grand Rapids: Eerdmans, 1997), 1:284.
130. G. Wallis, "*'āhabh*," in *Theological Dictionary of the Old Testament*, eds. G. J. Botterweck & H. Ringgren, trans. J. T. Willis (Grand Rapids: Eerdmans, 1977), 1:115.
131. In Exodus 20:6, the verb appears as a Qal participle in the masculine plural construct.
132. G. Sauer, "*šmr*," in *Theological Lexicon of the Old Testament*, eds. E. Jenni & C. Westermann, trans. M. E. Biddle (Peabody, MA: Hendrickson Publishers, 1997), 3:1380.
133. Koehler & Baumgartner, *The Hebrew and Aramaic Lexicon of the Old Testament*, 1:1582–1583.
134. J. E. Hartley, "*shāmar*," in *Theological Wordbook of the Old Testament*, eds. R. L. Harris, G. L. Archer, & B. K. Waltke (Chicago: Moody Press, 1980), 2:939.
135. K. N. Schoville, "*šmr*," in *New International Dictionary of Old Testament Theology & Exegesis*, ed. W. A. VanGemeren (Grand Rapids: Eerdmans, 1997), 4:182.
136. Brown, *The New Brown-Driver-Briggs-Gesenius Hebrew and English Lexicon with an Appendix Containing the Biblical Aramaic*, 845–846; cf. the discussion in chapter 2 regarding *mitswâ* and *tsāwâ*.
137. G. Liedke, "*tswh*," in *Theological Lexicon of the Old Testament*, eds. E. Jenni & C. Westermann, trans. M. E. Biddle (Peabody, MA: Hendrickson Publishers, 1997), 2:1062.
138. F. Garcia-López, "*tswh*," in *Theological Dictionary of the Old Testament*, eds. G. J. Botterweck, H. Ringgren, & H. J. Fabry, trans. D. W. Stott (Grand Rapids: Eerdmans, 2003), 12:278.
139. T. F. Williams, "*tswh*," in *New International Dictionary of Old Testament Theology & Exegesis*, ed. W. A. VanGemeren (Grand Rapids: Eerdmans, 1997), 3:777.
140. Koehler & Baumgartner, *The Hebrew and Aramaic Lexicon of the Old Testament*,

1:622.

141. J. E. Hartley, "*tsāwâ*," in *Theological Wordbook of the Old Testament*, eds. R. L. Harris, G. L. Archer, & B. K. Waltke (Chicago: Moody Press, 1980), 2:757.
142. R. F. Collins, "Commandment," in *The Anchor Bible Dictionary*, ed. D. N. Freedman (New York: Doubleday, 1992), 1:1098.
143. *The Net Bible.*
144. Ibid.; cf. Kalland, "Deuteronomy," 3:54. Sailhamer (*The Pentateuch as Narrative: A Biblical-Theological Commentary*, 285) likewise states, "[I]n God's grace, the love and obedience of a single generation can change the course of a family for thousands of future generations."
145. Cf. P. D. Miller, "The Place of the Decalogue in the Old Testament and Its Law," *Interpretation*, vol. 43 (1989), 235–236.
146. W. C. Kaiser, "Name," in *The Zondervan Pictorial Encyclopedia of the Bible*, ed. M. C. Tenny (Grand Rapids: Zondervan, 1976), 3:363; Smith, *Old Testament Theology: Its History, Method, and Message*, 116.
147. E. H. Merrill, "A Theology of the Pentateuch," in *A Biblical Theology of the Old Testament*, eds. R. B. Zuck, E. H. Merrill, & D. L. Bock (Chicago: Moody Press, 1991), 37.
148. Douma, *The Ten Commandments: Manual for the Christian Life*, 73; Quell, "*kýrios*," 3:1070.
149. R. A. Cole, "Exodus: An Introduction and Commentary," in *Tyndale Old Testament Commentaries*, ed. D. J. Wiseman (Downers Grove, IL: InterVarsity, 1973), 2:157.
150. J. Murray, *Principles of Conduct: Aspects of Biblical Ethics* (Grand Rapids: Eerdmans, 1957), 198–199.
151. Lange ("Exodus or the Second Book of Moses," 1:79) aptly notes that the "sin against the first commandment banishes the name of Jehovah by means of idol names; the sin against the second obscures and disfigures it; the sin against the third one abuses it."
152. J. Shepherd, "*šāw'*," in *New International Dictionary of Old Testament Theology & Exegesis*, ed. W. A. VanGemeren (Grand Rapids: Eerdmans, 1997), 4:53.
153. Ibid.
154. Koehler & Baumgartner, *The Hebrew and Aramaic Lexicon of the Old Testament*, 1425.
155. J. F. A. Sawyer, "*šāw'*," in *Theological Lexicon of the Old Testament*, eds. E. Jenni & C. Westermann, trans. M. E. Biddle (Peabody, MA: Hendrickson Publishers, 1997), 3:1310.
156. Brown, *The New Brown-Driver-Briggs-Gesenius Hebrew and English Lexicon with an Appendix Containing the Biblical Aramaic*, 996.
157. Shepherd, "*šāw'*," 4:54.
158. Cf. Tate ("Legal Traditions of the Books of Exodus," 490), who concludes that the evidence for the view espoused by Shepherd "is not very persuasive."
159. Marshall, "Decalogue," 176.
160. J. N. Oswalt, "Ten Commandments," in *Evangelical Dictionary of Biblical Theology*, ed. W. A. Elwell (Grand Rapids: Baker, 1996), 764.
161. Marshall, "Decalogue," 176.
162. Ibid.; cf. Merrill, *The New American Commentary: An Exegetical and Theological Exposition of Holy Scripture–Deuteronomy*, 149; Oswalt, "Ten Commandments," 764.
163. O. T. Allis, *God Spake By Moses: An Exposition of the Pentateuch* (Phillipsburg, NJ: Presbyterian and Reformed, 1951), 76; Noth, *Exodus: A Commentary*, 163; Keil & Delitzsch, "The Second Book of Moses (Exodus)," 2:118; Christensen, *Deuteronomy 1:1–21:9, Word Biblical Commentary*, 116.

164. C. Craigie, "Ten Commandments," in *Evangelical Dictionary of Theology* (2nd ed.), ed. W. A. Elwell (Grand Rapids: Baker, 2001), 1172.
165. Leibowitz, *Studies in Shemot: Exodus*, 328.
166. C. Hodge, *Systematic Theology* (Grand Rapids: Eerdmans, 1981), 3:305–306. R. J. Rushdoony (*The Institutes of Biblical Law* [Phillipsburg, NJ: Presbyterian & Reformed, 1973], 111–112) observed: "Where there is no fear of God, then the sanctity of oaths and vows disappears, and men shift the foundations of society from the truth to a lie....To despise, abuse, or profane the oath is therefore an offense which denies the validity of all law and order, of all courts and offices, and it is an act of anarchy and revolution."
167. G. Warmuth, "*nāqâ*," in *Theological Dictionary of the Old Testament*, eds. G. J. Botterweck, H. Ringgren, & H. J. Fabry, trans. D. E. Green (Grand Rapids: Eerdmans, 1998), 9:553–554.
168. M. C. Fisher & B. K. Waltke, "*nāqâ*," in *Theological Wordbook of the Old Testament*, eds. R. L. Harris, G. L. Archer, & B. K. Waltke (Chicago: Moody Press, 1980), 2:596.
169. Koehler & Baumgartner, *The Hebrew and Aramaic Lexicon of the Old Testament*, 1:720.
170. Holladay, *A Concise Hebrew and Aramaic Lexicon of the Old Testament*, 245.
171. J. J. Olivier, "*nqh*," in *New International Dictionary of Old Testament Theology & Exegesis*, ed. W. A. VanGemeren (Grand Rapids: Eerdmans, 1997), 3:152; cf. C. van Leeuwen, "*nqh*," in *Theological Lexicon of the Old Testament*, eds. E. Jenni & C. Westermann, trans. M. E. Biddle (Peabody, MA: Hendrickson Publishers, 1997), 2:763–764.
172. Dalman, *A People Come Out of Egypt: A Study of the Books of Exodus, Deuteronomy, and Judges*, 165; cf. the previous remarks about the belief ancient Near Eastern people had regarding the power of the spoken word.
173. Craigie, "Ten Commandments," 1172.
174. Douma, *The Ten Commandments: Manual for the Christian Life*, 79.
175. L. O. Richards, *Zondervan Expository Dictionary of Bible Words*, 1st ed. (Grand Rapids, Zondervan, 1991), 454.
176. Cf. Miller, "The Place of the Decalogue in the Old Testament and Its Law," 236.
177. The presence of the Hebrew pronoun אַתָּה, which is second person masculine singular in form, was not meant to exclude the female gender (Tigay, *The JPS Torah Commentary: Deuteronomy*, 68). As *The Net Bible* observes, "The 'you' of the commandments is addressed to the Israelites individually, male and female, just as God in the Garden of Eden held both the man and the woman responsible for their individual sins." And Christensen (*Deuteronomy 1:1–21:9, Word Biblical Commentary*, 119) opines as follows: "[T]his omission is probably not to be taken as an instance of sexism as such. It is rather an attempt to avoid any suggestion that the law applies to necessary domestic activities. In other words, the extreme legalism of observance in some Jewish households to the point that even a light switch cannot be turned on during the Sabbath is contrary to the spirit of the law itself."
178. Koehler & Baumgartner, *The Hebrew and Aramaic Lexicon of the Old Testament*, 270.
179. Merrill, *The New American Commentary: An Exegetical and Theological Exposition of Holy Scripture–Deuteronomy*, 150.
180. A. Bowling, "*zākar*," in *Theological Wordbook of the Old Testament*, eds. R. L. Harris, G. L. Archer, & B. K. Waltke (Chicago: Moody Press, 1980), 1:241.
181. G. A. Lint, *The Old Testament Hebrew-English Dictionary: Gimel–Zayin* (Springfield, Missouri: World Library Press, 1996), 402.

182. W. Schottroff, "*zkr,*" in *Theological Lexicon of the Old Testament* eds. E. Jenni & C. Westermann, trans. M. E. Biddle (Peabody, MA: Hendrickson Publishers, 1997), 1:383.
183. L. C. Allen, "*zkr,*" in *New International Dictionary of Old Testament Theology & Exegesis,* ed. W. A. VanGemeren (Grand Rapids: Eerdmans, 1997), 1:1101.
184. H. Eising, "*zākhar,*" in *Theological Dictionary of the Old Testament,* eds. G. J. Botterweck & H. Ringgren, trans. D. E. Green (Grand Rapids: Eerdmans, 1980), 4:68.
185. Schröeder, "Deuteronomy or The Fifth Book of Moses," 2:89.
186. Miller, *Deuteronomy–Interpretation, A Bible Commentary for Teaching and Preaching,* 80; A. G. Shead, "Sabbath," In *New Dictionary of Biblical Theology,* eds. T. D. Alexander, B. S. Rosner, D. A. Carson, & G. Goldsworthy (Downers Grove, IL: InterVarsity, 2000), 746–747.
187. D. W. Cover, *The Rest of God and Its Relationship to the Fourth Commandment* (Th.M. thesis, Dallas, TX: Dallas Theological Seminary, 1983), 1.
188. Koehler & Baumgartner (*The Hebrew and Aramaic Lexicon of the Old Testament,* 1407) note that there is scholarly disagreement over whether the noun is derived from the verb or the verb from the noun.
189. Holladay, *A Concise Hebrew and Aramaic Lexicon of the Old Testament,* 360.
190. F. Stolz, "*šbt,*" in *Theological Lexicon of the Old Testament,* eds. E. Jenni & C. Westermann, trans. M. E. Biddle (Peabody, MA: Hendrickson Publishers, 1997), 3:1298.
191. Cf. S. Bacchiocchi, *Divine Rest for Human Restlessness: A Theological Study of the Good News of the Sabbath for Today* (Rome: Pontifical Gregorian University Press, 1980), 22; J. C. McCann, "Sabbath," in *The International Standard Bible Encyclopedia,* ed. G. W. Bromiley (Grand Rapids: Eerdmans, 1988), 2:248; G. H. Waterman, "Sabbath," in *The Zondervan Pictorial Encyclopedia of the Bible,* ed. M. C. Tenney (Grand Rapids: Zondervan, 1976), 5:182–183.
192. V. Hamilton, *Handbook on the Pentateuch* (Grand Rapids: Baker, 1982), 143. Childs (*The Book of Exodus: A Critical, Theological Commentary,* 413) observed that "possibilities of extra-biblical parallels from the Ancient Near East appeared to offer a solution respecting the actual historical origins of the commandment."
193. Bacchiocchi, *Divine Rest for Human Restlessness: A Theological Study of the Good News of the Sabbath for Today,* 56; Jacob, *The Second Book of the Bible: Exodus,* 568–569.
194. Dalman, *A People Come Out of Egypt: A Study of the Books of Exodus, Deuteronomy, and Judges,* 166; J. Moskala, "The Sabbath in the First Creation Account," *Journal of the Adventist Theological Society,* vol. 13, no. 1 (2002), 58.
195. McCann, "Sabbath," 2:248.
196. Smith, *Old Testament Theology: Its History, Method, and Message,* 323–324.
197. V. Hamilton, "*shābat,*" in *Theological Wordbook of the Old Testament,* eds. R. L. Harris, G. L. Archer, & B. K. Waltke (Chicago: Moody Press, 1980), 2:902.
198. H. L. Bosman, "Sabbath," in *New International Dictionary of Old Testament Theology & Exegesis,* ed. W. A. VanGemeren (Grand Rapids: Eerdmans, 1997), 5:1158.
199. H. C. Leupold, *Exposition of Genesis* (Grand Rapids: Baker, 1942), 102.
200. Moskala, "The Sabbath in the First Creation Account," 63.
201. Cover, *The Rest of God and Its Relationship to the Fourth Commandment,* 44.
202. Ibid., 70.
203. V. Hamilton, *The Book of Genesis: Chapters 1–17* (Grand Rapids: Eerdmans, 1990), 141.

204. Cairns, *Word and Presence: A Commentary on the Book of Deuteronomy*, 75.
205. Hertz, *The Pentateuch and Haftorahs*, 6.
206. In Genesis 2:3, the verb appears as a Piel imperfect waw consecutive, third person masculine singular form.
207. Cf. Brown, *The New Brown-Driver-Briggs-Gesenius Hebrew and English Lexicon with an Appendix Containing the Biblical Aramaic*, 138; J. N. Oswalt, "*bārak*," in *Theological Wordbook of the Old Testament*, eds. R. L. Harris, G. L. Archer, & B. K. Waltke (Chicago: Moody Press, 1980), 132.
208. M. L. Brown. "*brk*," in *New International Dictionary of Old Testament Theology & Exegesis*, ed. W. A. VanGemeren (Grand Rapids: Eerdmans, 1997), 1:757.
209. Koehler & Baumgartner, *The Hebrew and Aramaic Lexicon of the Old Testament*, 160.
210. Lint, *The Old Testament Hebrew-English Dictionary: Aleph-Beth*, 594; cf. Cover, *The Rest of God and Its Relationship to the Fourth Commandment*, 38.
211. J. Scharbert, "*brk*," in *Theological Dictionary of the Old Testament*, eds. G. J. Botterweck & H. Ringgren, trans. J. T. Willis (Grand Rapids: Eerdmans, 1977), 2:281–282.
212. C. A. Keller, "*brk*," in *Theological Lexicon of the Old Testament*, eds. E. Jenni & C. Westermann, trans. M. E. Biddle (Peabody, MA: Hendrickson Publishers, 1997), 1:272–273.
213. J. A. Naudé, "*qdš*," in *New International Dictionary of Old Testament Theology & Exegesis*, ed. W. A. VanGemeren (Grand Rapids: Eerdmans, 1997), 3:877.
214. T. E. McComiskey, "*qādash*," in *Theological Wordbook of the Old Testament*, eds. R. L. Harris, G. L. Archer, & B. K. Waltke (Chicago: Moody Press, 1980), 2:786–787.
215. Holladay, ed. *A Concise Hebrew and Aramaic Lexicon of the Old Testament*, 313.
216. Koehler & Baumgartner, *The Hebrew and Aramaic Lexicon of the Old Testament*, 1073–1074.
217. H. Ringgren, "*qdš*," in *Theological Dictionary of the Old Testament*, eds. G. J. Botterweck, H. Ringgren, & H. J. Fabry, trans. D. W. Stott (Grand Rapids: Eerdmans, 2003), 12:531.
218. H. Müller, "*qdš*," in *Theological Lexicon of the Old Testament*, eds. E. Jenni & C. Westermann, trans. M. E. Biddle (Peabody, MA: Hendrickson Publishers, 1997), 3:1104.
219. E. F. Harrison, "Holiness," in *The International Standard Bible Encyclopedia*, ed. G. W. Bromiley (Grand Rapids: Eerdmans, 1982), 2:726.
220. Moskala, "The Sabbath in the First Creation Account," 60.
221. Cf. the discussion in chapter 3 regarding the issue of the Sabbath in various religious traditions.
222. Leupold, *Exposition of Genesis*, 103.
223. Cover, *The Rest of God and Its Relationship to the Fourth Commandment*, 55; cf. A. W. Watson, *Jesus and the Law* (Athens, GA: The University of Georgia Press, 1996), 9–10. Wright (*New International Biblical Commentary: Deuteronomy*, 76) suggests that the Sabbath was "a sign of the covenant precisely because it embodied the essential vertical and horizontal dimensions of covenant commitment."
224. Shead, "Sabbath," 746. Sarna (*The JPS Torah Commentary: Exodus*, 111) accordingly noted that the "Sabbath is wholly an Israelite innovation. There is nothing analogous to it in the entire ancient Near Eastern world."
225. McCann, "Sabbath," 4:250.
226. Douma, *The Ten Commandments: Manual for the Christian Life*, 114.
227. Driver, *The International Critical Commentary: A Critical and Exegetical Commentary on Deuteronomy*, 85.
228. Bunch, *The Ten Commandments: The Law of Liberty*, 89–90; N. R. Gulley, "Basic

Issues between Science and Scripture: Theological Implications of Alternative Models and the Necessary Basis for the Sabbath in Genesis 1–2," *Journal of the Adventist Theological Society*, vol. 14, no. 1 (2003), 222.

229. Childs, *The Book of Exodus: A Critical, Theological Commentary*, 417.
230. Cover, *The Rest of God and Its Relationship to the Fourth Commandment*, 62.
231. Douma, *The Ten Commandments: Manual for the Christian Life*, 112.
232. Cf. Eichrodt, "The Law and the Gospel: The Meaning of the Ten Commandments in Israel and for Us," 36–37.
233. J. Calvin, *Institutes of the Christian Religion* (Grand Rapids: Zondervan, 1981), 1:339.
234. Cf. Miller, "The Place of the Decalogue in the Old Testament and Its Law," 236.
235. Douma, *The Ten Commandments: Manual for the Christian Life*, 114.
236. M. J. Erickson, *Christian Theology*, 2nd ed. (Grand Rapids: Baker, 1998), 702.
237. G. F. Hasel, "Sabbath," in *The Anchor Bible Dictionary*, ed. D. N. Freedman (New York: Doubleday, 1992), 5:854.
238 A. D. H. Mayes, "The Decalogue of Moses: An Enduring Ethical Programme?," *Ethics and the Christian*, ed. in S. Freyne (Dublin: The Columba Press, 1991), 39.
239. J. P. Hyatt, *New Century Bible Commentary: Exodus* (Grand Rapids: Eerdmans, 1980), 213.
240. Cf. similar remarks made by Hsu, *The Decalogue and Moral Conscience in the Ancient Near East: A Comparative Study*, 13; Sarna, *The JPS Torah Commentary: Exodus*, 113; Jacob, *The Second Book of the Bible: Exodus*, 570.
241. C. Craigie, "The Book of Deuteronomy," in *The New International Commentary on the Old Testament* (vol. 5), ed. R. K. Harrison (Grand Rapids: Eerdmans, 1976), 159.
242. Dalman, *A People Come Out of Egypt: A Study of the Books of Exodus, Deuteronomy, and Judges*, 167.
243. W. White, "Family," in *The Zondervan Pictorial Encyclopedia of the Bible*, ed. M. C. Tenney, (Grand Rapids: Zondervan, 1976), 2:496.
244. Collins, "Ten Commandments," 6:385.
245. In Exodus 20:12, the verb appears in the Piel imperative, masculine singular form.
246. Koehler & Baumgartner, *The Hebrew and Aramaic Lexicon of the Old Testament*, 456.
247. C. J. Collins, "*kbd*," in *New International Dictionary of Old Testament Theology & Exegesis*, ed. W. A. VanGemeren (Grand Rapids: Eerdmans, 1997), 2:577.
248. C. Westermann, "*kbd*," in *Theological Lexicon of the Old Testament*, eds. E. Jenni & C. Westermann, trans. M. E. Biddle (Peabody, MA: Hendrickson Publishers, 1997), 2:591–592.
249. C. Dohmen, "*kāḇēḏ*," in, *Theological Dictionary of the Old Testament*, eds. G. J. Botterweck, H. Ringgren, & H. J. Fabry, trans. D.E. Green (Grand Rapids: Eerdmans, 1995), 7:16.
250. J. N. Oswalt, "*kābēd*," in *Theological Wordbook of the Old Testament*, eds. R. L. Harris, G. L. Archer, & B. K. Waltke (Chicago: Moody Press, 1980), 1:426. *The Net Bible* nicely captures the sense of the verse by paraphrasing it, "give them the proper weight of authority that they deserve."
251. G. B. Funderbunk, "Honorable, Honor," in *The Zondervan Pictorial Encyclopedia of the Bible*, ed. M. C. Tenney (Grand Rapids: Zondervan, 1976), 3:197.
252. J. C. Durham, "Exodus," in *Word Biblical Commentary* (vol. 3), eds. D. A. Hubbard & G. W. Barker (Waco, TX: Word Books, 1987), 291; W. Barclay, *The Old Law and the New Law: The Ten Commandments and the Sermon on the Mount* (Edinburgh: The Saint Andrew Press, 1991), 5–6.
253. T. E. Fretheim, *Exodus: A Biblical Commentary for Teaching and Preaching* (Louisville, Kentucky: John Knox Press, 1991), 231; Walton, Matthews, & Chavalas, *The*

IVP Bible Background Commentary: Old Testament, 96.

254. Keil & Delitzsch, "The Second Book of Moses (Exodus)," 2:122; Kaiser, "Exodus," 2:424.
255. Allis, *God Spake By Moses: An Exposition of the Pentateuch*, 77.
256. Plaut, *The Torah: A Modern Commentary*, 556. Miller ("The Place of the Decalogue in the Old Testament and Its Law," 238) aptly noted that the fifth commandment "enjoins an attitude toward parents that parallels one's attitude toward God (honor, fear, reverence)."
257. Patai, *The Jewish Mind*, 487.
258. Douma, *The Ten Commandments: Manual for the Christian Life*, 167.
259. Tate, "Legal Traditions of the Books of Exodus," 492.
260. Cole, "Exodus: An Introduction and Commentary," 159.
261. Cf. Douma, *The Ten Commandments: Manual for the Christian Life*, 172.
262. Cf. Miller, "The Place of the Decalogue in the Old Testament and Its Law," 236.
263. C. H. Gordon, "Ten Commandments," *Christianity Today*, vol. 8 (1964), 5.
264. For example, when sitting at home, when walking along the road, when resting, and when getting up (Deut. 6:7).
265. In Exodus 20:13, the verb appears as a Qal perfect, second person masculine form.
266. Koehler & W. Baumgartner, *The Hebrew and Aramaic Lexicon of the Old Testament*, 1283.
267. W. R. Domeris, "*rtsh*," in *New International Dictionary of Old Testament Theology & Exegesis*, ed. W. A. VanGemeren (Grand Rapids: Eerdmans, 1997), 3:1186–1187.
268. Oswalt, "Ten Commandments," 765.
269. W. White, "*rātsāch*," in *Theological Wordbook of the Old Testament*, eds. R. L. Harris, G. L. Archer, & B. K. Waltke (Chicago: Moody Press, 1980), 2:860.
270. Ibid. Cf. Miller, *Deuteronomy–Interpretation, A Bible Commentary for Teaching and Preaching*, 87.
271. White, "*rātsāch*," 2:860; cf. Phillips, *Ancient Israel's Criminal Law: A New Approach to the Decalogue*, 83.
272. Harman, "Decalogue (Ten Commandments)," 4:518.
273. Douma, *The Ten Commandments: Manual for the Christian Life*, 210.
274. J. J. Davis, *Evangelical Ethics: Issues Facing the Church Today*, 2nd ed. (Phillipsburg, PA: Presbyterian and Reformed, 1993), 172–173.
275. Cf. Miller, "The Place of the Decalogue in the Old Testament and Its Law," 236.
276. In Exodus 20:14, the verb appears as a Qal imperfect, second person masculine singular form.
277. Koehler & Baumgartner, *The Hebrew and Aramaic Lexicon of the Old Testament*, 1:658.
278. A. M. Silbermann, *Chumash with Targum Onkelos, Haphtaroth and Rashi's Commentary: Devarim* (Jerusalem: Feldheim Publishers, 1989), 34.
279. D. N. Freedman, "Adultery," in *The International Standard Bible Encyclopedia*, ed. G. W. Bromiley (Grand Rapids: Eerdmans, 1979), 1:58.
280. Douma, *The Ten Commandments: Manual for the Christian Life*, 243.
281. G. Lambert, "Adultery," in *The Zondervan Pictorial Encyclopedia of the Bible*, ed. M. C. Tenney (Grand Rapids: Zondervan, 1976), 1:65. H. J. Fabry (*nā'ap̱*," in *Theological Dictionary of the Old Testament*, eds. G. J. Botterweck, H. Ringgren, and H. J. Fabry, trans. D.E. Green [Grand Rapids: Eerdmans, 1998], 9:114) correspondingly noted that, in later biblical usage, "the prophets borrowed this terminology to describe offenses against the covenant between Yahweh as husband and Israel as his wife."
282. Cairns, *Word and Presence: A Commentary on the Book of Deuteronomy*, 77.

283. J. B. Payne, *The Theology of the Older Testament* (Grand Rapids: Zondervan, 1975), 330; Tigay, *The JPS Torah Commentary: Deuteronomy*, 71.
284. L. J. Coppes, "*nā'ap*," in *Theological Wordbook of the Old Testament*, eds. R. L. Harris, G. L. Archer, & B. K. Waltke (Chicago: Moody Press, 1980), 2:542.
285. C. Craigie, "The Book of Deuteronomy," in *The New International Commentary on the Old Testament* (vol. 5), ed. R. K. Harrison (Grand Rapids: Eerdmans, 1976), 160.
286. Douma, *The Ten Commandments: Manual for the Christian Life*, 264.
287. McQuilkin, *An Introduction to Biblical Ethics*, 193–194.
288. Hyatt, *New Century Bible Commentary: Exodus*, 214.
289. Hamilton, *Handbook on the Pentateuch*, 206.
290. Cf. Sarna, *The JPS Torah Commentary: Exodus*, 114.
291. G. H. Hall, "*n'p*," in *New International Dictionary of Old Testament Theology & Exegesis*, ed. W. A. VanGemeren (Grand Rapids: Eerdmans, 1997), 3:3; cf. Bailey, "Decalogue as Morality and Ethics," 190.
292. J. T. Mueller, "Adultery," in *Evangelical Dictionary of Theology* (2nd ed.), ed. W. Elwell (Grand Rapids: Baker, 2001), 26–27.
293. In Exodus 20:15, the verb appears as a Qal imperfect, second person masculine singular form.
294. Lint, *The Old Testament Hebrew-English Dictionary: Gimel–Zayin*, 127.
295. J. E. Smith, "*gānab*," in *Theological Wordbook of the Old Testament*, eds. R. L. Harris, G. L. Archer, & B. K. Waltke (Chicago: Moody Press, 1980), 1:168.
296. V. Hamp, "*gānabh*," in *Theological Dictionary of the Old Testament*, eds. G. J. Botterweck & H. Ringgren, trans. J. T. Willis, G. W. Bromiley, & D. E. Green (Grand Rapids: Eerdmans, 1978), 3:41–42.
297. W. R. Domeris, "*gnb*," in *New International Dictionary of Old Testament Theology & Exegesis*, ed. W. A. VanGemeren (Grand Rapids: Eerdmans, 1997), 1:879.
298. Ibid.
299. McBain, *The Ten Commandments in the New Testament*, 92.
300. Douma, *The Ten Commandments: Manual for the Christian Life*, 286.
301. Craigie, "Ten Commandments," 1173–1174.
302. Cf. Miller, "The Place of the Decalogue in the Old Testament and Its Law," 236.
303. Cf. the discussion of F. J. Stendebach, "*'ānâ*," in *Theological Dictionary of the Old Testament*, eds. G. J. Botterweck, H. Ringgren, & H. J. Fabry, trans. D. E. Green (Grand Rapids: Eerdmans, 2001), 11:215–217.
304. In Exodus 20:16, the verb appears as a Qal imperfect, second person masculine singular form.
305. Koehler & Baumgartner, *The Hebrew and Aramaic Lexicon of the Old Testament*, 852; cf. J. A. Beck, "*'nh* I," in *New International Dictionary of Old Testament Theology & Exegesis*, ed. W. A. VanGemeren (Grand Rapids: Eerdmans, 1997), 3:447.
306. C. J. Labuschagne, "*'nh*," in *Theological Lexicon of the Old Testament*, eds. E. Jenni & C. Westermann, trans. M. E. Biddle (Peabody, MA: Hendrickson Publishers, 1997), 2:928.
307. Noth, *Exodus: A Commentary*, 166; Phillips, *Ancient Israel's Criminal Law: A New Approach to the Decalogue*, 142.
308. Tate, "Legal Traditions of the Books of Exodus," 496; C. Schultz, "*'ûd*," in *Theological Wordbook of the Old Testament*, eds. R. L. Harris, G. L. Archer, & B. K. Waltke (Chicago: Moody Press, 1980), 2:648.
309. R. B. Allen, "*'ānâ*," in *Theological Wordbook of the Old Testament*, eds. R. L. Harris, G. L. Archer, & B. K. Waltke (Chicago: Moody Press, 1980), 2:680.
310. Bailey, "Decalogue as Morality and Ethics," 192.

311. Koehler & Baumgartner, *The Hebrew and Aramaic Lexicon of the Old Testament,* 1262.
312. J. Kühlewein, "*rēaʿ*," in *Theological Lexicon of the Old Testament,* eds. E. Jenni & C. Westermann, trans. M. E. Biddle (Peabody, MA: Hendrickson Publishers, 1997), 3:1243–1244.
313. R. L. Harris, "*rāʿâ*," in *Theological Wordbook of the Old Testament,* eds. R. L. Harris, G. L. Archer, & B. K. Waltke (Chicago: Moody Press, 1980), 2:853.
314. J. J. Hughes & N. J. Opperwall, "Neighbor," in *The International Standard Bible Encyclopedia,* ed. G. W. Bromiley (Grand Rapids: Eerdmans, 1986), 3:517.
315. R. L. Thomas, "Neighbor," in *The Zondervan Pictorial Encyclopedia of the Bible,* ed. M. C. Tenney (Grand Rapids: Zondervan, 1976), 4:408.
316. Douma, *The Ten Commandments: Manual for the Christian Life*, 320.
317. Hughes & Opperwall, "Neighbor," 3:518.
318. R. B. Chisholm, "*ʿwd,*" in *New International Dictionary of Old Testament Theology & Exegesis,* ed. W. A. VanGemeren (Grand Rapids: Eerdmans, 1997), 3:335; cf. the discussion in chapter 2 regarding '*ēḏûṯ* and *ʿûd.*
319. H. Simian-Yofre, "*ʿwd,*" in *Theological Dictionary of the Old Testament,* eds. G. J. Botterweck, H. Ringgren, and H. J. Fabry, trans. D. W. Scott (Grand Rapids: Eerdmans, 1999), 10:497.
320. C. van Leeuwen, "*ʿēd,*" in *Theological Lexicon of the Old Testament,* eds. E. Jenni & C. Westermann, trans. M. E. Biddle (Peabody, MA: Hendrickson Publishers, 1997), 2:840.
321. Douma, *The Ten Commandments: Manual for the Christian Life*, 315.
322. Brown, *The New Brown-Driver-Briggs-Gesenius Hebrew and English Lexicon with an Appendix Containing the Biblical Aramaic*, 1055.
323. Holladay, *A Concise Hebrew and Aramaic Lexicon of the Old Testament*, 383.
324. Koehler & Baumgartner, *The Hebrew and Aramaic Lexicon of the Old Testament,* 1647.
325. E. E. Carpenter & M. A. Grisanti, "*šqr*," in *New International Dictionary of Old Testament Theology & Exegesis,* ed. W. A. VanGemeren (Grand Rapids: Eerdmans, 1997), 4:247.
326. M. A. Klopfenstein, "*šqr*," in *Theological Lexicon of the Old Testament,* eds. E. Jenni & C. Westermann, trans. M. E. Biddle (Peabody, MA: Hendrickson Publishers, 1997), 3:1401.
327. Koehler & Baumgartner, *The Hebrew and Aramaic Lexicon of the Old Testament,* 1648.
328. H. J. Austel, "*shāqar*," in *Theological Wordbook of the Old Testament,* eds. R. L. Harris, G. L. Archer, & B. K. Waltke (Chicago: Moody Press, 1980), 2:955–956.
329. Cf. the previous discussion concerning Exodus 20:7 and Deuteronomy 5:11.
330. Collins, "Ten Commandments," 6:386; cf. Sailhamer, *The Pentateuch as Narrative: A Biblical-Theological Commentary*, 287.
331. Sawyer, "*šāwʾ*," 3:1310.
332. Schultz, "*ʿûd,*" 2:649.
333. In Exodus 20:17, the verb appears as a Qal imperfect, second person masculine singular form.
334. E. Gerstenberger, "*chmd,*" in *Theological Lexicon of the Old Testament,* eds. E. Jenni & C. Westermann, trans. M. E. Biddle (Peabody, MA: Hendrickson Publishers, 1997), 1:434.
335. D. Talley, "*chmd,*" in *New International Dictionary of Old Testament Theology & Exegesis,* ed. W. A. VanGemeren (Grand Rapids: Eerdmans, 1997), 2:167.

336. G. Wallis, "*chāmadh*," in *Theological Dictionary of the Old Testament,* eds. G. J. Botterweck & H. Ringgren, trans. D. E. Green (Grand Rapids: Eerdmans, 1980), 4:453–454.
337. For example, to seek wholesome relationships with others and to desire righteousness to prevail (Douma, *The Ten Commandments: Manual for the Christian Life*, 349).
338. Brown, *The New Brown-Driver-Briggs-Gesenius Hebrew and English Lexicon with an Appendix Containing the Biblical Aramaic*, 326; cf. J. B. Payne, "*chāmad*," in *Theological Wordbook of the Old Testament,* eds. R. L. Harris, G. L. Archer, & B. K. Waltke (Chicago: Moody Press, 1980), 1:295.
339. Wright, *New International Biblical Commentary: Deuteronomy*, 86.
340. Craigie ("Ten Commandments," 1174) noted the following: "The genius of the commandment lies in its therapeutic nature. It is not enough merely to deal with crime once it has been committed; the law must also attempt to attack the roots of crime. The root of almost all evil and crime lies within the self; it lies in the desires of the individual. Thus evil desires are prohibited. If the tenth commandment is fully and profoundly understood, then the significance of the first nine is much better understood. If covetous desires are gradually eliminated, then the natural desire which is rooted within each person may be directed more and more toward God."
341. Leibowitz, *Studies in Shemot: Exodus*, 344. Tate ("Legal Traditions of the Books of Exodus," 498) made this pertinent statement: "Obedience requires a harmony between the heart and the hand; it requires a quality of commitment that pervades and transforms everything that the obedient one is and does."
342. Douma, *The Ten Commandments: Manual for the Christian Life*, 339.
343. Hertz, *The Pentateuch and Haftorahs*, 300.
344. Cf. Bailey, "Decalogue as Morality and Ethics," 191–192.
345. Cf. Brown, *The Message of Deuteronomy: Not by Bread Alone*, 79.
346. Farrar, *The Voice from Sinai: The Eternal Bases of the Mosaic Law*, 29.
347. Brown, *The Message of Deuteronomy: Not by Bread Alone*, 92; emphases are his.

Chapter 5: An Overview of the Sermon on the Mount

1. A. Gearey, "The Bible, Law and Liberation: Towards a Politico-Legal Hermeneutics of the Sermon on the Mount," in eds. *Law and Literature: Current Legal Issues 1999, Volume 2,* M. Freeman and A. D. E. Lewis (Oxford: Oxford University Press, 1999), 274.
2. L. J. White, "Grid and Group in Matthew's Community: The Righteousness/Honor Code in the Sermon on the Mount," *Semeia,* vol. 35 (1986), 61.
3. H. A. Sturz, "The Sermon on the Mount and Its Application to the Present Age," *Grace Theological Journal,* vol. 4, no. 3 (1963), 3; R. McQuilkin, *An Introduction to Biblical Ethics,* 2nd. ed. (Wheaton, IL: Tyndale House Publishers, 1995), 48.
4. C. Gore, *The Sermon on the Mount: A Practical Exposition* (London: John Murray, 1900), 1.
5. C. H. Kang, *The Literary Affinities Of The Sermon On The Mount With Special Reference To Deuteronomic Features* (Ph.D. dissertation, Pasadena, CA: Fuller Theological Seminary, School Of Theology, 1987), 301; cf. similar remarks made by Gearey, "The Bible, Law and Liberation: Towards a Politico-Legal Hermeneutics of the Sermon on the Mount," 275.
6. S. B. Ferguson, *Kingdom Life In A Fallen World: Living Out the Sermon on the Mount* (Colorado Springs, CO: Nav Press, 1986), 17; R. A. Guelich, "Interpreting the Sermon

on the Mount," *Interpretation,* vol. 41, no. 2 (1987), 129; D. A. Hagner, *Word Biblical Commentary: Matthew 1–13* (Dallas, TX: Word Books, 1993), 82–83, 97–98, 112; G. T. Burke, "Sermon on the Mount," in *Evangelical Dictionary of Theology* (2nd ed.), ed. W. A. Elwell (Grand Rapids: Baker, 2001), 1093.

7. T. D. Bonham, *A Study of the Relevance of the Sermon on the Mount in Matthew 5–7* (Th.D. dissertation, Fort Worth, TX: Southwestern Baptist Theological Seminary, 1963), 5; R. A. Guelich, *The Sermon on the Mount: A Foundation for Understanding* (Waco, TX: Word, 1982), 13.
8. R. S. McConnell, *Law and Prophecy in Matthew's Gospel: The Authority and Use of the Old Testament in the Gospel of St. Matthew* (Basel: Friedrich Reinhardt Kommissionverlag, 1969), 8.
9. J. Phillips, *Exploring the Gospels: Matthew* (Neptune, NJ: Loizeaux Brothers, 1999), 84.
10. R. H. Mounce, "Sermon on the Mount," in *The International Standard Bible Encyclopedia,* ed. G. W. Bromiley (Grand Rapids: Eerdmans, 1988), 4:413.
11. J. A. Draper, "The Genesis and Narrative Thrust of the Paraenesis in the Sermon on the Mount," *Journal for the Study of the New Testament,* vol. 75 (1999), 27.
12. Ibid.
13. J. Lange, "The Gospel According to Matthew: Together With A General Theological And Homiletical Introduction To The New Testament," in *Lange's Commentary on the Holy Scriptures: Critical, Doctrinal, and Homiletical,* ed. Schaff (Grand Rapids: Zondervan, 1978), 8:99.
14. D. D. Kupp, *Matthew's Emmanuel: Divine Presence and God's People in the First Gospel* (Cambridge: Cambridge University Press, 1996), 66.
15. Ibid.
16. D. R. Bauer, *The Structure of Matthew's Gospel: A Study in Literary Design* (Sheffield, England: Sheffield Academic Press, 1988), 130; cf. K. C. Asahu-Ejere, *The Kingdom of God and Healing-Exorcism (Mt 4:17–5:12)* (Frankfurt: Peter Lang, 2003), 78, 107.
17. Bonham, *A Study of the Relevance of the Sermon on the Mount in Matthew 5–7,* 144; S. Westerholm, "The Law in the Sermon on the Mount: Matt 5:17–48," *Criswell Theological Review,* vol. 6, no. 1 (1992), 45; G. E. Ladd, "Kingdom of Christ, God, Heaven," in *Evangelical Dictionary of Theology,* ed. W. Elwell (Grand Rapids: Baker, 2001), 657; cf. the various reasons given by R. H. Stein ("Kingdom of God," in *Evangelical Dictionary of Biblical Theology,* ed. W. A. Elwell [Grand Rapids: Baker, 1996], 451) for the validity of seeing the two phrases as being synonymous.
18. J. Meier, *Law and History in Matthew's Gospel: A Redactional Study of Mt. 5:17–48* (Rome: Biblical Institute Press, 1976), 98; B. Klappert, "*basileía,*" in *New International Dictionary of New Testament Theology,* ed. C. Brown (Grand Rapids, MI: Zondervan, 1986), 2:381; D. Flusser and R. S. Notley, *Jesus* (Jerusalem: Magnes Press, 2001), 105.
19. J. W. Kim, *The Function and Meaning of the Lord's Prayer in the Sermon on the Mount* (Th.M. thesis, Grand Rapids: Calvin Theological Seminary, 1991), 97; J. H. Choi, *The Isaianic Background for the First Four Beatitudes in Matthew* (Th.M. thesis, Grand Rapids: Calvin Theological Seminary, 1993), 63–64.
20. F. W. Danker, ed., *A Greek-English Lexicon of the New Testament and Other Early Christian Literature*, 3rd ed. (Chicago, IL: The University of Chicago Press, 2000), 168; cf. B. H. Young, *Jesus the Jewish Theologian* (Peabody, MA: Hendrickson Publishers, 1995), 70.
21. J. P Louw & E. A. Nida, eds., *Greek-English Lexicon of the New Testament: Based on*

Semantic Domains, 2nd ed., vol. 1: Introduction and Domains, vol. 2: Indices (New York, New York: United Bible Societies, 1989), 1:480.

22. Ibid.; cf. B. H. Young, *The Jewish Background to the Lord's Prayer* (Tulsa, OK: Gospel Research Foundation Inc., 1984), 13.
23. U. Luz, "*basileia*," in *Exegetical Dictionary of the New Testament*, eds. H. Balz & G. Schneider, trans. J. W. Thompson & J. W. Medendorp (Grand Rapids: Eerdmans, 1991), 1:202; cf. G. Strecker, *Theology of the New Testament*, ed. F. W. Horn, trans. M. E. Boring (Berlin: Walter de Gruyter & Co., 2000), 255–256. C. C. Caragounis ("Kingdom of God/Heaven," in *Dictionary of Jesus and the Gospels*, eds. J. B. Green, S. McKnight, & I. H. Marshall [Downers Grove, IL: InterVarsity, 1992], 417) echoes this sentiment in the following remarks: "As proclaimed by Jesus the kingdom of God had continuity with the OT promise as well as with Jewish apocalyptic thinking, but differed from them in important respects. For example, it denoted God's eternal rule rather than an earthly kingdom, its scope was universal rather than limited to the Jewish nation, and it was imminent and potentially present in him rather than a vague future hope, being inextricably connected with his own person and mission."
24. C. Spicq, *Theological Lexicon of the New Testament*, trans. & ed. J. D. Ernest (Peabody, MA: Hendrickson Publishers, 1994), 1:262–264. D. J. Harrington & J. F. Keenan, *Jesus and Virtue Ethics: Building Bridges between New Testament Studies and Moral Theology* (Lanham, MD: Sheed & Ward, 2002), 37. D. C. Duling ("Kingdom of God/Kingdom of Heaven, in *The Anchor Bible Dictionary*, ed. D. N. Freedman [New York: Doubleday, 1992], 4:58) aptly noted that the "Kingdom of Heaven in Matthew" is "anticipated in the present which flows from the past."
25. E. Lohse, *Theological Ethics of the New Testament*, trans. M. B. Boring (Minneapolis: Fortress Press, 1991), 39; Stein, "Kingdom of God," 453.
26. G. Goldsworthy, "Kingdom of God," in *New Dictionary of Biblical Theology*, eds. T. D. Alexander, B. S. Rosner, D. A. Carson, & G. Goldsworthy (Downers Grove, IL: InterVarsity, 2000), 617, 620.
27. Collins, "Beatitudes," 1:630.
28. J. L. Benson, *The Kingdom Proffered and Postponed* (Unpublished notes, Johnson City, New York: Baptist Bible Seminary, 1967), 50.
29. Cf. the similar and more extensive discussion of T. M. Dang, *Christ's Beatitudes, Kingdom and the Spiritual Life* (M.A. thesis, La Mirada, CA: Talbot Theological Seminary, 1987), 11–17.
30. E. Linnemann, *Is There a Synoptic Problem? Rethinking the Literary Dependence of the First Three Gospels* (Grand Rapids: Baker, 1992), 175.
31. Cf. Strecker, *Theology of the New Testament*, 341.
32. Danker, *A Greek-English Lexicon of the New Testament and Other Early Christian Literature*, 402.
33. Louw & Nida, *Greek-English Lexicon of the New Testament: Based on Semantic Domains*, 1:413; J. K. Chamblin, "Gospel," in *Evangelical Dictionary of Biblical Theology*, ed. W. A. Elwell (Grand Rapids: Baker, 1996), 306.
34. C. C. Broyles, "Gospel (Good News)," in *Dictionary of Jesus and the Gospels*, eds. J. B. Green, S. McKnight, and I. H. Marshall (Downers Grove, IL: InterVarsity Press, 1992), 283.
35. U. Becker, "*euangélion*," in *New International Dictionary of New Testament Theology*, ed. C. Brown (Grand Rapids, MI: Zondervan, 1986), 2:108.
36. G. Friedrich, "*euangélion*," in, *Theological Dictionary of the New Testament*, ed. G. Kittel, trans. G. W. Bromiley (Grand Rapids, MI: Eerdmans, 1999), 2:714–715.

37. Spicq, *Theological Lexicon of the New Testament,* 2:83, 87.
38. G. Strecker, "*euangélion,*" in *Exegetical Dictionary of the New Testament,* eds. H. Balz & G. Schneider, trans. V. Howard & J. W. Thompson (Grand Rapids: Eerdmans, 1990), 2:70; Young, *Jesus the Jewish Theologian,* 61; G. Goldsworthy, "Gospel," in *New Dictionary of Biblical Theology,* eds. T. D. Alexander, B. S. Rosner, D. A. Carson, & G. Goldsworthy (Downers Grove, IL: InterVarsity 2000), 522.
39. U. Luz, *Matthew 1–7: A Commentary,* trans. W. C. Linss (Minneapolis, MN: Augsburg Fortress, 1989), 224; I. A. Massey, *Interpreting the Sermon on the Mount in the Light of Jewish Tradition as Evidenced in the Palestinian Targums of the Pentateuch: Selected Themes* (Lewiston, New York: The Edwin Mellen Press, 1991), 113, 162.
40. Draper, "The Genesis and Narrative Thrust of the Paraenesis in the Sermon on the Mount," 30.
41. C. S. Keener, *The IVP New Testament Commentary Series: Matthew,* ed. G. R. Osborne (Downers Grove, IL: InterVarsity, 1997), 103; cf. C. S. Keener, *A Commentary on the Gospel of Matthew* (Grand Rapids: Eerdmans, 1999), 164.
42. R. H. Gundry, *Matthew: A Commentary on His Literary and Theological Art* (Grand Rapids: Eerdmans, 1982), 66.
43. Bonham, *A Study of the Relevance of the Sermon on the Mount in Matthew 5–7,* 1–2, 160; E. G. Nutz, *The Unity of the Sermon on the Mount* (Ph.D. Dissertation, Greenville, SC: Bob Jones University, 1972), 15–16; R. H. Mounce, "Sermon on the Mount," in *The International Standard Bible Encyclopedia,* ed. G. W. Bromiley (Grand Rapids: Eerdmans, 1988), 4:411; Burke, "Sermon on the Mount," 1094.
44. R. C. H. Lenski, *The Interpretation of St. Matthew's Gospel* (Minneapolis, MN: Augsburg Publishing House, 1964), 179.
45. H. N. Ridderbos, *The Bible Student's Commentary: Matthew,* trans. R. Togtman (Grand Rapids: Zondervan, 1987), 81.
46. Ibid., 82.
47. Emphasis in the original.
48. N. B. Stonehouse, *The Witness of Matthew and Mark to Christ* (Philadelphia: The Presbyterian Guardian, 1944), 134.
49. R. H. Mounce, "Sermon on the Mount," in *New Bible Dictionary: Second Edition,* ed. J. D. Douglas (Wheaton, IL: Tyndale, 1982), 1090.
50. Louw & Nida, *Greek-English Lexicon of the New Testament: Based on Semantic Domains,* 1:11; Danker, *A Greek-English Lexicon of the New Testament and Other Early Christian Literature,* 724.
51. Capernaum not only was the home of some of Jesus' disciples, but also served as the Lord's headquarters during a large portion of His public ministry.
52. Hendriksen, *New Testament Commentary: The Gospel of Matthew,* 259.
53. R. L. Alden, "Mount of Beatitudes," in *The Zondervan Pictorial Encyclopedia of the Bible,* ed. M. C. Tenney (Grand Rapids: Zondervan, 1976), 4:299.
54. Cf. Mounce, "Sermon on the Mount," 1089.
55. D. A. Carson, "Matthew," in *The Expositor's Bible Commentary,* ed. F. E. Gaebelein (Grand Rapids: Zondervan, 1984), 8:125.
56. Mounce, "Sermon on the Mount," 4:411.
57. F. D. Bruner, *Matthew, A Commentary, Volume 1* (Dallas, Word Publishing, 1987), 133; D. C. Allison, "Mountain and Wilderness," in *Dictionary of Jesus and the Gospels,* eds. J. B. Green, S. McKnight, and I. H. Marshall (Downers Grove, IL: InterVarsity Press, 1992), 563; W. R. G. Loader, *Jesus' Attitude Towards the Law: A Study of the Gospels* (Tübingen: J.C.B. Mohr [Paul Siebeck], 1997), 162; W. Foerster, "*óros,*" in *Theological Dictionary of the New Testament,* ed. G. Kittel, trans. G. W.

Bromiley (Grand Rapids, MI: Eerdmans, 1999), 5:485; Gearey, "The Bible, Law and Liberation: Towards a Politico-Legal Hermeneutics of the Sermon on the Mount," 270–271.

58. H. Kleine, "*óros*," in *Exegetical Dictionary of the New Testament*, eds. H. Balz & G. Schneider, trans. J. W. Thompson & J. W. Medendorp (Grand Rapids: Eerdmans, 1991), 2:534; D. Scaer, "Sermon on the Mount," in *Evangelical Dictionary of Biblical Theology*, ed. W.A. Elwell (Grand Rapids: Baker, 1996), 724.

59. B. H. Branscomb, *Jesus and the Law of Moses* (New York: Richard R. Smith, Inc., 1930), 97; B. Häring, "Normative Value of the Sermon on the Mount," *Catholic Biblical Quarterly*, vol. 29, no. 3 (1967), 375–376; Lapide, *The Sermon on the Mount: Utopia or Program for Action?* trans. A. Swidler (Maryknoll, NY: Orbis Books, 1986), 11–12; U. Luz, *The Theology of the Gospel of Matthew*, trans. J. B. Robinson (Cambridge: Cambridge University Press, 1995), 44–45, 48; Draper, "The Genesis and Narrative Thrust of the Paraenesis in the Sermon on the Mount," 30–31; G. T. Burke, "Sermon on the Mount," in *Evangelical Dictionary of Theology* (2nd ed.), ed. W. A. Elwell (Grand Rapids: Baker, 2001), 1094. Bauer (*The Structure of Matthew's Gospel: A Study in Literary Design*, 136) goes so far as to suggest that "Matthew shaped his Gospel in order to conform to the five books of the Pentateuch, thus presenting Jesus as a new Moses who presents a new law to his church." For a dissenting view, cf. W. F. Albright & C. S. Mann, *The Anchor Bible: Matthew* (New York: Doubleday, 1971), 49–50; Choi, *The Isaianic Background for the First Four Beatitudes in Matthew*, 14–15.

60. W. D. Dumbrell, "The Logic of the Role of the Law in Matthew 5:1–20," *Novum Testamentum*, vol. 23, no. 1 (1981), 5.

61. Ibid., 6.

62. Ibid.

63. Ibid., 5. C. Brown ("*óros*," in *New International Dictionary of New Testament Theology*, ed. C. Brown [Grand Rapids, MI: Zondervan, 1986], 3:1011) offers this cautionary note: "[T]he mountain on which Jesus gave his Sermon with its authoritative comments on the law (Matt. 5–7) may represent a new Sinai, though this association rests on other assumptions regarding the intention of Matthew to establish an exodus motif in his narrative, with some uncertainties in this regard preventing a dogmatic conclusion."

64. M. G. Klein, "The Old Testament Origins of the Gospel Genre," *Westminster Theological Journal, vol. 38, no* 1 (1975), 20.

65. Ibid.; cf. R. Mohrlang, *Matthew and Paul: A Comparison of Ethical Perspectives* (Cambridge: Cambridge University Press, 1984), 23, 25; W. D. Davies & D. C. Allison, *A Critical and Exegetical Commentary on the Gospel According to Saint Matthew* (Edinburgh: T. & T. Clark, 1988), 1:423; R. T. France, *Matthew: Evangelist & Teacher* (Downers Grove, IL: InterVarsity, 1989), 187; G. Strecker, "The Law in the Sermon on the Mount, and the Sermon on the Mount as Law," in *The Promise and Practice of Biblical Theology*, ed. J. Reumann (Minneapolis, MN: Augsburg Fortress, 1991), 44.

66. D. Senior, *Abingdon New Testament Commentary Series: Matthew* (Nashville: Abingdon Press, 1998), 67; cf. similar remarks made by McConnell, *Law and Prophecy in Matthew's Gospel: The Authority and Use of the Old Testament in the Gospel of St. Matthew*, 9; M. M. Lie, *An Examination if Jesus Abolished the Law in Matthew 5:21–48* (M.A. thesis, Portland, OR: Multnomah School of the Bible, 1986), 2; S. Freyne, "The Ethic of Jesus: The Sermon on the Mount Then and Now," in *Ethics and the Christian*, ed. S. Freyne (Dublin: The Columba Press, 1991), 46; Kupp, *Matthew's*

Emmanuel: Divine Presence and God's People in the First Gospel, 71.

67. Loader, *Jesus' Attitude Towards the Law: A Study of the Gospels*, 163.
68. B. L. Martin, "Matthew on Christ and the Law," *Theological Studies*, vol. 44, no. 1 (1983), 58; cf. the discussion in chapter 2 regarding *tôrâ*.
69. G. A. Tuttle, "The Sermon On The Mount: Its Wisdom Affinities And Their Relation To Its Structure," *Journal of the Evangelical Theological Society*, vol. 20, no. 3 (1997), 214.
70. C. H. Kang, *The Literary Affinities Of The Sermon On The Mount With Special Reference To Deuteronomic Features*, 60.
71. Ibid., 240; cf. Davies & Allison, *A Critical and Exegetical Commentary on the Gospel According to Saint Matthew*, 1:426–427; D. E. Garland, *Reading Matthew: A Literary and Theological Commentary on the First Gospel* (New York: The Crossroad Publishing Company, 1993), 52; Hagner, *Word Biblical Commentary: Matthew 1–13*, 86.
72. Kang, *The Literary Affinities Of The Sermon On The Mount With Special Reference To Deuteronomic Features*, 246.
73. Cf. Linnemann, *Is There a Synoptic Problem? Rethinking the Literary Dependence of the First Three Gospels*, 76.
74. R. B. Miller, "Sermon on the Mount," in *The International Standard Bible Encyclopedia*, ed. J. Orr (Grand Rapids: Eerdmans, 1955), 4:2733. Concerning the interrelationship between the two Sermons, cf. J. A. Brooks, "The Unity and Structure of the Sermon on the Mount," *Criswell Theological Review*, vol. 6, no. 1 (1992), 15–24.
75. H. L. Drumwright, "The Sermon on the Mount," in *The Zondervan Pictorial Encyclopedia of the Bible*, ed. M. C. Tenny (Grand Rapids: Zondervan, 1976), 5:352.
76. J. O. Buswell, "Sermon on the Mount," in *The Zondervan Pictorial Bible Dictionary*, ed. M. C. Tenny (Grand Rapids: Zondervan, 1963), 773; Burke, "Sermon on the Mount," 1094.
77. G. N. Stanton, "Sermon on the Mount/Plain," in *Dictionary of Jesus and the Gospels*, eds. J. B. Green, S. McKnight, & I. H. Marshall (Downers Grove, IL: InterVarsity, 1992), 736.
78. Cf. S. Zeitlin, "Prolegomenon," in *The Jewish Sources of the Sermon on the Mount*, ed. G. Friedlander (New York: Ktav Publishing House, 1969), xv–xvi; G. T. Burke, "Sermon on the Mount," 1094.
79. Ridderbos, *The Bible Student's Commentary: Matthew*, 83–84.
80. W. Hendriksen, *New Testament Commentary: The Gospel of Matthew* (Grand Rapids: Baker, 1973), 260.
81. Carson, "Matthew," 8:125.
82. D. Guthrie, *New Testament Introduction* (Downers Grove, IL: InterVarsity, 1970), 122.
83. H. D. Betz, "Sermon on the Mount/Plain," in *The Anchor Bible Dictionary*, ed. D. N. Freedman (New York: Doubleday, 1992), 5:1106.
84. H. D. Betz, *The Sermon on the Mount* (Minneapolis, MN: Fortress Press, 1995), 23–24.
85. Scaer ("Sermon on the Mount," 723–724) reflected this view when he stated that Matthew was "arranging and editing preexisting material spoken by Jesus on more than one occasion....Matthew is more the editor of sayings collected in the Sermon on the Mount than he is the their author." Betz ("Sermon on the Mount/Plain," 5:1106–1107) similarly remarks, "Matthew received the basic material from Q and expanded it with other sources he found in his tradition or which he made up himself; he also made editorial changes in the material."
86. For example, the teaching on prayer in Matthew 6:1–11.

87. Cf. Mounce, "Sermon on the Mount," 1089.
88. Cf. R. A. Guelich, *The Sermon on the Mount: A Foundation for Understanding* (Waco, TX: Word, 1982), 117.
89. Cf. Linnemann, *Is There a Synoptic Problem? Rethinking the Literary Dependence of the First Three Gospels*, 167–168.
90. Drumwright, "The Sermon on the Mount," 5:350.
91. D. L. Bock, *Jesus According to Scripture: Restoring the Portrait from the Gospels* (Grand Rapids: Baker, 2002), 126.
92. Miller, "Sermon on the Mount," 4:2733.
93. Mounce, "Sermon on the Mount," 1090; G. H. Stassen, "The Fourteen Triads of the Sermon on the Mount (Matthew 5:21–7:12)," *Journal of Biblical Literature,* vol. 122, no. 2 (2003), 267–268, 274.
94. D. M. Lloyd-Jones, *Studies in the Sermon on the Mount* (Grand Rapids: Eerdmans, 1977), 1:22.
95. Nutz, *The Unity of the Sermon on the Mount,* 1.
96. Bonham, *A Study of the Relevance of the Sermon on the Mount in Matthew 5–7,* 9, 23; D. L. Turner, "Whom Does God Approve? The Context, Structure, Purpose, and Exegesis of Matthew's Beatitudes," *Criswell Theological Review*, vol. 6, no. 1 (1992), 31. Contra C. Burchard ("The Theme of the Sermon on the Mount," in *Essays on the Love Commandment*, eds. L. Schottroff, R. H. Fuller, C. Burchard, & M. J. Suggs, trans. R. H. Fuller & I. Fuller [Philadelphia: Fortress Press, 1978], 57), who makes the following claim: "Sooner or later we are bound to realize that Matthew is the author of the Sermon in its finished form and the last to give shape to its constituent parts."
97. A. Plummer, *An Exegetical Commentary on The Gospel According to St. Matthew* (Grand Rapids: Baker, 1982), 57.
98. L. Morris, *The Gospel According to Matthew* (Grand Rapids: Eerdmans, 1992), 92.
99. Ibid.; cf. L. S. Chafer, "The Teachings of Christ Incarnate, Part 1: The Sermon on the Mount," *Bibliotheca Sacra,* vol. 108, no. 432 (1951), 398; Ridderbos, *The Bible Student's Commentary: Matthew*, 84–85. Contra D. Stoutenburg (*With One Voice: The Sermon on the Mount and Rabbinic Literature* [San Francisco: International Scholars Publications, 1996], 72), who asserts that a "final editor" collected "the salient ethical teaching points ascribed to Jesus" and presented them "in a local setting that would popularize them, thus rendering them easy to remember and recount to others."
100. J. D. Kingsbury, "The Place, Structure, and Meaning of the Sermon of the Mount Within Matthew, *Interpretation, vol.* 31, no. 2 (1987), 136.
101. Cf. Lange, "The Gospel According to Matthew: Together With A General Theological And Homiletical Introduction To The New Testament," 8:101.
102. D. K. Campbell, *Interpretation And Exposition Of The Sermon On The Mount* (Th.D. dissertation, Dallas, TX: Dallas Theological Seminary, 1953), 69.
103. Cf. Nutz, *The Unity of the Sermon on the Mount*, 14.
104. Betz, "Sermon on the Mount/Plain," 5:1106.
105. Carson, "Matthew," 8:128.
106. Drumwright, "The Sermon on the Mount," 5:350.
107. G. Strecker, *The Sermon On The Mount: An Exegetical Commentary,* trans. O. C. Dean (Nashville: Abingdon Press, 1988), 25.
108. Betz, "Sermon on the Mount/Plain," 5:1106; Stanton, "Sermon on the Mount/Plain," 740; Scaer, "Sermon on the Mount," 725.
109. W. Carter, *What Are They Saying About Matthew's Sermon On The Mount?* (New York: Paulist Press, 1994), 85.
110. N. W. Lund, *Chiasmus in the New Testament* (Peabody, MS: Hendrickson Publishers,

1970), 255.

111. H. D. Betz, *The Sermon on the Mount* (Minneapolis, MN: Fortress Press, 1995), 62.

112. I. A. Massey, *Interpreting the Sermon on the Mount in the Light of Jewish Tradition as Evidenced in the Palestinian Targums of the Pentateuch: Selected Themes* (Lewsiston, New York: The Edwin Mellen Press, 1991), 115.

113. J. Lambrecht, *The Sermon on the Mount: Proclamation and Exhortation* (Wilmington, Delaware: Michael Glazier, 1985), 28–29.

114. Carson, "Matthew," 8:142; U. Luz, *The Theology of the Gospel of Matthew*, trans. J. B. Robinson (Cambridge: Cambridge University Press, 1995), 49.

115. McConnell, *Law and Prophecy in Matthew's Gospel: The Authority and Use of the Old Testament in the Gospel of St. Matthew*, 11.

116. Kang, *The Literary Affinities Of The Sermon On The Mount With Special Reference To Deuteronomic Features*, 5. While Kang's theory is suggestive, I think he goes too far when he asserts that the "author of the Sermon, in a typological manner, deliberately, but implicitly, reflected the setting, format and some contents of Deuteronomy in order to give the readers the impression that the Sermon is the authentic word of Jesus for the heirs of the coming Kingdom of God."

117. Lund, *Chiasmus in the New Testament*, 255.

118. In this discussion, the law refers to what was taught in the first five books of the Hebrew Scriptures.

119. M. J. Suggs, *Wisdom, Christology, and Law in Matthew's Gospel* (Cambridge, MA: Harvard University Press, 1970), 109.

120. J. D. Charles, "The Greatest Or The Least In The Kingdom?: The Disciple's Relationship To The Law (Matt 5:17–20)," *Trinity Journal*, vol. 13, no. 2 (1992), 145.

121. H. D. Betz, "The Problem of Christology in the Sermon the Mount," in *Text and Logos: The Humanistic Interpretation of the New Testament*, ed. T. W. Jennings (Atlanta: Scholars Press, 1990), 193.

122. Ibid.

123. Ibid., 194.

124. Cf. Kim, *The Function and Meaning of the Lord's Prayer in the Sermon on the Mount*, 28, 40, 153; Choi, *The Isaianic Background for the First Four Beatitudes in Matthew*, 11, 68; Loader, *Jesus' Attitude Towards the Law: A Study of the Gospels*, 165, 168.

125. Strecker, "The Law in the Sermon on the Mount, and the Sermon on the Mount as Law," 36; cf. R. B. Sisson, "Voices of Authority in the Sermon on the Mount," in *Society of Biblical Literature 1997 Seminar Papers. Number 36* (Atlanta: Scholars Press, 1997), 552.

126. J. D. Kingsbury, "The Title 'Kyrios' in Matthew's Gospel," *Journal of Biblical Literature*, vol. 94, no. 2 (1975), 249; cf. Loader, *Jesus' Attitude Towards the Law: A Study of the Gospels*, 172–173.

127. Ferguson, *Kingdom Life In A Fallen World: Living Out the Sermon on the Mount*, 21.

128. Cf. E. Linnemann, *Is There a Synoptic Problem? Rethinking the Literary Dependence of the First Three Gospels* (Grand Rapids: Baker, 1992), 166.

129. Kingsbury, "The Place, Structure, and Meaning of the Sermon of the Mount Within Matthew, 136.

130. Luz, *The Theology of the Gospel of Matthew*, 48.

131. Stanton, "Sermon on the Mount/Plain," 740.

132. D. C. Allison, "The Structure of the Sermon on the Mount," *Journal of Biblical Literature*, vol. 106 (1987), 424; Hagner, *Word Biblical Commentary: Matthew 1–13*, 83; J. B. Breck, *The Shape of Biblical Language: Chiasmus in the Scriptures and Beyond* (Crestwood, NJ: St. Vladimir's Seminary Press, 1994), 123, 132.

133. E. M. Skibbe, "Pentateuchal Themes In The Sermon On The Mount," *Lutheran Quarterly,* vol. 20, no. 1 (1968), 44.
134. For a more recent chronological survey and critique of proposed structures of Jesus' discourse, cf. J. E. Wyse, *The Structure of the Sermon on the Mount and Its Relationship to Interpretation* (M.A. thesis, Deerfield, IL: Trinity Evangelical Divinity School, 1997), 3–40.
135. Carter, *What Are They Saying About Matthew's Sermon On The Mount?*, 35–52.
136. Cf. Stanton, "Sermon on the Mount/Plain," 741.
137. Cf. the detailed discussion of Allison, "The Structure of the Sermon on the Mount," 426–429.
138. Kim, *The Function and Meaning of the Lord's Prayer in the Sermon on the Mount*, 20.
139. With respect to the first theological idea, cf. Asahu-Ejere, *The Kingdom of God and Healing-Exorcism (Mt 4:17–5:12)*, 82–83, 93. With respect to the second theological idea, cf. Lohse, *Theological Ethics of the New Testament,* 63. Kang (*The Literary Affinities Of The Sermon On The Mount With Special Reference To Deuteronomic Features*, 104) defines "the genre of the Sermon as an apocalyptic wisdom work with an emphasis on the promotion of righteousness." Also, Kingsbury ("The Place, Structure, and Meaning of the Sermon of the Mount Within Matthew, 136) maintains that "greater righteousness" is the central "theme of the Sermon on the Mount." Moreover, M. V. Terzian (*The Homiletical Style of Christ in the Sermon on the Mount* [M.Div. thesis, Winona Lake, IN: Grace Theological Seminary, 1984], 22–23) sees "true righteousness" as the key focus of Jesus' discourse.
140. E.g. Lund, *Chiasmus in the New Testament,* 241; D. Patte, *The Gospel According to Matthew: A Structural Commentary on Matthew's Faith* (Philadelphia: Fortress Press, 1987), 63–65; Luz, *Matthew 1–7: A Commentary*, 40; Breck, *The Shape of Biblical Language: Chiasmus in the Scriptures and Beyond*, 132; Carter, *What Are They Saying About Matthew's Sermon On The Mount?*, 39; H. W. Hernandez, *The Chiastic Structure of the Sermon on the Mount* (Th.M. thesis, Dallas, TX: Dallas Theological Seminary, 1994), 2; Wyse, *The Structure of the Sermon on the Mount and Its Relationship to Interpretation*, 49–50; Draper, "The Genesis and Narrative Thrust of the Paraenesis in the Sermon on the Mount," 32–34.
141. R. E. Man, "The Value of Chiasm for New Testament Interpretation," *Bibliotheca Sacra*, vol. 141, no. 562 (1984), 146.
142. W. W. Klein, C. L. Blomberg, P. & R. L. Hubbard, *Introduction to Biblical Interpretation* (Dallas, TX: Word Publishing, 1993), 237–238.
143. Breck, *The Shape of Biblical Language: Chiasmus in the Scriptures and Beyond,* 1.
144. Klein, Blomberg, and Hubbard, *Introduction to Biblical Interpretation*, 237.
145. Man, "The Value of Chiasm for New Testament Interpretation," 148.
146. R. B. Zuck, *Basic Bible Interpretation: A Practical Guide to Discovering Biblical Truth* (CO Springs, CO: Victor Books, 1991), 138–139.
147. Man, "The Value of Chiasm for New Testament Interpretation," 148.
148. Klein, Blomberg, and Hubbard, *Introduction to Biblical Interpretation*, 238.
149. Lund, *Chiasmus in the New Testament*, 23.
150. Breck, *The Shape of Biblical Language: Chiasmus in the Scriptures and Beyond*, 2–3.
151. M. Webb, *Revelation and Chiasm: The Drama of Supernatural Warfare* (M.A. thesis, Denver, CO: Denver Conservative Baptist Seminary, 1996), 33.
152. Allison, "The Structure of the Sermon on the Mount," 431.
153. Turner, "Whom Does God Approve? The Context, Structure, Purpose, and Exegesis of Matthew's Beatitudes," 33.
154. Wyse, *The Structure of the Sermon on the Mount and Its Relationship to Interpreta-*

tion, 50, 62–63.

155. Cf. Burchard ("The Theme of the Sermon on the Mount," 72–74), who espouses a similar demarcation for the macro-structure of Jesus' discourse.
156. Cf. a somewhat similar delineation in Choi, *The Isaianic Background for the First Four Beatitudes in Matthew*, 30.
157. Lund, *Chiasmus in the New Testament*, 240.
158. Ibid., 241–250.
159. Breck, *The Shape of Biblical Language: Chiasmus in the Scriptures and Beyond,* 123.
160. Ibid., 135.
161. Luz (*Matthew 1–7: A Commentary*, 40, 211, 213) also sees the Lord's Prayer as being at the center of the Sermon, though he offers a different approach for the symmetrical, ring-shaped arrangement of the material in Jesus' discourse; cf. Luz's diagram on page 212 of his commentary for further details. Senior (*Abingdon New Testament Commentary Series: Matthew*, 68), in his discussion of Luz's approach, noted that "proposals such as this are enticing but extraordinarily subtle and often depend on subjective judgments about what constitutes a 'parallel.'"
162. Breck, *The Shape of Biblical Language: Chiasmus in the Scriptures and Beyond*, 136.
163. Ibid.
164 Hernandez (*The Chiastic Structure of the Sermon on the Mount*) also sees "the concept of righteousness" as being at "the center of [his] proposed chiasm" (58; cf. 30). The difference is that various ideations define his chiastic approach. In contrast, Breck adopts a literary (rather than a conceptual) chiastic structure.
165. Breck, *The Shape of Biblical Language: Chiasmus in the Scriptures and Beyond*, 136; cf. the comments I made earlier in this chapter on the Lord's Prayer.
166. Draper, "The Genesis and Narrative Thrust of the Paraenesis in the Sermon on the Mount," 32.
167. Wyse, *The Structure of the Sermon on the Mount and Its Relationship to Interpretation*, 70; emphasis his.
168. Ibid., 71; cf. Kim, *The Function and Meaning of the Lord's Prayer in the Sermon on the Mount*, 22–23.
169. Cf. Kingsbury ("The Place, Structure, and Meaning of the Sermon of the Mount Within Matthew, 140–141), who also regards Matthew 6:1–18 as the literary and thematic center of Jesus' Sermon.
170. Even Breck acknowledges "the major weight [of] the relationship between Jesus and the Mosaic law" (*The Shape of Biblical Language: Chiasmus in the Scriptures and Beyond*, 130). Of course, he argues that an excessive stress on this aspect of the passage "tends to draw attention away from another more fundamental purpose of Jesus' Sermon: *to chart for his followers the way that leads to the Kingdom of Heaven*" (131, emphasis his). While I agree that this is an important truth taught in the Sermon, I do not consider it the foremost one.
171. Hernandez, *The Chiastic Structure of the Sermon on the Mount*, 2.
172. Ibid., 29; cf. his chart on page 30 for further details.
173. Ibid., 32.
174. Cf. Wyse, *The Structure of the Sermon on the Mount and Its Relationship to Interpretation*, 10–11.
175. Breck, *The Shape of Biblical Language: Chiasmus in the Scriptures and Beyond*, 123.
176. Ibid.
177. Draper, "The Genesis and Narrative Thrust of the Paraenesis in the Sermon on the Mount," 32; cf. my earlier critique of Breck's chiastic structure as it relates to the theme of righteousness being an overarching emphasis of Jesus' Sermon. Also, cf. the

discussion of G. H. Stassen, "Grace and Deliverance in the Sermon on the Mount," *Review & Expositor,* vol. 89, no. 2 (1992), 230–231.

178. Draper, "The Genesis and Narrative Thrust of the Paraenesis in the Sermon on the Mount," 33–34, 45.
179. Ibid., 34.
180. Breck, *The Shape of Biblical Language: Chiasmus in the Scriptures and* Beyond, 132.
181. Hernandez, *The Chiastic Structure of the Sermon on the Mount*, 5–6.
182. E. S. Fiorenza, *The Book of Revelation: Justice and Judgment*, 2nd ed. (Minneapolis, MN: Augsburg Fortress, 1998), 176.
183. Lund, *Chiasmus in the New Testament: A Study of the Form and Function of Chiastic Structures*, xviii–xix; Breck, *The Shape of Biblical Language: Chiasmus in the Scriptures and Beyond*, 59–61.
184. Guelich, *The Sermon on the Mount: A Foundation for Understanding*, 37.
185. Ibid., 39.
186. Betz, *The Sermon on the Mount*, 50–58.
187. Cf. Betz, "Sermon on the Mount/Plain," 5:1107; Stanton, "Sermon on the Mount/Plain," 740.
188. Kang, *The Literary Affinities Of The Sermon On The Mount With Special Reference To Deuteronomic Features*, 190.
189. Ibid., 191.
190. Ibid., 177. Kang also proposes that the author "seemingly had the Book of Deuteronomy before him when he composed the Sermon" (295) and that he "had an eye on the Book of Deuteronomy for the composition of the Sermon on the Mount" (297).
191. In this regard, Kang states that "Matthew, in the Sermon, is primarily concerned with the re-establishment of the law by interpreting it in terms of Christian ethics" (303).
192. Ibid., 194 (cf. 195).
193. Kang's view is unmistakable in the following statement he made (283): "Our examination reveals that in the Sermon, Matthew redacts his materials to fit the setting of Deuteronomy so that the Sermon can sound like an authentic word, which gives the final answer to ethical questions raised in his Christian community." Also, cf. H. D. Betz ("The Hermeneutical Principles of the Sermon on the Mount [Matt. 5:17–20]," *Journal of Theology for Southern Africa,* vol. 42 [1983], 20), who likewise asserts that the "Sermon the Mount is a secondary literary creation, a critical compilation of sayings of Jesus which have been recognized as decisive for instruction in proper theological thought and practice."
194. Cf. W. D. Dumbrell, "The Logic of the Role of the Law in Matthew 5:1–20," 18.
195. Kang, *The Literary Affinities Of The Sermon On The Mount With Special Reference To Deuteronomic Features*, 191.
196. This supposition is borne out by Kang's admission that the "distinction between the basic stipulations and the specific stipulations from Deuteronomy and the Sermon on the Mount is largely dependent on the general character of the section in which each stipulation is located, rather than the nature of each stipulation" (197). He then adds that "some specific stipulations may be found in the section on the basic stipulations, or the reverse."
197. In terms of literary arrangement, Kang acknowledges that in "Deuteronomy, the blessings are placed with the curses at the end of the book (Dt. 28; 33:1–29), while in the Sermon, blessings are placed in the introductory part of the work" (191).
198. Ibid., 200.
199. A. A. Trites, "The Blessings and Warnings of the Kingdom (Matthew 5:3–12; 7:13–27)," *Review & Expositor,* vol. 89, no. 2 (1992), 181.

200. Ibid.; cf. Sturz, "The Sermon on the Mount and Its Application to the Present Age," 4. For a thorough overview of formative studies concerning the relationship between Jesus' discourse and rabbinic literature, cf. Stoutenburg, *With One Voice: The Sermon on the Mount and Rabbinic Literature*, 9–30. For a detailed survey of the history of interpretation of Jesus' Sermon, cf. L. Allen, "The Sermon on the Mount in the History of the Church," *Review & Expositor,* vol. 89, no. 2 (1992), 245–261. At the end of his investigation, he offers this poignant conclusion: "The Sermon on the Mount in the history of the church is the story of a moral compass pointing beyond itself to a vision of Christian life, character, and thought which the community of faith has been unable either to domesticate or isolate from the common life" (259). Also, cf. C. Bauman, *The Sermon on the Mount: The Modern Quest for Its Meaning* (Macon, GA: Mercer University Press, 1985), especially his conclusion on pages 418–423; W. S. Fawley, *Matthew 5:17: An Interpretation* (M.Div. thesis, Winona Lake, IN: Grace Theological Seminary, 1985), 12–19; Lohse, *Theological Ethics of the New Testament,* 64–67; D. Crump, "Applying the Sermon on the Mount: Once You Have Read It What Do You Do With It?," *Criswell Theological Review*, vol. 6, no. 1 (1992), 4–9; Keener, *A Commentary on the Gospel of Matthew,* 160–161.
201. Bauman, *The Sermon on the Mount: The Modern Quest for Its Meaning*, 383.
202. Luz, *Matthew 1–7: A Commentary*, 276; cf. a similar observation made by McConnell, *Law and Prophecy in Matthew's Gospel: The Authority and Use of the Old Testament in the Gospel of St. Matthew*, 41.
203. D. J. Moo, "Jesus and the Authority of the Mosaic Law," *Journal for the Study of the New Testament,* vol. 20 (1984), 4–5.
204. Cf. Guelich, *The Sermon on the Mount: A Foundation for Understanding*, 138–142.
205. Cf. R. Banks, *Jesus and the Law in the Synoptic Tradition* (London: Cambridge University Press, 1975), 242, 251; Stanton, "Sermon on the Mount/Plain," 742.
206. Cf. E. Linnemann, *Historical Criticism of the Bible: Methodology or Ideology? Reflections of a Bultmannian Turned Evangelical* (Grand Rapids: Baker, 1990), 92.
207. Cf. the discussion in chapter 6 on this issue; also, Lenski, *The Interpretation of St. Matthew's Gospel*, 209–210.
208. Cf. Bauman, *The Sermon on the Mount: The Modern Quest for Its Meaning*, 390–391.
209. Cf. R. A. Hawkins, "Covenant Relations of the Sermon on the Mount," *Restoration Quarterly,* vol. 12, no. 1 (1969), 3.
210. K. L. Barker, "False dichotomies Between the Testaments," *Journal of the Evangelical Theological Society,* vol. 25, no. 1 (1982), 6, 8. Worth (*The Sermon on the Mount: Its Old Testament Roots*, 61) gave this pertinent summary thought: "[Jesus] is not so much introducing a teaching that is new as recovering the implications and requirements of teachings that those 'of old' either knew or should have known."
211. D. Greenwood, "Moral Obligation in the Sermon on the Mount," *Theological Studies,* vol. 31 (1970), 301.
212. Lambrecht, *The Sermon on the Mount: Proclamation and Exhortation*, 93–94; P. Fairbairn, *The Revelation of the Law in Scripture* (Phillipsburg, NJ: P. & R. Publishing, 1996), 225–226; Reisinger, *The Law and the Gospel*, 106. Bornkamm, Gerhard, & Held (*Tradition and Interpretation in Matthew,* 93–94) remark as follows: "It is plain that the antitheses are not directed primarily against the Old Testament itself, but against the interpretation of it in the Rabbinate."
213. W. C. Kaiser, "The Place of Law and Good Works In Evangelical Christianity," in *A Time to Speak: The Evangelical-Jewish Encounter,* ed. A. Rudin & M. Wilson (Austin, TX: Center for Judaic-Christian Studies, 1987), 120.
214. Ferguson, *Kingdom Life In A Fallen World: Living Out the Sermon on the Mount*, 112.

215. W. Harrington, "The Law, The Prophets, And The Gospel," *Irish Theological Quarterly*, vol. 31 (1964), 283.
216. McClain, *Law and Grace* (Winona Lake, IN: BMH Books, 1973), 12–13; I. A. Audu, *Christ's Interpretation of the Law* (Th.M. thesis, Dallas, TX: Dallas Theological Seminary, 1990), 9, 28.
217. As Meier (*Law and History in Matthew's Gospel: A Redactional Study of Mt. 5:17–48*, 129) notes, the "precise wording and length of the formula differ from antithesis to antithesis." The reason for this remains unclear, however, despite all the conjecture among scholars. In any case, "the variation in the introductory formula seems to carry no great theological significance."
218. H. G. Link, "*egō eimi*," in *New International Dictionary of New Testament Theology*, ed. C. Brown (Grand Rapids, MI: Zondervan, 1986), 2:281. Kang (*The Literary Affinities Of The Sermon On The Mount With Special Reference To Deuteronomic Features*, 233) reflects this sentiment in the "three hermeneutical principles" he enunciates for making sense of the Jesus' various quotations: "(1) The Torah is authoritative Scripture; (2) Jesus is the fulfiller of the Torah (cf. Mt. 5:17f.); (3) Jesus' interpretation of the Torah is on par with the Torah itself (cf. Mt. 19:8)."
219. Link, "*egō eimi*," 2:281; cf. Hegg, "What Does πληρῶσαι Mean in Matthew 5:17?", 15.
220. Link, "*egō eimi*," 2:281. Link goes on to say, "The *egō de legō hymin* is directed in the name of God against contemporary Judaism's misrepresentations of his will. To this extent Matt. understands the antitheses not as a contradiction but as the fulfillment of the original intention of the Torah (Matt. 5:17)."
221. G. L. Bahnsen, *Theonomy in Christian Ethics*, 2nd ed. (Phillipsburg, NJ: Presbyterian and Reformed, 1984), 90–91.
222. Bonham, *A Study of the Relevance of the Sermon on the Mount in Matthew 5–7*, 143; Nutz, *The Unity of the Sermon on the Mount*, 89.
223. S. D. Toussaint, *Behold The King: A Study of Matthew*, 1st ed. (Portland: Multnomah Press, 1981), 101.
224. Ladd, *A Theology of the New Testament: Revised Edition*, 223.
225. Carson, "Matthew," 8:144.
226. J. M. Grier, "The Relationship of the Law to Christ in Matthew 5:17–20 and Its Implications for Moral Theology," in *New Testament Essays In Honor of Homer A Kent, Jr.*, ed. G. T. Meadors (Winona Lake, IN: BMH Books, 1991), 173.
227. Cf. Guelich, "Interpreting the Sermon on the Mount," 129–130.
228. Cf. L. S. Cahill, "The Ethical Implications of the Sermon on the Mount," *Interpretation*, vol. 41, no. 2 (1987), 144.
229. Bonham, *A Study of the Relevance of the Sermon on the Mount in Matthew 5–7*, 3, 93–94, 96; Mounce, "Sermon on the Mount," 4:414.
230. Burke, "Sermon on the Mount," 1094.
231. Mounce, "Sermon on the Mount," 4:414.
232. D. Greenwood, "Moral Obligation in the Sermon on the Mount," *Theological Studies*, vol. 31 (1970), 303.
233. Guelich, *The Sermon on the Mount: A Foundation for Understanding*, 17.
234. W. S. Reid, "The New Testament Belief in an Old Testament Church," *Evangelical Quarterly*, vol. 24 (1952), 196.
235. G. F. Hershberger, "Peace and War in the New Testament," *Mennonite Quarterly Review*, vol. 17 (1943a), 59.
236. Cahill, "The Ethical Implications of the Sermon on the Mount," 145.
237. Carson, "Matthew," 8:127.

238. Mounce, "Sermon on the Mount," 4:414. Hershberger ("Mennonites and the Modern Peace Movement, *Mennonite Quarterly Review*, vol. 2 [1928], 163) reflected this view when he wrote the following: "The Mennonite Church...believes that war should be avoided by the state, but also insists that war is morally wrong now, and that it always was wrong because it is a violation of God's moral law. Therefore the individual actually sins when he takes any part in war at all."
239. G. F. Hershberger, "Peace and War in the New Testament," *Mennonite Quarterly Review*, vol. 17 (1943), 5.
240. C. F. Henry, *Christian Personal Ethics* (Grand Rapids: Eerdmans, 1957), 307.
241. N. L. Geisler, *Christian Ethics: Options and Issues* (Grand Rapids: Baker, 1989), 230.
242. J. J. Davis, *Evangelical Ethics: Issues Facing the Church Today*, 2nd ed. (Phillipsburg, PA: Presbyterian and Reformed, 1993), 217.
243. J. Murray, *Principles of Conduct: Aspects of Biblical Ethics* (Grand Rapids: Eerdmans, 1957), 179.
244. Henry, *Christian Personal Ethics*, 305.
245. Davis, *Evangelical Ethics: Issues Facing the Church Today*, 217–218.
246. R. Gordon, "War," in *New Bible Dictionary: Second Edition*, ed. J. D. Douglas (Wheaton, IL: Tyndale, 1982), 1241.
247. McQuilkin, *An Introduction to Biblical Ethics*, 342.
248. R. G. Clouse, "War and Peace," in *New Dictionary of Theology*, eds. S. B. Ferguson & D. F. Wright (Downers Grove, IL: InterVarsity, 1988), 715.
249. Davis, *Evangelical Ethics: Issues Facing the Church Today*, 214.
250. R. G. Clouse, "War," in *Evangelical Dictionary of Theology* (2nd ed.), ed. W. A. Elwell (Grand Rapids: Baker, 2001), 1255.
251. Davis, *Evangelical Ethics: Issues Facing the Church Today*, 215.
252. W. Klassen, "War in the NT," in *The Anchor Bible Dictionary*, ed. D. N. Freedman (New York: Doubleday, 1992), 6:873.
253. Clouse, "War," 1255.
254. McQuilkin, *An Introduction to Biblical Ethics*, 336.
255. Geisler, *Christian Ethics: Options and Issues*, 230.
256. R. H. Mounce, "Sermon on the Mount," in *New Bible Dictionary: Second Edition*, ed. J. D. Douglas (Wheaton, IL: Tyndale, 1982), 1090.
257. Mounce, "Sermon on the Mount," 4:413. H. L. Drumwright ("The Sermon on the Mount," in *The Zondervan Pictorial Encyclopedia of the Bible*, ed. M. C. Tenny [Grand Rapids: Zondervan, 1976], 5:352) made this point: "Crude literalism had always been a danger in the interpretation of the proverbial. It is the principle underlying the proverb that is important and not the literal meaning (Matt 5:29, 30)."
258. Guelich, *The Sermon on the Mount: A Foundation for Understanding*, 19.
259. Mounce, "Sermon on the Mount," 4:415.
260. E. Linnemann, *Historical Criticism of the Bible: Methodology or Ideology? Reflections of a Bultmannian Turned Evangelical* (Grand Rapids: Baker, 1990), 26.
261. R. A. Hawkins, "Covenant Relations of the Sermon on the Mount," *Restoration Quarterly*, vol. 12, no. 1 (1969), 2. Henry (*Christian Personal Ethics*, 279) noted the following about the humanistic point of view: "Humanistic moralists either dismiss the Sermon on the Mount as the passé ethical prejudice of a past age which, in common with all early traditions, must be superseded, or they attack it as inadequate for the complexities of contemporary life."
262. Cf. Linnemann, *Historical Criticism of the Bible: Methodology or Ideology? Reflections of a Bultmannian Turned Evangelical*, 36.

263. R. H. Mounce, "Sermon on the Mount," in *New Bible Dictionary: Second Edition,* ed. J. D. Douglas (Wheaton, IL: Tyndale, 1982), 1090.
264. R. G. Gromacki, *New Testament Survey* (Grand Rapids: Baker, 1974), 78.
265. Mounce, "Sermon on the Mount," 1089.
266. Burke, "Sermon on the Mount," 1094.
267. Drumwright, "The Sermon on the Mount," 5:352.
268. Burke, "Sermon on the Mount," 1094.
269. Miller, "Sermon on the Mount," 4:2735.
270. W. Hendriksen, *New Testament Commentary: The Gospel of Matthew* (Grand Rapids: Baker, 1973), 262.
271. Carson, "Matthew," 8:126.
272. Ferguson, *Kingdom Life In A Fallen World: Living Out the Sermon on the Mount*, 21.
273. A. W. Pink, *An Exposition of the Sermon on the Mount* (Grand Rapids: Baker, 1953), 12.
274. Henry, *Christian Personal Ethics*, 296.
275. Mounce, "Sermon on the Mount," 4:415.
276. Hendriksen, *New Testament Commentary: The Gospel of Matthew*, 261.
277. Keener, *A Commentary on the Gospel of Matthew*, 161.
278. Nixon, "Matthew," 822.
279. Greenwood ("Moral Obligation in the Sermon on the Mount," 308) makes this apt observation: "To put the ideals of the Sermon on the Mount into practice may well be impossible for most men; to follow humbly in the direction indicated by Christ is impossible for no morally responsible individual."
280. Stanton, "Sermon on the Mount/Plain," 738.
281. Mounce, "Sermon on the Mount," 4:415. Guelich (*The Sermon on the Mount: A Foundation for Understanding,* 16) provided this helpful summary: "In his 'two-kingdom' approach, Luther...distinguished between one's 'office' and one's 'person.' The former represents the God-ordained order for the kingdom of this world, the latter one's 'heart' or 'spiritual' relationship to God and others. Thus, the Sermon's demands are to be carried out continually within the Christian's 'heart' even if the 'office' demands conduct to the contrary."
282. A. Schweitzer, *The Quest for the Historical Jesus*, trans. W. Montgomery (New York: Macmillan, 1961), 354.
283. Mounce, "Sermon on the Mount," 4:415.
284. Stanton, "Sermon on the Mount/Plain," 739.
285. Burke, "Sermon on the Mount," 1095.
286. Carson, "Matthew," 8:127.
287. Cf. Breck, *The Shape of Biblical Language: Chiasmus in the Scriptures and Beyond,* 132.
288. Hendriksen, *New Testament Commentary: The Gospel of Matthew*, 261.
289. Henry, *Christian Personal Ethics*, 303–304.
290. J. F. Walvoord, *Matthew: Thy Kingdom Come* (Chicago: Moody Press, 1974), 45.
291. D. K. Campbell, *Interpretation And Exposition Of The Sermon On The Mount* (Th.D. dissertation, Dallas, TX: Dallas Theological Seminary, 1953), 39.
292. C. C. Ryrie, *Biblical Theology of the New Testament* (Chicago: Moody Press, 1959), 78. The remarks of Pentecost (*Things to Come: A Study in Biblical Eschatology* [Grand Rapids: Eerdmans 1958], 130) serve as an example of this view: "Even a causal glance at the Sermon on the Mount ought to be sufficient to show that this discourse was not spoken as the guide to salvation, either of the individual or of society.

There is no mention of the death of Christ for sin nor of faith as related to salvation, nor of justification, the new creation, the position 'in Christ' which occupies so much of the soteriological passages of the New Testament, no security offered, no enablement of the Holy Spirit for a new life as a result of salvation. It is evident from the clear teaching of the rest of the New Testament that the Lord's purpose was not to address the unbelieving world in this discourse to show them the way of life, either individual or social."

293. L. S. Chafer, "The Teachings of Christ Incarnate, Part 1: The Sermon on the Mount," 392; J. F. Rand, "Problems in Literal Interpretation of the Sermon on the Mount: Part I," *Bibliotheca Sacra,* vol. 112, no. 445 (1955), 31; S. D. Toussaint, *Behold The King: A Study of Matthew,* 1st ed. (Portland: Multnomah Press, 1981), 88–89.
294. Ryrie, *Biblical Theology of the New Testament*, 80. Pentecost (*The Sermon on the Mount: Contemporary Insights for a Christian Lifestyle* [Portland, OR: Multnomah Press, 1980], 16) seems to echo this orientation when he says concerning Jesus' Sermon, "we realize that it has a present-day application."
295. Campbell, *Interpretation And Exposition Of The Sermon On The Mount*, 2–3.
296. Hendriksen, *New Testament Commentary: The Gospel of Matthew*, 261.
297. McConnell, *Law and Prophecy in Matthew's Gospel: The Authority and Use of the Old Testament in the Gospel of St. Matthew*, 34; Mounce, "Sermon on the Mount," 1089; Keener, *The IVP New Testament Commentary Series: Matthew*, 103–104; Sisson, "Voices of Authority in the Sermon on the Mount," 552–553, 564.
298. D. M. Lloyd-Jones, *Studies in the Sermon on the Mount* (Grand Rapids: Eerdmans, 1977), 1:15.
299. Pink, *An Exposition of the Sermon on the Mount*, 13; cf. Audu (*Christ's Interpretation of the Law*, 38), who makes the following candid admission: "Even though Matthew compiled the narratives of Jesus' life and teaching in the prechurch age, Matthew himself never made the distinction that we now make in our dispensational approach to the Sermon. We should also bear in mind always when we read the Sermon on the Mount that Matthew's immediate readers is the Church."
300. J. O. Buswell, "Sermon on the Mount," in *The Zondervan Pictorial Bible Dictionary,* ed. M. C. Tenny (Grand Rapids: Zondervan, 1963), 773.
301. Lange, "The Gospel According to Matthew: Together With A General Theological And Homiletical Introduction To The New Testament," 8:97.
302. A. Plummer, *An Exegetical Commentary on The Gospel According to St. Matthew* (Grand Rapids: Baker, 1982), 53.
303. Bonham, *A Study of the Relevance of the Sermon on the Mount in Matthew 5–7,* 165; Lambrecht (*The Sermon on the Mount: Proclamation and Exhortation,* 30) aptly remarked, "In Matthew's conception, the listening people form a more distant circle than do the disciples, but the present and listening people are, after all, potential disciples. Thus, it is better not to invoke the introductory verses to argue that the Sermon on the Mount is not for everybody, that it does not apply to ordinary Christians but is rather a kind of supplementary course for advanced students."
304. Kupp, *Matthew's Emmanuel: Divine Presence and God's People in the First Gospel*, 67, 69.
305. Hendriksen, *New Testament Commentary: The Gospel of Matthew*, 264; Luz, *The Theology of the Gospel of Matthew*, 42–43.
306. Carson, "Matthew," 8:128.
307. Henry, *Christian Personal Ethics*, 291.
308. Campbell, *Interpretation And Exposition Of The Sermon On The Mount*, 66.

309. Breck (*The Shape of Biblical Language: Chiasmus in the Scriptures and Beyond*, 132) made this insightful observation (emphasis his): "There are those who find in the Sermon on the Mount only Law without Grace, instruction in *what* to do with no indication as to how to do it. Such a reading is possible only through the lens of theological presuppositions drawn from sources other than the New Testament....[T]he Sermon from beginning to end is a proclamation of Grace."
310. Mounce, "Sermon on the Mount," 4:415.
311. Henry, *Christian Personal Ethics*, 292.
312. Lloyd-Jones, *Studies in the Sermon on the Mount*, 1:28.
313. D. Guthrie, *New Testament Theology* (Downers Grove, IL: InterVarsity, 1981), 154.

Chapter 6: A Content Analysis of the Sermon on the Mount

1. Cf. the remarks of R. C. H. Lenski, *The Interpretation of St. Matthew's Gospel* (Minneapolis, MN: Augsburg Publishing House, 1964), 179–180.
2. R. H. Mounce, "Sermon on the Mount," in *The International Standard Bible Encyclopedia*, ed. G. W. Bromiley (Grand Rapids: Eerdmans, 1988), 4:412.
3. R. B. Miller, "Sermon on the Mount," in *The International Standard Bible Encyclopedia*, ed. J. Orr (Grand Rapids: Eerdmans, 1955), 4:2733; cf. the remarks made in chapter 5 regarding the nature and purpose of the divine kingdom.
4. D. Scaer, "Sermon on the Mount," in *Evangelical Dictionary of Biblical Theology*, ed. W.A. Elwell (Grand Rapids: Baker, 1996), 723; G. Strecker, *Theology of the New Testament*, ed. F. W. Horn, trans. M. E. Boring (Berlin: Walter de Gruyter & Co., 2000), 378. J. Meier (*Law and History in Matthew's Gospel: A Redactional Study of Mt. 5:17–48* [Rome: Biblical Institute Press, 1976], 41) noted that these "five great discourses serve as the main pillars holding up the architectonic structure of Mt."
5. Cf. the previous chapter for a detailed discussion of pertinent issues related to the Prologue of Jesus' Sermon.
6. D. Guthrie, *New Testament Theology* (Downers Grove, IL: InterVarsity, 1981), 899.
7. W. R. Domeris, "'Blessed are you...' (Matthew 5:1–12)," *Journal of Theology for Southern Africa*, vol. 73 (1990), 68.
8. J. Tigwell, *Explaining the Gospels* (London: Scripture Union, 1981), 38.
9. D. K. Lowery, "A Theology of Matthew," in *A Biblical Theology of the New Testament*, ed. R. B. Zuck (Chicago: Moody Press, 1994), 42.
10. R. F. Collins, "Beatitudes," in *The Anchor Bible Dictionary*, ed. D. N. Freedman (New York: Doubleday, 1992), 1:639.
11. W. R. G. Loader, *Jesus' Attitude Towards the Law: A Study of the Gospels* (Tübingen: J.C.B. Mohr [Paul Siebeck], 1997), 164.
12. Campbell, *Interpretation And Exposition Of The Sermon On The Mount*, 71.
13. L. S. Chafer, *Chafer's Systematic Theology* (Dallas: Dallas Seminary Press, 1978), 4:216.
14. J. P Louw & E. A. Nida (*Greek-English Lexicon of the New Testament: Based on Semantic Domains*, 2nd ed., vol. 1: Introduction and Domains, vol. 2: Indices [New York, New York: United Bible Societies, 1989], 1:302) note that this "passive construction in Greek...is generally regarded as a so-called 'passive of avoidance,' that is to say, the use of the passive form in order to avoid a direct reference to God."
15. W. D. Davies & D. C. Allison, *A Critical and Exegetical Commentary on the Gospel According to Saint Matthew* (Edinburgh: T. & T. Clark, 1988), 440, 466. D. Scaer ("Beatitudes," in *Evangelical Dictionary of Biblical Theology*, ed. W. A. Elwell

[Grand Rapids: Baker, 1996], 54) made this pertinent observation: "Blessedness should not be seen as a reward for religious accomplishments, but as an act of God's grace in believers' lives. Rather than congratulating them on spiritual or moral achievements, the beatitude underscores the fact that sinners stand within a forgiving relationship made possible by Christ's atonement."

16. Strecker, *The Sermon On The Mount: An Exegetical Commentary*, 33.
17. A common view in New Testament scholarship is that Paul's teachings were either at variance with or a corruption of Jesus' teachings; cf. the discussion of R. Mohrlang, *Matthew and Paul: A Comparison of Ethical Perspectives* (Cambridge: Cambridge University Press, 1984), 42–47, 67–71, 89–93, 106–110, 123–132. D. Wenham has written two works that explore and refute this view: *Paul: Follower of Jesus or Founder of Christianity?* (Grand Eerdmans: Eerdmans, 1995; esp. pp. 373–378, 397–402, 408–410) and *Paul and Jesus: The True Story* (Grand Rapids: Eerdmans, 2002; esp. pp. 76, 109–110, 167–168, 181–186). In brief, Wenham maintains that Paul's own thought and evangelism were indebted to the ministry and teaching of Jesus. Wenham also argues that Paul drew extensively on the traditions of Jesus and worked tirelessly to herald His message to the known world; cf. E. Andrews, *The Meaning of Christ for Paul* (Nashville: Abingdon-Cokesbury Press, 1949), 223, 231, 233, 240–241; A. J. M. Wedderburn, ed., *Paul and Jesus: Collected Essays* (Sheffield: Sheffield Academic Press, 1989), 113–115, 143, 187–189; V. P. Furnish, *Jesus According to Paul* (Cambridge: Cambridge University Press, 1993), 64–65.
18. Christ's followers would be those who had made or would make a faith commitment to Him.
19. S. B. Ferguson, *Kingdom Life In A Fallen World: Living Out the Sermon on the Mount* (Colorado Springs, CO: Nav Press, 1986), 29.
20. Davies & Allison, *A Critical and Exegetical Commentary on the Gospel According to Saint Matthew*, 1:430–431; J. H. Choi, *The Isaianic Background for the First Four Beatitudes in Matthew* (Th.M. thesis, Grand Rapids: Calvin Theological Seminary, 1993), 31.
21. A. Kodjak, *A Structural Analysis Of The Sermon On The Mount* (New York: Mouton de Gruyter, 1986), 42.
22. Cf. D. A. Hagner, *Word Biblical Commentary: Matthew 1–13* (Dallas, TX: Word Books, 1993), 89.
23. W. DeBoer, "Beatitudes," in *The International Standard Bible Encyclopedia*, ed. G. W. Bromiley (Grand Rapids: Eerdmans, 1979), 1:443.
24. R. A. Guelich, *The Sermon on the Mount: A Foundation for Understanding* (Waco, TX: Word, 1982), 63.
25. J. Lambrecht, *The Sermon on the Mount: Proclamation and Exhortation* (Wilmington, Delaware: Michael Glazier, 1985), 45; Lapide, *The Sermon on the Mount: Utopia or Program for Action?*, 27.
26. Collins, "Beatitudes," 1:629.
27. J. C. Lambert, "Beatitudes," in *The International Standard Bible Encyclopedia*, ed. J. Orr (Grand Rapids: Eerdmans, 1955), 1:419.
28. J. H. Neyrey, *Honor and Shame in the Gospel of Matthew* (Louisville: Westminster John Knox Press, 1998), 165–166.
29. Ibid., 167; cf. 187.
30. U. Becker, "*makários*," in *New International Dictionary of New Testament Theology*, ed. C. Brown (Grand Rapids, MI: Zondervan, 1986), 1:215.
31. F. W. Danker, ed., *A Greek-English Lexicon of the New Testament and Other Early Christian Literature*, 3rd ed. (Chicago, IL: The University of Chicago Press, 2000),

610.

32. G. Strecker, "*makários,*" in *Exegetical Dictionary of the New Testament,* eds. H. Balz & G. Schneider, trans. V. Howard & J. W. Thompson (Grand Rapids: Eerdmans, 1990), 2:377.
33. F. Hauck, "*makários,*" in *Theological Dictionary of the New Testament,* ed. G. Kittel, trans. G. W. Bromiley (Grand Rapids, MI: Eerdmans, 1999), 4:367. D. E. Garland ("Blessing and Woe," in *Dictionary of Jesus and the Gospels,* eds. J. B. Green, S. McKnight, & I. H. Marshall [Downers Grove, IL: InterVarsity, 1992], 79) reflects this sentiment when he writes the following: "[T]he long-awaited blessings of the future age are perceived to have broken into the present. Jesus directly addresses his disciples as blessed because they are able to see and hear what the prophets and the righteous longed to see."
34. Plummer, *An Exegetical Commentary on The Gospel According to St. Matthew,* 57–58; T. M. Dang, *Christ's Beatitudes, Kingdom and the Spiritual Life* (M.A. thesis, La Mirada, CA: Talbot Theological Seminary, 1987), 29.
35. C. Spicq, *Theological Lexicon of the New Testament,* trans. & ed. J. D. Ernest (Peabody, MA: Hendrickson Publishers, 1994), 2:438; cf. G. von Rad, "*basileús,*" in *Theological Dictionary of the New Testament,* ed. G. Kittel, trans. G. W. Bromiley (Grand Rapids, MI: Eerdmans, 1999), 1:565–571.
36. Spicq, *Theological Lexicon of the New Testament,* 2:438.
37. I. H. Marshall, *Commentary on Luke* (Grand Rapids: Eerdmans, 1978), 250.
38. Guthrie, *New Testament Theology,* 415, 421.
39. Tigwell, *Explaining the Gospels,* 37.
40. A. A. Di Lella, "The Structure and Composition of the Matthean Beatitudes," in *To Touch the Text: Biblical and Related Studies in Honor of Joseph A. Fitzmyer,* eds. M. P. Horgan & P. J. Kobelski (New York: The Crossroad Publishing Company, 1989), 237; cf. Plummer, *An Exegetical Commentary on The Gospel According to St. Matthew,* 58; Betz, *The Sermon on the Mount,* 105–109.
41. Stanton, "Sermon on the Mount/Plain," 741.
42. Cf. A. H. McNeile, *The Gospel According to St. Matthew* (Grand Rapids: Baker, 1980), 49; Kodjak, *A Structural Analysis Of The Sermon On The Mount,* 48–51.
43. D. C. Allison, "The Structure of the Sermon on the Mount," *Journal of Biblical Literature,* vol. 106 (1987), 429.
44. Betz, *The Sermon on the Mount,* 147.
45. Nutz, *The Unity of the Sermon on the Mount,* 37.
46. Plummer, *An Exegetical Commentary on The Gospel According to St. Matthew,* 61.
47. Cf. Lambert, "Beatitudes," 1:419–420; Di Lella, "The Structure and Composition of the Matthean Beatitudes," 238–241; Betz, "Sermon on the Mount/Plain," 5:1107–1108.
48. A. Farrer, *St. Matthew and St. Mark* (London: Dacre Press, 1954), 174–177.
49. Cf. V. C. Grounds, "Mountain Manifesto," *Bibliotheca Sacra,* vol. 128, no. 510 (1971), 136.
50. R. Schnackenburg, *The Moral Teaching of the New Testament,* trans. J. Holland-Smith & W. J. O'Hara (New York: The Seabury Press, 1965), 146; R. T. France, *Jesus and the Old Testament: His Application of Old Testament Passages to Himself and His Mission* (Downers Grove, IL: InterVarsity, 1971), 134–135; R. K. Rogers, *The Old Testament Origins of the First Three Beatitudes* (Th.M. thesis, Dallas, TX: Dallas Theological Seminary, 1984), 5–6; Davies & Allison, *A Critical and Exegetical Commentary on the Gospel According to Saint Matthew,* 1:436–437, 466; K. C. Asahu-Ejere, *The Kingdom of God and Healing-Exorcism (Mt 4:17–5:12)* (Frankfurt: Peter

Lang, 2003), 201.
51. Betz, *The Sermon on the Mount*, 115–116.
52. The noun appears in the neuter singular dative form.
53. Strecker, *The Sermon On The Mount: An Exegetical Commentary*, 32.
54. F. D. Bruner, *Matthew, A Commentary, Volume 1* (Dallas, Word Publishing, 1987), 136. Contra Domeris, "'Blessed are you…' (Matthew 5:1–12)," 68–69.
55. Cf. Campbell, *Interpretation And Exposition Of The Sermon On The Mount*, 72–73; Betz, *The Sermon on the Mount*, 111.
56. For example, the phrase, τῷ πνεύματι, which is a dative of reference, relation, or sphere.
57. T. D. Bonham, *A Study of the Relevance of the Sermon on the Mount in Matthew 5–7* (Th.D. dissertation, Fort Worth, TX: Southwestern Baptist Theological Seminary, 1963), 168; W. C. Allen, *A Critical and Exegetical Commentary on the Gospel According to St. Matthew* (Edinburgh: T. & T. Clark, 1965), 39; G. T. Meadors, "The 'Poor' in the Beatitudes of Matthew and Luke," *Grace Theological Journal, vol. 6, no.* 2 (1985), 305; Ferguson, *Kingdom Life In A Fallen World: Living Out the Sermon on the Mount*, 32; cf. Davies & Allison (*A Critical and Exegetical Commentary on the Gospel According to Saint Matthew*, 1:443), who maintain that both a "religious state of poverty" and "literal poverty" (or as a minimum the personal experience of "economic inequities") are in view.
58. J. D. Pentecost, *The Words and Works of Jesus Christ* (Chicago: Moody Press, 1974), 173; Dang, *Christ's Beatitudes, Kingdom and the Spiritual Life*, 31–32; E. Lohse, *Theological Ethics of the New Testament*, trans. M. B. Boring (Minneapolis: Fortress Press, 1991), 69.
59. Rogers, *The Old Testament Origins of the First Three Beatitudes*, 12–13.
60. DeBoer, "Beatitudes," 1:444.
61. R. McQuilkin, *An Introduction to Biblical Ethics*, 2nd. ed. (Wheaton, IL: Tyndale House Publishers, 1995), 122.
62. D. E. Garland, *Reading Matthew: A Literary and Theological Commentary on the First Gospel* (New York: The Crossroad Publishing Company, 1993), 55; D. C. Jones, *Biblical Christian Ethics* (Grand Rapids: Baker, 1994), 26.
63. C. Vaught, *The Sermon on the Mount: A Theological Interpretation* (New York: State University of New York Press, 1986), 18.
64. Kang, *The Literary Affinities Of The Sermon On The Mount With Special Reference To Deuteronomic Features*, (Ph.D. dissertation, Pasadena, CA: Fuller Theological Seminary, School Of Theology, 1987), 86.
65. L. Morris, *The Gospel According to Matthew* (Grand Rapids: Eerdmans, 1992), 96.
66. Plummer, *An Exegetical Commentary on The Gospel According to St. Matthew*, 62.
67. Lenski, *The Interpretation of St. Matthew's Gospel*, 184; Grounds, "Mountain Manifesto," 137.
68. Trites, "The Blessings and Warnings of the Kingdom (Matthew 5:3–12; 7:13–27)," 185.
69. V. C. Grounds, "The Beatitudes," in *The Zondervan Pictorial Encyclopedia of the Bible*, ed. M. C. Tenney (Grand Rapids: Zondervan, 1976), 1:499; D. J. Harrington & J. F. Keenan, *Jesus and Virtue Ethics: Building Bridges between New Testament Studies and Moral Theology* (Lanham, MD: Sheed & Ward, 2002), 62, 131.
70. Guthrie, *New Testament Theology*, 900.
71. Dang, *Christ's Beatitudes, Kingdom and the Spiritual Life*, 35; Betz, *The Sermon on the Mount*, 119.
72. Rogers, *The Old Testament Origins of the First Three Beatitudes*, 17; Davies & Alli-

son, *A Critical and Exegetical Commentary on the Gospel According to Saint Matthew*, 1:448; Asahu-Ejere, *The Kingdom of God and Healing-Exorcism (Mt 4:17–5:12)*, 204–205.

73. Grounds, "Mountain Manifesto," 138; Ferguson, *Kingdom Life In A Fallen World: Living Out the Sermon on the Mount*, 36; Trites, "The Blessings and Warnings of the Kingdom (Matthew 5:3–12; 7:13–27)," 185. Contra Domeris, "'Blessed are you...' (Matthew 5:1–12)," 69, who maintains that "the literal sense militates against such a reading."
74. Grounds, "The Beatitudes," 1:499.
75. Lange, "The Gospel According to Matthew: Together With A General Theological And Homiletical Introduction To The New Testament," 8:102.
76. Lloyd-Jones, *Studies in the Sermon on the Mount*, 1:32.
77. Guelich, *The Sermon on the Mount: A Foundation for Understanding*, 81.
78. Betz, *The Sermon on the Mount*, 126.
79. Rogers, *The Old Testament Origins of the First Three Beatitudes*, 23, 29; France, *Jesus and the Old Testament: His Application of Old Testament Passages to Himself and His Mission*, 62; cf. Asahu-Ejere (*The Kingdom of God and Healing-Exorcism [Mt 4:17–5:12]*, 207–208), who maintains that, while Matthew 5:5 quotes Psalm 37:11, the third beatitude most likely recalls Isaiah 61:7 and serves as a "fulfillment of the salvation promised" in Isaiah 61.
80. Guelich, *The Sermon on the Mount: A Foundation for Understanding*, 82.
81. Ferguson, *Kingdom Life In A Fallen World: Living Out the Sermon on the Mount*, 39.
82. A. W. Pink, *An Exposition of the Sermon on the Mount* (Grand Rapids: Baker, 1953), 23.
83. Grounds, "The Beatitudes," 1:500; J. Phillips, *Exploring the Gospels: Matthew* (Neptune, NJ: Loizeaux Brothers, 1999), 88.
84. Trites, "The Blessings and Warnings of the Kingdom (Matthew 5:3–12; 7:13–27)," 186.
85. Grounds, "Mountain Manifesto," 138; Guthrie, *New Testament Theology*, 901; Dang, *Christ's Beatitudes, Kingdom and the Spiritual Life*, 38–39.
86. Betz, *The Sermon on the Mount*, 127.
87. Allen, *A Critical and Exegetical Commentary on the Gospel According to St. Matthew*, 40, 42; Strecker, *The Sermon On The Mount: An Exegetical Commentary*, 31; Morris, *The Gospel According to Matthew*, 98; cf. W. Schrage, *The Ethics of the New Testament*, trans. D.E. Green (Philadelphia: Fortress Press, 1988), 35–37.
88. Grounds, "The Beatitudes," 1:500.
89. Trites, "The Blessings and Warnings of the Kingdom (Matthew 5:3–12; 7:13–27)," 187.
90. Ibid.
91. Danker, *A Greek-English Lexicon of the New Testament and Other Early Christian Literature*, 248; cf. Nutz, *The Unity of the Sermon on the Mount*, 49.
92. Danker, *A Greek-English Lexicon of the New Testament and Other Early Christian Literature*, 248. In the latter case, these might be understood as "observances or practices required by one's religion" (Louw & Nida, *Greek-English Lexicon of the New Testament: Based on Semantic Domains*, 1:532). This explains why, in Matthew 6:1, the NRSV renders *dikaiosýnē* as "piety."
93. Spicq, *Theological Lexicon of the New Testament*, 1:331.
94. Louw & Nida, *Greek-English Lexicon of the New Testament: Based on Semantic Domains*, 1:744; cf. Davies & Allison, *A Critical and Exegetical Commentary on the Gospel According to Saint Matthew*, 1:452–453.

95. Danker, *A Greek-English Lexicon of the New Testament and Other Early Christian Literature*, 248; cf. R. T. France, *Matthew: Evangelist & Teacher* (Downers Grove, IL: InterVarsity, 1989), 267–268.
96. Danker, *A Greek-English Lexicon of the New Testament and Other Early Christian Literature*, 248.
97. D. W. Diehl, "Righteousness," in *Evangelical Dictionary of Theology* (2nd ed.), ed. W. Elwell (Grand Rapids: Baker, 2001), 1033.
98. S. McKnight, "Justice, Righteousness," in *Dictionary of Jesus and the Gospels,* eds. J. B. Green, S. McKnight, and I. H. Marshall (Downers Grove, IL: InterVarsity Press, 1992), 414. O. Schrenk ("*dikaiosýnē*," in *Theological Dictionary of the New Testament,* ed. G. Kittel, trans. G. W. Bromiley [Grand Rapids, MI: Eerdmans, 1999], 2:198) put it this way: "δικαιοσύνην is almost always used in the NT for the right conduct of man which follows the will of God and is pleasing to Him, for rectitude of life before God, for uprightness before His judgment."
99. Toon, "Righteousness," in *Evangelical Dictionary of Biblical Theology,* ed. W. A. Elwell (Grand Rapids: Baker, 1996), 688.
100. B. Przybylski, *Righteousness in Matthew and His World of Thought* (Cambridge: Cambridge University Press, 1980), 2; Strecker, *Theology of the New Testament*, 382.
101. H. Seabass, "*dikaiosýnē*," in *New International Dictionary of New Testament Theology,* ed. C. Brown (Grand Rapids, MI: Zondervan, 1986), 3:360.
102. K. Kertelge, "*dikaiosýnē*," in *Exegetical Dictionary of the New Testament,* eds. H. Balz & G. Schneider, trans. J. W. Thompson & J. W. Medendorp (Grand Rapids: Eerdmans, 1991), 1:329.
103. Ibid.
104. Ibid.; cf. Przybylski, *Righteousness in Matthew and His World of Thought*, 84–85, 96–97, 105–106; Mohrlang, *Matthew and Paul: A Comparison of Ethical Perspectives*, 114; C. T. Brown, *Beyond Obedience: Jesus and the Law in Matthew 5:17–20* (M.A. thesis, Chicago, IL: The Catholic Theological Union, 1991), 67–68; J. W. Kim, *The Function and Meaning of the Lord's Prayer in the Sermon on the Mount* (Th.M. thesis, Grand Rapids: Calvin Theological Seminary, 1991), 44–45.
105. Jones, *Biblical Christian Ethics*, 33.
106. Guelich, *The Sermon on the Mount: A Foundation for Understanding*, 87.
107. Cf. Ferguson, *Kingdom Life In A Fallen World: Living Out the Sermon on the Mount*, 46–49; J. D. Charles, "The Greatest Or The Least In The Kingdom?: The Disciple's Relationship To The Law (Matt 5:17–20)," *Trinity Journal*, vol. 13, no. 2 (1992), 157–158.
108. Grounds, "The Beatitudes," 1:498.
109. Guthrie, *New Testament Theology*, 901.
110. Vaught, *The Sermon on the Mount: A Theological Interpretation*, 24–25.
111. Bonham, *A Study of the Relevance of the Sermon on the Mount in Matthew 5–7,* 170; Lange, "The Gospel According to Matthew: Together With A General Theological And Homiletical Introduction To The New Testament," 8:102; Schrage, *The Ethics of the New Testament,* 152; Garland, *Reading Matthew: A Literary and Theological Commentary on the First Gospel*, 56.
112. Massey, *Interpreting the Sermon on the Mount in the Light of Jewish Tradition as Evidenced in the Palestinian Targums of the Pentateuch: Selected Themes*, 166.
113. Morris, *The Gospel According to Matthew*, 100.
114. Lenski, *The Interpretation of St. Matthew's Gospel*, 191, 197–198.
115. Guthrie, *New Testament Theology*, 901.
116. Lloyd-Jones, *Studies in the Sermon on the Mount*, 98.

117. Ferguson, *Kingdom Life In A Fallen World: Living Out the Sermon on the Mount*, 50.
118. Pink, *An Exposition of the Sermon on the Mount*, 30.
119. Pentecost, *The Words and Works of Jesus Christ*, 174.
120. Guelich, *The Sermon on the Mount: A Foundation for Understanding*, 89.
121. For example, by being sensitive to the needs of the helpless and homeless (Jones, *Biblical Christian Ethics*, 92; cf. Ps. 41:1).
122. Grounds, "The Beatitudes," 1:500.
123. Bruner, *Matthew, A Commentary, Volume 1*, 147–148; Garland, *Reading Matthew: A Literary and Theological Commentary on the First Gospel*, 57.
124. For example, the intellectual, the emotional, the rational, the volitional, and the spiritual dimensions; cf. Harrington & Keenan, *Jesus and Virtue Ethics: Building Bridges between New Testament Studies and Moral Theology*, 164.
125. Davies & Allison, *A Critical and Exegetical Commentary on the Gospel According to Saint Matthew*, 1:456; Luz, *Matthew 1–7: A Commentary*, 239.
126. Guthrie, *New Testament Theology*, 902.
127. Grounds, "The Beatitudes," 1:500.
128. Ferguson, *Kingdom Life In A Fallen World: Living Out the Sermon on the Mount*, 57.
129. Betz, *The Sermon on the Mount*, 136.
130. McQuilkin, *An Introduction to Biblical Ethics*, 341.
131. Ferguson, *Kingdom Life In A Fallen World: Living Out the Sermon on the Mount*, 58.
132. Vaught, *The Sermon on the Mount: A Theological Interpretation*, 33.
133. Guelich, *The Sermon on the Mount: A Foundation for Understanding*, 106.
134. Lange, "The Gospel According to Matthew: Together With A General Theological And Homiletical Introduction To The New Testament," 8:103; B. H. Young, *Jesus the Jewish Theologian* (Peabody, MA: Hendrickson Publishers, 1995), 89.
135. D. A. Carson, "Matthew," in *The Expositor's Bible Commentary*, ed. F. E. Gaebelein (Grand Rapids: Zondervan, 1984), 8:135; Hagner, *Word Biblical Commentary: Matthew 1–13*, 94.
136. Betz, *The Sermon on the Mount*, 140.
137. Guthrie, *New Testament Theology*, 902.
138. Plummer, *An Exegetical Commentary on The Gospel According to St. Matthew*, 68.
139. C. Gore, *The Sermon on the Mount: A Practical Exposition* (London: John Murray, 1900), 43.
140. Grounds, "The Beatitudes," 1:450.
141. Pentecost, *The Words and Works of Jesus Christ*, 175.
142. Betz, *The Sermon on the Mount*, 142.
143. Kodjak, *A Structural Analysis Of The Sermon On The Mount*, 45; Draper, "The Genesis and Narrative Thrust of the Paraenesis in the Sermon on the Mount," 35; Asahu-Ejere, *The Kingdom of God and Healing-Exorcism (Mt 4:17–5:12)*, 31, 88, 111–112, 212.
144. Betz, *The Sermon on the Mount*, 142.
145. Przybylski, *Righteousness in Matthew and His World of Thought*, 98.
146. Grounds, "The Beatitudes," 1:498.
147. Guthrie, *New Testament Theology*, 903.
148. Ferguson, *Kingdom Life In A Fallen World: Living Out the Sermon on the Mount*, 62.
149. Plummer, *An Exegetical Commentary on The Gospel According to St. Matthew*, 69.
150. W. D. Dumbrell, "The Logic of the Role of the Law in Matthew 5:1–20," *Novum Testamentum*, vol. 23, no. 1 (1981), 2.
151. Choi, *The Isaianic Background for the First Four Beatitudes in Matthew*, 31.

152 Grounds, "The Beatitudes," 1:501.
153. Lange, "The Gospel According to Matthew: Together With A General Theological And Homiletical Introduction To The New Testament," 8:103.
154. A. Bowling, "Salt," in *The Zondervan Pictorial Encyclopedia of the Bible,* ed. M. C. Tenney (Grand Rapids: Zondervan, 1976), 5:220.
155. R. K. Harrison, "Salt," in *New Bible Commentary: Second Edition,* ed. J. D. Douglas (Wheaton, IL: Tyndale, 1982), 1056.
156. Louw & Nida, *Greek-English Lexicon of the New Testament: Based on Semantic Domains*, 1:52.
157. L. G. Herr, "Salt," in *The International Standard Bible Encyclopedia,* ed. G. W. Bromiley (Grand Rapids: Eerdmans, 1988), 4:287.
158. N. Hillyer, "*halas,*" in *New International Dictionary of New Testament Theology,* ed. C. Brown (Grand Rapids, MI: Zondervan, 1986), 3:446.
159. Danker, *A Greek-English Lexicon of the New Testament and Other Early Christian Literature*, 41.
160. Herr, "Salt," 4:286; W. Barclay, *The Old Law and the New Law: The Ten Commandments and the Sermon on the Mount* (Edinburgh: The Saint Andrew Press, 1991), 56.
161. I. H. Marshall, *Commentary on Luke* (Grand Rapids: Eerdmans, 1978), 597; R. H. Gundry, *Matthew: A Commentary on His Literary and Theological Art* (Grand Rapids: Eerdmans, 1982), 75.
162. Carson, "Matthew," 8:138.
163. W. F. Albright & C. S. Mann, *The Anchor Bible: Matthew* (New York: Doubleday, 1971), 54–55.
164. Betz, *The Sermon on the Mount*, 159.
165. Allen, *A Critical and Exegetical Commentary on the Gospel According to St. Matthew*, 43; Marshall, *Commentary on Luke*, 596; W. L. Liefield, "Luke," in *The Expositor's Bible Commentary,* ed. F. E. Gaebelein (Grand Rapids: Eerdmans, 1984), 8:980.
166. C. S. Keener, *The IVP New Testament Commentary Series: Matthew*, ed. G. R. Osborne (Downers Grove, IL: InterVarsity, 1997), 109.
167. F. Hauck, "*halas,*" in *Theological Dictionary of the New Testament,* ed. G. Kittel, trans. G. W. Bromiley (Grand Rapids, MI: Eerdmans, 1999), 1:229.
168. Bowling, "Salt," 5:220.
169. Herr, "Salt," 4:286.
170. Ferguson, *Kingdom Life In A Fallen World: Living Out the Sermon on the Mount*, 83.
171. McNeile, *The Gospel According to St. Matthew*, 55.
172. L. Morris, "Light," in *The International Standard Bible Encyclopedia,* ed. G. W. Bromiley (Grand Rapids: Eerdmans, 1986), 3:135; M. J. Wilkins, "Light," in *Evangelical Dictionary of Biblical Theology,* ed. W. A. Elwell (Grand Rapids: Baker, 1996), 486–487.
173. H. C. Hahn, "*phōs,*" in *New International Dictionary of New Testament Theology,* ed. C. Brown (Grand Rapids, MI: Zondervan, 1986), 2:493–494; G. L. Borchert, "Light," in *New Dictionary of Biblical Theology,* eds.T. D. Alexander, B. S. Rosner, D. A. Carson, & G. Goldsworthy (Downers Grove, IL: InterVarsity, 2000), 645.
174. H. Ritt, "*phōs,*" in *Exegetical Dictionary of the New Testament,* eds. H. Balz & G. Schneider, trans. J. W. Thompson & J. W. Medendorp (Grand Rapids: Eerdmans, 1991), 3:447–448; G. F. Shirbroun, "Light," in *Dictionary of Jesus and the Gospels,* eds. J. B. Green, S. McKnight, & I. H. Marshall (Downers Grove, IL: InterVarsity, 1992), 472.
175. Carson, "Matthew," 8:139.
176. Spicq, *Theological Lexicon of the New Testament,* 3:480.

177. Guelich, *The Sermon on the Mount: A Foundation for Understanding*, 123.
178. Louw & Nida, *Greek-English Lexicon of the New Testament: Based on Semantic Domains*, 1:66; Danker, *A Greek-English Lexicon of the New Testament and Other Early Christian Literature*, 606.
179. G. Schneider, "*lychnos*," in *Exegetical Dictionary of the New Testament*, eds. H. Balz & G. Schneider, trans. J. W. Thompson & J. W. Medendorp (Grand Rapids: Eerdmans, 1991), 2:367; Betz, *The Sermon on the Mount*, 162.
180. Hendriksen, *New Testament Commentary: The Gospel of Matthew*, 285–286.
181. Bonham, *A Study of the Relevance of the Sermon on the Mount in Matthew 5–7*, 176–177; G. F. Hasel, "Lamp," in *The International Standard Bible Encyclopedia*, ed. G. W. Bromiley (Grand Rapids: Eerdmans, 1986), 3:69.
182. Plummer, *An Exegetical Commentary on The Gospel According to St. Matthew*, 73.
183. H. C. Hahn, "*lychnos*," in *New International Dictionary of New Testament Theology*, ed. C. Brown (Grand Rapids, MI: Zondervan, 1986), 2:487; W. Michaelis, "*lychnos*," in *Theological Dictionary of the New Testament*, ed. G. Kittel, trans. G. W. Bromiley (Grand Rapids, MI: Eerdmans, 1999), 4:326.
184. Draper, "The Genesis and Narrative Thrust of the Paraenesis in the Sermon on the Mount," 41.
185. Cf. the discussion of Allison, "The Structure of the Sermon on the Mount," 431.
186. Davies & Allison, *A Critical and Exegetical Commentary on the Gospel According to Saint Matthew*, 1:484; J. E. Wyse, *The Structure of the Sermon on the Mount and Its Relationship to Interpretation* (M.A. Thesis, Deerfield, IL: Trinity Evangelical Divinity School, 1997), 43.
187. R. S. McConnell, *Law and Prophecy in Matthew's Gospel: The Authority and Use of the Old Testament in the Gospel of St. Matthew* (Basel: Friedrich Reinhardt Kommissionverlag, 1969), 13.
188. J. C. Slemp, *Twelve Laws of Life: A Study of the Ten Commandments and Related Teachings of Jesus* (Philadelphia: The Judson Press, 1950), 11–12.
189. Dumbrell, "The Logic of the Role of the Law in Matthew 5:1–20," 17.
190. Betz, *The Sermon on the Mount*, 177.
191. Guelich, *The Sermon on the Mount: A Foundation for Understanding*, 138.
192. Lloyd-Jones, *Studies in the Sermon on the Mount*, 1:185.
193. Hagner, *Word Biblical Commentary: Matthew 1–13*, 105.
194. Lenski, *The Interpretation of St. Matthew's Gospel*, 204–205; Hendriksen, *New Testament Commentary: The Gospel of Matthew*, 288.
195. Gundry, *Matthew: A Commentary on His Literary and Theological Art*, 79.
196. Slemp, *Twelve Laws of Life: A Study of the Ten Commandments and Related Teachings of Jesus* 12; Pink, *An Exposition of the Sermon on the Mount*, 49; Stanton, "Sermon on the Mount/Plain," 741.
197. W. S. Fawley, *Matthew 5:17: An Interpretation* (M.Div. thesis, Winona Lake, IN: Grace Theological Seminary, 1985), 38, 41, 64.
198. Hendriksen, *New Testament Commentary: The Gospel of Matthew*, 288.
199. G. Strecker ("The Law in the Sermon on the Mount, and the Sermon on the Mount as Law," in *The Promise and Practice of Biblical Theology*, ed. J. Reumann [Minneapolis, MN: Augsburg Fortress, 1991], 36) aptly stated that for "Jesus it is not a matter of a theoretical disagreement with the authority of Moses; rather, he takes aim at the tradition in which his listeners live."
200. The verb is in the aorist active infinitive form.
201. H. Hübner, "*katalyō*," in *Exegetical Dictionary of the New Testament*, eds. H. Balz & G. Schneider, trans. J. W. Thompson & J. W. Medendorp (Grand Rapids: Eerdmans,

1991), 2:264.

202. Danker, *A Greek-English Lexicon of the New Testament and Other Early Christian Literature*, 522.

203. Meier, *Law and History in Matthew's Gospel: A Redactional Study of Mt. 5:17–48*, 70; G. P. Johnson, *A Semantic and Discourse Analysis of Matthew 5:17–20* (Th.M. thesis, Portland, OR: Western Conservative Baptist Seminary, 1984), 29; C. Brown, "*katalyō*," in *New International Dictionary of New Testament Theology*, ed. C. Brown (Grand Rapids, MI: Zondervan, 1986), 3:189; Louw & Nida, *Greek-English Lexicon of the New Testament: Based on Semantic Domains*, 1:682.

204. The noun is in the masculine singular form, accusative case; cf. the discussion in chapter 2 regarding *nómos*.

205. Danker, *A Greek-English Lexicon of the New Testament and Other Early Christian Literature*, 678; cf. the discussion in chapter 2 regarding this term; also, Meier, *Law and History in Matthew's Gospel: A Redactional Study of Mt. 5:17–48*, 52; H. H. Esser, "*nómos*," in *New International Dictionary of New Testament Theology*, ed. C. Brown (Grand Rapids, MI: Zondervan, 1986), 2:443; H. Hübner, "*nómos*," in *Exegetical Dictionary of the New Testament*, eds. H. Balz & G. Schneider, trans. J. W. Thompson & J. W. Medendorp (Grand Rapids: Eerdmans, 1991), 2:475; W. Gutbrod, "*nómos*," in *Theological Dictionary of the New Testament*, G. Kittel, ed., G.W. Bromiley, trans. (Grand Rapids, MI: Eerdmans, 1999), 4:1059.

206. Plummer, *An Exegetical Commentary on The Gospel According to St. Matthew*, 77; cf. the discussion of E. P. Sanders, "When Is a Law a Law? The Case of Jesus and Paul," in *Religion and Law: Biblical-Judaic and Islamic Perspectives*, eds. E. B. Firmage, B. G. Weiss, & J. W. Welch (Winona Lake, IL: Eisenbrauns, 1990), 140–142.

207. J. H. Gerstner, "Law in the NT," In *The International Standard Bible Encyclopedia*, ed. G. W. Bromiley (Grand Rapids: Eerdmans, 1986), 3:85; H. N. Ridderbos, *The Bible Student's Commentary: Matthew*, trans. R. Togtman (Grand Rapids: Zondervan, 1987), 98, 101–102.

208. Ferguson, *Kingdom Life In A Fallen World: Living Out the Sermon on the Mount*, 100.

209. The verb, which is in the aorist active infinitive form, "expresses the purpose of Jesus' coming" (Morris, *The Gospel According to Matthew*, 108).

210. Mohrlang, *Matthew and Paul: A Comparison of Ethical Perspectives*, 8; Davies & Allison, *A Critical and Exegetical Commentary on the Gospel According to Saint Matthew*, 1:485–486. G. Bornkamm, B. Gerhard, & H. J. Held (*Tradition and Interpretation in Matthew*, trans. Scott [Philadelphia: The Westminster Press, 1976], 67) state that this issue is "hotly disputed." Moreover, Sigal (*The Halakah of Jesus of Nazareth According to the Gospel of Matthew* [Lanham, MD: University Press of America, 1986], 19) observed that despite the "massive work" that has been done, it has "imparted a legacy of little clarity."

211. Cf. Johnson, *A Semantic and Discourse Analysis of Matthew 5:17–20*, 9–10; U. Luz, *Matthew 1–7: A Commentary*, trans. W. C. Linss (Minneapolis, MN: Augsburg Fortress, 1989), 260–261.

212. Danker, *A Greek-English Lexicon of the New Testament and Other Early Christian Literature*, 829; cf. Fawley, *Matthew 5:17: An Interpretation*, 43–44; Louw & Nida, *Greek-English Lexicon of the New Testament: Based on Semantic Domains*, 1:161, 405, 598, 658; Y. E. Yang, *Jesus and the Sabbath in Matthew's Gospel* (Sheffield, England: Sheffield Academic Press, 1997), 109.

213. Cf. Hendriksen, *New Testament Commentary: The Gospel of Matthew*, 290; H. H. Rowdon, "Ethics of Jesus," in *The Zondervan Pictorial Encyclopedia of the Bible*, ed. M. C. Tenney (Grand Rapids: Zondervan, 1976), 2:405; L. I. Hodges, "A Defense of

the Tripartite Understanding of the Law Articulated in the 'The Westminster Confession,'" in *Evangelical Philosophical Society*, paper read at the meeting held during November 1990 (Portland, OR: Theological Research Exchange Network, 1990), 19; S. Westerholm, "The Law in the Sermon on the Mount: Matt 5:17–48," *Criswell Theological Review*, vol. 6, no. 1 (1992), 46; E. C. Reisinger, *The Law and the Gospel* (Phillipsburg, NJ: P. & R. Publishing, 1997), 112–117.

214. H. D. Betz, "The Hermeneutical Principles of the Sermon on the Mount (Matt. 5:17–20)," *Journal of Theology for Southern Africa*, vol. 42 (1983), 17; R. Schippers, "*plēroō*," in *New International Dictionary of New Testament Theology*, ed. C. Brown (Grand Rapids, MI: Zondervan, 1986), 1:738; D. G. Bloesch, "Law and Gospel in Reformed Perspective," *Grace Theological Journal*, vol. 12, no. 2 (1991), 183.

215. T. G. Bunch, *The Ten Commandments: The Law of Liberty* (Washington, DC: Review and Herald, 1944), 177; McClain, *Law and Grace* (Winona Lake, IN: BMH Books, 1973), 15; C. S. Keener, *A Commentary on the Gospel of Matthew* (Grand Rapids: Eerdmans, 1999), 177.

216. A. M'Caig, "Law in the NT," in *The International Standard Bible Encyclopedia*, ed. J. Orr (Grand Rapids: Eerdmans, 1955), 3:1847; McConnell, *Law and Prophecy in Matthew's Gospel: The Authority and Use of the Old Testament in the Gospel of St. Matthew*, 19, 22, 25; M. J. Suggs, *Wisdom, Christology, and Law in Matthew's Gospel* (Cambridge, MA: Harvard University Press, 1970), 118–119; D. Senior, *Abingdon New Testament Commentary Series: Matthew* (Nashville: Abingdon Press, 1998), 74–75.

217. Meier, *Law and History in Matthew's Gospel: A Redactional Study of Mt. 5:17–48*, 63–64, 79–80, 123, 165.

218. R. Banks, *Jesus and the Law in the Synoptic Tradition* (London: Cambridge University Press, 1975), 210, 217; D. A. Anderson, *The Meaning and Application of Matthew 5:38–42* (Th.M. thesis, Dallas, TX: Dallas Theological Seminary, 1985), 21; France, *Matthew: Evangelist & Teacher*, 194–196.

219. Cf. B. L. Martin, "Matthew on Christ and the Law," *Theological Studies*, vol. 44, no. 1 (1983), 67; Davies & Allison, *A Critical and Exegetical Commentary on the Gospel According to Saint Matthew*, 1:486–487; R. H. Fuller, "The Decalogue in the New Testament," *Interpretation*, vol. 43, no. 3 (1989), 247; D. J. Moo, "Law," in *Dictionary of Jesus and the Gospels*, J. B. Green, S. McKnight, & I. H. Marshall, eds. (Downers Grove, IL: InterVarsity, 1992), 457; Yang, *Jesus and the Sabbath in Matthew's Gospel*, 110–111; D. L. Bock, *Jesus According to Scripture: Restoring the Portrait from the Gospels* (Grand Rapids: Baker, 2002), 132.

220. M. W. Baird, *Jesus' Use of the Decalogue in the Synoptics: An Exegetical Study* (Ph.D. dissertation, Fort Worth, TX: Southwestern Baptist Theological Seminary, 1982), 135–136; Kang, *The Literary Affinities Of The Sermon On The Mount With Special Reference To Deuteronomic Features*, 166–167; Charles, "The Greatest Or The Least In The Kingdom?: The Disciple's Relationship To The Law (Matt 5:17–20)," 142; Hagner, *Word Biblical Commentary: Matthew 1–13*, 106, 108; Young, *Jesus the Jewish Theologian*, 269; J. D. Hays, "Applying the Old Testament Law Today," *Bibliotheca Sacra*, vol. 158, no. 629 (2001), 29.

221. Carson, "Matthew," 8:144.

222. S. Osborne, "The Christian and the Law," *Bibliotheca Sacra*, vol. 109, no. 435 (1952), 242–243; J. F. Rand, "Problems in Literal Interpretation of the Sermon on the Mount: Part II," *Bibliotheca Sacra*, vol. 112, no. 446 (1955), 127; R. D. Brinsmead, "Jesus and the Law," *Verdict* (Duranbah, NSW, Australia: Verdict Publications, 1981). [article online] (accessed 1 April 2003); available from http://quango.net/ brinsmead/ je-

susandthelaw.htm; Internet.

223. Cf. Strecker, "The Law in the Sermon on the Mount, and the Sermon on the Mount as Law," 43; G. Delling, "*plēroō*," in *Theological Dictionary of the New Testament*, ed. G. Kittel, trans. G. W. Bromiley (Grand Rapids, MI: Eerdmans, 1999), 6:294.

224. Cf. W. R. Estep, "Law and Gospel in the Anabaptist/Baptist Tradition," *Grace Theological Journal*, vol. 12, no. 2 (1991), 192–193.

225. J. J. Davis, *Evangelical Ethics: Issues Facing the Church Today*, 2nd ed. (Phillipsburg, PA: Presbyterian and Reformed, 1993), 4.

226. Keener, *The IVP New Testament Commentary Series: Matthew*, 110.

227. J. Murray, *Principles of Conduct: Aspects of Biblical Ethics* (Grand Rapids: Eerdmans, 1957), 150; cf. G. Vermes (*The Religion of Jesus the Jew* [Minneapolis, MN: Fortress Press, 1993], 11–12), who maintains that "it is reasonable to infer that [Jesus] accepted, respected and observed the laws and customs regulating private and public existence which were in force among his companions in his age."

228. D. R. Bauer (*The Structure of Matthew's Gospel: A Study in Literary Design* [Sheffield, England: Sheffield Academic Press, 1988], 60) fittingly noted that "in Matthew's Gospel Jesus is the epitome of obedience to the will of God." Cf. Bonham, *A Study of the Relevance of the Sermon on the Mount in Matthew 5–7*, 178; Fawley, *Matthew 5:17: An Interpretation*, 51–52; T. Hegg, "What Does πληρῶσαι Mean in Matthew 5:17?" in *Evangelical Theological Society*, paper read at the Northwest Regional Meeting of ETS in Tacoma, Washington on 28 February 1999 (Portland, OR: Theological Research Exchange Network, 1998), 4, 6, 19; H. Hübner, "*plēroō*," in *Exegetical Dictionary of the New Testament*, eds. H. Balz & G. Schneider, trans. J. W. Thompson & J. W. Medendorp (Grand Rapids: Eerdmans, 1991), 3:109; McKnight, "Justice, Righteousness," 413–414.

229. Cf. D. Patte, *The Gospel According to Matthew: A Structural Commentary on Matthew's Faith* (Philadelphia: Fortress Press, 1987), 72–74; Garland, *Reading Matthew: A Literary and Theological Commentary on the First Gospel*, 63.

230. Cf. Bornkamm, Gerhard, & Held, *Tradition and Interpretation in Matthew*, 69–71; Lambrecht, *The Sermon on the Mount: Proclamation and Exhortation*, 84; Sigal, *The Halakah of Jesus of Nazareth According to the Gospel of Matthew*, 20.

231. Contra M. J. Cook ("Interpreting 'Pro-Jewish' Passages in Matthew," *Hebrew Union College Annual*, vol. 54 [1983], 135), who asserts that Jesus, in the Gospel of Matthew, "manifests a persistent anti-Jewish animus." In particular, Cook sees 5:17ff. as "severely denigrat[ing] Judaism" (143). Furthermore, he insists that Jesus' discourse should be "understood as displacing and superseding the Mosaic law." In contrast, this study maintains that the Savior neither denigrated the law of Moses nor used a discussion of that written code as a pretext to "catapult Jesus' law" into a status that is "much more superior" (144). Cf. L. Swidler ("The Jewishness of Jesus: Some Religious Implications for Christians," *Journal of Ecumenical Studies*, vol. 18, no. 1 [1981], 105), who concludes that Jesus was not anti-Jewish; rather, He was "a very observant Jew." Likewise, D. Flusser and R. S. Notley (*Jesus* [Jerusalem: Magnes Press, 2001], 58) maintain that "the synoptic gospels, if read through the eyes of their own time, still portray a picture of Jesus as a faithful, law-observant Jew." Similarly, M. Bockmuehl (*Jewish Law in Gentile Churches: Halakhah and the Beginning of Christian Public Ethics* [Grand Rapids: Baker, 2003], viii–ix) notes that a careful scrutiny of "the synoptic tradition produces little evidence that Jesus deliberately contravened the Torah in any substantive point." In fact, the Savior's ethical teachings were "conversant with contemporary Jewish legal debate and readily accommodated on the spectrum of 'mainstream' first-century Jewish opinion."

232. R. H. Worth, *The Sermon on the Mount: Its Old Testament Roots* (New York: Paulist Press, 1997), 37, 40, 53.
233. Cf. Lenski, *The Interpretation of St. Matthew's Gospel*, 217–218.
234. W. C. Kaiser, "Response to Douglas Moo," in *The Law, the Gospel, and the Modern Christian: Five Views*, ed. W. G. Strickland (Grand Rapids: Zondervan, 1993), 399.
235. M. Lie, *An Examination if Jesus Abolished the Law in Matthew 5:21–48* (M.A. thesis, Portland, OR: Multnomah School of the Bible, 1986), 12–13, 21–22; Vaught, *The Sermon on the Mount: A Theological Interpretation*, 55.
236. N. B. Stonehouse, *The Witness of Matthew and Mark to Christ* (Philadelphia: The Presbyterian Guardian, 1944), 199, 201; Ridderbos, *The Bible Student's Commentary: Matthew*, 102–103; Cf. Anderson, *The Meaning and Application of Matthew 5:38–42*, 10, 25.
237. K. Ahn, *The Sinaitic Covenant and Law in the Theology of Dispensationalism* (Ph.D. dissertation, Berrien Springs, MI: Andrews University, Seventh-day Adventist Theological Seminary, 1989), 281; Hagner, *Word Biblical Commentary: Matthew 1–13*, 111–112, 331.
238. Cf. Nutz, *The Unity of the Sermon on the Mount*, 83.
239. Gerstner, "Law in the NT," 3:85.
240. Worth, *The Sermon on the Mount: Its Old Testament Roots*, 41.
241. Cf. Charles, "The Greatest Or The Least In The Kingdom?: The Disciple's Relationship To The Law (Matt 5:17–20)," 154.
242. Schnackenburg, *The Moral Teaching of the New Testament*, 59.
243. B. H. Branscomb, *Jesus and the Law of Moses* (New York: Richard R. Smith, Inc., 1930), 214; G. Friedlander, *The Jewish Sources of the Sermon on the Mount* (New York: Ktav Publishing House, 1969), 33.
244. The verb is in the third person singular, aorist middle subjective form.
245. Danker, *A Greek-English Lexicon of the New Testament and Other Early Christian Literature*, 197.
246. Ibid.; cf. Meier, *Law and History in Matthew's Gospel: A Redactional Study of Mt. 5:17–48*, 53; Yang, *Jesus and the Sabbath in Matthew's Gospel*, 113.
247. W. Hackenberg, "*ginomai*," in *Exegetical Dictionary of the New Testament*, eds. H. Balz & G. Schneider, trans. J. W. Thompson & J. W. Medendorp (Grand Rapids: Eerdmans, 1991), 1:247.
248. Pink, *An Exposition of the Sermon on the Mount*, 50; Davies & Allison, *A Critical and Exegetical Commentary on the Gospel According to Saint Matthew*, 1:495; Brown, *Beyond Obedience: Jesus and the Law in Matthew 5:17–20*, 76–77.
249. J. Douma, *The Ten Commandments: Manual for the Christian Life*, trans. N. D. Kloosterman (Phillipsburg, NJ: P. & R. Publishing, 1996), 377.
250. C. Blaising & D. L. Bock, *Progressive Dispensationalism* (Wheaton, IL: Victor Books, 1993), 195.
251. Carson, "Matthew," 8:143; cf. similar arguments put forward by Moo, "Law," 458.
252. Cf. G. L. Bahnsen & K. L. Gentry, *House Divided: The Break-Up Of Dispenational Theology* (Tyler, TX: Institute for Christian Economics, 1989), 107.
253. Nutz, *The Unity of the Sermon on the Mount*, 87–88.
254. A. D. Verhey, "Ethics: NT Ethics," in *The International Standard Bible Encyclopedia*, ed. G. W. Bromiley (Grand Rapids: Eerdmans, 1982), 2:175.
255. C. M. Horne, "Law in the New Testament," in *The Zondervan Pictorial Encyclopedia of the Bible*, ed. M. C. Tenny (Grand Rapids: Zondervan, 1976), 3:894.
256. Morris, *The Gospel According to Matthew*, 111.
257. Lloyd-Jones, *Studies in the Sermon on the Mount*, 1:207.

258. Cf. J. M. Sprinkle, "Law," in *Evangelical Dictionary of Biblical Theology*, ed. W. A. Elwell, (Grand Rapids: Baker, 1996), 470.
259. Vaught, *The Sermon on the Mount: A Theological Interpretation*, 56.
260. McNeile, *The Gospel According to St. Matthew*, 59; Harrington & Keenan, *Jesus and Virtue Ethics: Building Bridges between New Testament Studies and Moral Theology*, 78.
261. Lambrecht, *The Sermon on the Mount: Proclamation and Exhortation*, 87; Hegg, "What Does πληρῶσαι Mean in Matthew 5:17?", 9–12.
262. Meier, *Law and History in Matthew's Gospel: A Redactional Study of Mt. 5:17–48*, 90–92; Luz, *Matthew 1–7: A Commentary*, 267.
263. Bunch, *The Ten Commandments: The Law of Liberty*, 186.
264. Strecker, *The Sermon On The Mount: An Exegetical Commentary*, 57.
265. Guelich, *The Sermon on the Mount: A Foundation for Understanding*, 152.
266. Ibid.
267. G. L. Bahnsen, "Theonomic Reformed Approach to Law and Gospel," in *The Law, the Gospel, and the Modern Christian: Five Views*, ed. W. G. Strickland (Grand Rapids: Zondervan, 1993), 117.
268. M. G. Klein, "Comments on an Old-New Error," *Westminster Theological Journal*, vol. 41 (1978), 178.
269. J. Zens, "The Believer's Rule of Life: A Study of Two Extremes. Postponed Ethics: Lewis Sperry Chafer. Retrogressive Ethics: Greg Bahnsen," *Baptist Reformation Review*, vol. 8, no. 4 (1979), 16.
270. Chafer, *Chafer's Systematic Theology*, 4:220.
271. Cf. Campbell, *Interpretation And Exposition Of The Sermon On The Mount*, 103; Rand, "Problems in Literal Interpretation of the Sermon on the Mount: Part II," 126; Pentecost, *Things to Come: A Study in Biblical Eschatology* (Grand Rapids: Eerdmans 1958), 317.
272. Chafer, *Chafer's Systematic Theology*, 5:105.
273. Cf. L. S. Chafer, "The Teachings of Christ Incarnate, Part 1: The Sermon on the Mount," *Bibliotheca Sacra*, vol. 108, no. 432 (1951), 391–394 J. L. Benson, *The Kingdom Proffered and Postponed* (Unpublished notes, Johnson City, New York: Baptist Bible Seminary, 1967), 53–54.
274. G. E. Ladd, *A Theology of the New Testament: Revised Edition*, ed. D. A. Hagner (Grand Rapids: Eerdmans, 1993), 132.
275. Hendriksen, *New Testament Commentary: The Gospel of Matthew*, 292.
276. J. Stalker, "Ethics of Jesus," in *The International Standard Bible Encyclopedia*, ed. J. Orr (Grand Rapids: Eerdmans, 1939), 2:1027.
277. Cf. Toon, "Righteousness," 687.
278. Carson, "Matthew," 8:147; Mohrlang, *Matthew and Paul: A Comparison of Ethical Perspectives*, 19; Worth, *The Sermon on the Mount: Its Old Testament Roots*, 56.
279. D. G. Bloesch, *Freedom for Obedience: Evangelical Ethics in Contemporary Times* (San Francisco: Harper & Row, Publishers, 1987), 71; Betz, *The Sermon on the Mount*, 193.
280. Yang, *Jesus and the Sabbath in Matthew's Gospel*, 118.
281. Gerstner, "Law in the NT," 3:85; Davies & Allison, *A Critical and Exegetical Commentary on the Gospel According to Saint Matthew*, 1:499–500; contra Nutz, *The Unity of the Sermon on the Mount*, 84.
282. Diehl, "Righteousness," 1033.
283. Ferguson, *Kingdom Life In A Fallen World: Living Out the Sermon on the Mount*, 106.
284. Murray, *Principles of Conduct: Aspects of Biblical Ethics*, 155.

285. Chafer, *Chafer's Systematic Theology*, 5:106.
286. Lloyd-Jones, *Studies in the Sermon on the Mount*, 1:208.
287. K. R. Snodgrass, "Matthew's Understanding of the Law," *Interpretation*, vol. 46, no. 4 (1992), 373.
288. Cf. the discussion in chapter 2 regarding the purposes of the law.
289. S. E. Lauer, "Must We Obey the Law?," *A Journal of Biblical-Theological Preaching*, vol. 8 (1993), 12.
290. K. L. Barker, "False dichotomies Between the Testaments," *Journal of the Evangelical Theological Society*, vol. 25, no. 1 (1982), 5–6.
291. Cf. I. A. Audu, *Christ's Interpretation of the Law* (Th.M. thesis, Dallas, TX: Dallas Theological Seminary, 1990), 69; A. W. Watson, *Jesus and the Law* (Athens, GA: The University of Georgia Press, 1996), 101–102.
292. Lie, *An Examination if Jesus Abolished the Law in Matthew 5:21–48*, 23; Charles, "The Greatest Or The Least In The Kingdom?: The Disciple's Relationship To The Law (Matt 5:17–20)," 142–143; Morris, *The Gospel According to Matthew*, 112.
293. Carson, "Matthew," 8:148.
294. Kang, *The Literary Affinities Of The Sermon On The Mount With Special Reference To Deuteronomic Features*, 196.
295. M. J. Erickson, *Christian Theology*, 2nd ed. (Grand Rapids: Baker, 1998), 989–990.
296. Cf. McConnell, *Law and Prophecy in Matthew's Gospel: The Authority and Use of the Old Testament in the Gospel of St. Matthew*, 43, 91; R. E. Nixon, "Matthew," in *The New Bible Commentary Revised*, eds. D. Guthrie & J. A. Motyer (Grand Rapids: Eerdmans, 1970), 822; Albright & Mann, *The Anchor Bible: Matthew*, 60.
297. M. C. Tenny, *New Testament Survey* (Grand Rapids: Eerdmans, 1961), 146.
298. Contra Strecker, *Theology of the New Testament*, 385; cf. R. Banks, *Jesus and the Law in the Synoptic Tradition* (London: Cambridge University Press, 1975), 184–185. In connection with this discussion, Draper ("The Genesis and Narrative Thrust of the Paraenesis in the Sermon on the Mount," 32) not only affirms the continuity of Jesus' teaching "with the Torah," but also that this "continuity is more likely at the root of Matthew's usage" of the Torah.
299. C. Vaught, *The Sermon on the Mount: A Theological Interpretation* (New York: State University of New York Press, 1986), xii; Charles, "The Greatest Or The Least In The Kingdom?: The Disciple's Relationship To The Law (Matt 5:17–20)," 144; P. Fairbairn, *The Revelation of the Law in Scripture* (Phillipsburg, NJ: P. & R. Publishing, 1996), 227–230; Worth, *The Sermon on the Mount: Its Old Testament Roots*, 37–38.
300. H. G. Link, "*egō eimi*," in *New International Dictionary of New Testament Theology*, ed. C. Brown (Grand Rapids, Michigan: Zondervan, 1986), 2:281.
301. Lapide (*The Sermon on the Mount: Utopia or Program for Action?* trans. A. Swidler [Maryknoll, NY: Orbis Books, 1986], 14) offered this clarifying thought: "Matthew saw his Master not as a new lawgiver but as the legitimate interpreter of God's will as contained in the Torah. Jesus is no anti-Moses to Matthew, but rather one who carries on from Moses who had begun to expound the teaching of Sinai in his own time."
302. H. Weder, "'But I Say to You...' Concerning the Foundations of Jesus' Interpretation of the Law in the 'Sermon on the Mount,'" in *Text and Logos: The Humanistic Interpretation of the New Testament*, ed. T. W. Jennings (Atlanta: Scholars Press, 1990), 221.
303. Ferguson, *Kingdom Life In A Fallen World: Living Out the Sermon on the Mount*, 22.
304. Keener, *The IVP New Testament Commentary Series: Matthew*, 114; Keener, *A Commentary on the Gospel of Matthew*, 182.
305. McConnell, *Law and Prophecy in Matthew's Gospel: The Authority and Use of the*

Old Testament in the Gospel of St. Matthew, 49.

306. Betz, *The Sermon on the Mount*, 216.
307. Baird, *Jesus' Use of the Decalogue in the Synoptics: An Exegetical Study*, 137.
308. Cf. Kang, *The Literary Affinities Of The Sermon On The Mount With Special Reference To Deuteronomic Features*, 118.
309. Ferguson, *Kingdom Life In A Fallen World: Living Out the Sermon on the Mount*, 114.
310. Hendriksen, *New Testament Commentary: The Gospel of Matthew*, 296–297.
311. Plummer, *An Exegetical Commentary on The Gospel According to St. Matthew*, 79.
312. McNeile, *The Gospel According to St. Matthew*, 60; Baird, *Jesus' Use of the Decalogue in the Synoptics: An Exegetical Study*, 117, 122, 126; J. D. Nystrom, *A Semantic Structure Analysis of Matthew 5:33–48* (M.A. thesis, Deerfield, IL: Trinity Evangelical Divinity School, 1986), 45–46; Loader, *Jesus' Attitude Towards the Law: A Study of the Gospels*, 181.
313. Some Greek manuscripts add "without cause" (εἰκῆ, *eikē*). Regarding this variant, D. A. Black ("Jesus on Anger: The Text of Matthew 5:22a Revisited," *Novum Testamentum*, vol. 30 [1988], 2) maintains that "the text of Matt 5:22a remains open" and that the variant, "if not original, should at least be reconsidered in scholarly discussions of this passage."
314. R. D. Congdon, "Did Jesus Sustain The Law In Matthew 5?," *Bibliotheca Sacra*, vol. 135, no. 538 (1978), 118.
315. Toussaint, *Behold The King: A Study of Matthew*, 100.
316. Louw & Nida, *Greek-English Lexicon of the New Testament: Based on Semantic Domains*, 1:388.
317. Davies & Allison, *A Critical and Exegetical Commentary on the Gospel According to Saint Matthew*, 1:513; Danker, *A Greek-English Lexicon of the New Testament and Other Early Christian Literature*, 903.
318. Allen, *A Critical and Exegetical Commentary on the Gospel According to St. Matthew*, 318; Guelich, *The Sermon on the Mount: A Foundation for Understanding*, 186; Luz, *Matthew 1–7: A Commentary*, 282.
319. Cf. Phillips, *Exploring the Gospels: Matthew*, 98.
320. O. Böcher, "*geenna*," in *Exegetical Dictionary of the New Testament*, eds. H. Balz & G. Schneider, trans. J. W. Thompson & J. W. Medendorp (Grand Rapids: Eerdmans, 1991), 1:239.
321. G. A. Lee, "Gehenna," in *The International Standard Bible Encyclopedia*, ed. G. W. Bromiley (Grand Rapids: Eerdmans, 1982), 2:423.
322. H. Bietenhard, "*gehenna*," in *New International Dictionary of New Testament Theology*, ed. C. Brown (Grand Rapids, MI: Zondervan, 1986), 2:208.
323. R. E. Davies, "Gehenna," in *The Zondervan Pictorial Encyclopedia of the Bible*, ed. M. C. Tenney (Grand Rapids: Zondervan, 1976), 2:671.
324. Pentecost, *Things to Come: A Study in Biblical Eschatology*, 559; Gundry, *Matthew: A Commentary on His Literary and Theological Art*, 85.
325. Garland, *Reading Matthew: A Literary and Theological Commentary on the First Gospel*, 65.
326. Betz, *The Sermon on the Mount*, 226.
327. The monetary unit Jesus mentioned was a quadrans, the smallest copper Roman coin and equal to 1/64 of a denarius (Lange, "The Gospel According to Matthew: Together With A General Theological And Homiletical Introduction To The New Testament," 8:114).
328. Ridderbos, *The Bible Student's Commentary: Matthew*, 107.

329. Carson, "Matthew," 8:150.
330. Lenski, *The Interpretation of St. Matthew's Gospel*, 225; Strecker, *The Sermon On The Mount: An Exegetical Commentary*, 77; Hodges, "A Defense of the Tripartite Understanding of the Law Articulated in the 'The Westminster Confession,'" 15.
331. Hendriksen, *New Testament Commentary: The Gospel of Matthew*, 302; Lie, *An Examination if Jesus Abolished the Law in Matthew 5:21–48*, 28–29; Ridderbos, *The Bible Student's Commentary: Matthew*, 109–110.
332. Ferguson, *Kingdom Life In A Fallen World: Living Out the Sermon on the Mount*, 119.
333. Lloyd-Jones, *Studies in the Sermon on the Mount*, 1:232.
334. Betz, *The Sermon on the Mount*, 233.
335. Kang, *The Literary Affinities Of The Sermon On The Mount With Special Reference To Deuteronomic Features*, 261–262; Worth, *The Sermon on the Mount: Its Old Testament Roots*, 96–97; Keener, *A Commentary on the Gospel of Matthew*, 189.
336. Hendriksen, *New Testament Commentary: The Gospel of Matthew*, 302; Baird, *Jesus' Use of the Decalogue in the Synoptics: An Exegetical Study*, 160.
337. Congdon, "Did Jesus Sustain The Law In Matthew 5?," 120.
338. Morris, *The Gospel According to Matthew*, 118–119.
339. Nutz, *The Unity of the Sermon on the Mount*, 94; Davies & Allison, *A Critical and Exegetical Commentary on the Gospel According to Saint Matthew*, 1:524; G. H. Stassen, "The Fourteen Triads of the Sermon on the Mount (Matthew 5:21–7:12)," *Journal of Biblical Literature*, vol. 122, no. 2 (2003), 275.
340. Plummer, *An Exegetical Commentary on The Gospel According to St. Matthew*, 81.
341. J. F. Walvoord, *Matthew: Thy Kingdom Come* (Chicago: Moody Press, 1974), 49. Guelich (*The Sermon on the Mount: A Foundation for Understanding*, 196) fittingly remarked: "The action prescribed here and later regarding amputating one's hand could hardly be more pointed. It clearly intends to convey drastic measures."
342. Betz, *The Sermon on the Mount*, 237.
343. J. D. M. Derrett, *Law in the New Testament* (London: Darton, Longman & Todd Limited, 1970), 380.
344. Douma, *The Ten Commandments: Manual for the Christian Life*, 271.
345. Betz, *The Sermon on the Mount*, 244.
346. H. S. Songer, "The Sermon on the Mount and Its Jewish Foreground," *Review & Expositor*, vol. 89, no. 2 (1992), 168–169.
347. Toussaint, *Behold The King: A Study of Matthew*, 102; Harrington & Keenan, *Jesus and Virtue Ethics: Building Bridges between New Testament Studies and Moral Theology*, 152.
348. Carson, "Matthew," 8:152.
349. Douma, *The Ten Commandments: Manual for the Christian Life*, 273.
350. Nutz, *The Unity of the Sermon on the Mount*, 98.
351. Lloyd-Jones, *Studies in the Sermon on the Mount*, 1:257.
352. Derrett, *Law in the New Testament*, 377.
353. Lie, *An Examination if Jesus Abolished the Law in Matthew 5:21–48*, 34; Audu, *Christ's Interpretation of the Law*, 56.
354. Strecker, *The Sermon On The Mount: An Exegetical Commentary*, 75.
355. Sigal, *The Halakah of Jesus of Nazareth According to the Gospel of Matthew*, 98.
356. Derrett, *Law in the New Testament*, 384.
357. Hegg, "What Does πληρῶσαι Mean in Matthew 5:17?", 16; cf. Stonehouse, *The Witness of Matthew and Mark to Christ*, 204–205.
358. Sigal, *The Halakah of Jesus of Nazareth According to the Gospel of Matthew*, 91.

359. Hegg, "What Does πληρῶσαι Mean in Matthew 5:17?", 16.
360. Luz, *Matthew 1–7: A Commentary*, 310.
361. Keener, *A Commentary on the Gospel of Matthew*, 192.
362. Ferguson, *Kingdom Life In A Fallen World: Living Out the Sermon on the Mount*, 131; Lie, *An Examination if Jesus Abolished the Law in Matthew 5:21–48*, 35–36.
363. Plummer, *An Exegetical Commentary on The Gospel According to St. Matthew*, 82.
364. Toussaint, *Behold The King: A Study of Matthew*, 103.
365. Cf. Congdon, "Did Jesus Sustain The Law In Matthew 5?," 122; Kang, *The Literary Affinities Of The Sermon On The Mount With Special Reference To Deuteronomic Features*, 91; Songer, "The Sermon on the Mount and Its Jewish Foreground," 169; D. Garlington, "Oath-Taking In The Community Of The New Age (Matthew 5:33–37)," *Trinity Journal*, vol. 16, no. 2 (1995), 161–163; Stassen, "The Fourteen Triads of the Sermon on the Mount (Matthew 5:21–7:12)," 278.
366. Slemp, *Twelve Laws of Life: A Study of the Ten Commandments and Related Teachings of Jesus*, 35–36.
367. Carson, "Matthew," 8:153.
368. Hendriksen, *New Testament Commentary: The Gospel of Matthew*, 308; Garlington, "Oath-Taking In The Community Of The New Age (Matthew 5:33–37)," 163–164.
369. Garland, *Reading Matthew: A Literary and Theological Commentary on the First Gospel*, 72.
370. Douma, *The Ten Commandments: Manual for the Christian Life*, 89.
371. Nystrom, *A Semantic Structure Analysis of Matthew 5:33–48*, 69.
372. Betz, *The Sermon on the Mount*, 270.
373. For example, Anabaptists, Quakers, and Jehovah's Witnesses (Douma, *The Ten Commandments: Manual for the Christian Life*, 92).
374. Carson, "Matthew," 8:154; Davies & Allison, *A Critical and Exegetical Commentary on the Gospel According to Saint Matthew*, 1:535.
375. McNeile, *The Gospel According to St. Matthew*, 67.
376. Pink, *An Exposition of the Sermon on the Mount*, 106.
377. Lange, "The Gospel According to Matthew: Together With A General Theological And Homiletical Introduction To The New Testament," 8:116.
378. Cf. Kang, *The Literary Affinities Of The Sermon On The Mount With Special Reference To Deuteronomic Features*, 52.
379. Bonham, *A Study of the Relevance of the Sermon on the Mount in Matthew 5–7*, 156; Audu, *Christ's Interpretation of the Law*, 59; Hagner, *Word Biblical Commentary: Matthew 1–13*, 129.
380. Martin, "Matthew on Christ and the Law," 56.
381. Betz, *The Sermon on the Mount*, 283.
382. Morris, *The Gospel According to Matthew*, 126.
383. Anderson, *The Meaning and Application of Matthew 5:38–42*, 26–27.
384. Ferguson, *Kingdom Life In A Fallen World: Living Out the Sermon on the Mount*, 135.
385. Guelich, *The Sermon on the Mount: A Foundation for Understanding*, 250.
386. Lloyd-Jones, *Studies in the Sermon on the Mount*, 1:273.
387. Hendriksen, *New Testament Commentary: The Gospel of Matthew*, 310.
388. Lie, *An Examination if Jesus Abolished the Law in Matthew 5:21–48*, 39; Phillips, *Exploring the Gospels: Matthew*, 105.
389. Ridderbos, *The Bible Student's Commentary: Matthew*, 113.
390. Hegg ("What Does πληρῶσαι Mean in Matthew 5:17?", 18) reflects this view when he writes as follows: "Yeshua, then, is teaching His disciples to favor the life of kindness

and mercy and to entrust themselves to the care of the Father Who would meet all their needs."

391. Carson, "Matthew," 8:155.
392. Plummer, *An Exegetical Commentary on The Gospel According to St. Matthew*, 85; Davies & Allison, *A Critical and Exegetical Commentary on the Gospel According to Saint Matthew*, 1:540.
393. Guelich, *The Sermon on the Mount: A Foundation for Understanding*, 221–222; Nystrom, *A Semantic Structure Analysis of Matthew 5:33–48*, 81–82, 84; Keener, *The IVP New Testament Commentary Series: Matthew*, 128.
394. Barclay, *The Old Law and the New Law: The Ten Commandments and the Sermon on the Mount*, 72; Songer, "The Sermon on the Mount and Its Jewish Foreground," 173; Betz, *The Sermon on the Mount*, 289–290.
395. "Coat" (Matt. 5:40), or tunic, refers to a long garment worn under a cloak next to the skin.
396. "Cloak" (Matt. 5:40) refers to a loose outer garment.
397. For example, as a guide or as a burden carrier; cf. L. J. White, "Grid and Group in Matthew's Community: The Righteousness/Honor Code in the Sermon on the Mount," *Semeia*, vol. 35 (1986), 76.
398. Nutz, *The Unity of the Sermon on the Mount*, 106.
399. Pentecost, *The Words and Works of Jesus Christ*, 181.
400. Carson, "Matthew," 8:156–157.
401. McNeile, *The Gospel According to St. Matthew*, 70.
402. Lange, "The Gospel According to Matthew: Together With A General Theological And Homiletical Introduction To The New Testament," 8:117–118.
403. Anderson, *The Meaning and Application of Matthew 5:38–42*, 37.
404. Schnackenburg, *The Moral Teaching of the New Testament*, 80–81.
405. Cf. Keener, *The IVP New Testament Commentary Series: Matthew*, 133.
406. Cf. Congdon, "Did Jesus Sustain The Law In Matthew 5?," 124.
407. Lohse, *Theological Ethics of the New Testament*, 57; Garland, *Reading Matthew: A Literary and Theological Commentary on the First Gospel*, 76–77.
408. Lenski, *The Interpretation of St. Matthew's Gospel*, 245; Kang, *The Literary Affinities Of The Sermon On The Mount With Special Reference To Deuteronomic Features*, 97–98; Ridderbos, *The Bible Student's Commentary: Matthew*, 116.
409. McNeile, *The Gospel According to St. Matthew*, 72; Nystrom, *A Semantic Structure Analysis of Matthew 5:33–48*, 105–106, 132; Davies & Allison, *A Critical and Exegetical Commentary on the Gospel According to Saint Matthew*, 1:550. Baird (*Jesus' Use of the Decalogue in the Synoptics: An Exegetical Study*, 109) notes that "in Jesus' day the definition was not commonly agreed upon." While "the Old Testament context and a part of Jewish interpretation restricted the meaning to fellow-Israelites, the terms were recognized for their all-inclusive nature" and "came to be interpreted by many as embracing all or the greater part of mankind." Baird moreover states that "both views were present in the debate"; cf. Schrage, *The Ethics of the New Testament*, 73–74.
410. Lie, *An Examination if Jesus Abolished the Law in Matthew 5:21–48*, 42.
411. Hendriksen, *New Testament Commentary: The Gospel of Matthew*, 313.
412. Ferguson, *Kingdom Life In A Fallen World: Living Out the Sermon on the Mount*, 140.
413. Ibid., 88.
414. Massey, *Interpreting the Sermon on the Mount in the Light of Jewish Tradition as Evidenced in the Palestinian Targums of the Pentateuch: Selected Themes*, 55, 60.
415. Carson, "Matthew," 8:158–159.

416. Plummer (*An Exegetical Commentary on The Gospel According to St. Matthew*, 89) cogently noted: "To return evil for good is devilish; to return good for good is human; to return good for evil is divine."
417. Betz, *The Sermon on the Mount*, 318.
418. Nystrom, *A Semantic Structure Analysis of Matthew 5:33–48*, 114–115. *The Net Bible* (Garland, Texas: Biblical Studies Press, L.L.C., and the authors [Web:] http://www.bible.org/netbible/index.htm. [Date of access: 13 March 2003], 2001) offers this helpful explanatory note (emphasis theirs): "The *tax collectors* would bid to collect taxes for the Roman government and then add a surcharge, which they kept. Since tax collectors worked for Rome, they were viewed as traitors to their own people and were not well liked."
419. Kodjak, *A Structural Analysis Of The Sermon On The Mount*, 99.
420. Carson ("Matthew," 8:159) suggested that Jesus was referring to like-minded followers of God.
421. France, *Jesus and the Old Testament: His Application of Old Testament Passages to Himself and His Mission*, 61; Douma, *The Ten Commandments: Manual for the Christian Life*, 23–24. Friedlander (*The Jewish Sources of the Sermon on the Mount*, 84) appropriately commented as follows: "This statement is clearly intended to be a summary of all that Jesus has said in the Sermon up to this point. From the artistic standpoint, it must be granted that no finer culminating passage could possibly have been selected."
422. Danker, *A Greek-English Lexicon of the New Testament and Other Early Christian Literature*, 996; cf. Davies & Allison, *A Critical and Exegetical Commentary on the Gospel According to Saint Matthew*, 1:561.
423. Louw & Nida, *Greek-English Lexicon of the New Testament: Based on Semantic Domains*, 1:754.
424. Kang, *The Literary Affinities Of The Sermon On The Mount With Special Reference To Deuteronomic Features*, 223; cf. Fuller, "The Decalogue in the New Testament," 247–248.
425. Allen, *A Critical and Exegetical Commentary on the Gospel According to St. Matthew*, 56; R. Schippers, "*telos*," in *New International Dictionary of New Testament Theology*, ed. C. Brown (Grand Rapids, MI: Zondervan, 1986), 2:63. G. H. Stassen ("Grace and Deliverance in the Sermon on the Mount," *Review & Expositor*, vol. 89, no. 2 [1992], 232) aptly notes that "love is at the heart of the Sermon on the Mount."
426. G. Delling, "*téleios*," in *Theological Dictionary of the New Testament*, ed. G. Kittel, trans. G. W. Bromiley (Grand Rapids, MI: Eerdmans, 1999), 8:74; cf. Flusser & Notley, *Jesus*, 83.
427. Bruner, *Matthew, A Commentary, Volume 1*, 224; Schrage, *The Ethics of the New Testament*, 40; Stassen, "The Fourteen Triads of the Sermon on the Mount (Matthew 5:21–7:12)," 282. Meier (*Law and History in Matthew's Gospel: A Redactional Study of Mt. 5:17–48*, 131) reflects this sentiment when he notes that *téleios* conveys the "idea of whole-hearted, sincere, honest, undivided devotion to Yahweh."
428. A site in Palestine near the northwest shore of the Dead Sea.
429. H. Hübner, "*teleios*," in *Exegetical Dictionary of the New Testament*, eds. H. Balz & G. Schneider, trans. J. W. Thompson & J. W. Medendorp (Grand Rapids: Eerdmans, 1991), 3:343; cf. Luz, *Matthew 1–7: A Commentary*, 346. Häring ("Normative Value of the Sermon on the Mount," 378–379) fittingly noted that "the requirement of perfection must not be confused with an ethic of anthropocentric self-perfection or with an abstract virtuous ideal of perfection." This position is contra that of Przybylski

(*Righteousness in Matthew and His World of Thought*, 85–87), who maintains that the concept of absolute moral perfection (as seen in a meticulous observance of the law) was being emphasized.

430. Hendriksen, *New Testament Commentary: The Gospel of Matthew*, 317.
431. J. G. Williams, "Paraenesis, Excess, and Ethics: Matthew's Rhetoric in the Sermon on the Mount," *Semeia*, vol. 50 (1990), 171, 177.
432. Toussaint, *Behold The King: A Study of Matthew*, 105; Nystrom, *A Semantic Structure Analysis of Matthew 5:33–48*, 124–126.
433. Walvoord, *Matthew: Thy Kingdom Come*, 51.
434. Betz, *The Sermon on the Mount*, 323–324.
435. Strecker, *The Sermon On The Mount: An Exegetical Commentary*, 113.
436. Lenski, *The Interpretation of St. Matthew's Gospel*, 254.
437. Luz, *Matthew 1–7: A Commentary*, 354.
438. Carson, "Matthew," 162–163.
439. This included charitable giving (cf. 6:2–4), praying (cf. vss. 5–15), and fasting (cf. vss. 16–18).
440. Morris, *The Gospel According to Matthew*, 135–136.
441. Guelich, *The Sermon on the Mount: A Foundation for Understanding*, 1982.
442. Σαλπίσῃς is the second person singular, aorist active subjunctive of σαλπίζω.
443. Keener, *The IVP New Testament Commentary Series: Matthew*, 137.
444. Plummer, *An Exegetical Commentary on The Gospel According to St. Matthew*, 91.
445. McNeile, *The Gospel According to St. Matthew*, 74.
446. Lange, "The Gospel According to Matthew: Together With A General Theological And Homiletical Introduction To The New Testament," 8:122.
447. Carson, "Matthew," 8:164.
448. For example, when the benefactors were in the synagogues and streets.
449. Hendriksen, *New Testament Commentary: The Gospel of Matthew*, 320; Davies & Allison, *A Critical and Exegetical Commentary on the Gospel According to Saint Matthew*, 1:579.
450. Betz, *The Sermon on the Mount*, 355.
451. Gore, *The Sermon on the Mount: A Practical Exposition*, 109–110.
452. Spicq, *Theological Lexicon of the New Testament*, 3:407–408.
453. Danker, *A Greek-English Lexicon of the New Testament and Other Early Christian Literature*, 1038.
454. Louw & Nida, *Greek-English Lexicon of the New Testament: Based on Semantic Domains*, 1:766.
455. W. Günther, "*hypokrino*," in *New International Dictionary of New Testament Theology*, ed. C. Brown (Grand Rapids, MI: Zondervan, 1986), 2:469.
456. Strecker, *The Sermon On The Mount: An Exegetical Commentary*, 99.
457. Ferguson, *Kingdom Life In A Fallen World: Living Out the Sermon on the Mount*, 148.
458. Plummer, *An Exegetical Commentary on The Gospel According to St. Matthew*, 91.
459. McNeile, *The Gospel According to St. Matthew*, 73. U. Wilckens ("*hypokrínomai*," in *Theological Dictionary of the New Testament*, ed. G. Kittel, trans. G. W. Bromiley [Grand Rapids, MI: Eerdmans, 1999], 8:568) made the following cogent observation: "The ὑπόκρισις of the adversaries consists in the fact that they are concerned about their status with men rather than their standing before God. They thus fail to achieve the righteousness which they pretend to have. Their hypocrisy will be their ruin in God's judgment."
460. Friedlander, *The Jewish Sources of the Sermon on the Mount*, 93–94.

461. Nutz, *The Unity of the Sermon on the Mount*, 129–130.
462. Gundry, *Matthew: A Commentary on His Literary and Theological Art*, 103.
463. Guelich, *The Sermon on the Mount: A Foundation for Understanding*, 281.
464. *The Net Bible* states that Greek noun rendered "room" (ταμεῖον, Matt. 6:6) refers to the "inner room of a house." This chamber was "normally without any windows opening outside." It thus was "the most private location possible."
465. Lange, "The Gospel According to Matthew: Together With A General Theological And Homiletical Introduction To The New Testament," 8:123.
466. Hendriksen, *New Testament Commentary: The Gospel of Matthew*, 322.
467. D. E. Garland, "The Lord's Prayer in the Gospel of Matthew," *Review & Expositor*, vol. 89, no. 2 (1992), 216.
468. Carson, "Matthew," 8:166.
469. Douma, *The Ten Commandments: Manual for the Christian Life*, 86.
470. Betz, *The Sermon on the Mount*, 367.
471. Morris, *The Gospel According to Matthew*, 142; Garland, *Reading Matthew: A Literary and Theological Commentary on the First Gospel*, 79.
472. Plummer, *An Exegetical Commentary on The Gospel According to St. Matthew*, 93–94.
473. Cf. B. Gerhardsson, "The Matthaean Version of the Lord's Prayer," in *The New Testament Age: Essays in Honor of Bo Reicke*, ed. W. C. Weinrich (Macon, GA: Mercer University Press, 1984), 208.
474. Albright & Mann, *The Anchor Bible: Matthew*, 75; Bock, *Jesus According to Scripture: Restoring the Portrait from the Gospels*, 140.
475. T. E. Mills, "The Significance of The Lord's Prayer For Understanding The New Testament Today," in *Evangelical Theological Society*, paper read at the Annual Meeting of the Southeast Division of ETS on March 16, 2002 (Portland, OR: Theological Research Exchange Network, 2002), 4.
476. Kim, *The Function and Meaning of the Lord's Prayer in the Sermon on the Mount*, 61; cf. B. H. Young, *The Jewish Background to the Lord's Prayer* (Tulsa, OK: Gospel Research Foundation Inc., 1984), 1.
477. D. E. Lanier, "The Lord's Prayer: Matt 6:9–13–A Thematic and Semantic-Structural Analysis," *Criswell Theological Review*, vol. 6, no. 1 (1992), 60–61.
478. Marshall, *Commentary on Luke*, 455.
479. J. F. Rand, "Problems in Literal Interpretation of the Sermon on the Mount: Part I," *Bibliotheca Sacra*, vol. 112, no. 445 (1955), 37; Campbell, *Interpretation And Exposition Of The Sermon On The Mount*, 151.
480. R. E. Brown, "The Pater Noster As An Eschatological Prayer," *Theological Studies*, vol. 22 (1961), 175.
481. Garland, "The Lord's Prayer in the Gospel of Matthew," 215.
482. Pink, *An Exposition of the Sermon on the Mount*, 159–160.
483. Cf. Gerhardsson, "The Matthaean Version of the Lord's Prayer," 210; Davies & Allison, *A Critical and Exegetical Commentary on the Gospel According to Saint Matthew*, 1:590–599.
484. A. A. Trites, "The Blessings and Warnings of the Kingdom (Matthew 5:3–12; 7:13–27)," *Review & Expositor*, vol. 89, no. 2 (1992), 183.
485. Guelich, *The Sermon on the Mount: A Foundation for Understanding*, 284.
486. Carson, "Matthew," 8:168; Ridderbos, *The Bible Student's Commentary: Matthew*, 126; J. C. O'Neill, "The Lord's Prayer," *Journal for the Study of the New Testament*, vol. 51 (1993), 5–6.
487. J. C. Jeffries, *The Law in the Prayer: The Ten Commandments in the Lord's Prayer*

(New York: Exposition Press, 1952), 16–17; Lenski, *The Interpretation of St. Matthew's Gospel*, 265; Kim, *The Function and Meaning of the Lord's Prayer in the Sermon on the Mount*, 65–66, 149–150.

488. *The Net Bible;* cf. Luz, *Matthew 1–7: A Commentary*, 375–377; Mills, "The Significance of The Lord's Prayer For Understanding The New Testament Today," 5.
489. It appears in the third person singular, aorist passive imperative form.
490. Danker, *A Greek-English Lexicon of the New Testament and Other Early Christian Literature*, 10.
491. Louw & Nida, *Greek-English Lexicon of the New Testament: Based on Semantic Domains*, 1:745–746.
492. C. Brown, "*hagios*," in *New International Dictionary of New Testament Theology*, ed. C. Brown (Grand Rapids, MI: Zondervan, 1986), 2:229; cf. Young, *The Jewish Background to the Lord's Prayer*, 7–8.
493. Toussaint, *Behold The King: A Study of Matthew*, 108.
494. O. Procksch, "*hágios*," in *Theological Dictionary of the New Testament*, ed. G. Kittel, trans. G. W. Bromiley (Grand Rapids, MI: Eerdmans, 1999), 1:101; cf. Stassen ("The Fourteen Triads of the Sermon on the Mount [Matthew 5:21–7:12]," 305), who considers "the first petition of the Lord's prayer" as most likely being "connected with the revelation of YHWH in Exod 19 and 20."
495. Strecker, *The Sermon On The Mount: An Exegetical Commentary*, 112; Hagner, *Word Biblical Commentary: Matthew 1–13*, 147.
496. Jeffries, *The Law in the Prayer: The Ten Commandments in the Lord's Prayer*, 20–21.
497. Plummer, *An Exegetical Commentary on The Gospel According to St. Matthew*, 97.
498. Gerhardsson, "The Matthaean Version of the Lord's Prayer," 211.
499. Garland, "The Lord's Prayer in the Gospel of Matthew," 218.
500. Jeffries, *The Law in the Prayer: The Ten Commandments in the Lord's Prayer*, 48–49, 51.
501. L. Morris, *The Gospel According to St. Luke* (Grand Rapids: Eerdmans, 1974), 194; Kim, *The Function and Meaning of the Lord's Prayer in the Sermon on the Mount*, 101–102, 107, 110.
502. Young, *The Jewish Background to the Lord's Prayer*, 20; Ferguson, *Kingdom Life In A Fallen World: Living Out the Sermon on the Mount*, 164; Garland, "The Lord's Prayer in the Gospel of Matthew," 221.
503. C. Müller, "*epiousios*," in *Exegetical Dictionary of the New Testament*, eds. H. Balz & G. Schneider, trans. J. W. Thompson & J. W. Medendorp (Grand Rapids: Eerdmans, 1991), 2:32; cf. Brown, "The Pater Noster As An Eschatological Prayer," 195; E. M. Yamauchi, "The 'Daily Bread' Motif In Antiquity," *Westminster Theological Journal*, vol. 28, no. 2 (1966), 145; O'Neill, "The Lord's Prayer," 12.
504. Danker, *A Greek-English Lexicon of the New Testament and Other Early Christian Literature*, 376–377; cf. Louw & Nida, *Greek-English Lexicon of the New Testament: Based on Semantic Domains*, 1:652, 654; R. W. Byargeon, "Echoes Of Wisdom In The Lord's Prayer (Matt 6:9–13)," *Journal of the Evangelical Theological Society*, vol. 41, no. 3 (1998), 360.
505. Cf. W. Mundle, "*epiousios*," in *New International Dictionary of New Testament Theology*, ed. C. Brown (Grand Rapids, MI: Zondervan, 1986), 1:251–252; Davies & Allison, *A Critical and Exegetical Commentary on the Gospel According to Saint Matthew*, 1:607–609; Kim, *The Function and Meaning of the Lord's Prayer in the Sermon on the Mount*, 119–128; W. Foerster, "*epioúsios*," in *Theological Dictionary of the New Testament*, ed. G. Kittel, trans. G. W. Bromiley (Grand Rapids, MI: Eerdmans, 1999), 2:595–599.

506. Ridderbos, *The Bible Student's Commentary: Matthew*, 131; Spicq, *Theological Lexicon of the New Testament*, 2:56; contra Mills, "The Significance of The Lord's Prayer For Understanding The New Testament Today," 7; cf. Yamauchi, "The 'Daily Bread' Motif In Antiquity," 146–147, 155–156.
507. McNeile, *The Gospel According to St. Matthew*, 79–80; cf. Brown, "The Pater Noster As An Eschatological Prayer," 198–199.
508. Toussaint, *Behold The King: A Study of Matthew*, 110.
509. Carson, "Matthew," 8:171.
510. Gerhardsson, "The Matthaean Version of the Lord's Prayer," 215; contra Byargeon, "Echoes Of Wisdom In The Lord's Prayer (Matt 6:9–13)," 360.
511. Plummer, *An Exegetical Commentary on The Gospel According to St. Matthew*, 101.
512. Strecker, *The Sermon On The Mount: An Exegetical Commentary*, 118.
513. Ferguson, *Kingdom Life In A Fallen World: Living Out the Sermon on the Mount*, 171; Songer, "The Sermon on the Mount and Its Jewish Foreground," 172.
514. Mills, "The Significance of The Lord's Prayer For Understanding The New Testament Today," 7.
515. Plummer, *An Exegetical Commentary on The Gospel According to St. Matthew*, 102.
516. Campbell, *Interpretation And Exposition Of The Sermon On The Mount*, 151. Chafer (*Chafer's Systematic Theology*, 4:221) similarly remarked: "This, again, is purely legal....The legal character of this great kingdom-prayer should not be overlooked."
517. Jeffries, *The Law in the Prayer: The Ten Commandments in the Lord's Prayer*, 72–73.
518. Young, *The Jewish Background to the Lord's Prayer*, 28; Ridderbos, *The Bible Student's Commentary: Matthew*, 132.
519. Betz, *The Sermon on the Mount*, 406.
520. J. Dahms, "Lead Us Not Into Temptation," *Journal of the Evangelical Theological Society*, vol. 17, no. 4 (1974), 220, 229; Gerhardsson, "The Matthaean Version of the Lord's Prayer," 216; Kim, *The Function and Meaning of the Lord's Prayer in the Sermon on the Mount*, 143.
521. McNeile, *The Gospel According to St. Matthew*, 81; Young, *The Jewish Background to the Lord's Prayer*, 31.
522. Liefield, "Luke," 8:948.
523. Toussaint, *Behold The King: A Study of Matthew*, 111; Davies & Allison, *A Critical and Exegetical Commentary on the Gospel According to Saint Matthew*, 1:613–614; Keener, *The IVP New Testament Commentary Series: Matthew*, 145; Keener, *A Commentary on the Gospel of Matthew*, 224.
524. Dahms, "Lead Us Not Into Temptation," 229; Ferguson, *Kingdom Life In A Fallen World: Living Out the Sermon on the Mount*, 173.
525. Hendriksen, *New Testament Commentary: The Gospel of Matthew*, 338.
526. *The Net Bible* offers this clarifying explanation regarding the longer reading: "The addition can easily be explained as a scribal alteration for liturgical purposes. The phrase was probably composed for liturgy of the early church and most likely was based on 1 Chr 29:11–13; a scribe probably added the phrase at this point in the text for use in public scripture reading." Cf. Mills, "The Significance of The Lord's Prayer For Understanding The New Testament Today," 4.
527. Cf. Lanier, "The Lord's Prayer: Matt 6:9–13–A Thematic and Semantic-Structural Analysis," 68, 72; Morris, *The Gospel According to Matthew*, 149.
528. Lenski, *The Interpretation of St. Matthew's Gospel*, 271–272; Ridderbos, *The Bible Student's Commentary: Matthew*, 133.
529. Bruner, *Matthew, A Commentary, Volume 1*, 255.
530. The noun appears in the neuter plural accusative case.

531. Danker, *A Greek-English Lexicon of the New Testament and Other Early Christian Literature*, 770.
532. Louw & Nida, *Greek-English Lexicon of the New Testament: Based on Semantic Domains*, 1:774.
533. M. Wolter, "*paraptōma*," in *Exegetical Dictionary of the New Testament*, eds. H. Balz & G. Schneider, trans. J. W. Thompson & J. W. Medendorp (Grand Rapids: Eerdmans, 1991), 3:33.
534. W. Bauder, "*paraptōma*," in *New International Dictionary of New Testament Theology*, ed. C. Brown (Grand Rapids, MI: Zondervan, 1986), 3:586. W. Michaelis ("*parapíptō*," in *Theological Dictionary of the New Testament*, ed. G. Kittel, trans. G. W. Bromiley, [Grand Rapids, MI: Eerdmans, 1999], 6:171) notes that "there are no παραπτώματα against one's neighbour which do not affect one's relation to God, and *vice versa*" (emphasis his).
535. Patte, *The Gospel According to Matthew: A Structural Commentary on Matthew's Faith*, 89.
536. Morris, *The Gospel According to St. Luke*, 194.
537. Kim, *The Function and Meaning of the Lord's Prayer in the Sermon on the Mount*, 56, 137–138.
538. Pink, *An Exposition of the Sermon on the Mount*, 179.
539. Guelich, *The Sermon on the Mount: A Foundation for Understanding*, 305.
540. Plummer, *An Exegetical Commentary on The Gospel According to St. Matthew*, 104.
541. For example, by bowing their heads, wearing sackcloth, and covering themselves with ashes (cf. Isa. 58:5; Matt. 11:21).
542. Songer, "The Sermon on the Mount and Its Jewish Foreground," 172.
543. Benson, *The Kingdom Proffered and Postponed*, 57.
544. Ferguson, *Kingdom Life In A Fallen World: Living Out the Sermon on the Mount*, 180.
545. Betz, *The Sermon on the Mount*, 433.
546. Danker, *A Greek-English Lexicon of the New Testament and Other Early Christian Literature*, 184; cf. Gundry, *Matthew: A Commentary on His Literary and Theological Art*, 112.
547. Louw & Nida, *Greek-English Lexicon of the New Testament: Based on Semantic Domains*, 1:28.
548. H. J. van der Minde, "*brōsis*," in *Exegetical Dictionary of the New Testament*, eds. H. Balz & G. Schneider, trans. V. Howard & J. W. Thompson (Grand Rapids: Eerdmans, 1990), 1:229; cf. H. Kropatschek, "*brōsis*," in *New International Dictionary of New Testament Theology*, ed. C. Brown (Grand Rapids, MI: Zondervan, 1986), 2:268.
549. Hendriksen, *New Testament Commentary: The Gospel of Matthew*, 344.
550. Jesus was referring to whatever one does in this life that has eternal value (Carson, "Matthew," 8:177).
551. *The Net Bible* makes the pertinent observation that in Matthew 6:19–20 the pronouns are plural, whereas in verse 21 the pronoun is singular. "The change to singular emphasizes personal responsibility as opposed to corporate responsibility; even if others do not listen, the one who hears Jesus' commands should obey."
552. Guelich, *The Sermon on the Mount: A Foundation for Understanding*, 329.
553. Cf. the discussion of Kang, *The Literary Affinities Of The Sermon On The Mount With Special Reference To Deuteronomic Features*, 119–122.
554. Allen, *A Critical and Exegetical Commentary on the Gospel According to St. Matthew*,62; Ferguson, *Kingdom Life In A Fallen World: Living Out the Sermon on the Mount*, 183.

555. Slemp, *Twelve Laws of Life: A Study of the Ten Commandments and Related Teachings of Jesus*, 23; cf. Harrington & Keenan, *Jesus and Virtue Ethics: Building Bridges between New Testament Studies and Moral Theology*, 18–19.
556. Betz, *The Sermon on the Mount*, 458.
557. Pentecost, *The Words and Works of Jesus Christ*, 184.
558. Ferguson, *Kingdom Life In A Fallen World: Living Out the Sermon on the Mount*, 188.
559. "As opposed to domesticated fowl" (*The Net Bible*).
560. McNeile, *The Gospel According to St. Matthew*, 87.
561. Ferguson, *Kingdom Life In A Fallen World: Living Out the Sermon on the Mount*, 189.
562. Gundry, *Matthew: A Commentary on His Literary and Theological Art*, 117.
563. Pink, *An Exposition of the Sermon on the Mount*, 230–231.
564. Nutz, *The Unity of the Sermon on the Mount*, 154.
565. Liefield, "Luke," 8:963.
566. The lilies may be representative of all types of flowers (McNeile, *The Gospel According to St. Matthew*, 88).
567. Lange, "The Gospel According to Matthew: Together With A General Theological And Homiletical Introduction To The New Testament," 8:134.
568. *The Net Bible* states that these rounded clay ovens were "used for baking bread, which was heated by burning wood and dried grass."
569. Betz, *The Sermon on the Mount*, 479.
570. Morris, *The Gospel According to St. Luke*, 215.
571. T. E. Schmidt, "Burden, Barrier, Blasphemy: Wealth In Matt 6:33, Luke 14:33, And Luke 16:15," *Trinity Journal*, vol. 9, no. 2 (1988), 176–177.
572. Cf. Keener, *A Commentary on the Gospel of Matthew*, 236–237.
573. Morris, *The Gospel According to St. Luke*, 215.
574. Draper, "The Genesis and Narrative Thrust of the Paraenesis in the Sermon on the Mount," 41.
575. Carson, "Matthew," 8:182.
576. Morris, *The Gospel According to Matthew*, 164.
577. Plummer, *An Exegetical Commentary on The Gospel According to St. Matthew*, 111.
578. Betz, *The Sermon on the Mount*, 490.
579. Ferguson, *Kingdom Life In A Fallen World: Living Out the Sermon on the Mount*, 199; Patte, *The Gospel According to Matthew: A Structural Commentary on Matthew's Faith*, 96; Hagner, *Word Biblical Commentary: Matthew 1–13*, 169.
580. *The Net Bible* points out that the word rendered "speck" (Matt. 7:3) refers to "a small piece of wood, chaff, or straw."
581. *The Net Bible* points out that the word rendered "log" refers to "a very big piece of wood, the main beam of a building."
582. Morris, *The Gospel According to St. Luke*, 133.
583. Betz, *The Sermon on the Mount*, 492.
584. Kang, *The Literary Affinities Of The Sermon On The Mount With Special Reference To Deuteronomic Features*, 122.
585. Bonham, *A Study of the Relevance of the Sermon on the Mount in Matthew 5–7*, 187–188; Gundry, *Matthew: A Commentary on His Literary and Theological Art*, 123; Davies & Allison, *A Critical and Exegetical Commentary on the Gospel According to Saint Matthew*, 1:675; Songer, "The Sermon on the Mount and Its Jewish Foreground," 173.
586. Bock, *Jesus According to Scripture: Restoring the Portrait from the Gospels*, 416.
587. Lenski, *The Interpretation of St. Matthew's Gospel*, 291.
588. Ridderbos, *The Bible Student's Commentary: Matthew*, 146; Morris, *The Gospel Ac-*

cording to Matthew*, 168–169; Keener, *A Commentary on the Gospel of Matthew*, 243.
589. Morris, *The Gospel According to St. Luke*, 196.
590. Pink, *An Exposition of the Sermon on the Mount*, 296.
591. McNeile (*The Gospel According to St. Matthew,* 92) offered this helpful comment: "Fish would be, next to bread, one of the most common articles of food near the Sea of Galilee; the town of Traicheae, at the S.W. corner of the lake, derived its name from the curing of fish. Stones on the shore, and possibly water-snakes, suggested themselves as substitutes."
592. Carson, "Matthew," 8:187.
593. Campbell, *Interpretation And Exposition Of The Sermon On The Mount*, 182–183.
594. Plummer, *An Exegetical Commentary on The Gospel According to St. Matthew*, 113. For a brief overview of the history of research on and origin of the Golden Rule, cf. J. Topel, "The Tarnished Golden Rule (Luke 6:31): The Inescapable Radicalness of Christian Ethics," *Theological Studies,* vol. 59, no. 3 (1998), 475–477, 481–485.
595. Lohse, *Theological Ethics of the New Testament,* 67–68; M. A. Inch, "Golden Rule," in *Evangelical Dictionary of Theology* (2nd ed.), ed. W. A. Elwell (Grand Rapids: Baker, 2001), 509. Nevertheless, as Stanton ("Sermon on the Mount/Plain," 743) notes, "the positive formulation of Matthew 7:12" is "found in some Jewish writings." Thus "it is a mistake to claim that the positive form of the Golden Rule is distinctively Christian." S. Freyne ("The Ethic of Jesus: The Sermon on the Mount Then and Now," in *Ethics and the Christian,* ed. S. Freyne [Dublin: The Columba Press, 1991], 46) also echoes this sentiment. This position, however, is contra Topel ("The Tarnished Golden Rule [Luke 6:31]: The Inescapable Radicalness of Christian Ethics," 485), who insists that "Jesus' formulation . . . has no precedents in the thought world of his time. It is unique."
596. Carson, "Matthew," 8:187.
597. R. F. Collins, "Golden Rule," in *The Anchor Bible Dictionary,* ed. D. N. Freedman (New York: Doubleday, 1992), 2:1071; Vermes, *The Religion of Jesus the Jew*, 41.
598. Senior, *Abingdon New Testament Commentary Series: Matthew*, 89.
599. Luz, *Matthew 1–7: A Commentary*, 427.
600. W. A. Simmons, "Golden Rule," in *Evangelical Dictionary of Biblical Theology,* ed. W. A. Elwell (Grand Rapids: Baker, 1996), 304.
601. Strecker, *The Sermon On The Mount: An Exegetical Commentary,* 152; Topel, "The Tarnished Golden Rule (Luke 6:31): The Inescapable Radicalness of Christian Ethics," 479–480.
602. McQuilkin, *An Introduction to Biblical Ethics,* 8.
603. J. A. Brooks, "The Unity and Structure of the Sermon on the Mount," *Criswell Theological Review*, vol. 6, no. 1 (1992), 27; Flusser & Notley, *Jesus*, 87. Allison ("The Structure of the Sermon on the Mount," 436) stated that the "golden rule sums up in one sentence the right conduct toward others."
604. Lambrecht, *The Sermon on the Mount: Proclamation and Exhortation,* 182; Davies & Allison, *A Critical and Exegetical Commentary on the Gospel According to Saint Matthew*, 1:685–686; Collins, "Golden Rule," 2:1071; cf. R. B. Sisson, "Voices of Authority in the Sermon on the Mount," in *Society of Biblical Literature 1997 Seminar Papers. Number 36* (Atlanta: Scholars Press, 1997), 558.
605. Draper, "The Genesis and Narrative Thrust of the Paraenesis in the Sermon on the Mount," 43; cf. Stanton, "Sermon on the Mount/Plain," 743.
606. Cf. J. B. Breck, *The Shape of Biblical Language: Chiasmus in the Scriptures and Beyond* (Crestwood, NJ: St. Vladimir's Seminary Press, 1994), 131.

607. Pink, *An Exposition of the Sermon on the Mount*, 323.
608. Campbell, *Interpretation And Exposition Of The Sermon On The Mount*, 187.
609. G. E. Ladd, "Kingdom of God," in *The International Standard Bible Encyclopedia*, ed. G. W. Bromiley (Grand Rapids: Eerdmans, 1986), 3:24.
610. Hendriksen, *New Testament Commentary: The Gospel of Matthew*, 369.
611. Draper, "The Genesis and Narrative Thrust of the Paraenesis in the Sermon on the Mount," 44.
612. The repetition of the term "Lord" denoted a sense of urgency and desperation (*The Net Bible*).
613. The noun is in the masculine singular vocative form.
614. Danker, *A Greek-English Lexicon of the New Testament and Other Early Christian Literature*, 577.
615. Louw & Nida, *Greek-English Lexicon of the New Testament: Based on Semantic Domains*, 1:739.
616. J. A. Fitzmyer, "*kyrios*," in *Exegetical Dictionary of the New Testament*, eds. H. Balz & G. Schneider, trans. J. W. Thompson & J. W. Medendorp (Grand Rapids: Eerdmans, 1991), 2:329.
617. H. Bietenhard, "*kyrios*," in *New International Dictionary of New Testament Theology*, ed. C. Brown (Grand Rapids, MI: Zondervan, 1986), 2:512.
618. Spicq, *Theological Lexicon of the New Testament*, 349.
619. W. Foerster, "*kýrios*," in *Theological Dictionary of the New Testament*, ed. G. Kittel, trans. G. W. Bromiley (Grand Rapids, MI: Eerdmans, 1999), 3:1094; contra Ridderbos, *The Bible Student's Commentary: Matthew*, 153.
620. H. D. Betz, "The Problem of Christology in the Sermon the Mount," in *Text and Logos: The Humanistic Interpretation of the New Testament*, ed. T. W. Jennings (Atlanta: Scholars Press, 1990), 198.
621. J. D. Kingsbury, "The Title 'Kyrios' in Matthew's Gospel," *Journal of Biblical Literature*, vol. 94, no. 2 (1975), 248.
622. Betz, "The Problem of Christology in the Sermon the Mount," 198.
623. Ibid.
624. Keener, *A Commentary on the Gospel of Matthew*, 254; cf. McConnell, *Law and Prophecy in Matthew's Gospel: The Authority and Use of the Old Testament in the Gospel of St. Matthew*, 96–97; Patte, *The Gospel According to Matthew: A Structural Commentary on Matthew's Faith*, 100; France, *Matthew: Evangelist & Teacher*, 288.
625. Kingsbury, "The Title 'Kyrios' in Matthew's Gospel," 249; cf. Loader, *Jesus' Attitude Towards the Law: A Study of the Gospels*, 186.
626. As in verse 21, so also in verse 22, the repetition of the Lord's name denotes a sense of urgency and desperation; cf. Luz, *Matthew 1–7: A Commentary*, 444.
627. Ridderbos, *The Bible Student's Commentary: Matthew*, 154.
628. Schnackenburg, *The Moral Teaching of the New Testament*, 70.
629. An objective examination of Jesus' Sermon has demonstrated this.
630. Bock, *Jesus According to Scripture: Restoring the Portrait from the Gospels*, 152.
631. Ferguson, *Kingdom Life In A Fallen World: Living Out the Sermon on the Mount*, 223; Barclay, *The Old Law and the New Law: The Ten Commandments and the Sermon on the Mount*, 114–115.
632. Slemp, *Twelve Laws of Life: A Study of the Ten Commandments and Related Teachings of Jesus*, 11; M. V. Terzian, *The Homiletical Style of Christ in the Sermon on the Mount* (M.Div. thesis, Winona Lake, IN: Grace Theological Seminary, 1984), 35–36, 42.

633. Plummer, *An Exegetical Commentary on The Gospel According to St. Matthew*, 120.
634. Phillips, *Exploring the Gospels: Matthew*, 133.
635. Patte, *The Gospel According to Matthew: A Structural Commentary on Matthew's Faith*, 60–61.
636. Gundry, *Matthew: A Commentary on His Literary and Theological Art*, 137.
637. Keener, *The IVP New Testament Commentary Series: Matthew*, 168.
638. Luz, *Matthew 1–7: A Commentary*, 456.
639. Cf. Linnemann, *Historical Criticism of the Bible: Methodology or Ideology? Reflections of a Bultmannian Turned Evangelical*, 113.
640. Draper, "The Genesis and Narrative Thrust of the Paraenesis in the Sermon on the Mount," 46–47.

Chapter 7: Affirming the Moral Law's Enduring Relevance

1. J. Calvin, *Institutes of the Christian Religion* (Grand Rapids: Zondervan, 1981), 1:339.
2. Cf. the discussion in chapter 4 regarding *gānab.*
3. Pentecost, *Things to Come: A Study in Biblical Eschatology* (Grand Rapids: Eerdmans 1958), 133.
4. Ibid., 317.
5. W. Hendriksen, *New Testament Commentary: The Gospel of Matthew* (Grand Rapids: Baker, 1973), 261.
6. R. H. Mounce, "Sermon on the Mount," in *New Bible Dictionary: Second Edition,* ed. J. D. Douglas (Wheaton, IL: Tyndale, 1982), 1089.
7. Pentecost, *Things to Come: A Study in Biblical Eschatology*, 318.
8. Mounce, "Sermon on the Mount," 1090.

Bibliography

Ahn, K. 1989. *The Sinaitic Covenant and Law in the Theology of Dispensationalism.* Berrien Springs: Andrews University, Seventh-day Adventist Theological Seminary. (Dissertation-Ph.D.)

Albright, W.F. & Mann, C.S. 1971. *The Anchor Bible: Matthew.* New York: Doubleday.

Alden, R.L. 1976. Mount of Beatitudes. In M.C. Tenney, ed. *The Zondervan Pictorial Encyclopedia of the Bible* (4:297–299). Grand Rapids: Zondervan.

Alderson, R. 1986. The Law–Civic, Ceremonial, and Moral. In R. Alderson. *No Holiness, No Heaven!: Antinomianism Today* (Carlisle, PA: Banner of Truth Trust) [Web:] http://www.the-highway.com/law1_Alderson.html. [Date of access: 27 November 2003].

Aldrich, R.L. 1959. Has the Mosaic Law Been Abolished? *Bibliotheca Sacra, 116*(464), 322–335.

———. 1961. The Mosaic Ten Commandments Compared To Their Restatements In The New Testament. *Bibliotheca Sacra, 118,* 251–258.

Alexander, A. 1939. Ethics. In J. Orr, ed. *The International Standard Bible Encyclopedia* (2:1013–1026). Grand Rapids: Eerdmans.

Allen, L. 1992. The Sermon on the Mount in the History of the Church. *Review & Expositor, 89*(2), 245–262.

Allen, L.C. 1997. *zkr*. In W.A. VanGemeren, ed. *New International Dictionary of Old Testament Theology & Exegesis* (1:1100–1106). Grand Rapids: Eerdmans.

Allen, R.B. 1980. *'ānâ*. In R.L. Harris, G.L. Archer, & B.K. Waltke, eds. *Theological Wordbook of the Old Testament* (2:679–680). Chicago: Moody Press.

Allen, W.C. 1965. *A Critical and Exegetical Commentary on the Gospel According to St. Matthew.* Edinburgh: T. & T. Clark.

Allis, O.T. 1951. *God Spake By Moses: An Exposition of the Pentateuch.* Phillipsburg, NJ: Presbyterian and Reformed.

Allison, D.C. 1987. The Structure of the Sermon on the Mount. *Journal of Biblical Literature, 106*, 423–445.

———. 1992. Mountain and Wilderness. In J.B. Green, S. McKnight, & I.H. Marshall, eds. *Dictionary of Jesus and the Gospels* (563–566). Downers Grove, IL: InterVarsity.

Anderson, D.A. 1985. *The Meaning and Application of Matthew 5:38–42.* Dallas, TX: Dallas Theological Seminary. (Thesis-Th.M.)

Anderson, J.C. 1994. *Matthew's Narrative Web: Over, and Over, and Over Again.* Sheffield, England: Sheffield Academic Press.

André, G. 2003. *pāqaḏ*. In G.J. Botterweck, H. Ringgren, & H.J. Fabry, eds. D.W. Stott, trans. *Theological Dictionary of the Old Testament* (12:50–63). Grand Rapids: Eerdmans.

Andrews, E. 1949. *The Meaning of Christ for Paul.* Nashville: Abingdon-Cokesbury Press.

Asahu-Ejere, K.C. 2003. *The Kingdom of God and Healing-Exorcism (Mt 4:17–5:12).* Frankfurt: Peter Lang.

Audu, I.A. 1990. *Christ's Interpretation of the Law.* Dallas, TX: Dallas Theological Seminary. (Thesis-Th.M.)

Austel, H.J. 1980. *shāqar*. In R.L. Harris, G.L. Archer, & B.K. Waltke, eds. *Theological Wordbook of the Old Testament* (2:955–956). Chicago: Moody Press.

Bacchiocchi, S. 1977. *From Sabbath to Sunday: A Historical Investigation of the Rise of Sunday Observance in Early Christianity.* Rome: Pontifical Gregorian University Press.

———. 1980. *Divine Rest for Human Restlessness: A Theological Study of the Good News of*

the Sabbath for Today. Rome: Pontifical Gregorian University Press.
Baer, D.A. & Gordon, R.P. 1997. *chesed.* In W.A. VanGemeren, ed. *New International Dictionary of Old Testament Theology & Exegesis* (2:211–218). Grand Rapids: Eerdmans.
Bahnsen, G.L. 1978. The Authority of God's Law. *The Presbyterian Journal, 6,* 11.
———. 1984. *Theonomy in Christian Ethics* (2nd ed.). Phillipsburg, NJ: Presbyterian and Reformed.
———. 1985. *By This Standard: The Authority Of God's Law Today.* Tyler, TX: Institute for Christian Economics.
———. 1985a. Should We Uphold Unchanging Moral Absolutes? *Journal of the Evangelical Theological Society, 28*(3), 309–315.
———. 1991. *No Other Standard: Theonomy And Its Critics.* Tyler, TX: Institute for Christian Economics.
———. 1993. Theonomic Reformed Approach to Law and Gospel. In W.G. Strickland, ed. *The Law, the Gospel, and the Modern Christian: Five Views* (93–143). Grand Rapids: Zondervan.
Bahnsen, G.L. & Gentry, K.L. 1989. *House Divided: The Break-Up Of Dispensational Theology.* Tyler, TX: Institute for Christian Economics.
Bailey, K. 1963. Decalogue as Morality and Ethics. *Theology Today, 20*(2), 183–195.
Baird, M.W. 1982. *Jesus' Use of the Decalogue in the Synoptics: An Exegetical Study.* Fort Worth, TX: Southwestern Baptist Theological Seminary. (Dissertation-Ph.D.)
Baker, A.L. 1919. *Belief and Work of Seventh-Day Adventists.* Washington, DC: Review and Herald Publishing Association.
Baker, D.W. 2003. God, Names of. In T.D. Alexander & D.W. Baker, eds. *Dictionary of the Old Testament: Pentateuch* (359–368). Downers Grove, IL: InterVarsity.
Balz, H. 1990. *énnomos.* In H. Balz & G. Schneider, eds. V.P. Howard & J.W. Thompson, trans. *Exegetical Dictionary of the New Testament* (1:455–456). Grand Rapids: Eerdmans.
Banks, R. 1974. Matthew's Understanding of the Law: Authenticity and Interpretation in Matthew 5:17–20. *Journal of Biblical Literature, 93,* 226–242.
———. 1975. *Jesus and the Law in the Synoptic Tradition.* London: Cambridge University Press.
Barcellos, R.C. 2001. *In Defense of the Decalogue: A Critique of New Covenant Theology.* Enumclaw, WA: WinePress Publishing.
Barclay, W. 1991. *The Old Law and the New Law: The Ten Commandments and the Sermon on the Mount.* Edinburgh: The Saint Andrew Press.
Barker, K.L. 1982. False dichotomies Between the Testaments. *Journal of the Evangelical Theological Society, 25*(1), 3–16.
Barré, M.L. 1992. Treaties in the ANE. In D.N. Freedman, ed. *The Anchor Bible Dictionary* (6:653–656). New York: Doubleday.
Bauder, W. 1986. *paraptōma.* In C. Brown, ed. *New International Dictionary of New Testament Theology* (3:585–587). Grand Rapids: Zondervan.
Bauer, D.R. 1988. *The Structure of Matthew's Gospel: A Study in Literary Design.* Sheffield, England: Sheffield Academic Press.
Bauman, C. 1985. *The Sermon on the Mount: The Modern Quest for Its Meaning.* Macon, GA: Mercer University Press.
Baumgärtel, F. 1952. *Zur Frage des evangelischen Verständnisses des Alten Testaments.*

Gütersloh: Bertelsmann Verlag.

Bauslin, D.H. 1939. Gospel. In J. Orr, ed. *The International Standard Bible Encyclopedia* (2:1281). Grand Rapids: Eerdmans.

Beauchamp, P. 1997. *mîn*. In G.J. Botterweck & H. Ringgren, eds. D.W. Scott, trans. *Theological Dictionary of the Old Testament* (8:288–290). Grand Rapids: Eerdmans.

Beck, J.A. 1997. *'nh* I. In W.A. VanGemeren, ed. *New International Dictionary of Old Testament Theology & Exegesis* (3:447–449). Grand Rapids: Eerdmans.

Becker, U. 1986. *euangélion*. In C. Brown, ed. *New International Dictionary of New Testament Theology* (2:107–115). Grand Rapids: Zondervan.

———. 1986a. *makários*. In C. Brown, ed. *New International Dictionary of New Testament Theology* (1:215–218). Grand Rapids: Zondervan.

Benson, J.L. 1967. *The Kingdom Proffered and Postponed.* Unpublished notes. Johnson City, NY: Baptist Bible Seminary.

Berkhof, L. 1981. *Systematic Theology*. Grand Rapids: Eerdmans.

Betz, H.D. 1983. The Hermeneutical Principles of the Sermon on the Mount (Matt. 5:17–20). *Journal of Theology for Southern Africa, 42*, 17–28.

———. 1985. *Essays on the Sermon on the Mount.* Philadelphia: Fortress Press.

———. 1990. The Problem of Christology in the Sermon the Mount. In T.W. Jennings, ed. *Text and Logos: The Humanistic Interpretation of the New Testament* (191–209). Atlanta: Scholars Press.

———. 1992. Sermon on the Mount/Plain. In D.N. Freedman, ed. *The Anchor Bible Dictionary* (5:1106–1112). New York: Doubleday.

———. 1995. *The Sermon on the Mount.* Minneapolis, MN: Fortress Press.

Bible. 1989. *New Revised Standard Version of the Bible*. Nashville, TN: Thomas Nelson Publishers.

Bietenhard, H. 1986. *kyrios*. In C. Brown, ed. *New International Dictionary of New Testament Theology* (2:510–520). Grand Rapids: Zondervan.

———. 1986a. *gehenna*. In C. Brown, ed. *New International Dictionary of New Testament Theology* (2:208–209). Grand Rapids: Zondervan.

Black, D.A. 1988. Jesus on Anger: The Text of Matthew 5:22a Revisited. *Novum Testamentum, 30*, 1–8.

Blaiklock, E.M. 1976. Acts of the Apostles. In M.C. Tenney, ed. *The Zondervan Pictorial Encyclopedia of the Bible* (1:39–53). Grand Rapids: Zondervan.

———. 1976a. Septuagint. In M.C. Tenney, ed. *The Zondervan Pictorial Encyclopedia of the Bible* (5:342–347). Grand Rapids: Zondervan.

Blaising, C. 2001. Dispensation, Dispensationalism. In W.A. Elwell, ed. *Evangelical Dictionary of Theology*. 2nd ed. (343–345). Grand Rapids: Baker Book House.

Blaising, C. & Bock, D.L. 1993. *Progressive Dispensationalism.* Wheaton, IL: Victor Books.

Blaney, H.J.S. 1976. Light. In M.C. Tenney, ed. *The Zondervan Pictorial Encyclopedia of the Bible* (3:932–934). Grand Rapids: Zondervan.

Blenkinsopp, J. 1992. *The Pentateuch: An Introduction to the First Five Books of the Bible.* New York: Doubleday.

Bloesch, D.G. 1987. *Freedom for Obedience: Evangelical Ethics in Contemporary Times.* San Francisco: Harper & Row, Publishers.

———. 1991. Law and Gospel in Reformed Perspective. *Grace Theological Journal, 12*(2), 179–188.

Blomberg, C.L. 1986. Parable. In G.W. Bromiley, ed. *The International Standard Bible Encyclopedia* (3:655–659). Grand Rapids: Eerdmans.

Böcher, O. 1991. *geenna*. In H. Balz & G. Schneider, eds. J.W. Thompson & J.W. Medendorp, trans. *Exegetical Dictionary of the New Testament* (1:239–240). Grand Rapids: Eerdmans.

Bock, D.L. 2002. *Jesus According to Scripture: Restoring the Portrait from the Gospels*. Grand Rapids: Baker.

Bockmuehl, M. 2003. *Jewish Law in Gentile Churches: Halakhah and the Beginning of Christian Public Ethics*. Grand Rapids: Baker.

Bolton, S. 2000. The Moral Law: A Rule of Obedience. [Web:] http://www.thehighway.com/articleFeb00.html. [Date of access: 27 November 2003].

Bonham, T.D. 1963. *A Study of the Relevance of the Sermon on the Mount in Matthew 5–7*. Fort Worth, TX: Southwestern Baptist Theological Seminary. (Dissertation-Th.D.)

Borchert, G.L. 2000. Light. In T.D. Alexander, B.S. Rosner, D.A. Carson, & G. Goldsworthy, eds. *New Dictionary of Biblical Theology* (644–646). Downers Grove, IL: InterVarsity.

Bornkamm, G., Gerhard, B., & Held, H.J. 1976. *Tradition and Interpretation in Matthew*. P. Scott, trans. Philadelphia: The Westminster Press.

Bosman, H.L. 1997. Sabbath. In W.A. VanGemeren, ed. *New International Dictionary of Old Testament Theology & Exegesis* (5:1157–1162). Grand Rapids: Eerdmans.

Bowling, A. 1976. Salt. In M.C. Tenney, ed. *The Zondervan Pictorial Encyclopedia of the Bible* (5:220). Grand Rapids: Zondervan.

———. 1980. *zākar*. In R.L. Harris, G.L. Archer, & B.K. Waltke, eds. *Theological Wordbook of the Old Testament* (1:241–243). Chicago: Moody Press.

Branscomb, B.H. 1930. *Jesus and the Law of Moses*. New York: Richard R. Smith, Inc.

Bray, G.L. 2000. God. In T.D. Alexander, B.S. Rosner, D.A. Carson, & G. Goldsworthy, eds. *New Dictionary of Biblical Theology* (511–521). Downers Grove, IL: InterVarsity.

Breck, J.B. 1994. *The Shape of Biblical Language: Chiasmus in the Scriptures and Beyond*. Crestwood, NJ: St. Vladimir's Seminary Press.

Brinsmead, R.D. 1981. Jesus and the Law. *Verdict*. Duranbah, NSW, Australia: Verdict Publications. [Web:] http://quango.net/brinsmead/jesusandthelaw.htm. [Date of access: 1 April 2003].

Broekhoven, H.V. 1982. Eagle. In G.W. Bromiley, ed. *The International Standard Bible Encyclopedia* (2:1–2). Grand Rapids: Eerdmans.

Brooks, J.A. 1992. The Unity and Structure of the Sermon on the Mount. *Criswell Theological Review*, *6*(1), 15–28.

Brown, C. 1986. *hagios*. In C. Brown, ed. *New International Dictionary of New Testament Theology* (2:229–232). Grand Rapids: Zondervan.

———. 1986a. *katalyō*. In C. Brown, ed. *New International Dictionary of New Testament Theology* (3:189). Grand Rapids: Zondervan.

———. 1986b. *óros*. In C. Brown, ed. *New International Dictionary of New Testament Theology* (3:1009–1013). Grand Rapids: Zondervan.

Brown, C.T. 1991. *Beyond Obedience: Jesus and the Law in Matthew 5:17–20*. Chicago, IL: The Catholic Theological Union. (Thesis-M.A.)

Brown, F. 1983. *The New Brown-Driver-Briggs-Gesenius Hebrew and English Lexicon with an Appendix Containing the Biblical Aramaic*. Christian Copyrights.

Brown, M.L. 1995. *Israel's Divine Healer*. Grand Rapids: Zondervan.

———. 1997. *brk*. In W.A. VanGemeren, ed. *New International Dictionary of Old Testament Theology & Exegesis* (1:757–767). Grand Rapids: Eerdmans.

Brown, R. 1993. *The Message of Deuteronomy: Not by Bread Alone*. Downers Grove, IL: InterVarsity.

Brown, R.E. 1961. The Pater Noster As An Eschatological Prayer. *Theological Studies, 22*, 175–208.

Broyles, C.C. 1992. Gospel (Good News). In J.B. Green, S. McKnight, & I.H. Marshall, eds. *Dictionary of Jesus and the Gospels* (282–286). Downers Grove, IL: InterVarsity.

Bruner, F.D. 1987. *Matthew, A Commentary, Volume 1*. Dallas: Word Publishing.

Büchsel, F. 1999. *krínō*. In G. Kittel, ed. G.W. Bromiley, trans. *Theological Dictionary of the New Testament* (3:921–923). Grand Rapids: Eerdmans.

Burchard, C. 1978. The Theme of the Sermon on the Mount. In L. Schottroff, R.H. Fuller, C. Burchard, & M.J. Suggs, eds. R.H. Fuller & I. Fuller, trans. *Essays on the Love Commandment* (57–91). Philadelphia: Fortress Press.

Bullock, C.H. 2001. Old Testament Theology. In W.A. Elwell, ed. *Evangelical Dictionary of Theology*. 2nd ed. (860–865). Grand Rapids: Baker Book House.

Bultmann, R. 1964. The Significance of the Old Testament for the Christian Faith. In B.W. Anderson, ed. *The Old Testament and Christian Faith: A Theological Discussion* (8–35). New York: Harper & Row.

Bunch, T.G. 1944. *The Ten Commandments: The Law of Liberty*. Washington, DC: Review and Herald.

Burke, D.G. 1986. Murder. In G.W. Bromiley, ed. *The International Standard Bible Encyclopedia* (3:434–435). Grand Rapids: Eerdmans.

Burke, G.T. 2001. Sermon on the Mount. In W.A. Elwell, ed. *Evangelical Dictionary of Theology*, 2nd ed. (1093–1095). Grand Rapids: Baker.

Burtness, J.H. 1975. Life Style and Law: Some Reflections on Matthew 5:17. *Dialog, 14*, 13–20.

Buswell, J.O. 1962. *A Systematic Theology of the Christian Religion*. (Vols. 1–3). Grand Rapids: Zondervan.

———. 1963. Sermon on the Mount. In M.C. Tenny, ed. *The Zondervan Pictorial Bible Dictionary* (773). Grand Rapids: Zondervan.

Byargeon, R.W. 1998. Echoes Of Wisdom In The Lord's Prayer (Matt 6:9–13). *Journal of the Evangelical Theological Society, 41*(3), 353–365.

Cahill, L.S. 1987. The Ethical Implications of the Sermon on the Mount, *Interpretation, 41*(2), 144–156.

Cairns, I. 1992. *Word and Presence: A Commentary on the Book of Deuteronomy*. Grand Rapids: Eerdmans.

Calvin, J. 1981. *Institutes of the Christian Religion*. Grand Rapids: Zondervan.

Campbell, D.K. 1953. *Interpretation And Exposition Of The Sermon On The Mount*. Dallas, TX: Dallas Theological Seminary. (Dissertation-Th.D.)

Caragounis, C.C. 1992. Kingdom of God/Heaven. In J.B. Green, S. McKnight, & I.H. Marshall, eds. *Dictionary of Jesus and the Gospels* (417–430). Downers Grove, IL: InterVarsity.

Carl, W.J. 1989. The Decalogue in Liturgy, Preaching, and Life. *Interpretation, 33*(3), 267–281.

Carmichael, C.M. 1985. *Law and Narrative in the Bible: The Evidence of the Deuteronomic Laws and the Decalogue*. Ithaca, NY: Cornell University Press.

Carpenter, E.E. 1986. Pentateuch. In G.W. Bromiley, ed. *The International Standard Bible Encyclopedia* (3:741–753). Grand Rapids: Eerdmans.

Carpenter, E.E. & Grisanti, M.A. 1997. *šqr*. In W.A. VanGemeren, ed. *New International Dictionary of Old Testament Theology & Exegesis* (4:247–249). Grand Rapids: Eerdmans.

Carson, D.A. 1984. Matthew. In F.E. Gaebelein, ed. *The Expositor's Bible Commentary.* (Vol. 8). Grand Rapids: Zondervan.

Carson, D.A., Moo, D.J., & Morris, L. 1992. *An Introduction to the New Testament.* Grand Rapids: Zondervan.

Carter, W. 1994. *What Are They Saying About Matthew's Sermon On The Mount?* New York: Paulist Press.

Cassuto, U. 1978. *A Commentary on the Book of Genesis. Part I: From Adam to Noah.* Jerusalem: Magnes Press.

———. 1983. *A Commentary on the Book of Exodus.* Jerusalem: Magnes Press.

Chafer, L.S. 1922. *Grace.* Grand Rapids: Zondervan.

———. 1951. The Teachings of Christ Incarnate, Part 1: The Sermon on the Mount. *Bibliotheca Sacra, 108*(432), 389–413.

———. 1978. *Chafer's Systematic Theology.* (Vols. 1–8). Dallas: Dallas Seminary Press.

Chamblin, J.K. 1988. The Law of Moses and the Law of Christ. In J.S. Feinberg, ed. *Continuity and Discontinuity: Perspectives on the Relationship Between the Old and New Testaments* (181–202). Westchester, IL: Crossway Books.

———. 1996. Gospel. In W.A. Elwell, ed. *Evangelical Dictionary of Biblical Theology* (305–308). Grand Rapids: Baker.

Charles, J.D. 1992. The Greatest Or The Least In The Kingdom?: The Disciple's Relationship To The Law (Matt 5:17–20). *Trinity Journal, 13*(2), 139–162.

Childs, B.S. 1974. *The Book of Exodus: A Critical, Theological Commentary.* Philadelphia: Westminster.

Chisholm, R.B. 1997. *'wd.* In W.A. VanGemeren, ed. *New International Dictionary of Old Testament Theology & Exegesis* (3:335–340). Grand Rapids: Eerdmans.

Chismar, D.E., & Rausch, D.A. 1984. Regarding Theonomy: An Essay of Concern. *Journal of the Evangelical Theological Society, 27,* 315–323.

Choi, J.H. 1993. *The Isaianic Background for the First Four Beatitudes in Matthew.* Grand Rapids: Calvin Theological Seminary. (Thesis-Th.M.)

Christensen, D.L. 2001. *Deuteronomy 1:1–21:9, Word Biblical Commentary.* Dallas: Word Books.

Clouse, R.G. 1988. War and Peace. In S.B. Ferguson & D.F. Wright, eds. *New Dictionary of Theology* (714–716). Downers Grove, IL: InterVarsity.

———. 2001. War. In W.A. Elwell, ed. *Evangelical Dictionary of Theology*, 2nd ed. (1255–1257). Grand Rapids: Baker.

Clutter, R.T. 1991. Law and Gospel in the Brethren Tradition. *Grace Theological Journal, 12*(2), 215–232.

Coffman, J.B. 1985. *Commentary on Exodus: The Second Book of Moses.* Abilene, TX: Abilene Christian University Press.

Cole, R.A. 1973. Exodus: An Introduction and Commentary. In D.J. Wiseman, ed. *Tyndale Old Testament Commentaries.* (Vol. 2). Downers Grove, IL: InterVarsity.

———. 1976. Law in the Old Testament. In M.C. Tenny, ed. *The Zondervan Pictorial Encyclopedia of the Bible* (3:883–894). Grand Rapids: Zondervan.

Collins, C.J. 1997. *kbd*. In W.A. VanGemeren, ed. *New International Dictionary of Old Testament Theology & Exegesis* (2:577–587). Grand Rapids: Eerdmans.

Collins, R.F. 1992. Beatitudes. In D.N. Freedman, ed. *The Anchor Bible Dictionary* (1:629–631). New York: Doubleday.

———. 1992a. Commandment. In D.N. Freedman, ed. *The Anchor Bible Dictionary* (1:1097–1099). New York: Doubleday.

———. 1992b. Golden Rule. In D.N. Freedman, ed. *The Anchor Bible Dictionary* (2:1070–1071). New York: Doubleday.

———. 1992c. Ten Commandments. In D.N. Freedman, ed. *The Anchor Bible Dictionary* (6:383–387). New York: Doubleday.

Congdon, R.D. 1978. Did Jesus Sustain The Law In Matthew 5? *Bibliotheca Sacra, 135*(538), 117–125.

Cook, M.J. 1983. Interpreting "Pro-Jewish" Passages in Matthew. *Hebrew Union College Annual, 54*, 135–146.

Coppes, L.J. 1980. *nā'ap*. In R.L. Harris, G.L. Archer, & B.K. Waltke, eds. *Theological Wordbook of the Old Testament* (2:542–543). Chicago: Moody Press.

———. 1980. *qānā'*. In R.L. Harris, G.L. Archer, & B.K. Waltke, eds. *Theological Wordbook of the Old Testament* (2:802–803). Chicago: Moody Press.

Cotton, J.P. 1933. *From Sabbath to Sunday*. Bethlehem, PA: Times Publishing Co.

Cover, D.W. 1983. *The Rest of God and Its Relationship to the Fourth Commandment*. Dallas, TX: Dallas Theological Seminary. (Thesis-Th.M.)

Cover, R.C. 1992. Sin, Sinners (OT). In D.N. Freedman, ed. *The Anchor Bible Dictionary* (6:31–40). New York: Doubleday.

Crafts, W.F. 1885. *The Sabbath for Man*. New York: Funk and Wagnalls.

Craigie, P.C. 1976. The Book of Deuteronomy. In R.K. Harrison, ed. *The New International Commentary on the Old Testament*. (Vol. 5). Grand Rapids: Eerdmans.

———. 2001. Idolatry. In W.A. Elwell, ed. *Evangelical Dictionary of Theology*. 2nd ed. (588–589). Grand Rapids: Baker.

———. 2001a. Ten Commandments. In W.A. Elwell, ed. *Evangelical Dictionary of Theology*. 2nd ed. (1171–1174). Grand Rapids: Baker.

Cranfield, C.E.B. 1975. *A Critical and Exegetical Commentary on the Epistle to the Romans* (Vol. 1). Edinburgh: T. & T. Clark.

Crossan, J.D. 1992. Parable. In D.N. Freedman, ed. *The Anchor Bible Dictionary* (5:146–152). New York: Doubleday.

Crump, D. 1992. Applying the Sermon on the Mount: Once You Have Read It What Do You Do With It? *Criswell Theological Review, 6*(1), 3–14.

Culver, R.D. 1980. *mishpāt*. In R.L. Harris, G.L. Archer, & B.K. Waltke, eds. *Theological Wordbook of the Old Testament* (2:948–949). Chicago: Moody Press.

Dabney, R.L. 1882. *The Christian Sabbath: Its Nature, Design and Proper Observance*. Philadelphia: Presbyterian Board of Publication.

Dahms, J. 1974. Lead Us Not Into Temptation. *Journal of the Evangelical Theological Society, 17*(4), 220–330.

Dalman, R.W. 2002. *A People Come Out of Egypt: A Study of the Books of Exodus, Deuteronomy, and Judges*. Concord, MT: Send the Light Press.

———. 2002a. *Sojourners in the Promise: Genesis and the Origin of Abraham's Faith*. New Hope, MN: Rodger W. Dalman.

Dang, T.M. 1987. *Christ's Beatitudes, Kingdom and the Spiritual Life*. La Mirada, CA: Talbot Theological Seminary. (Thesis-M.A.)

Danker, F.W., ed. 2000. *A Greek-English Lexicon of the New Testament and Other Early Christian Literature*. 3rd ed. Chicago: The University of Chicago Press.

Davidson, A.B. 1904. *The Theology of the Old Testament*. Edinburgh: T. & T. Clark.

Davies, R.E. 1976. Gehenna. In M.C. Tenney, ed. *The Zondervan Pictorial Encyclopedia of the Bible* (2:670–672). Grand Rapids: Zondervan.

Davies, T.W. 1979. Apocrypha. In G.W. Bromiley, ed. *The International Standard Bible Encyclopedia* (1:161–165). Grand Rapids: Eerdmans.

Davies, W.D. & Allison, D.C. 1988. *A Critical and Exegetical Commentary on the Gospel According to Saint Matthew*. (Vol. 1). Edinburgh: T. & T. Clark.

Davis, J.J. 1983. *Moses and the Gods of Egypt: Studies in the Book of Exodus*. Grand Rapids: Baker.

———. 1993. *Evangelical Ethics: Issues Facing the Church Today*. (2nd ed.). Phillipsburg, PA: Presbyterian and Reformed.

Dayton, D.W. 1991. Law and Gospel in the Wesleyan Tradition. *Grace Theological Journal, 12*(2), 233–243.

Dayton, W.T. 1976. Luke, the Evangelist. In M.C. Tenney, ed. *The Zondervan Pictorial Encyclopedia of the Bible* (3:999–1000). Grand Rapids: Zondervan.

———. 1976a. The Gospel of Luke. In M.C. Tenney, ed. *The Zondervan Pictorial Encyclopedia of the Bible* (3:1000–1008). Grand Rapids: Zondervan.

DeBoer, W.P. 1979. Beatitudes. In G.W. Bromiley, ed. *The International Standard Bible Encyclopedia* (1:443–444). Grand Rapids: Eerdmans.

Delling, G. 1999. *plēroō*. In G. Kittel, ed. G.W. Bromiley, trans. *Theological Dictionary of the New Testament* (6:286–298). Grand Rapids: Eerdmans.

———. 1999a. *téleios*. In G. Kittel, ed. G.W. Bromiley, trans. *Theological Dictionary of the New Testament* (8:67–78). Grand Rapids: Eerdmans.

Derrett, J.D.M. 1970. *Law in the New Testament*. London: Darton, Longman & Todd Limited.

Diehl, D.W. 2001. Righteousness. In W. Elwell, ed. *Evangelical Dictionary of Theology*. 2nd ed. (1033–1034). Grand Rapids: Baker.

Di Lella, A.A. 1989. The Structure and Composition of the Matthean Beatitudes. In M.P. Horgan & P.J. Kobelski, eds. *To Touch the Text: Biblical and Related Studies in Honor of Joseph A. Fitzmyer* (237–242). New York: The Crossroad Publishing Company.

Dohmen, C. 1995. *kābēḏ*. In G.J. Botterweck, H. Ringgren, & H.J. Fabry, eds. D.E. Green, trans. *Theological Dictionary of the Old Testament* (7:13–17). Grand Rapids: Eerdmans.

———. 2003. *pāsîl*. In G.J. Botterweck, H. Ringgren, & H.J. Fabry, eds. D.W. Stott, trans. *Theological Dictionary of the Old Testament* (12:30–38). Grand Rapids: Eerdmans.

Domeris, W.R. 1990. "Blessed are you..." (Matthew 5:1–12). *Journal of Theology for Southern Africa, 73*, 67–76.

———. 1997. *gnb*. In W.A. VanGemeren, ed. *New International Dictionary of Old Testament Theology & Exegesis* (1:878–880). Grand Rapids: Eerdmans.

———. 1997a. *rtsh*. In W.A. VanGemeren, ed. *New International Dictionary of Old Testament Theology & Exegesis* (3:1186–1188). Grand Rapids: Eerdmans.

Dorsey, D.A. 1991. The Law of Moses and the Christian: A Compromise. *Journal of the Evangelical Theological Society, 34*(3), 321–334.

Dosker, H.E. 1955. Between the Testaments. In J. Orr, ed. *The International Standard Bible

Encyclopedia (1:455–458). Grand Rapids: Eerdmans.

Douma, J. 1996. *The Ten Commandments: Manual for the Christian Life*. N.D. Kloosterman, trans. Phillipsburg, NJ: P. & R. Publishing.

Draper, J.A. 1999. The Genesis and Narrative Thrust of the Paraenesis in the Sermon on the Mount. *Journal for the Study of the New Testament, 75*, 25–48.

Driver, S.R. 1902. *The International Critical Commentary: A Critical and Exegetical Commentary on Deuteronomy.* New York: Charles Scribner's Sons.

Drumwright, H.L. 1976. The Sermon on the Mount. In M.C. Tenny, ed. *The Zondervan Pictorial Encyclopedia of the Bible* (5:350–356). Grand Rapids: Zondervan.

Duling, D.C. 1992. Kingdom of God/Kingdom of Heaven. In D.N. Freedman, ed. *The Anchor Bible Dictionary* (4:49–69). New York: Doubleday.

———. 1992a. Matthew. In D.N. Freedman, ed. *The Anchor Bible Dictionary* (4:618–622). New York: Doubleday.

Dumbrell, W.D. 1981. The Logic of the Role of the Law in Matthew 5:1–20. *Novum Testamentum, 23*(1), 1–21.

Durham, J.C. 1987. Exodus. In D.A. Hubbard & G.W. Barker, eds. *Word Biblical Commentary.* (Vol. 3). Waco, TX: Word Books.

Dyrness, W. 1977. *Themes in Old Testament Theology.* Downers Grove, IL: InterVarsity.

Edwards, D.M. & Harrison, R.K. 1979. Deuteronomy. In G.W. Bromiley, ed. *The International Standard Bible Encyclopedia* (1:934–940). Grand Rapids: Eerdmans.

Eichrodt, W. 1957. The Law and the Gospel: The Meaning of the Ten Commandments in Israel and for Us. C.F. McRae, trans. *Interpretation, 11*, 23–40.

———. 1963. Is Typological Exegesis an Appropriate Method? In C. Westermann, ed. *Essays on Old Testament Hermeneutics* (224–245). Richmond: John Knox Press.

Eising, H. 1980. *zākhar.* In G.J. Botterweck & H. Ringgren, eds. D.E. Green, trans. *Theological Dictionary of the Old Testament* (4:64–82). Grand Rapids: Eerdmans.

Elliot, E.E. 1982. Light. In J. D. Douglas, ed. *New Bible Dictionary: Second Edition* (701). Wheaton, IL: Tyndale House Publishers.

Ellis, E.E. 1983. *The New Century Bible Commentary: The Gospel of Luke.* Grand Rapids: Eerdmans.

———. 1986. Gospel According to Luke. In G.W. Bromiley, ed. *The International Standard Bible Encyclopedia* (3:180–186). Grand Rapids: Eerdmans.

Els, P.J.J.S. 1997. *'hb.* In W.A. VanGemeren, ed. *New International Dictionary of Old Testament Theology & Exegesis* (1:277–299). Grand Rapids: Eerdmans.

Enns, P. 1997. *chōq.* In W.A. VanGemeren, ed. *New International Dictionary of Old Testament Theology & Exegesis* (2:250–251). Grand Rapids: Eerdmans.

———. 1997a. *tôrâ.* In W.A. VanGemeren, ed. *New International Dictionary of Old Testament Theology & Exegesis* (4:893–900). Grand Rapids: Eerdmans.

Erickson, M.J. 1998. *Christian Theology.* 2nd ed. Grand Rapids: Baker.

Esser, H.H. 1986. *nómos.* In C. Brown, ed. *New International Dictionary of New Testament Theology* (2:438–451). Grand Rapids: Zondervan.

Estep, W.R. 1991. Law and Gospel in the Anabaptist/Baptist Tradition. *Grace Theological Journal, 12*(2), 189–214.

Everts, W.W. 1974. *The Sabbath: It's Permanence, Promise and Defense.* New York: Revell.

Fabry, H.J. 1998. *nā'ap̱.* In G.J. Botterweck, H. Ringgren, and H.J. Fabry, eds. D.E. Green, trans. *Theological Dictionary of the Old Testament* (9:113–118). Grand Rapids: Eerdmans.

Fagen, R.S. 1992. Phylacteries. In D.N. Freedman, ed. *The Anchor Bible Dictionary* (5:368–370). New York: Doubleday.

Fairbairn, P. 1996. *The Revelation of the Law in Scripture*. Phillipsburg, NJ: P. & R. Publishing.

Farrar, F.W. 1896. *The Voice from Sinai: The Eternal Bases of the Mosaic Law*. London: Isbister and Company.

Farrer, A. 1954. *St. Matthew and St. Mark*. London: Dacre Press.

Fawley, W.S. 1985. *Matthew 5:17: An Interpretation*. Winona Lake, IN: Grace Theological Seminary. (Thesis-M.Div.)

Feinberg, J.S. 1988. Systems of Discontinuity. In J.S. Feinberg, ed. *Continuity and Discontinuity: Perspectives on the Relationship Between the Old and New Testaments* (63–86). Westchester, IL: Crossway Books.

Ferguson, S.B. 1986. *Kingdom Life In A Fallen World: Living Out the Sermon on the Mount*. Colorado Springs, CO: Nav Press.

Filson, F.V. 1982. Synoptic Gospels. In G.W. Bromiley, ed. *The International Standard Bible Encyclopedia* (2:532–536). Grand Rapids: Eerdmans.

Fiorenza, E.S. 1998. *The Book of Revelation: Justice and Judgment*. 2nd ed. Minneapolis, MN: Augsburg Fortress.

Fischer, J. 1989. Covenant, Fulfillment and Judaism in Hebrews. *Evangelical Review of Theology, 13*, 175–187.

Fisher, M.C. & Waltke, B.K. 1980. *nāqâ*. In R.L. Harris, G.L. Archer, & B.K. Waltke, eds. *Theological Wordbook of the Old Testament* (2:596–598). Chicago: Moody Press.

Fitzmyer, J.A. 1991. *kyrios*. In H. Balz & G. Schneider, eds. J.W. Thompson & J.W. Medendorp, trans. *Exegetical Dictionary of the New Testament* (2:328–331). Grand Rapids: Eerdmans.

Floody, R.J. 1906. *Scientific Basis of Sabbath and Sunday*. Boston: Herbert B. Turner.

Flusser, D. & Notley, R.S. 2001. *Jesus*. Jerusalem: Magnes Press.

Foerster, W. 1999. *epioúsios*. In G. Kittel, ed. G.W. Bromiley, trans. *Theological Dictionary of the New Testament* (2:590–599). Grand Rapids: Eerdmans.

———. 1999a. *kýrios*. In G. Kittel, ed. G.W. Bromiley, trans. *Theological Dictionary of the New Testament* (3:1081–1095). Grand Rapids: Eerdmans.

———. 1999b. *óros*. In G. Kittel, ed. G.W. Bromiley, trans. *Theological Dictionary of the New Testament* (5:475–487). Grand Rapids: Eerdmans.

France, R.T. 1971. *Jesus and the Old Testament: His Application of Old Testament Passages to Himself and His Mission*. Downers Grove, IL: InterVarsity.

———. 1989. *Matthew: Evangelist & Teacher*. Downers Grove, IL: InterVarsity.

Freedman, D.N. 1960. The Name of the God of Moses. *Journal of Biblical Literature, 79*, 152–153.

———. 1979. Adultery. In G.W. Bromiley, ed. *The International Standard Bible Encyclopedia* (1:58–59). Grand Rapids: Eerdmans.

Freedman, D.N. & O'Connor, M.P. 1986. *yhwh*. In G.J. Botterweck & H. Ringgren, eds. D.E. Green, trans. *Theological Dictionary of the Old Testament* (5:500–521). Grand Rapids: Eerdmans.

Fretheim, T.E. 1991. *Exodus: A Biblical Commentary for Teaching and Preaching*. Louisville, Kentucky: John Knox Press.

———. 1997. *'ĕlōhîm*. In W.A. VanGemeren, ed. *New International Dictionary of Old Testament Theology & Exegesis* (1:405–406). Grand Rapids: Eerdmans.

———. 1997a. *yahweh*. In W.A. VanGemeren, ed. *New International Dictionary of Old Testament Theology & Exegesis* (4:1295–1300). Grand Rapids: Eerdmans.

Freyne, S. 1991. The Ethic of Jesus: The Sermon on the Mount Then and Now. In S. Freyne, ed. *Ethics and the Christian* (41–57). Dublin: The Columba Press.

Friedlander, G. 1969. *The Jewish Sources of the Sermon on the Mount.* New York: KTAV Publishing House.

Friedman, R.E. 1992. Torah (Pentateuch). In D.N. Freedman, ed. *The Anchor Bible Dictionary* (6:605–622). New York: Doubleday.

Friedrich, G. 1999. *euangélion*. In G. Kittel, ed. G. W. Bromiley, trans. *Theological Dictionary of the New Testament* (2:707–737). Grand Rapids: Eerdmans.

Fruchtenbaum, A. 1999. Israelology: Part 3 of 6. *Chafer Theological Seminary Journal, 5*(4), 27–46.

Fuller, R.H. 1989. The Decalogue in the New Testament. *Interpretation, 43*(3), 243–255.

Funderbunk, G.B. 1976. Honorable, Honor. In M.C. Tenney, ed. *The Zondervan Pictorial Encyclopedia of the Bible* (3:197). Grand Rapids: Zondervan.

Furnish, V.P. 1993. *Jesus According to Paul.* Cambridge: Cambridge University Press.

Gamble, H.R. 1901. *Sunday and the Sabbath.* New York: Dutton.

Gane, R. 1999. Sabbath and the New Covenant. *Journal of the Adventist Theological Society. 10*(1–2), 311–322.

Garber, P.L. & Wyatt, R.J. 1982. Idol. In G.W. Bromiley, ed. *The International Standard Bible Encyclopedia* (2:794–796). Grand Rapids: Eerdmans.

Garcia-López, F. 2003. *tswh*. In G.J. Botterweck, H. Ringgren, & H.J. Fabry, eds. D.W. Stott, trans. *Theological Dictionary of the Old Testament* (12:276–296). Grand Rapids: Eerdmans.

Garland, D.E. 1992. Blessing and Woe. In J.B. Green, S. McKnight, & I.H. Marshall, eds. *Dictionary of Jesus and the Gospels* (77–81). Downers Grove, IL: InterVarsity.

———. 1992a. The Lord's Prayer in the Gospel of Matthew. *Review & Expositor, 89*(2), 215–228.

———. 1993. *Reading Matthew: A Literary and Theological Commentary on the First Gospel.* New York: The Crossroad Publishing Company.

Garlington, D. 1995. Oath-Taking In The Community Of The New Age (Matthew 5:33–37). *Trinity Journal. 16*(2), 139–170.

Gasque, W.W. 1986. Luke. In G.W. Bromiley, ed. *The International Standard Bible Encyclopedia* (3:178–180). Grand Rapids: Eerdmans.

Gearey, A. 1999. The Bible, Law and Liberation: Towards a Politico-Legal Hermeneutics of the Sermon on the Mount. In M. Freeman and A.D.E. Lewis, eds. *Law and Literature: Current Legal Issues 1999, Volume 2* (263–283). Oxford: Oxford University Press.

Geisler, N.L. 1985. *False Gods of Our Time: A Defense of the Christian Faith.* Eugene, OR: Harvest House.

———. 1989. *Christian Ethics: Options and Issues.* Grand Rapids: Baker.

Geldenhuys, N. 1983. *Commentary on the Gospel of Luke.* Grand Rapids: Eerdmans.

Gerhardsson, B. 1984. The Matthaean Version of the Lord's Prayer. In W.C. Weinrich, ed. *The New Testament Age: Essays in Honor of Bo Reicke* (207–220). Macon, GA: Mercer University Press.

Gerleman, G. 1997. *dābār*. In E. Jenni & C. Westermann, eds. M.E. Biddle, trans. *Theologi-*

cal Lexicon of the Old Testament (1:325–332). Peabody, MA: Hendrickson Publishers.

Gerstenberger, E. 1997. *chmd.* In E. Jenni & C. Westermann, eds. M.E. Biddle, trans. *Theological Lexicon of the Old Testament* (1:433–435). Peabody, MA: Hendrickson Publishers.

Gerstner, J.H. 1986. Law in the NT. In G.W. Bromiley, ed. *The International Standard Bible Encyclopedia* (3:85–91). Grand Rapids: Eerdmans.

Gianotti, C.R. 1985. The Meaning of the Divine Name YHWH. *Bibliotheca Sacra, 142*(565), 38–51.

Godfrey, W.R. 1988. Law and Gospel. In S. Ferguson, D.F. Wright, & J.I. Packer, eds. *New Dictionary of Theology* (379–380). Downers Grove, IL: InterVarsity.

Goldsworthy, G. 2000. Gospel. In T.D. Alexander, B.S. Rosner, D.A. Carson, & G. Goldsworthy, eds. *New Dictionary of Biblical Theology* (521–524). Downers Grove, IL: InterVarsity.

———. 2000a. Kingdom of God. In T.D. Alexander, B.S. Rosner, D.A. Carson, & G. Goldsworthy, eds. *New Dictionary of Biblical Theology* (615–620). Downers Grove, IL: InterVarsity.

Goodfriend, E.A. 1992. Adultery. In D.N. Freedman, ed. *The Anchor Bible Dictionary* (1:82–87). New York: Doubleday.

Gordon, C.H. 1964. Ten Commandments. *Christianity Today, 8,* 3–6.

Gordon, R.P. 1982. War. In J. D. Douglas, ed. *New Bible Dictionary: Second Edition* (1240–1242). Wheaton, IL: Tyndale.

Gordon, T.D. 1994. Critique of Theonomy: A Taxonomy. *Westminster Theological Journal, 56,* 23–43.

Gore, C. 1900. *The Sermon on the Mount: A Practical Exposition.* London: John Murray.

Gowan, D.E. 1994. *Theology in Exodus: Biblical Theology in the Form of a Commentary.* Louisville, KY: Westminster John Knox Press.

Grant, R.M. 1947. The Decalogue in Early Christianity. *Harvard Theological Review, 40,* 1–17.

Greengus, S. 1992. Law. In D.N. Freedman, ed. *The Anchor Bible Dictionary* (4:242–252). New York: Doubleday.

Greenwood, D. 1970. Moral Obligation in the Sermon on the Mount. *Theological Studies, 31,* 301–309.

Grier, J.M. 1991. The Relationship of the Law to Christ in Matthew 5:17–20 and Its Implications for Moral Theology. In G.T. Meadors, ed. *New Testament Essays In Honor of Homer A Kent, Jr.* (165–177). Winona Lake, IN: BMH Books.

Grogan, G.W. 1986. Isaiah. In F.E. Gaebelein, ed. *The Expositor's Bible Commentary* (Vol. 6). Grand Rapids: Eerdmans.

Gromacki, R.G. 1974. *New Testament Survey.* Grand Rapids: Baker.

Grosheide, F.W. 1953. *The First Epistle to the Corinthians.* Grand Rapids: Eerdmans.

Grounds, V.C. 1971. Mountain Manifesto. *Bibliotheca Sacra, 128*(510), 135–141.

———. 1976. The Beatitudes. In M.C. Tenney, ed. *The Zondervan Pictorial Encyclopedia of the Bible* (1:497–501). Grand Rapids: Zondervan.

Guelich, R.A. 1982. *The Sermon on the Mount: A Foundation for Understanding.* Waco, TX: Word.

———. 1987. Interpreting the Sermon on the Mount. *Interpretation, 41*(2), 117–130.

Gulley, N.R. 2003. Basic Issues between Science and Scripture: Theological Implications of

Alternative Models and the Necessary Basis for the Sabbath in Genesis 1–2. *Journal of the Adventist Theological Society*, *14*(1), 195–228.

Gundry, R.H. 1982. *Matthew: A Commentary on His Literary and Theological Art.* Grand Rapids: Eerdmans.

Günther, W. 1986. *hypokrino*. In C. Brown, ed. *New International Dictionary of New Testament Theology* (2:468–470). Grand Rapids: Zondervan.

Gutbrod, W. 1999. *nómos*. In G. Kittel, ed. G.W. Bromiley, trans. *Theological Dictionary of the New Testament* (4:1036–1091). Grand Rapids: Eerdmans.

Guthrie, D. 1970. *New Testament Introduction.* Downers Grove, IL: InterVarsity.

———. 1981. *New Testament Theology.* Downers Grove, IL: InterVarsity.

Hackenberg, W. 1991. *ginomai*. In H. Balz & G. Schneider, eds. J.W. Thompson & J.W. Medendorp, trans. *Exegetical Dictionary of the New Testament* (1:247). Grand Rapids: Eerdmans.

Hagner, D.A. 1986. Gospel According to Matthew. In G.W. Bromiley, ed. *The International Standard Bible Encyclopedia* (3:280–288). Grand Rapids: Eerdmans.

———. 1988. Tax Collector. In G.W. Bromiley, ed. *The International Standard Bible Encyclopedia* (4:742–743). Grand Rapids: Eerdmans.

———. 1993. *Word Biblical Commentary: Matthew 1–13.* Dallas, TX: Word Books.

Hahn, H.C. 1986. *lychnos*. In C. Brown, ed. *New International Dictionary of New Testament Theology* (2:486–487). Grand Rapids: Zondervan.

———. 1986a. *phōs*. In C. Brown, ed. *New International Dictionary of New Testament Theology* (2:490–495). Grand Rapids: Zondervan.

Hall, G.H. 1997. *n'p*. In W.A. VanGemeren, ed. *New International Dictionary of Old Testament Theology & Exegesis* (3:2–5). Grand Rapids: Eerdmans.

Hamilton, V.P. 1980. *pāqad*. In R.L. Harris, G.L. Archer, & B.K. Waltke, eds. *Theological Wordbook of the Old Testament* (2:731–732). Chicago: Moody Press.

———. 1980. *shābat*. In R.L. Harris, G.L. Archer, & B.K. Waltke, eds. *Theological Wordbook of the Old Testament* (2:902–903). Chicago: Moody Press.

———. 1982. *Handbook on the Pentateuch.* Grand Rapids: Baker.

———. 1990. *The Book of Genesis: Chapters 1–17.* Grand Rapids: Eerdmans.

Hammerton-Kelly, R.G. 1972. Attitudes to the Law in Matthew's Gospel: A Discussion of Matthew 5:18. *Biblical Research, 17,* 19–32.

Hamp, V. 1978. *gānabh*. In G.J. Botterweck & H. Ringgren, eds. J.T. Willis, G.W. Bromiley, & D.E. Green, trans. *Theological Dictionary of the Old Testament* (3:39–45). Grand Rapids: Eerdmans.

Häring, B. 1967. Normative Value of the Sermon on the Mount. *Catholic Biblical Quarterly, 29*(3), 375–385.

Harm, F.R. 2001. Sabbatarianism. In W. Elwell, ed. *Evangelical Dictionary of Theology.* 2nd ed. (1045–1046). Grand Rapids: Baker.

Harman, A.M. 1997. Decalogue (Ten Commandments). In W.A. VanGemeren, ed. *New International Dictionary of Old Testament Theology & Exegesis* (4:513–519). Grand Rapids: Eerdmans.

Harrington, D.J. & Keenan, J.F. 2002. *Jesus and Virtue Ethics: Building Bridges between New Testament Studies and Moral Theology.* Lanham, MD: Sheed & Ward.

Harrington, W. 1964. The Law, The Prophets, And The Gospel. *Irish Theological Quarterly, 31,* 283–302.

Harris, R.L. 1980. *rā'â*. In R.L. Harris, G.L. Archer, & B.K. Waltke, eds. *Theological Wordbook of the Old Testament* (2:853). Chicago: Moody Press.

Harrison, E. F. 1971. *Introduction to the New Testament.* Grand Rapids: Eerdmans.

———. 1982. Holiness. In G.W. Bromiley, ed. *The International Standard Bible Encyclopedia* (2:725–729). Grand Rapids: Eerdmans.

Harrison, R.K. 1969. *Introduction to the Old Testament.* London: The Tyndale Press.

———. 1976. Dead Sea Scrolls. In M.C. Tenney, ed. *The Zondervan Pictorial Encyclopedia of the Bible* (2:53–68). Grand Rapids: Zondervan.

———. 1982. Book of Exodus. In G.W. Bromiley, ed. *The International Standard Bible Encyclopedia* (2:222–230). Grand Rapids: Eerdmans.

———. 1982a. Salt. In J.D. Douglas, ed. *New Bible Commentary: Second Edition* (1056). Wheaton, IL: Tyndale.

———. 1986. Law in the OT. In G.W. Bromiley, ed. *The International Standard Bible Encyclopedia* (3:76–85). Grand Rapids: Eerdmans.

Hartley, J.E. 1980. *shāmar*. In R.L. Harris, G.L. Archer, & B.K. Waltke, eds. *Theological Wordbook of the Old Testament* (2:939–940). Chicago: Moody Press.

———. 1980a. *tôrâ*. In R.L. Harris, G.L. Archer, & B.K. Waltke, eds. *Theological Wordbook of the Old Testament* (1:403–405). Chicago: Moody Press.

———. 1980b. *tsāwâ*. In R.L. Harris, G.L. Archer, & B.K. Waltke, eds. *Theological Wordbook of the Old Testament* (2:757–758). Chicago: Moody Press.

Hasel, G.F. 1986. Lamp. In G.W. Bromiley, ed. *The International Standard Bible Encyclopedia* (3:68–69). Grand Rapids: Eerdmans.

———. 1991. *Old Testament Theology: Basic Issues In the Current Debate.* (4th ed.). Grand Rapids: Eerdmans.

———. 1992. Sabbath. In D.N. Freedman, ed. *The Anchor Bible Dictionary* (5:849–856). New York: Doubleday.

Hauck, F. 1999. *halas*. In G. Kittel, ed. G.W. Bromiley, trans. *Theological Dictionary of the New Testament* (1:228–229). Grand Rapids: Eerdmans.

———. 1999a. *makários*. In G. Kittel, ed. G.W. Bromiley, trans. *Theological Dictionary of the New Testament* (4:367–370). Grand Rapids: Eerdmans.

Hawkins, R.A. 1969. Covenant Relations of the Sermon on the Mount. *Restoration Quarterly, 12*(1), 1–9.

Hawthorne, G.F. 1986. Name. In G.W. Bromiley, ed. *The International Standard Bible Encyclopedia* (3:480–483). Grand Rapids: Eerdmans.

Hays, J.D. 2001. Applying the Old Testament Law Today. *Bibliotheca Sacra, 158*(629), 21–35.

Heath, E.A. 2003. Grace. In T.D. Alexander & D.W. Baker, eds. *Dictionary of the Old Testament: Pentateuch* (371–375). Downers Grove, IL: InterVarsity.

Hegg, T. 1998. What Does πληρῶσαι Mean in Matthew 5:17? In *Evangelical Theological Society.* Paper read at the Northwest Regional Meeting of ETS in Tacoma, Washington on 28 February 1999 (1–19). Portland, OR: Theological Research Exchange Network.

Heideman, P. 1998. Dispensational Theology. *Chafer Theological Seminary Journal, 4*(3), 31–42.

Hendriksen, W. 1967. *New Testament Commentary: Exposition of Ephesians.* Grand Rapids: Baker.

———. 1968. *New Testament Commentary: Exposition of Galatians.* Grand Rapids: Baker.

———. 1973. *New Testament Commentary: The Gospel of Matthew*. Grand Rapids: Baker.

Henry, C.F. 1957. *Christian Personal Ethics*. Grand Rapids: Eerdmans.

———. 1976. God. In M.C. Tenney, ed. *The Zondervan Pictorial Encyclopedia of the Bible* (2:742–758). Grand Rapids: Zondervan.

Hernandez, H.W. 1994. *The Chiastic Structure of the Sermon on the Mount*. Dallas, TX: Dallas Theological Seminary. (Thesis-Th.M.)

Herr, L.G. 1988. Salt. In G.W. Bromiley, ed. *The International Standard Bible Encyclopedia* (4:286–287). Grand Rapids: Eerdmans.

Hershberger, G.F. 1928. Mennonites and the Modern Peace Movement. *Mennonite Quarterly Review, 2*, 163.

———. 1943. Peace and War in the New Testament. *Mennonite Quarterly Review, 17*, 5–8.

———. 1943a. Peace and War in the New Testament. *Mennonite Quarterly Review, 17*, 59–60.

Hertz, J.H. 1981. *The Pentateuch and Haftorahs*. (2nd ed.). London: Soncino Press.

Hesse, F. 1966. *Das Alte Testament als Buch der Kirche*. Gütersloh: Mohn.

Hessey, J.A. 1889. *Sunday: Its Origin, History and Present Obligation*. London: Cassell.

Hillyer, N. 1986. *halas*. In C. Brown, ed. *New International Dictionary of New Testament Theology* (3:443–449). Grand Rapids: Zondervan.

Hodge, A.A. 1922. *The Day Changed and the Sabbath Preserved*. Philadelphia: Presbyterian Board of Publication and Sabbath School Work.

Hodge, C. 1981. *Systematic Theology*. (Vols. 1–3). Grand Rapids: Eerdmans.

Hodges, L.I. 1990. A Defense of the Tripartite Understanding of the Law Articulated in the "The Westminster Confession." In *Evangelical Philosophical Society*. Paper read at the meeting held during November 1990 (1–21). Portland, OR: Theological Research Exchange Network.

Holladay, W.L., ed. 1988. *A Concise Hebrew and Aramaic Lexicon of the Old Testament*. Leiden, the Netherlands: E.J. Brill.

Hordern, R.P. 1983. Law and Gospel as Hermeneutic: Martin Luther and the Lutheran Tradition. *Consensus, 9*, 3–15.

Horne, C.M. 1976. Law in the New Testament. In M.C. Tenny, ed. *The Zondervan Pictorial Encyclopedia of the Bible* (3:894–896). Grand Rapids: Zondervan.

Hsu, J. 1986. *The Decalogue and Moral Conscience in the Ancient Near East: A Comparative Study*. Deerfield, IL: Trinity Evangelical Divinity School. (Thesis-Th.M.)

Hübner, H. 1991. *katalyō*. In H. Balz & G. Schneider, eds. J.W. Thompson & J.W. Medendorp, trans. *Exegetical Dictionary of the New Testament* (2:264). Grand Rapids: Eerdmans.

———. 1991a. *nomikós*. In H. Balz & G. Schneider, eds. J.W. Thompson & J.W. Medendorp, trans. *Exegetical Dictionary of the New Testament* (2:470–471). Grand Rapids: Eerdmans.

———. 1991b. *nómos*. In H. Balz & G. Schneider, eds. J.W. Thompson & J.W. Medendorp, trans. *Exegetical Dictionary of the New Testament* (2:471–477). Grand Rapids: Eerdmans.

———. 1991c. *plēroō*. In H. Balz & G. Schneider, eds. J.W. Thompson & J.W. Medendorp, trans. *Exegetical Dictionary of the New Testament* (3:108–110). Grand Rapids: Eerdmans.

———. 1991d. *teleios*. In H. Balz & G. Schneider, eds. J.W. Thompson & J.W. Medendorp, trans. *Exegetical Dictionary of the New Testament* (3:342–344). Grand Rapids: Eerdmans.

Huey, F.B. 1976. Idolatry. In M.C. Tenny, ed. *The Zondervan Pictorial Encyclopedia of the Bible* (3:242–248). Grand Rapids: Zondervan.

Hughes, J.J. & Opperwall, N.J. 1986. Neighbor. In G.W. Bromiley, ed. *The International Standard Bible Encyclopedia* (3:517–518). Grand Rapids: Eerdmans.

Hughes, P.E. 1962. *Paul's Second Epistle to the Corinthians.* Grand Rapids: Eerdmans.

———. 1990. *The Book of Revelation: A Commentary.* Grand Rapids: Eerdmans.

Hutchinson, J.P. 1942. *Our Obligations to the Day of Rest and Worship.* Colorado Springs, CO: Lord's Day Alliance.

Hyatt, J.P. 1980. *New Century Bible Commentary: Exodus.* Grand Rapids: Eerdmans.

Inch, M.A. 2001. Golden Rule. In W.A. Elwell, ed. *Evangelical Dictionary of Theology.* 2nd ed. (509). Grand Rapids: Baker.

Iverach, J. 1955. The Synoptic Gospels. In J. Orr, ed. *The International Standard Bible Encyclopedia* (2:1281–1286). Grand Rapids: Eerdmans.

Jackson, D.R. 1976. Gospel (Message). In M.C. Tenny, ed. *The Zondervan Pictorial Encyclopedia of the Bible* (2:779–784). Grand Rapids: Zondervan.

Jacob, B. 1992. *The Second Book of the Bible: Exodus.* W. Jacob, trans. Hoboken, NJ: KTAV Publishing House.

Jeffries, J.C. 1952. *The Law in the Prayer: The Ten Commandments in the Lord's Prayer.* New York: Exposition Press.

Jenni, E. 1997. *'hb.* In E. Jenni & C. Westermann, eds. M.E. Biddle, trans. *Theological Lexicon of the Old Testament* (1:45–54). Peabody, MA: Hendrickson Publishers.

———. 1997a. *śn'.* In E. Jenni & C. Westermann, eds. M.E. Biddle, trans. *Theological Lexicon of the Old Testament* (3:1277–1279). Peabody, MA: Hendrickson Publishers.

———. 1997b. *yhwh.* In E. Jenni & C. Westermann, eds. M.E. Biddle, trans. *Theological Lexicon of the Old Testament* (2:522–526). Peabody, MA: Hendrickson Publishers.

Jewett, P. 1976. Monotheism. In M.C. Tenney, ed. *The Zondervan Pictorial Encyclopedia of the Bible* (4:271–272). Grand Rapids: Zondervan.

Jocz, J. 1976. Torah. In M.C. Tenney, ed. *The Zondervan Pictorial Encyclopedia of the Bible* (5:779–780). Grand Rapids: Zondervan.

Johnson, G.P. 1984. *A Semantic and Discourse Analysis of Matthew 5:17–20.* Portland, OR: Western Conservative Baptist Seminary. (Thesis-Th.M.)

Johnson, T.F. 1988. Steal. In G.W. Bromiley, ed. *The International Standard Bible Encyclopedia* (4:614–615). Grand Rapids: Eerdmans.

Jones, D.C. 1994. *Biblical Christian Ethics.* Grand Rapids: Baker.

Josephus, F. 1978. *Josephus Complete Works.* W. Whiston, trans. Grand Rapids: Kregel.

Kaiser, W.C. 1976. Name. In M.C. Tenny, ed. *The Zondervan Pictorial Encyclopedia of the Bible* (4:360–366). Grand Rapids: Zondervan.

———. 1978. *Toward an Old Testament Theology.* Grand Rapids: Zondervan.

———. 1980. *myn, mwn.* In R.L. Harris, G.L. Archer, & B.K. Waltke, eds. *Theological Wordbook of the Old Testament* (1:503–504). Chicago: Moody Press.

———. 1983. *Toward Old Testament Ethics.* Grand Rapids: Zondervan.

———. 1987. The Place of Law and Good Works In Evangelical Christianity. In A. Rudin & M. Wilson, eds. *A Time to Speak: The Evangelical-Jewish Encounter* (120–133). Austin, TX: Center for Judaic-Christian Studies.

———. 1990. Exodus. In F.E. Gabelein, ed. *The Expositor's Bible Commentary.* (Vol. 2). Grand Rapids: Zondervan.

———. 1990a. God's Promise Plan and His Glorious Law. *Journal of the Evangelical Theological Society, 33*(3), 289–302.

———. 1993. Response to Douglas Moo. In W.G. Strickland, ed. *The Law, the Gospel, and the Modern Christian: Five Views* (393–400). Grand Rapids: Zondervan.

Kalland, E.S. 1980. *dābār.* In R.L. Harris, G.L. Archer, & B.K. Waltke, eds. *Theological Wordbook of the Old Testament* (1:180). Chicago: Moody Press.

———. 1992. Deuteronomy. In F.E. Gabelein, ed. *The Expositor's Bible Commentary.* (Vol. 3). Grand Rapids: Zondervan.

Kang, C.H. 1987. *The Literary Affinities Of The Sermon On The Mount With Special Reference To Deuteronomic Features.* Pasadena, CA: Fuller Theological Seminary, School Of Theology. (Dissertation-Ph.D.)

Kearsley, R. 1988. Repentance. In S. Ferguson, D.F. Wright, & J.I. Packer, eds. *New Dictionary of Theology* (580–581). Downers Grove, IL: InterVarsity.

Keener, C.S. 1997. *The IVP New Testament Commentary Series: Matthew.* G.R. Osborne, ed. Downers Grove, IL: InterVarsity.

———. 1999. *A Commentary on the Gospel of Matthew.* Grand Rapids: Eerdmans.

Keil, C.F. & Delitzsch, F. 1981. The Second Book of Moses (Exodus). In J. Martin, trans. *Biblical Commentary on the Old Testament.* Vol. 2. Grand Rapids: Eerdmans.

Keller, C.A. 1997. *brk.* In E. Jenni & C. Westermann, eds. M.E. Biddle, trans. *Theological Lexicon of the Old Testament* (1:266–274). Peabody, MA: Hendrickson Publishers.

Kelso, J.L. 1976. Idol Makers. In M.C. Tenny, ed. *The Zondervan Pictorial Encyclopedia of the Bible* (3:242). Grand Rapids: Zondervan.

Kertelge, K. 1991. *dikaiosýnē.* In H. Balz & G. Schneider, eds. J.W. Thompson & J.W. Medendorp, trans. *Exegetical Dictionary of the New Testament* (1:325–330). Grand Rapids: Eerdmans.

Kevan, E. 2002. The Moral Law and its Relation to Believers. [Web:] http://www.the-highway.com/articleSept02.html. [Date of access: 26 November 2003].

———. 2003. The Law not Abrogated by Christ to Believers. [Web:] http://www.the-highway.com/law_Kevan.html. [Date of access: 27 November 2003].

Kidner, D. 1976. Ten Commandments. In M.C. Tenny, ed. *The Zondervan Pictorial Encyclopedia of the Bible* (5:672–676). Grand Rapids: Zondervan.

Kim, H.D. 2003. *The Mosaic Law in the Old Testament and the New Testament.* South Hamilton, MA: Gordon-Conwell Theological Seminary. (Thesis-M.A.)

Kim, J.W. 1991. *The Function and Meaning of the Lord's Prayer in the Sermon on the Mount.* Grand Rapids: Calvin Theological Seminary. (Thesis-Th.M.)

Kingsbury, J.D. 1975. The Title "Kyrios" in Matthew's Gospel. *Journal of Biblical Literature, 94*(2), 246–255.

———. 1987. The Place, Structure, and Meaning of the Sermon of the Mount Within Matthew. *Interpretation, 41*(2), 131–143.

Kistemaker, S.J. 1984. *New Testament Commentary: Exposition of Hebrews.* Grand Rapids: Baker.

———. 1984a. Parables of Jesus. In W. Elwell, ed. *Evangelical Dictionary of Theology* (824–826). Grand Rapids: Baker.

Kitchen, K.A. 1992. The Exodus. In D.N. Freedman, ed. *The Anchor Bible Dictionary*

(2:700–708). New York: Doubleday.
Klappert, B. 1986. *basileía*. In C. Brown, ed. *New International Dictionary of New Testament Theology* (2:372–390). Grand Rapids: Zondervan.
Klassen, W. 1992. War in the NT. In D.N. Freedman, ed. *The Anchor Bible Dictionary* (6:867–875). New York: Doubleday.
Klein, M.G. 1963. *Treaty of the Great King*. Grand Rapids: Eerdmans.
———. 1975. The Old Testament Origins of the Gospel Genre. *Westminster Theological Journal, 38*(1), 1–20.
———. 1978. Comments on an Old-New Error. *Westminster Theological Journal, 41*, 172–189.
Klein, W.W., Blomberg, C.L., & Hubbard, R.L. 1993. *Introduction to Biblical Interpretation*. Waco, TX: Word.
Kleine, H. 1991. *óros*. In H. Balz & G. Schneider, eds. J.W. Thompson & J.W. Medendorp, trans. *Exegetical Dictionary of the New Testament* (2:533–534). Grand Rapids: Eerdmans.
Klopfenstein, M.A. 1997. *šqr*. In E. Jenni & C. Westermann, eds. M.E. Biddle, trans. *Theological Lexicon of the Old Testament* (3:1399–1405). Peabody, MA: Hendrickson Publishers.
Knierim, R. 1997. *'āwōn*. In E. Jenni & C. Westermann, eds. M.E. Biddle, trans. *Theological Lexicon of the Old Testament* (2:862–866). Peabody, MA: Hendrickson Publishers.
Knight, G.A.F. 1976. *Theology as Narration: A Commentary on the Book of Exodus*. Grand Rapids: Eerdmans.
Koch, K. 1999. *'āwōn*. In G.J. Botterweck, H. Ringgren, & H.J. Fabry, eds. D.W. Scott, trans. *Theological Dictionary of the Old Testament* (10:546–562). Grand Rapids: Eerdmans.
Kodjak, A. 1986. *A Structural Analysis Of The Sermon On The Mount*. New York: Mouton de Gruyter.
Koehler, L. & Baumgartner, W. 2001. *The Hebrew and Aramaic Lexicon of the Old Testament*. Study Edition. 2 vols. M.E.J. Richardson, trans. Leiden, the Netherlands: Koninklijke Brill NV.
Konkel, A.H. 1997. *śn'*. In W.A. VanGemeren, ed. *New International Dictionary of Old Testament Theology & Exegesis* (3:1256–1260). Grand Rapids: Eerdmans.
Kromminga, C.G. 1984. Repentance. In W. Elwell, ed. *Evangelical Dictionary of Theology* (936–937). Grand Rapids: Baker.
Kropatschek, H. 1986. *brōsis*. In C. Brown, ed. *New International Dictionary of New Testament Theology* (2:268–269). Grand Rapids: Zondervan.
Kühlewein, J. 1997. *rēa'*. In E. Jenni & C. Westermann, eds. M.E. Biddle, trans. *Theological Lexicon of the Old Testament* (3:1243–1246). Peabody, MA: Hendrickson Publishers.
Kuhn, H.B. 1976. Names of God. In M.C. Tenney, ed. *The Zondervan Pictorial Encyclopedia of the Bible* (2:760–766). Grand Rapids: Zondervan.
Kupp, D.D. 1996. *Matthew's Emmanuel: Divine Presence and God's People in the First Gospel*. Cambridge: Cambridge University Press.
Labuschagne, C.J. 1997. *'nh*. In E. Jenni & C. Westermann, eds. M.E. Biddle, trans. *Theological Lexicon of the Old Testament* (2:926–930). Peabody, MA: Hendrickson Publishers.
Ladd, G.E. 1986. Kingdom of God. In G.W. Bromiley, ed. *The International Standard Bible Encyclopedia* (3:23–29). Grand Rapids: Eerdmans.

———. 1993. *A Theology of the New Testament: Revised Edition.* D.A. Hagner, ed. Grand Rapids: Eerdmans.

———. 2001. Kingdom of Christ, God, Heaven. In W. Elwell, ed. *Evangelical Dictionary of Theology* (657–661). Grand Rapids: Baker.

Lambert, G. 1976. Adultery. In M.C. Tenney, ed. *The Zondervan Pictorial Encyclopedia of the Bible* (1:65–66). Grand Rapids: Zondervan.

Lambert, J.C. 1955. Beatitudes. In J. Orr, ed. *The International Standard Bible Encyclopedia* (1:419–420). Grand Rapids: Eerdmans.

Lambrecht, J. 1985. *The Sermon on the Mount: Proclamation and Exhortation.* Wilmington, Delaware: Michael Glazier.

Lane, W.L. 1974. *The Gospel According to Mark.* Grand Rapids: Eerdmans.

Lange, J.P. 1978. Exodus or the Second Book of Moses. In J.P. Lange, ed. P. Schaff & C.M. Mead, trans. *Commentary on the Holy Scriptures: Critical, Doctrinal, and Homiletical.* Vol. 1. Grand Rapids: Zondervan.

———. 1978. The Gospel According to Matthew: Together With A General Theological And Homiletical Introduction To The New Testament. In P. Schaff, ed. *Lange's Commentary on the Holy Scriptures: Critical, Doctrinal, and Homiletical.* (Vol. 8). Grand Rapids: Zondervan.

Lanier, D.E. 1992. The Lord's Prayer: Matt 6:9–13–A Thematic and Semantic-Structural Analysis. *Criswell Theological Review, 6*(1), 57–72.

Lapide, P. 1986. *The Sermon on the Mount: Utopia or Program for Action?* A. Swidler, trans. Maryknoll, NY: Orbis Books.

LaSor, W.S. 1979. Dead Sea Scrolls. In G.W. Bromiley, ed. *The International Standard Bible Encyclopedia* (1:883–897). Grand Rapids: Eerdmans.

———. 1982. Galilee. In G.W. Bromiley, ed. *The International Standard Bible Encyclopedia* (2:386–391). Grand Rapids: Eerdmans.

LaSor, W.S., Hubbard, D.A., & Bush, F.W. 1982. *Old Testament Survey: The Message, Form, and Background of the Old Testament.* Grand Rapids: Eerdmans.

Lauer, S.E. 1993. Must We Obey the Law? *A Journal of Biblical-Theological Preaching, 8,* 3–183.

Lee, G.A. 1982. Gehenna. In G.W. Bromiley, ed. *The International Standard Bible Encyclopedia* (2:423). Grand Rapids: Eerdmans.

Leibowitz, N. 1981. *Studies in Shemot: Exodus.* Jerusalem: Homanim Press.

Lenski, R.C.H. 1964. *The Interpretation of St. Matthew's Gospel.* Minneapolis, MN: Augsburg Publishing House.

Leslie, C.W. 1954. No Graven Images: The Contemporary Relevance of the Ten Commandments. *Canadian Journal of Theology, 1,* 129–131.

Leupold, H.C. 1942. *Exposition of Genesis.* Grand Rapids: Baker.

Lewis, J.P. 1980. *chōq.* In R.L. Harris, G.L. Archer, & B.K. Waltke, eds. *Theological Wordbook of the Old Testament* (1:317). Chicago: Moody Press.

Lie, M.M. 1986. *An Examination if Jesus Abolished the Law in Matthew 5:21–48.* Portland, OR: Multnomah School of the Bible. (Thesis-M.A.)

Liedke, G. 1997. *tswh.* In E. Jenni & C. Westermann, eds. M.E. Biddle, trans. *Theological Lexicon of the Old Testament* (2:1062–1065). Peabody, MA: Hendrickson Publishers.

Liefield, W.L. 1984. Luke. In F.E. Gaebelein, ed. *The Expositor's Bible Commentary* (Vol. 8). Grand Rapids: Eerdmans.

Lightner, R.P. 1986. Theological Perspectives on Theonomy; Part 1: Theonomy and Dispensationalism. *Bibliotheca Sacra, 143,* 26–36.
———. 1986a. Theological Perspectives on Theonomy; Part 2: Nondispensational Responses to Theonomy. *Bibliotheca Sacra, 143,* 134–145.
———. 1986b. Theological Perspectives on Theonomy; Part 3: A Dispensational Response to Theonomy. *Bibliotheca Sacra, 143,* 228–245.
———. 2000. Progressive Dispensationalism. *Conservative Theological Journal, 4*(11), 46–64.
Link, H.G. 1986. *egō eimi*. In C. Brown, ed. *New International Dictionary of New Testament Theology* (2:281–283). Grand Rapids: Zondervan.
Linnemann, E. 1990. *Historical Criticism of the Bible: Methodology or Ideology? Reflections of a Bultmannian Turned Evangelical.* Grand Rapids: Baker.
———. 1992. *Is There a Synoptic Problem? Rethinking the Literary Dependence of the First Three Gospels.* Grand Rapids: Baker.
Lint, G.A., ed. 1995. *The Old Testament Hebrew-English Dictionary: Aleph-Beth.* Springfield, Missouri: World Library Press.
———. 1996. *The Old Testament Hebrew-English Dictionary: Gimel–Zayin.* Springfield, Missouri: World Library Press.
Lloyd-Jones, D.M. 1977. *Studies in the Sermon on the Mount.* Grand Rapids: Eerdmans.
Loader, W.R.G. 1997. *Jesus' Attitude Towards the Law: A Study of the Gospels.* Tübingen: J.C.B. Mohr (Paul Siebeck).
Lochman, J.M. 1982. *Signposts to Freedom: The Ten Commandments and Christian Ethics.* D. Lewis, trans. Minneapolis, MN: Augsburg Publishing House.
Lohse, E. 1991. *Theological Ethics of the New Testament.* M.B. Boring, trans. Minneapolis: Fortress Press.
Louw, J.P. & Nida, E.A., eds. 1989. *Greek-English Lexicon of the New Testament: Based on Semantic Domains.* Second Edition. Vol. 1: Introduction and Domains. Vol. 2: Indices. New York, New York: United Bible Societies.
Love, W.D. 1896. *Sabbath and Sunday.* Chicago: Revell.
Lowery, D.K. 1994. A Theology of Matthew. In R.B. Zuck, ed. *A Biblical Theology of the New Testament* (19–63). Chicago: Moody Press.
———. 2001. Lord's Day. In W. Elwell, ed. *Evangelical Dictionary of Theology.* 2nd ed. (700–702). Grand Rapids: Baker.
Luc, A. 1997. *'āwōn*. In W.A. VanGemeren, ed. *New International Dictionary of Old Testament Theology & Exegesis* (3:351). Grand Rapids: Eerdmans.
Lucas, R. 1966. Considerations of Method in Old Testament Hermeneutics. *The Dunwoodie Review, 6,* 35.
Lund, N.W. 1970. *Chiasmus in the New Testament.* Peabody, MS: Hendrickson Publishers.
Luz, U. 1989. *Matthew 1–7: A Commentary.* W.C. Linss, trans. Minneapolis, MN: Augsburg Fortress.
———. 1991. *basileía*. In H. Balz & G. Schneider, eds. J.W. Thompson & J.W. Medendorp, trans. *Exegetical Dictionary of the New Testament* (1:201–205). Grand Rapids: Eerdmans.
———. 1995. *The Theology of the Gospel of Matthew.* J.B. Robinson, trans. Cambridge: Cambridge University Press.
MacKenzie, R.A. 1964. The Formal Aspect of Ancient Near Eastern Law. In W.S.

McCollough, ed. *The Seed of Wisdom: Essays in Honor of T. J. Meek* (39). Toronto: University of Toronto Press.

MacRae, A.A. 1976. Book of Exodus. In M.C. Tenney, ed. *The Zondervan Pictorial Encyclopedia of the Bible* (2:436–450). Grand Rapids: Zondervan.

Man, R.E. 1984. The Value of Chiasm for New Testament Interpretation. *Bibliotheca Sacra. 141* (562), 146–157.

Mankin, J. 1992. The Meaning of the Ten Commandments for Today. *Restoration Quarterly, 34* (4), 238–244.

Marshall, I.H. 1976. Kingdom of God, of Heaven. In M.C. Tenney, ed. *The Zondervan Pictorial Encyclopedia of the Bible* (3:801–809). Grand Rapids: Zondervan.

———. 1978. *Commentary on Luke*. Grand Rapids: Eerdmans.

Marshall, J.W. 2003. Decalogue. In T.D. Alexander & D.W. Baker, eds. *Dictionary of the Old Testament: Pentateuch* (171–182). Downers Grove, IL: InterVarsity.

Martens, E.A. 1996. God, Names of. In W.A. Elwell, ed. *Evangelical Dictionary of Biblical Theology* (297–300). Grand Rapids: Baker.

———. 2003. Sin, Guilt. In T.D. Alexander & D.W. Baker, eds. *Dictionary of the Old Testament: Pentateuch* (764–778). Downers Grove, IL: InterVarsity.

Martin, B.L. 1983. Matthew on Christ and the Law. *Theological Studies, 44*(1), 53–70.

Martin, R.P. 1982. Gospel. In G.W. Bromiley, ed. *The International Standard Bible Encyclopedia* (2:529–532). Grand Rapids: Eerdmans.

Martin, W.M. 1977. *The Kingdom of the Cults: An Analysis of the Major Cult Systems in the Present Christian Era.* Minneapolis, MN: Bethany Fellowship Publishers.

Massey, I.A. 1991. *Interpreting the Sermon on the Mount in the Light of Jewish Tradition as Evidenced in the Palestinian Targums of the Pentateuch: Selected Themes.* Lewiston, New York: The Edwin Mellen Press.

Mayes, A.D.H. 1981. *New Century Bible Commentary: Deuteronomy.* Grand Rapids: Eerdmans.

———. 1991. The Decalogue of Moses: An Enduring Ethical Programme? In S. Freyne, ed. *Ethics and the Christian* (25–40). Dublin: The Columba Press.

M'Caig, A. 1955. Law in the NT. In J. Orr, ed. *The International Standard Bible Encyclopedia* (3:1844–1852). Grand Rapids: Eerdmans.

McBain, J.M. 1977. *The Ten Commandments in the New Testament.* Nashville: Broadman Press.

McCann, J.C. 1988. Sabbath. In G.W. Bromiley, ed. *The International Standard Bible Encyclopedia* (4:247–252). Grand Rapids: Eerdmans.

McClain, A.J. 1953. What Is "the Law"? *Bibliotheca Sacra, 110*(440), 333–341.

———. 1973. *Law and Grace*. Winona Lake, IN: BMH Books.

McComiskey, T.E. 1980. *qādash.* In R.L. Harris, G.L. Archer, & B.K. Waltke, eds. *Theological Wordbook of the Old Testament* (2:786–789). Chicago: Moody Press.

———. 1982. Idolatry. In G.W. Bromiley, ed. *The International Standard Bible Encyclopedia* (2:796–799). Grand Rapids: Eerdmans.

———. 2001. God, Names of. In W.A. Elwell, ed. *Evangelical Dictionary of Theology.* 2nd ed. (504–508). Grand Rapids: Baker.

McConnell, R.S. 1969. *Law and Prophecy in Matthew's Gospel: The Authority and Use of the Old Testament in the Gospel of St. Matthew.* Basel: Friedrich Reinhardt Kommissionverlag.

McKnight, S. 1992. Justice, Righteousness. In J.B. Green, S. McKnight, and I.H. Marshall, eds. *Dictionary of Jesus and the Gospels* (411–416). Downers Grove, IL: InterVarsity.
McNeile, A.H. 1980. *The Gospel According to St. Matthew.* Grand Rapids: Baker.
McQuilkin, R. 1995. *An Introduction to Biblical Ethics.* (2nd. ed.). Wheaton, IL: Tyndale House Publishers.
Meadors, G.T. 1985. The "Poor" in the Beatitudes of Matthew and Luke. *Grace Theological Journal, 6*(2), 305–314.
Meier, J.P. 1976. *Law and History in Matthew's Gospel: A Redactional Study of Mt. 5:17–48.* Rome: Biblical Institute Press.
———. 1992. Gospel of Matthew. In D.N. Freedman, ed. *The Anchor Bible Dictionary* (4:622–641). New York: Doubleday.
Mendenhall, G.E. 1954. Covenant Forms in Israelite Tradition. *Biblical Archaeologist, 17*(3), 50–76.
Mendenhall, G.E. & Herion, G.A. 1992. Covenant. In D.N. Freedman, ed. *The Anchor Bible Dictionary* (1:1179–1202). New York: Doubleday.
Merrill, E.H. 1991. A Theology of the Pentateuch. In R.B. Zuck, E.H. Merrill, & D.L. Bock, eds. *A Biblical Theology of the Old Testament* (7–87). Chicago: Moody Press.
———. 1994. *The New American Commentary: An Exegetical and Theological Exposition of Holy Scripture–Deuteronomy.* Nashville, TN: Broadman & Holman Publishers.
Michaelis, W. 1999. *lychnos*. In G. Kittel, ed. G.W. Bromiley, trans. *Theological Dictionary of the New Testament* (4:324–327). Grand Rapids: Eerdmans.
———. 1999a. *parapíptō*. In G. Kittel, ed. G.W. Bromiley, trans. *Theological Dictionary of the New Testament* (6:170–172). Grand Rapids: Eerdmans.
Miller, P.D. 1989. The Place of the Decalogue in the Old Testament and Its Law, *Interpretation, 43*, 229–242.
———. 1990. *Deuteronomy–Interpretation, A Bible Commentary for Teaching and Preaching.* Louisville, KY: John Knox Press.
Miller, R.B. 1955. Sermon on the Mount. In J. Orr, ed. *The International Standard Bible Encyclopedia* (4:2732–2736). Grand Rapids: Eerdmans.
Milligram, A.E. 1944. *Sabbath: The Day of Delight.* Philadelphia: Jewish Publication Society of America.
Mills, T.E. 2002. The Significance of The Lord's Prayer For Understanding The New Testament Today. In *Evangelical Theological Society.* Paper read at the Annual Meeting of the Southeast Division of ETS on March 16, 2002 (1–20). Portland, OR: Theological Research Exchange Network.
Mohrlang, R. 1984. *Matthew and Paul: A Comparison of Ethical Perspectives.* Cambridge: Cambridge University Press.
Moo, D.J. 1984. Jesus and the Authority of the Mosaic Law. *Journal for the Study of the New Testament, 20,* 3–49.
———. 1988. The Law of Moses or the Law of Christ. In John S. Feinberg, ed. *Continuity and Discontinuity: Perspectives on the Relationship Between the Old and New Testaments* (203–218). Westchester, IL: Crossway Books.
———. Law. In J.B. Green, S. McKnight, & I.H. Marshall, eds. *Dictionary of Jesus and the Gospels* (450–461). Downers Grove, IL: InterVarsity.
———. 1993. The Law of Christ as the Fulfillment of the Law of Moses: A Modified Lutheran View. In W.G. Strickland, ed. *The Law, the Gospel, and the Modern Christian:*

Five Views (319–376). Grand Rapids: Zondervan.
Morris, L. 1974. *The Gospel According to St. Luke*. Grand Rapids: Eerdmans.
———. 1986. Light. In G.W. Bromiley, ed. *The International Standard Bible Encyclopedia* (3:134–136). Grand Rapids: Eerdmans.
———. 1992. *The Gospel According to Matthew*. Grand Rapids: Eerdmans.
Moskala, J. 2002. The Sabbath in the First Creation Account. *Journal of the Adventist Theological Society. 13*(1), 55–66.
Motyer, J.A. 2001. Law, Biblical Concept of. In W. Elwell, ed. *Evangelical Dictionary of Theology* (674–676). Grand Rapids: Baker.
Motyer, S. 1996. The Old Testament in the New Testament. In W.A. Elwell, ed. *Evangelical Dictionary of Biblical Theology* (582–585). Grand Rapids: Baker.
Mounce, R.H. 1977. *The Book of Revelation*. Grand Rapids: Eerdmans.
———. 1982. Sermon on the Mount. In J. D. Douglas, ed. *New Bible Dictionary: Second Edition* (1088–1091). Wheaton, IL: Tyndale.
———. 1988. Sermon on the Mount. In G.W. Bromiley, ed. *The International Standard Bible Encyclopedia* (4:411–416). Grand Rapids: Eerdmans.
Mueller, J.T. 2001. Adultery. In W. Elwell, ed. *Evangelical Dictionary of Theology*, 2nd ed. (26–27). Grand Rapids: Baker.
Müller, C. 1991. *epiousios*. In H. Balz & G. Schneider, eds. J.W. Thompson & J.W. Medendorp, trans. *Exegetical Dictionary of the New Testament* (2:31–32). Grand Rapids: Eerdmans.
Müller, H.P. 1997. *qdš*. In E. Jenni & C. Westermann, eds. M.E. Biddle, trans. *Theological Lexicon of the Old Testament* (3:1103–1118). Peabody, MA: Hendrickson Publishers.
Mundle, W. 1986. *epiousios*. In C. Brown, ed. *New International Dictionary of New Testament Theology* (1:251–252). Grand Rapids: Zondervan.
Murphy, R.E. 1964. The Relationship Between the Testaments. *Catholic Biblical Quarterly, 26*, 349–359.
Murray, J. 1957. *Principles of Conduct: Aspects of Biblical Ethics*. Grand Rapids: Eerdmans.
Naudé, J.A. 1997. *qdš*. In W.A. VanGemeren, ed. *New International Dictionary of Old Testament Theology & Exegesis* (3:877–887). Grand Rapids: Eerdmans.
Neyrey, J.H. 1998. *Honor and Shame in the Gospel of Matthew*. Louisville: Westminster John Knox Press.
Nichol, F.D. 1957. *Questions in Doctrine: An Explanation of Certain Major Aspects of Seventh Day Adventist Leaders, Bible Teachers and Editors*. Washington, DC: Review and Herald Publishing Association.
Nicholson, E.W. 1977. Decalogue as the Direct Address of God. *Vetus Testamentum, 27*(4), 422–433.
Nixon, R.E. 1970. Matthew. In D. Guthrie & J.A. Motyer, eds. *The New Bible Commentary Revised* (813–850). Grand Rapids: Eerdmans.
North, G. & DeMar, G. 1991. *Christian Reconstruction: What It Is, What It Isn't*. Tyler, TX: Institute for Christian Economics.
Noth, M. 1962. *Exodus: A Commentary*. J.S. Bowden, trans. Philadelphia: The Westminster Press.
Nutz, E.G. 1972. *The Unity of the Sermon on the Mount*. Greenville, SC: Bob Jones University. (Dissertation-Ph.D.)
Nystrom, J.D. 1986. *A Semantic Structure Analysis of Matthew 5:33–48*. Deerfield, IL: Trin-

ity Evangelical Divinity School. (Thesis-M.A.)
Olivier, J.P.J. 1997. *nqh*. In W.A. VanGemeren, ed. *New International Dictionary of Old Testament Theology & Exegesis* (3:152–154). Grand Rapids: Eerdmans.
O'Neill, J.C. 1993. The Lord's Prayer. *Journal for the Study of the New Testament, 51*, 3–25.
Osborne, S. 1952. The Christian and the Law. *Bibliotheca Sacra, 109*(435), 239–247.
Oss, D.A. 1989. The Influence of Hermeneutical Frameworks in the Theonomy Debate. *Westminster Theological Journal, 51*, 227–258.
Oswalt, J.N. 1980. *bārak*. In R.L. Harris, G.L. Archer, & B.K. Waltke, eds. *Theological Wordbook of the Old Testament* (1:132–133). Chicago: Moody Press.
———. 1980a. *kābēd*. In R.L. Harris, G.L. Archer, & B.K. Waltke, eds. *Theological Wordbook of the Old Testament* (1:426–428). Chicago: Moody Press.
———. 1996. Ten Commandments. In W.A. Elwell, ed. *Evangelical Dictionary of Biblical Theology* (763–765). Grand Rapids: Baker.
Packer, J.I. 1988. God. In S. Ferguson, D.F. Wright, & J.I. Packer, eds. *New Dictionary of Theology* (274–277). Downers Grove, IL: InterVarsity.
Park, J.E. 1952. The Book of Exodus. In G.A. Buttrick, ed. *The Interpreter's Bible* (1:833–939). New York: Abingdon Press.
Patai, R. 1977. *The Jewish Mind*. New York: Charles Scribner's Sons.
Patrick, D. 1973. Cauistic Law Governing Primary Rights and Duties. *Journal of Biblical Literature, 92*, 180.
Patte, D. 1987. *The Gospel According to Matthew: A Structural Commentary on Matthew's Faith*. Philadelphia: Fortress Press.
Payne, J.B. 1975. *The Theology of the Older Testament*. Grand Rapids: Zondervan.
———. 1980a. *chāmad*. In R.L. Harris, G.L. Archer, & B.K. Waltke, eds. *Theological Wordbook of the Old Testament* (1:294–295). Chicago: Moody Press.
———. 1980a. *hāwâ*. In R.L. Harris, G.L. Archer, & B.K. Waltke, eds. *Theological Wordbook of the Old Testament* (1:210–212). Chicago: Moody Press.
Pentecost, J.D. 1958. The Purpose of the Sermon on the Mount. *Bibliotheca Sacra, 115*, 128–135.
———. 1958a. The Purpose of the Sermon on the Mount. *Bibliotheca Sacra, 115*, 313–319.
———. 1958b. *Things to Come: A Study in Biblical Eschatology*. Grand Rapids: Eerdmans.
———. 1974. *The Words and Works of Jesus Christ*. Chicago: Moody Press.
———. 1980. *The Sermon on the Mount: Contemporary Insights for a Christian Lifestyle*. Portland, OR: Multnomah Press.
Perkins, P. 1992. Ethics (NT). In D.N. Freedman, ed. *The Anchor Bible Dictionary* (2:652–665). New York: Doubleday.
Phillips, A. 1970. *Ancient Israel's Criminal Law: A New Approach to the Decalogue*. New York: Schocken Books.
Phillips, J. 1999. *Exploring the Gospels: Matthew*. Neptune, NJ: Loizeaux Brothers.
Philo. 1937. On the Decalogue, On the Special Laws, On the Virtues. In E.H. Warmington, ed. F.H. Colson, trans. *The Loeb Classical Library*. Cambridge: Harvard University.
Pink, A.W. 1953. *An Exposition of the Sermon on the Mount*. Grand Rapids: Baker.
———. 2003. The Law and the Saint. [Web:] http://www.the-highway.com/Law_Pink.html. [Date of access: 27 November 2003].
Plaut, W.G. 1981. *The Torah: A Modern Commentary*. New York: Union of American Hebrew Congregations.

Plummer, A. 1982. *An Exegetical Commentary on The Gospel According to St. Matthew*. Grand Rapids: Baker.

Preuss, H.D. 1995. *Old Testament Theology: Volume 1*. L.G. Perdue, trans. Louisville, KY: Westminster John Knox Press.

Procksch, O. 1999. *hágios*. In G. Kittel, ed. G.W. Bromiley, trans. *Theological Dictionary of the New Testament* (1:100–115). Grand Rapids: Eerdmans.

Przybylski, B. 1980. *Righteousness in Matthew and His World of Thought*. Cambridge: Cambridge University Press.

Quell, G. 1999. *kýrios*. In G. Kittel, ed. G.W. Bromiley, trans. *Theological Dictionary of the New Testament* (3:1058–1081). Grand Rapids: Eerdmans.

Rand, J.F. 1955. Problems in Literal Interpretation of the Sermon on the Mount: Part I. *Bibliotheca Sacra, 112*(445), 28–38.

———. 1955. Problems in Literal Interpretation of the Sermon on the Mount: Part II. *Bibliotheca Sacra, 112*(446), 125–136.

Reid, W.S. 1952. The New Testament Belief in an Old Testament Church. *Evangelical Quarterly, 24*, 194–205.

Reisinger, E.C. 1997. *The Law and the Gospel*. Phillipsburg, NJ: P. & R. Publishing.

Richards, L.O. 1991. *Zondervan Expository Dictionary of Bible Words*. (1st ed.). Grand Rapids, Zondervan.

Ridderbos, H.N. 1987. *The Bible Student's Commentary: Matthew*. R. Togtman, trans. Grand Rapids: Zondervan.

Ringgren, H. 1974. *'ĕlōhîm*. In G.J. Botterweck & H. Ringgren, eds. J.T. Willis, trans. *Theological Dictionary of the Old Testament* (1:267–284). Grand Rapids: Eerdmans.

———. 1986. *chāqâ*. In G.J. Botterweck & H. Ringgren, eds. D.E. Green, trans. *Theological Dictionary of the Old Testament* (5:139–147). Grand Rapids: Eerdmans.

———. 2003. *qdš*. In G.J. Botterweck, H. Ringgren, & H.J. Fabry, eds. D.W. Stott, trans. *Theological Dictionary of the Old Testament* (12:530–543). Grand Rapids: Eerdmans.

Rissi, M. 1991. *krínō*. In H. Balz & G. Schneider, eds. J.W. Thompson & J.W. Medendorp, trans. *Exegetical Dictionary of the New Testament* (2:318–321). Grand Rapids: Eerdmans.

Ritt, H. 1991. *phōs*. In H. Balz & G. Schneider, eds. J.W. Thompson & J.W. Medendorp, trans. *Exegetical Dictionary of the New Testament* (3:447–448). Grand Rapids: Eerdmans.

Rogers, R.K. 1984. *The Old Testament Origins of the First Three Beatitudes*. Dallas, TX: Dallas Theological Seminary. (Thesis-Th.M.)

Rordorf, W. 1968. *Sunday: The History of the Day of Rest and Worship in the Earliest Centuries of the Christian Church*. Philadelphia: Westminster Press.

Rose, M. 1992. Names of God in the OT. In D.N. Freedman, ed. *The Anchor Bible Dictionary* (4:1001–1011). New York: Doubleday.

Rowdon, H.H. 1976. Ethics of Jesus. In M.C. Tenney, ed. *The Zondervan Pictorial Encyclopedia of the Bible* (2:404–411). Grand Rapids: Zondervan.

———. 1988. Dispensational Theology. In S. Ferguson, D.F. Wright, & J.I. Packer, eds. *New Dictionary of Theology* (200–201). Downers Grove, IL: InterVarsity.

Rowlingson, D.T. 1964. The Theme of Promise and Fulfillment in Jesus' Thought. *Religion in Life, 33*, 80–89.

Rule, U.Z. 1955. Law in the OT. In J. Orr, ed. *The International Standard Bible Encyclopedia* (3:1852–1858). Grand Rapids: Eerdmans.

Rushdoony, R. J. 1973. *The Institutes of Biblical Law.* Phillipsburg, NJ: Presbyterian & Reformed.
Ryrie, C.C. 1959. *Biblical Theology of the New Testament.* Chicago: Moody Press.
———. 1965. *Dispensationalism Today.* Chicago: Moody Press.
———. 1986. *Basic Theology: A Popular Systematic Guide To Understanding Biblical Truth.* Wheaton, IL: Victor Books.
———. 1996. Dispensationalism. In M. Couch, ed. *Dictionary of Premillennial Theology* (93–98). Grand Rapids: Kregel.
Sailhamer, J.H. 1992. *The Pentateuch as Narrative: A Biblical-Theological Commentary.* Grand Rapids: Zondervan.
Sakenfeld, K.D. 1992. Love (OT). In D.N. Freedman, ed. *The Anchor Bible Dictionary* (4:375–381). New York: Doubleday.
Sanders, E.P. 1975. Torah and Christ. *Interpretation, 29,* 372–390.
———. 1990. When Is a Law a Law? The Case of Jesus and Paul. In E.B. Firmage, B.G. Weiss, & J.W. Welch, eds. *Religion and Law: Biblical-Judaic and Islamic Perspectives* (139–158). Winona Lake, IL: Eisenbrauns.
———. 1992. Law in Judaism of the NT Period. In D.N. Freedman, ed. *The Anchor Bible Dictionary* (4:254–265). New York: Doubleday.
Sanders, J.A. 1975. Torah and Christ. *Interpretation, 29,* 372–390.
Sarna, N.M. 1991. *The JPS Torah Commentary: Exodus.* Philadelphia: The Jewish Publication Society.
———. 2000. *Studies in Biblical Interpretation.* Philadelphia: The Jewish Publication Society.
Saucy, R.L. 1993. *The Case for Progressive Dispensationalism: The Interface Between Dispensational and Non-Dispensational Theology.* Grand Rapids: Zondervan.
Sauer, G. 1997. *qin'â.* In E. Jenni & C. Westermann, eds. M.E. Biddle, trans. *Theological Lexicon of the Old Testament* (3:1145–1147). Peabody, MA: Hendrickson Publishers.
———. 1997a. *šmr.* In E. Jenni & C. Westermann, eds. M.E. Biddle, trans. *Theological Lexicon of the Old Testament* (3:1380–1384). Peabody, MA: Hendrickson Publishers.
Sawyer, J.F.A. 1997. *šāw'.* In E. Jenni & C. Westermann, eds. M.E. Biddle, trans. *Theological Lexicon of the Old Testament* (3:1310–1312). Peabody, MA: Hendrickson Publishers.
Scaer, D.P. 1991. The Law and the Gospel in Lutheran Theology. *Grace Theological Journal, 12*(2), 163–178.
———. 1996. Beatitudes. In W.A. Elwell, ed. *Evangelical Dictionary of Biblical Theology* (53–55). Grand Rapids: Baker.
———. 1996a. Sermon on the Mount. In W.A. Elwell, ed. *Evangelical Dictionary of Biblical Theology* (723–725). Grand Rapids: Baker.
Schaff, P. 1979. *History of the Christian Church.* (Vols. 1–6). Grand Rapids: Eerdmans.
Scharbert, J. 1977. *brk.* In G.J. Botterweck & H. Ringgren, eds. J.T. Willis, trans. *Theological Dictionary of the Old Testament* (2:279–308). Grand Rapids: Eerdmans.
Schmidt, T.E. 1988. Burden, Barrier, Blasphemy: Wealth In Matt 6:33, Luke 14:33, And Luke 16:15. *Trinity Journal. 9*(2), 171–189.
Schmidt, W.H. 1978. *dābhar.* In G.J. Botterweck & H. Ringgren, eds. J.T. Willis, G.W. Bromiley, & D.E. Green, trans. *Theological Dictionary of the Old Testament* (3:94–125). Grand Rapids: Eerdmans.
———. 1997. *'ĕlōhîm.* In E. Jenni & C. Westermann, eds. M.E. Biddle, trans. *Theological*

Lexicon of the Old Testament (1:115–126). Peabody, MA: Hendrickson Publishers.

Schmidtbleicher, P.R. 2002. Balancing The Use Of The Old Testament. *Chafer Theological Seminary Journal, 8*(3), 39–62.

Schnackenburg, R. 1965. *The Moral Teaching of the New Testament*. J. Holland-Smith & W.J. O'Hara, trans. New York: The Seabury Press.

Schneider, G. 1991. *lychnos*. In H. Balz & G. Schneider, eds. J.W. Thompson & J.W. Medendorp, trans. *Exegetical Dictionary of the New Testament* (2:367–368). Grand Rapids: Eerdmans.

Schneider, W. 1986. *kríma*. In C. Brown, ed. *New International Dictionary of New Testament Theology* (2:362–367). Grand Rapids: Zondervan.

Schottroff, W. 1997. *zkr*. In E. Jenni & C. Westermann, eds. M.E. Biddle, trans. *Theological Lexicon of the Old Testament* (1:381–388). Peabody, MA: Hendrickson Publishers.

Schoville, K.N. 1997. *šmr*. In W.A. VanGemeren, ed. *New International Dictionary of Old Testament Theology & Exegesis* (4:182–184). Grand Rapids: Eerdmans.

Schrage, W. 1988. *The Ethics of the New Testament*. D.E. Green, trans. Philadelphia: Fortress Press.

Schrenk, O. 1999. *dikaiosýnē*. In G. Kittel, ed. G.W. Bromiley, trans. *Theological Dictionary of the New Testament* (2:192–210). Grand Rapids: Eerdmans.

Schröeder, W.J. 1978. Deuteronomy or The Fifth Book of Moses. In J.P. Lange, ed. P. Schaff & A. Gosman, trans. *Commentary on the Holy Scriptures: Critical, Doctrinal, and Homiletical*. Vol. 2. Grand Rapids: Zondervan.

Schultz, C. 1980. *'āwâ*. In R.L. Harris, G.L. Archer, & B.K. Waltke, eds. *Theological Wordbook of the Old Testament* (2:650–652). Chicago: Moody Press.

———. 1980a. *'ûd*. In R.L. Harris, G.L. Archer, & B.K. Waltke, eds. *Theological Wordbook of the Old Testament* (2:648–650). Chicago: Moody Press.

Schultz, R. 1997. *shāphat*. In W.A. VanGemeren, ed. *New International Dictionary of Old Testament Theology & Exegesis* (4:213–220). Grand Rapids: Eerdmans.

Schwarzwäller, K. 1969. Das Verhältnis Altes Testament–Neues Testament in Lichte der gegenwärtigen Bestimmungen. *Evangelische Theologie, 29*, 281–307.

Schweitzer, A. 1961. *The Quest for the Historical Jesus*. W. Montgomery, trans. New York: Macmillan.

Schwertley, B. 2003. God's Law for Modern Man. [Web:] http://www.reformed.com/pub/law.htm#f4. [Date of access: 26 November 2003].

Scott, J.B. 1980. *'ĕlōhîm*. In R.L. Harris, G.L. Archer, & B.K. Waltke, eds. *Theological Wordbook of the Old Testament* (1:44–45). Chicago: Moody Press.

Seabass, H. 1986. *dikaiosýnē*. In C. Brown, ed. *New International Dictionary of New Testament Theology* (3:358–365). Grand Rapids: Zondervan.

Selman, M.J. 2003. Law. In T.D. Alexander & D.W. Baker, eds. *Dictionary of the Old Testament: Pentateuch* (497–515). Downers Grove, IL: InterVarsity.

Senior, D. 1998. *Abingdon New Testament Commentary Series: Matthew*. Nashville: Abingdon Press.

Seow, C.L. 1992. Ark of the Covenant. In D.N. Freedman, ed. *The Anchor Bible Dictionary* (1:386–393). New York: Doubleday.

Shead, A.G. 2000. Sabbath. In T.D. Alexander, B.S. Rosner, D.A., & G. Goldsworthy, eds. *New Dictionary of Biblical Theology* (745–750). Downers Grove, IL: InterVarsity.

Shepherd, J. 1997. *šāw'*. In W.A. VanGemeren, ed. *New International Dictionary of Old Tes-*

tament Theology & Exegesis (4:53–55). Grand Rapids: Eerdmans.
Schippers, R. 1986. *plēroō*. In C. Brown, ed. *New International Dictionary of New Testament Theology* (1:733–741). Grand Rapids: Zondervan.
———. 1986a. *telos*. In C. Brown, ed. *New International Dictionary of New Testament Theology* (2:59–66). Grand Rapids: Zondervan.
Shirbroun, G.F. 1992. Light. In J.B. Green, S. McKnight, & I.H. Marshall, eds. *Dictionary of Jesus and the Gospels* (472–473). Downers Grove, IL: InterVarsity.
Sigal, P. 1986. *The Halakah of Jesus of Nazareth According to the Gospel of Matthew*. Lanham, MD: University Press of America.
Silbermann, A.M. 1988. *Chumash with Targum Onkelos, Haphtaroth and Rashi's Commentary: Shemoth*. Jerusalem: Feldheim Publishers.
———. 1989. *Chumash with Targum Onkelos, Haphtaroth and Rashi's Commentary: Devarim*. Jerusalem: Feldheim Publishers.
Simian-Yofre, H. 1999. *'wd*. In G.J. Botterweck, H. Ringgren, and H.J. Fabry, eds. D.W. Scott, trans. *Theological Dictionary of the Old Testament* (10:495–515). Grand Rapids: Eerdmans.
Simmons, W.A. 1996. Golden Rule. In W.A. Elwell, ed. *Evangelical Dictionary of Biblical Theology* (304–305). Grand Rapids: Baker.
Sisson, R.B. 1997. Voices of Authority in the Sermon on the Mount. In *Society of Biblical Literature 1997 Seminar Papers. Number 36* (551–566). Atlanta: Scholars Press.
Skibbe, E.M. 1968. Pentateuchal Themes In The Sermon On The Mount. *Lutheran Quarterly, 20*(1), 44–51.
Slemp, J.C. 1950. *Twelve Laws of Life: A Study of the Ten Commandments and Related Teachings of Jesus*. Philadelphia: The Judson Press.
Smith, J.E. 1980. *gānab*. In R.L. Harris, G.L. Archer, & B.K. Waltke, eds. *Theological Wordbook of the Old Testament* (1:168). Chicago: Moody Press.
Smith, M.A. 1977. Worship and the Christian Year. In Tim Dowley, ed. *Eerdman's Handbook to the History of Christianity*. Grand Rapids: Eerdmans.
Smith, R.L. 1993. *Old Testament Theology: Its History, Method, and Message*. Nashville, TN: Broadman & Holman, Publishers.
Snodgrass, K.R. 1992. Matthew's Understanding of the Law. *Interpretation, 46*(4), 368–378.
Songer, H.S. 1992. The Sermon on the Mount and Its Jewish Foreground. *Review & Expositor, 89*(2), 165–177.
Spicq, C. 1994. *Theological Lexicon of the New Testament*. J.D. Ernest, trans. & ed. Peabody, MA: Hendrickson Publishers.
Spong, J.S. & Haines, D.G. 1986. *Beyond Moralism: A Contemporary View Of The Ten Commandments*. San Francisco: Harper & Row.
Sprinkle, J.M. 1996. Law. In W.A. Elwell, ed. *Evangelical Dictionary of Biblical Theology* (467–471). Grand Rapids: Baker.
Stalker, J. 1939. Ethics of Jesus. In J. Orr, ed. *The International Standard Bible Encyclopedia* (2:1026–1031). Grand Rapids: Eerdmans.
Stanton, G.N. 1992. Sermon on the Mount/Plain. In J.B. Green, S. McKnight, & I.H. Marshall, eds. *Dictionary of Jesus and the Gospels* (735–744). Downers Grove, IL: InterVarsity.
Stassen, G.H. 1992. Grace and Deliverance in the Sermon on the Mount. *Review & Expositor, 89*(2), 229–244.

———. 2003. The Fourteen Triads of the Sermon on the Mount (Matthew 5:21–7:12). *Journal of Biblical Literature, 122*(2), 267–308.

Stein, R.H. 1996. Kingdom of God. In W.A. Elwell, ed. *Evangelical Dictionary of Biblical Theology* (451–454). Grand Rapids: Baker.

Steinmetz, D.C. 1989. The Reformation and the Ten Commandments. *Interpretation, 33*(3), 256–266.

Stendebach, F.J. 2001. *'ānâ*. In G.J. Botterweck, H. Ringgren, & H.J. Fabry, eds. D.E. Green, trans. *Theological Dictionary of the Old Testament* (11:215–230). Grand Rapids: Eerdmans.

Stevenson, H.F. 1956. *Titles of the Triune God.* Westwood, NJ: Revell.

Stewart, D.K. 1988. Steadfast Love. In G.W. Bromiley, ed. *The International Standard Bible Encyclopedia* (4:613–614). Grand Rapids: Eerdmans.

Stoebe, H.J. 1997. *chesed.* In E. Jenni & C. Westermann, eds. M.E. Biddle, trans. *Theological Lexicon of the Old Testament* (2:449–464). Peabody, MA: Hendrickson Publishers.

Stolz, F. 1997. *šbt.* In E. Jenni & C. Westermann, eds. M.E. Biddle, trans. *Theological Lexicon of the Old Testament* (3:1297–1302). Peabody, MA: Hendrickson Publishers.

Stonehouse, N.B. 1944. *The Witness of Matthew and Mark to Christ.* Philadelphia: The Presbyterian Guardian.

Stoutenburg, D. 1996. *With One Voice: The Sermon on the Mount and Rabbinic Literature.* San Francisco: International Scholars Publications.

Strecker, G. 1988. *The Sermon On The Mount: An Exegetical Commentary.* O.C. Dean, trans. Nashville: Abingdon Press.

———. 1990. *euangélion.* In H. Balz & G. Schneider, eds. V.P. Howard & J.W. Thompson, trans. *Exegetical Dictionary of the New Testament* (2:70–74). Grand Rapids: Eerdmans.

———. 1990a. *makários.* In H. Balz & G. Schneider, eds. V.P. Howard & J.W. Thompson, trans. *Exegetical Dictionary of the New Testament* (2:376–379). Grand Rapids: Eerdmans.

———. 1991. The Law in the Sermon on the Mount, and the Sermon on the Mount as Law. In J. Reumann, ed. *The Promise and Practice of Biblical Theology* (35–49). Minneapolis, MN: Augsburg Fortress.

———. 2000. *Theology of the New Testament.* F.W. Horn, ed. M.E. Boring, trans. Berlin: Walter de Gruyter & Co.

Strickland, W.G. 1993. The Inauguration of the Law of Christ with the Gospel of Christ: A Dispensational View. In W.G. Strickland, ed. *The Law, the Gospel, and the Modern Christian: Five Views* (229–279). Grand Rapids: Zondervan.

Sturz, H.A. 1963. The Sermon on the Mount and Its Application to the Present Age. *Grace Theological Journal. 4*(3), 3–15.

Suggs, M.J. 1970. *Wisdom, Christology, and Law in Matthew's Gospel.* Cambridge, MA: Harvard University Press.

Swidler, L. 1981. The Jewishness of Jesus: Some Religious Implications for Christians. *Journal of Ecumenical Studies, 18*(1), 104–113.

Talley, D. 1997. *chmd.* In W.A. VanGemeren, ed. *New International Dictionary of Old Testament Theology & Exegesis* (2:167–169). Grand Rapids: Eerdmans.

Tate, M.E. 1977. Legal Traditions of the Books of Exodus. *Review & Expositor. 74*, 483–510.

Tenny, M.C. 1961. *New Testament Survey.* Grand Rapids: Eerdmans.

Terzian, M.V. 1984. *The Homiletical Style of Christ in the Sermon on the Mount.* Winona

Lake, IN: Grace Theological Seminary. (Thesis-M.Div.)

The Net Bible. 2001. Garland, Texas: Biblical Studies Press, L.L.C., and the authors. [Web:] http://www.bible.org/netbible/index.htm. [Date of access: 13 March 2003].

The Westminster Confession of Faith. 3rd ed. 1990. Atlanta, GA: Committee for Christian Education & Publications, Presbyterian Church in America.

Thiessen, H.C. 1979. *Lectures in Systematic Theology.* (Rev. ed.). Grand Rapids: Eerdmans.

Thomas, R.L. 1976. Neighbor. In M.C. Tenney, ed. *The Zondervan Pictorial Encyclopedia of the Bible* (4:408–409). Grand Rapids: Zondervan.

———. 1995. The Hermeneutics of Progressive Dispensationalism. *The Master's Seminary Journal, 6*(1), 79–95.

Thompson, J.A. 1974. Deuteronomy: An Introduction and Commentary. In D.J. Wiseman, ed. *Tyndale Old Testament Commentaries.* (Vol. 5). Downers Grove, IL: InterVarsity.

———. 1979. Covenant (OT). In G.W. Bromiley, ed. *The International Standard Bible Encyclopedia* (1:790–793). Grand Rapids: Eerdmans.

Thurston, B.B. 1987. Matthew 5:43–48. *Interpretation, 41*(2), 170–173.

Tiessen, T. 1993. Toward A Hermeneutic For Discerning Universal Moral Absolutes. *Journal of the Evangelical Theological Society, 36*(2), 189–207.

Tigay, J.H. 1996. *The JPS Torah Commentary: Deuteronomy.* Philadelphia: The Jewish Publication Society.

Tigwell, J. 1981. *Explaining the Gospels.* London: Scripture Union.

Toon, P. 1996. Righteousness. In W.A. Elwell, ed. *Evangelical Dictionary of Biblical Theology* (687–689). Grand Rapids: Baker.

Topel, J. 1998. The Tarnished Golden Rule (Luke 6:31): The Inescapable Radicalness of Christian Ethics, *Theological Studies, 59*(3), 475–485.

Toussaint, S.D. 1981. *Behold The King: A Study of Matthew.* (1st ed.). Portland: Multnomah Press.

Trites, A.A. 1992. The Blessings and Warnings of the Kingdom (Matthew 5:3–12; 7:13–27). *Review & Expositor, 89*(2), 179–196.

Turner, D.L. 1992. Whom Does God Approve? The Context, Structure, Purpose, and Exegesis of Matthew's Beatitudes. *Criswell Theological Review, 6*(1), 29–42.

Turner, G.A. 1986. Love. In G.W. Bromiley, ed. *The International Standard Bible Encyclopedia* (3:173–176). Grand Rapids: Eerdmans.

Tuttle, G.A. 1997. The Sermon On The Mount: Its Wisdom Affinities And Their Relation To Its Structure. *Journal of the Evangelical Theological Society, 20*(3), 213–230.

Van der Minde, H.J. 1990. *brōsis.* In H. Balz & G. Schneider, eds. V.P. Howard & J.W. Thompson, trans. *Exegetical Dictionary of the New Testament* (1:228–229). Grand Rapids: Eerdmans.

VanGemeren, W.A. 1988. Systems of Continuity. In J.S. Feinberg, ed. *Continuity and Discontinuity: Perspectives on the Relationship Between the Old and New Testaments* (37–62). Westchester, IL: Crossway Books.

———. 1993. The Law Is the Perfection of Righteousness in Jesus Christ: A Reformed Perspective. In W.G. Strickland, ed. *The Law, the Gospel, and the Modern Christian: Five Views* (177–199). Grand Rapids: Zondervan.

———. 2001. Lovingkindness. In W. Elwell, ed. *Evangelical Dictionary of Theology.* 2nd ed. 713). Grand Rapids: Baker.

———. 2001a. Tetragammaton. In W.A. Elwell, ed. *Evangelical Dictionary of Theology.* 2nd ed. (1177–1178). Grand Rapids: Baker.

Van Groningen, G. 1980. *śānē'*. In R.L. Harris, G.L. Archer, & B.K. Waltke, eds. *Theological Wordbook of the Old Testament* (2:879–880). Chicago: Moody Press.

Van Leeuwen, R.C. 1997. *'ēd.* In E. Jenni & C. Westermann, eds. M.E. Biddle, trans. *Theological Lexicon of the Old Testament* (2:838–846). Peabody, MA: Hendrickson Publishers.

———. 1997a. Form, Image. In W.A. VanGemeren, ed. *New International Dictionary of Old Testament Theology & Exegesis* (4:643–648). Grand Rapids: Eerdmans.

———. 1997b. *nqh.* In E. Jenni & C. Westermann, eds. M.E. Biddle, trans. *Theological Lexicon of the Old Testament* (2:763–767). Peabody, MA: Hendrickson Publishers.

Van Ruler, A.A. 1971. *The Christian Church and the Old Testament.* Grand Rapids: Eerdmans.

Vaught, C. 1986. *The Sermon on the Mount: A Theological Interpretation.* New York: State University of New York Press.

Verhey, A.D. 1982. Ethics: NT Ethics. In G.W. Bromiley, ed. *The International Standard Bible Encyclopedia* (2:173–183). Grand Rapids: Eerdmans.

———. 1982a. Ethics: The Ethic of Jesus. In G.W. Bromiley, ed. *The International Standard Bible Encyclopedia* (2:169–173). Grand Rapids: Eerdmans.

Verhoef, P.A. 1970. The Relationship Between the Old and New Testaments. In J.B. Payne, ed. *New Perspectives on the Old Testament* (282–292). Waco, TX: Word.

Vermes, G. 1993. *The Religion of Jesus the Jew.* Minneapolis, MN: Fortress Press.

Vischer, W. 1934. *Das Christuszeugnis des Alte Testament.* Zurich. Translated *The Witness of the Old Testament to Christ.* London: Lutterworth. 1949.

Von Rad, G. 1962. *Old Testament Theology.* New York: Harper and Row.

———. 1963. Typological Interpretation of the Old Testament. In C. Westermann, ed. *Essays on Old Testament Hermeneutics* (17–39). Richmond: John Knox Press.

———. 1999. *basileús.* In G. Kittel, ed. G.W. Bromiley, trans. *Theological Dictionary of the New Testament* (1:565–571). Grand Rapids: Eerdmans.

Waffle, Albert E. 1885. *The Lord's Day: Its Universal and Perpetual Obligation.* Philadelphia: American Sunday School Union.

Wager, S. 1990. *yārâ.* In G.J. Botterweck & H. Ringgren, eds. D.E. Green, trans. *Theological Dictionary of the Old Testament* (6:330–335). Grand Rapids: Eerdmans.

Wallace, R.S. 1965. *The Ten Commandments: A Study of Ethical Freedom.* Grand Rapids: Eerdmans.

Wallis, G. 1977. *'āhabh.* In G.J. Botterweck & H. Ringgren, eds. J.T. Willis, trans. *Theological Dictionary of the Old Testament* (1:101–118). Grand Rapids: Eerdmans.

———. 1980. *chāmadh.* In G.J. Botterweck & H. Ringgren, eds. D.E. Green, trans. *Theological Dictionary of the Old Testament* (4:452–461). Grand Rapids: Eerdmans.

Walton, J.H., Matthews, V.H., & Chavalas, M.K. 2000. *The IVP Bible Background Commentary: Old Testament.* Downers Grove, IL: InterVarsity.

Walvoord, J.F. 1966. *The Revelation of Jesus Christ.* Chicago: Moody Press.

———. 1974. *Matthew: Thy Kingdom Come.* Chicago: Moody Press.

Warmuth, G. 1998. *nāqâ.* In G.J. Botterweck, H. Ringgren, & H.J. Fabry, eds. D.E. Green, trans. *Theological Dictionary of the Old Testament* (5:500–521). Grand Rapids: Eerdmans.

Waterman, G.H. 1976. Sabbath. In M.C. Tenney, ed. *The Zondervan Pictorial Encyclopedia of the Bible* (5:181–189). Grand Rapids: Zondervan.

Watson, A.W. 1996. *Jesus and the Law.* Athens, GA: The University of Georgia Press.

Webb, P.M. 1996. *Revelation and Chiasm: The Drama of Supernatural Warfare.* Denver, CO: Denver Conservative Baptist Seminary. (Thesis-M.A.)

Wedderburn, A.J.M., ed. 1989. *Paul and Jesus: Collected Essays.* Sheffield: Sheffield Academic Press.

Weder, H. 1990. "But I Say to You..." Concerning the Foundations of Jesus' Interpretation of the Law in the "Sermon on the Mount." In T.W. Jennings, ed. *Text and Logos: The Humanistic Interpretation of the New Testament* (211–228). Atlanta: Scholars Press.

Weinfield, M. 1990. The Decalogue: Its Significance, Uniqueness, and Place in Israel's Tradition. In E.B. Firmage, B.G. Weiss, & J.W. Welch, eds. *Religion and Law: Biblical-Judaic and Islamic Perspectives* (3–47). Winona Lake, IL: Eisenbrauns.

Wenham, D. 1995. *Paul: Follower of Jesus or Founder of Christianity?* Grand Rapids: Eerdmans.

———. 2002. *Paul and Jesus: The True Story.* Grand Rapids: Eerdmans.

Wenham, G. 1978. Law and the Legal System in the Old Testament. In B. Kaye and G. Wenham (eds.), *Law, Morality, and the Bible* (28–29). Downers Grove, IL: InterVarsity.

———. 1979. *The Book of Leviticus.* Grand Rapids: Eerdmans.

Westerholm, S. 1992. The Law in the Sermon on the Mount: Matt 5:17–48. *Criswell Theological Review, 6*(1), 43–56.

Westermann, C. 1997. *kbd.* In E. Jenni & C. Westermann, eds. M.E. Biddle, trans. *Theological Lexicon of the Old Testament* (2:590–602). Peabody, MA: Hendrickson Publishers.

White, E.G. 1926. *The Great Controversy.* Washington, DC: Review and Herald Publishing Association.

White, L.J. 1986. Grid and Group in Matthew's Community: The Righteousness/Honor Code in the Sermon on the Mount. *Semeia, 35*, 61–90.

White, W. 1976. Family. In M.C. Tenney, ed. *The Zondervan Pictorial Encyclopedia of the Bible* (2:496–501). Grand Rapids: Zondervan.

———. 1980. *rātsāch.* In R.L. Harris, G.L. Archer, & B.K. Waltke, eds. *Theological Wordbook of the Old Testament* (2:860). Chicago: Moody Press.

Wilckens, U. 1999. *hypokrinomai.* In G. Kittel, ed. G.W. Bromiley, trans. *Theological Dictionary of the New Testament* (8:559–571). Grand Rapids: Eerdmans.

Wilkins, M.J. 1996. Light. In W.A. Elwell, ed. *Evangelical Dictionary of Biblical Theology* (486–487). Grand Rapids: Baker.

Williams, J.G. 1990. Paraenesis, Excess, and Ethics: Matthew's Rhetoric in the Sermon on the Mount. *Semeia, 50*, 163–187.

Williams, T.F. 1997. *pqd.* In W.A. VanGemeren, ed. *New International Dictionary of Old Testament Theology & Exegesis* (3:657–663). Grand Rapids: Eerdmans.

———. 1997. *tswh.* In W.A. VanGemeren, ed. *New International Dictionary of Old Testament Theology & Exegesis* (3:776–780). Grand Rapids: Eerdmans.

Wolter, M. 1991. *paraptōma.* In H. Balz & G. Schneider, eds. J.W. Thompson & J.W. Medendorp, trans. *Exegetical Dictionary of the New Testament* (3:33–34). Grand Rapids: Eerdmans.

Worth, R.H. 1997. *The Sermon on the Mount: Its Old Testament Roots.* New York: Paulist Press.

Wright, C.J.H. 1988. Ten Commandments. In G.W. Bromiley, ed. *The International Standard Bible Encyclopedia* (4:786–790). Grand Rapids: Eerdmans.

———. 1996. *New International Biblical Commentary: Deuteronomy*. Peabody, MA: Hendrickson Publishers.

Wyatt, R.J. 1982. Names of God. In G.W. Bromiley, ed. *The International Standard Bible Encyclopedia* (2:504–509). Grand Rapids: Eerdmans.

Wyse, J.E. 1997. *The Structure of the Sermon on the Mount and Its Relationship to Interpretation*. Deerfield, IL: Trinity Evangelical Divinity School. (Thesis-M.A.)

Yamauchi, E.M. 1966. The "Daily Bread" Motif In Antiquity. *Westminster Theological Journal*. *28*(2), 145–156.

Yang, Y.E. 1997. *Jesus and the Sabbath in Matthew's Gospel*. Sheffield, England: Sheffield Academic Press.

Young, B.H. 1984. *The Jewish Background to the Lord's Prayer*. Tulsa, OK: Gospel Research Foundation Inc.

———. 1995. *Jesus the Jewish Theologian*. Peabody, MA: Hendrickson Publishers.

Youngblood, R. 2001. Monotheism. In W. Elwell, ed. *Evangelical Dictionary of Theology*. 2nd ed. (788–789). Grand Rapids: Baker.

Zaspel, F.G. 1992. The Continuing Relevance of Divine Law. In *Evangelical Theological Society*. Paper read at the Eastern Regional Evangelical Theological Society in Lanham, Maryland on 3 April 1992 (1–16). Portland, OR: Theological Research Exchange Network.

Zeitlin, S. 1969. Prolegomenon. In G. Friedlander, ed. *The Jewish Sources of the Sermon on the Mount* (ix–xxxvi). New York: Ktav Publishing House.

Zens, J. 1978. This is My Beloved Son...Hear him: A Study of the Development of Law in the History of Redemption. *Baptist Reformation Review*, *7*(4), 15–52.

———. 1979. The Believer's Rule of Life: A Study of Two Extremes. Postponed Ethics: Lewis Sperry Chafer. Retrogressive Ethics: Greg Bahnsen. *Baptist Reformation Review*, *8*(4), 5–19.

Zimmerli, W. 1961. Promise and Fulfillment. *Interpretation*, *15*, 310–338.

Zoebel, H.J. 1986. *chesed*. In G.J. Botterweck & H. Ringgren, eds. D.E. Green, trans. *Theological Dictionary of the Old Testament* (5:44–64). Grand Rapids: Eerdmans.

Zuck, R.B. 1991. *Basic Bible Interpretation*. Wheaton, IL: Victor Books.

Subject Index

References Index

Old Testament

New Testament

Early Church Writings

Studies in Biblical Literature

This series invites manuscripts from scholars in any area of biblical literature. Both established and innovative methodologies, covering general and particular areas in biblical study, are welcome. The series seeks to make available studies that will make a significant contribution to the ongoing biblical discourse. Scholars who have interests in gender and sociocultural hermeneutics are particularly encouraged to consider this series.

For further information about the series and for the submission of manuscripts, contact:

Hemchand Gossai
Department of Religion
Muhlenberg College
2400 Chew Street
Allentown, PA 18104-5586